Deepening Democracy

The Real Utopias Project

Series editor: Erik Olin Wright

The Real Utopias Project embraces a tension between dreams and practice. It is founded on the belief that what is pragmatically possible is not fixed independently of our imaginations, but is itself shaped by our visions. The fulfillment of such a belief involves 'real utopias': utopian ideals that are grounded in the real potentials for redesigning social institutions.

In its attempt at sustaining and deepening serious discussion of radical alternatives to existing social practices, the Real Utopias Project examines various basic institutions – property rights and the market, secondary associations, the family, the welfare state, among others – and focusses on specific proposals for their fundamental redesign. The books in the series are the result of workshop conferences, at which groups of scholars are invited to respond to provocative manuscripts.

Deepening Democracy

Institutional Innovations in Empowered Participatory Governance

The Real Utopias Project IV

◆

ARCHON FUNG and ERIK OLIN WRIGHT

with contributions by
Rebecca Neaera Abers, Gianpaolo Baiocchi, Joshua Cohen,
Patrick Heller, Bradley C. Karkkainen, Rebecca S. Krantz,
Jane Mansbridge, Joel Rogers, Craig W. Thomas, and
T.M. Thomas Isaac

VERSO

London · New York

First published by Verso 2003
© in the collection Verso 2003
© in individual contributions the contributors 2003
All rights reserved

The moral rights of the authors and the editors have been asserted

Verso
UK: 6 Meard Street, London W1F 0EG
USA: 180 Varick Street, New York, NY 10014–4606
www.versobooks.com

Verso is the imprint of New Left Books

ISBN 1–85984–688–2
ISBN 1–85984–466–9 (pbk)

British Library Cataloguing in Publication Data
A catalogue record for this book is available from the British Library

Library of Congress Cataloging-in-Publication Data
A catalog record for this book is available from the Library of Congress

Typeset in Sabon by The Running Head Limited, www.therunninghead.com
Printed by Biddles Ltd, Guildford and King's Lynn, www. biddles.co.uk

Contents

CONTENTS

Preface
The Real Utopias Project
Erik Olin Wright

"Real Utopia" seems like a contradiction in terms. Utopias are fantasies, morally inspired designs for social life unconstrained by realistic considerations of human psychology and social feasibility. Realists eschew such fantasies. What is needed are hard-nosed proposals for pragmatically improving our institutions. Instead of indulging in utopian dreams we must accommodate to practical realities.

The Real Utopias Project embraces this tension between dreams and practice. It is founded on the belief that what is pragmatically possible is not fixed independently of our imaginations, but is itself shaped by our visions. Self-fulfilling prophecies are powerful forces in history, and while it may be Pollyanna-ish to say "where there is a will there is a way," it is certainly true that without "will" many "ways" become impossible. Nurturing clear-sighted understandings of what it would take to create social institutions free of oppression is part of creating a political will for radical social changes to reduce oppression. A vital belief in a utopian destination may be necessary to motivate people to leave on the journey from the status quo in the first place, even though the actual destination may fall short of the utopian ideal. Yet, vague utopian fantasies may lead us astray, encouraging us to embark on trips that have no real destinations at all, or worse still, which lead us over some unforeseen abyss. Along with "where there is a will there is a way," the human struggle for emancipation confronts "the road to hell is paved with good intentions." What we need, then, are "real utopias": utopian ideals that are grounded in the real potentials of humanity, utopian destinations that have pragmatically accessible waystations, utopian designs of institutions that can inform our practical tasks of muddling through in a world of imperfect conditions for social change. These are the goals of the Real Utopias Project.

The Real Utopias Project is an attempt at sustaining and deepening serious discussion of radical alternatives to existing institutions. The objective is to focus on specific proposals for the fundamental redesign of basic social institutions rather than on either vague, abstract formulations of grand designs, or on small reforms of existing practices. In practical terms, the Real Utopias Project consists of a series of workshop conferences, each revolving around a manuscript that lays out the basic outlines of a radical institutional proposal. The essays presented at these conferences are then revised for the books in the Real Utopias Project.

The conference which was the basis for this volume in the Real Utopias Project was held at the University of Wisconsin in Madison, Wisconsin in January 2000. For that conference four people who had done research on empirical cases of innovative forms of participatory democracy in different parts of the world were asked to write papers in which they analyzed their cases in terms of an earlier version of the model of empowered participatory governance which appears in revised form as chapter 1 in this book. Other participants at the conference then commented on these cases and on the ideas in the general model.

Acknowledgements

We would like to thank the Vilas Trust of the University of Wisconsin and the editorial board of *Politics & Society* for their generous support in funding the conference, "Experiments in Empowered Deliberative Democracy," held in January, 2000, in Madison, Wisconsin, which formed the basis for this book. The staff of the A.E. Havens Center – Patrick Barrett, Shamus Khan, and Grace Livingston – provided invaluable help in organizing the conference.

We would also like to express our special debt to Joel Rogers and Joshua Cohen, whose earlier work on association and democracy (volume I of the Real Utopias Project) provided the point of departure for the conference on empowered deliberative democracy.

Earlier versions of a number of papers included in this volume were previously published in a special issue of *Politics & Society*, copyright Sage Publications, Inc., March 2001, vol. 29, no. 1, and are reproduced here with permission. They are:

Archon Fung and Erik Olin Wright, "Deepening Democracy: Innovations in Empowered Participatory Governance," pp. 5–42

Gianpaolo Baiocchi, "Participation, Activism and Politics: the Porto Alegre Experiment and Deliberative Democratic Theory," pp. 43–72

Archon Fung, "Accountable Autonomy: Toward Empowered Deliberation in Chicago Schools and Policing," pp. 73–104

Craig Thomas, "Habitat Conservation Planning: Certainly Empowered, Somewhat Deliberative, Questionably Democratic," pp. 105–30

PART I

Introduction

Thinking about Empowered Participatory Governance
Archon Fung and Erik Olin Wright[*]

As the tasks of the state have become more complex and the size of polities larger and more heterogeneous, the institutional forms of liberal democracy developed in the nineteenth century – representative democracy plus techno-bureaucratic administration – seem increasingly ill suited to the novel problems we face in the twenty-first century. "Democracy" as a way of organizing the state has come to be narrowly identified with territorially based competitive elections of political leadership for legislative and executive offices. Yet, increasingly, this mechanism of political representation seems ineffective in accomplishing the central ideals of democratic politics: facilitating active political involvement of the citizenry, forging political consensus through dialogue, devising and implementing public policies that ground a productive economy and healthy society, and, in more radical egalitarian versions of the democratic ideal, assuring that all citizens benefit from the nation's wealth.

The Right of the political spectrum has taken advantage of this apparent decline in the effectiveness of democratic institutions to escalate its attack on the very idea of the affirmative state. The only way the state can play a competent and constructive role, the Right typically argues, is to dramatically reduce the scope and depth of its activities. In addition to the traditional moral opposition of libertarians to the activist state on the grounds that it infringes on property rights and individual autonomy, it is now widely argued that the affirmative state has simply become too costly and inefficient. The benefits supposedly provided by the state are myths; the costs – both in terms of the resources directly absorbed by the state and of indirect negative effects on economic growth and efficiency – are real and increasing. Rather than seeking to deepen the democratic character of politics in response to these concerns, the thrust of much political energy in the developed industrial democracies in recent years has been to reduce the role of politics altogether. Deregulation, privatization, reduction of social services, and curtailments of state spending have been the watchwords, rather than participation, greater responsiveness, more creative and effective forms of democratic state intervention. As the slogan goes: "The state is the problem, not the solution."

In the past, the political Left in capitalist democracies vigorously defended the affirmative state against these kinds of arguments. In its most radical form, revolutionary socialists argued that public ownership of the principal means of production combined with centralized state planning offered the best hope for a just, humane, and egalitarian society. But even those on the Left who rejected revolutionary visions of ruptures with capitalism insisted that an activist state was essential to counteract a host of negative effects generated by the dynamics of capitalist economies – poverty, unemployment, increasing inequality, under-provision of public goods like training and public health. In the absence of such state interventions, the capitalist market becomes a "Satanic mill," in Karl Polanyi's metaphor, that erodes the social foundations of its own existence.[1] These defenses of the affirmative state have become noticeably weaker in recent years, both in their rhetorical force and in their practical political capacity to mobilize. Although the Left has not come to accept unregulated markets and a minimal state as morally desirable or economically efficient, it is much less certain that the institutions it defended in the past can achieve social justice and economic well-being in the present.

Perhaps this erosion of democratic vitality is an inevitable result of complexity and size. Perhaps we should expect no more than limited popular constraint on the activities of government through regular, weakly competitive elections. Perhaps the era of the "affirmative democratic state" – the state which plays a creative and active role in solving problems in response to popular demands – is over, and a retreat to privatism and political passivity is the unavoidable price of "progress." But perhaps the problem has more to do with the specific design of our institutions than with the tasks they face as such. If so, then a fundamental challenge for the Left is to develop transformative democratic strategies that can advance our traditional values – egalitarian social justice, individual liberty combined with popular control over collective decisions, community and solidarity, and the flourishing of individuals in ways which enable them to realize their potentials.

This volume explores a range of empirical responses to this challenge.

They constitute real-world experiments in the redesign of democratic institutions, innovations that elicit the energy and influence of ordinary people, often drawn from the lowest strata of society, in the solution of problems that plague them. Below, we briefly introduce four such experiments:

- *Neighborhood governance councils* in Chicago address the fears and hopes of inner-city Chicago residents by turning urban bureaucracy on its head and devolving substantial power over policing and public schools.
- *Habitat conservation planning* under the U.S. Endangered Species Act empowers stakeholders to develop governance arrangements that will satisfy the double imperatives of human development and the protection of endangered species.
- *The participatory budget* of Porto Alegre, Brazil enables residents of that city to participate directly in forging the city budget and thus use public monies previously diverted to patronage payoffs to secure common goods such as street paving and water services.
- *Panchayat reforms* in West Bengal and Kerala, India have created both direct and representative democratic channels that devolve substantial administrative and fiscal development power to individual villages.

Though these four reforms differ dramatically in the details of their design, issue areas, and scope, they all aspire to deepen the ways in which ordinary people can effectively participate in and influence policies which directly affect their lives. From their common features, we call this reform family *Empowered Participatory Governance* (EPG). They are participatory because they rely upon the commitment and capacities of ordinary people to make sensible decisions through reasoned deliberation and empowered because they attempt to tie action to discussion.

The exploration of empowered participation as a progressive institutional reform strategy advances the conceptual and empirical understanding of democratic practice. Conceptually, EPG presses the values of participation, deliberation, and empowerment to the apparent limits of prudence and feasibility. Taking participatory democracy seriously in this way throws both its vulnerabilities and advantages into sharp relief. We also hope that injecting empirically centered examination into current debates about deliberative democracy will paradoxically expand the imaginative horizons of that discussion at the same time that it injects a bit of realism. Much of that work has been quite conceptually focussed, and so has failed to detail or evaluate institutional designs to advance these values. By contrast, large and medium scale reforms like those mentioned above offer an array of real alternative political and administrative designs for deepening democracy. As we shall see, many of these ambitious designs are not just workable, but may surpass conventional democratic institutional forms on the quite practical aims of enhancing the responsiveness and effectiveness of the state while at the same time making it more fair, participatory, deliberative, and accountable. These benefits, however, may be offset by costs such as their alleged dependence on fragile political and cultural conditions, tendencies to compound background social and economic inequalities, and weak protection of minority interests.

We begin by briefly sketching four reform experiments.[2] Each of these will be examined extensively in the chapters that follow. We then lay out an abstract model of Empowered Participatory Governance that distills the distinctive features of these experiments into three central principles and three institutional design features. The next section explains why, in principle, such arrangements will generate a range of desirable social effects. We conclude this introduction with an agenda of questions to interrogate cases of actually existing EPG.

I Four Experiments in Empowered Participatory Governance

These institutional reforms vary widely in many dimensions, and none perfectly realizes the democratic values of citizen participation, deliberation, and empowerment. In its own way and quite imperfectly, however, each strives to advance these values and to an extent succeeds.

These cases can be usefully grouped into two general categories: first, reforms that primarily address failures of specific administrative and regulatory agencies and, second, reforms that attempt to restructure democratic decision-making more generally. Two of the cases fall under the first rubric. They attempt to remedy failures of state agencies by deploying participation and deliberation as tools to enhance effectiveness. One consists of functionally specific administrative reforms geared to improving the performance of the police and public education systems in the city of Chicago. The second attempts to balance human development and the protection of endangered species through stakeholder governance under reforms to the U.S. Endangered Species Act. The other two cases concern more broadly-scoped reforms in which left-wing political parties have captured state power and employed EPG forms to advance their social justice agenda. These are aimed explicitly at the problems of inequality and lack of democratic accountability. Participation and devolution are instruments toward those ends. One of these is an urban budgeting experiment in the city of Porto Alegre, Brazil. In the other, a left-wing party in the Indian state of Kerala and West Bengal created popular, participatory municipal governance bodies to supplant many of the functions performed by centralized administration.

Functionally Specific Neighborhood Councils in Chicago, USA

Our first experiment concerns public education and policing in a city characterized by great poverty and inequality: Chicago, Illinois, whose 2.5 million residents make it the third largest city in the United States. In the late 1980s, the Chicago Public School system suffered attacks from all sides – parents, community members, and area businessmen charged that the centralized school bureaucracy was failing to educate the city's children on a massive scale. These individuals and groups formed a small but vocal social movement that managed to turn the top-heavy, hierarchical school system on its head. In 1988, the Illinois legislature passed a law that decentralized and opened the governance of Chicago schools to direct forms of neighborhood participation.[3] The reform law shifted power and control from a centralized city-wide headquarters to the individual schools themselves. For each of some 560 elementary (grades K–8) and high (grades 9–12) schools, the law established a Local School Council (LSC). Each council is composed of six parents, two community members, two teachers, and the principal of the school, and its members (other than the principal) are elected every two years. The councils of high schools add to these eleven members one non-voting student representative. These councils are empowered, and required by law, to select principals, write principal performance contracts that they monitor and review every three years, develop annual School Improvement Plans that address staff, program, and infrastructure issues, monitor the implementation of those plans, and approve school budgets. Councils typically meet monthly during the school year, and less frequently in the summer. This reform created the most formally directly democratic system of school governance in the United States. Every year, more than five thousand parents, neighborhood residents, and school teachers are elected to run their schools. By a wide margin, the majority of elected Illinois public officials who are minorities serve on these councils.

Despite initial exuberance, the weaknesses of their decentralization soon became apparent. While many schools flourished through their new powers, other foundered from lack of capacity, knowledge, internal conflict, or bad luck. New regulations and departments within the Chicago Public Schools were refashioned to address these problems. For example, 1995 legislation required each local school council member to undergo three days of training, on topics such as budgeting, school improvement planning, principal selection, group process, and council responsibilities. The same law also created accountability provisions to identify the worst-performing schools in the city. These schools receive additional management supervision, resources, and, in some cases, disciplinary intervention.

The Chicago Police Department restructured itself in the mid 1990s along deeply decentralized and democratic lines that resemble (but were conceived and implemented quite independently from) that city's school reform. In response to the perception that conventional policing practices had proved largely ineffective in stemming the rise of crime or in maintaining safety in many Chicago neighborhoods, the Mayor's office, community organizations, and officials inside the police department began to explore "community policing" ideas in 1993. By 1995, reformers from these groups had implemented a wide-ranging program, called the Chicago Alternative Policing Strategy, that shifted the burden of maintaining public safety from police professionals to hundreds of neighborhood-level partnerships between police and neighborhood residents.

This program divides the city into some 280 neighborhood "beats"; beats are the administrative atoms of policing. It opens public safety operations in each of these beats to the observation, participation, and direction of neighborhood residents. Interested residents and police officers serving the area attend "community beat meetings" held monthly in each beat. The strategy also redefines the "how" of policing. In these meetings, residents and police discuss the neighborhood's public safety problems in order to establish, through deliberation, which problems should be counted as priorities that merit the concentrated attention of police and residents. They then develop strategies to address these problems. Often, responsibilities are divided between police (e.g. obtaining and executing search warrants) and residents (e.g. meeting with landlords to discuss building dilapidation). At successive meetings, participants assess the quality of implementation and effectiveness of their strategies, revise them if necessary, and raise new priorities.

As with the school reform experiment, the police department has joined with other public agencies and non-profit organizations to support and manage these decentralized problem-solving efforts on a city-wide basis. In the areas of citizen capacity and community mobilization, the city has hired community organizers and trainers to rove throughout the neighborhoods to teach group problem-solving skills. The strategies and plans developed in community beat meetings have been incorporated into ordinary reporting, evaluation, and management routines.

Habitat Conservation Planning Under the U.S. Endangered Species Act

The next experiment moves away from the reconstruction of municipal government to the problem of species preservation. For most of the time since its establishment in 1973, the U.S. Endangered Species Act has been the antithesis of participatory action. Section 9 of that Act prohibits the "taking" – killing or injuring – of any wildlife listed as an endangered species through either direct means or indirect action such as modification of its habitat. In practice, this often imposed a strict bar on any development or resource extraction activities in or near the habitats of endangered species. This law had two main defects.[4] First, it stopped productive development projects that may have had marginal impact on the ultimate viability of endangered species. Second, because the law protects only those species that receive administrative recognition,[5] it created a listing process that frequently amounted to a high stakes political battle between developers and conservationists. As a result, too few species receive protection and some are nearly decimated by the time they do qualify.

In 1982, Congress created an option to escape these deep deadlocks called an "incidental take permit." Under this provision, an applicant can obtain a waiver from strict enforcement by producing a "Habitat Conservation Plan" (HCP) that allows human activity in the habitat of an endangered species so long as "take" occurs only incidentally, the plan includes measures to mitigate take, and the human activity does not impair the chances of the species' survival and recovery. For a decade, however, this relief option was little used because permitting procedures were unclear and plan production costs high. Only fourteen HCPs were produced between 1982 and 1992. Since 1993, however, these plans and their associated permits have proliferated. By April 2002, 379 plans covering tens of millions of acres had been approved and dozens more were in various stages of development. This explosion in HCP activity grew out of an effort by Interior Secretary Bruce Babbitt and several associates to use incidental take permit provision to avoid the lose–lose outcomes generated by strict application of the

Endangered Species Act's ninth section. Under the new process, developers, environmentalists, and other stakeholders could potentially work together to construct large-scale habitat conservation plans.

The most advanced HCPs have served this ambition by incorporating significant elements of the design of EPG. For example, large acreage, multi-species conservation plans in Southern California were developed by stakeholder committees that include officials from local, state, and national environmental agencies, developers, environmental activists, and community organizations. Through deliberative processes, these stakeholders have developed sophisticated management plans that set out explicit numerical goals, measures to achieve those goals, monitoring regimes that assess plan effectiveness through time, and adaptive management provisions to incorporate new scientific information and respond to unforeseen events.

Beyond devolving responsibility and power for endangered species protection to local stakeholders, recent improvements to the national habitat conservation plan regime approved by the U.S. Fish and Wildlife Service attempt to create learning and accountability devices to mitigate the defects of excessive localism.[6] It has been widely recognized that high-quality HCPs possess common features such as quantitative biological goals, adaptive management plans, and careful monitoring regimes. Yet a study of more than two hundred plans revealed that less than half of all plans incorporate these basic features.[7] Its programs are participatory because they rely upon the commitment and capacities of ordinary people to make sensible decisions through reasoned deliberation and empowered because they tie discussion to action. To make habitat conservation plan provisions and performance a matter of transparent public accountability and to enable stakeholders of different HCPs to assess and learn from each other, this same Fish and Wildlife Service guidance attempts to establish an HCP information infrastructure that tracks the details of HCP permits as well as the performance of plans.

Participatory City Budgeting in Porto Alegre, Brazil

Porto Alegre is the capital of the state of Rio Grande do Sul in Brazil and home to some 1.3 million inhabitants. Like many other local and national states in Latin America, a clientelistic government has ruled the city in recent decades through the time-tested machinery of political patronage. This system allocated public funds not according to public needs, but rather in order to mobilize support for political personages. As a result, "the budget becomes a fiction, shocking evidence of the discrepancy between the formal institutional framework and the actual state practices."[8] Under similar arrangements elsewhere in Brazil, investigators revealed that this patronage-based "irregular allocation of social expenditures amounted to 64 percent of the total [budget]."[9]

In 1988, a left coalition led by the Workers' Party, or Partido dos Trabalhadores (PT), gained control of municipal government and continued to win successive elections in 1992 and 1996. Their most substantial reform measure, called "Participatory Budgeting" (PB), attempts to transform clientelistic, vote-for-money budgeting arrangements into a publicly accountable, bottom-up, deliberative system driven by expressed needs of city residents. This multi-tiered interest articulation and administrative arrangement begins with the sixteen administrative regions that compose the city. Within each region, a Regional Plenary Assembly meets twice per year to settle budgetary issues. City executives, administrators, representatives of community entities such as neighborhood associations, youth and health clubs, and any interested inhabitant of the city attends these assemblies, but only residents of the region can vote in them. They are jointly co-ordinated by members of municipal government and by community delegates.

At the first of these annual plenary meetings, held in March, a report reviewing and discussing the implementation of the prior year's budget is presented by representatives of the city government. Delegates are also elected from those attending the assembly to participate in meetings conducted over the following three months to work out the region's spending priorities. These delegate meetings are held in neighborhoods throughout the region. Participants consider a wide range of possible projects which the city might fund in the region, including issues such as transportation, sewage, land regulation, day care centers, and health care. At the end of three months, these delegates report back to the second regional plenary assembly with a set of regional budget proposals. At this second plenary, proposals are ratified and two delegates and substitutes are elected to represent the region in a city-wide body called the Participatory Budgeting Council which meets over the following five months to formulate a city-wide budget from these regional agendas.

The city-level budget council is composed of two elected delegates from each of the regional assemblies, two elected delegates from each of five "thematic plenaries" representing the city as a whole, a delegate from the municipal workers' union, one from the union of neighborhood associations, and two delegates from central municipal agencies. The group meets intensively, at least once per week from July to

September, to discuss and establish a municipal budget that conforms to priorities established at the regional level while still coordinating spending for the city as a whole. Since citizen representatives are in most cases non-professionals, city agencies offer courses and seminars on budgeting for council delegates as well as for interested participants from the regional assemblies. On September 30 of each year, the Council submits a proposed budget to the Mayor, who can either accept the budget or, through veto, remand it back to the Council for revision. The budget council responds by either amending the budget or by overriding the veto through a super-majoritian vote of two-thirds. City officials estimate that some hundred thousand people, or 8 percent of the adult population, participated in the 1996 round of regional assemblies and intermediate meetings.

Democratic Decentralization in India: West Bengal and Kerala

Like the participatory budgeting reforms in Porto Alegre, left-wing parties revitalized substantive local governance in West Bengal[10] and Kerala, India as central parts of their political program. Though Indian states have enjoyed many formal arrangements for local self-government since independence, these institutions have been doubly constrained. Externally, larger state bureaucracies enjoyed the lion's share of financing and formal authority over most areas of administration and development over this period. Internally, traditional elites used social and economic power to dominate formally democratic local structures. Until 1957, the franchise was restricted on status grounds.[11] But even after universal suffrage, traditional leaders managed to control these bodies and their resources. Corruption was rampant, many locally administered services were simply not performed, and development resources were squandered.

In a number of Indian states, significant reforms have addressed these problems of local governance by deepening their democratic character. The earliest of these began in the late 1970s in the state of West Bengal.[12] The Left Front Government, which took power there in 1977 and has enjoyed a growing base of support ever since, saw the Panchayat village governance system as an opportunity for popular mobilization and empowerment.[13] In addition to instituting one of the most radical programs of land reform in India in order to break the hold of traditional power at the village level, the Left Front Government has, in several distinct stages from 1977 to the present, transformed the Bengali panchayats to increase opportunities for members of disadvantaged classes to wield public power.

The first important step in panchayat empowerment came in 1988, when the state government shifted responsibility for implementing many development programs from state ministries directly to panchayats. Simultaneous with this expansion in function, their budgets more than doubled to approximately two million rupees per panchayat. Then, in 1993, a series of Constitutional and state statutory amendments dramatically enhanced the potential for further expansion of panchayat democracy. Three changes were particularly important. First, these reforms increased the financing capacity of the lowest-level panchayat authorities – the gram panchayats – by imposing a revenue-sharing scheme with the districts and giving the gram panchayats their own taxing power. Second, these measures stipulated that one-third of the seats in panchayat assemblies and leadership positions would be occupied by women and that lower-caste – Scheduled Caste and Scheduled Tribe (SC/ST) – persons would occupy leadership positions in all of these bodies in proportion to their population in the district. Finally, and most importantly for our purposes, the 1993 reforms established two kinds of directly deliberative bodies, called gram sabhas, to increase the popular accountability of gram panchayat representatives. The gram sabha consists of all of the persons within a gram panchayat area (typically around ten thousand) and meets once per year in the month of December. At this meeting, elected gram panchayat representatives review the proposed budget for the following year and review the accomplishment (or lack thereof) of the previous year's budget and action items. Similar meetings occur twice a year at an even more disaggregated level of panchayat governance.

Officials in the southwestern state of Kerala watched these democratic developments closely and then embarked on a bold initiative to adopt and extend them in their own state in 1996. There, the ruling Communist Party of India/Marxist (CPM) pursued a devolutionary program of village-level participatory planning as a strategy to both shore up its waning electoral base and enhance administrative effectiveness. Under the program, some 40 percent of the state's public budget would be taken from traditionally powerful line departments in the bureaucracy and devolved to some nine hundred individual panchayat village planning councils.[14] In order to spend these monies, however, each village was required to produce a detailed development plan that specified assessments of need, development reports, specific projects, supplemental financing, arrangements for deciding and documenting plan beneficiaries, and monitoring arrangements. These plans, in principle, are then approved or rejected by direct vote in popular village assemblies. In addition to these procedural requirements, there are some categorical limitations: some 40–50 percent of each pan-chayat's funds were to be invested in economic development, while 40 percent was earmarked for social spending including slum improve-ment, a maximum of 30 percent could be spent on roads, and 10 percent of funds were to be targeted to programs for women. Outside of these general requirements, village planning bodies were left to their own devices.

A large-scale political and administrative mobilization effort has been organized to support this basic reform of devolution-for-account-ability.[15] One component of this effort has been to build village capacity to conduct rural assessments and formulate development plans. In 1997–98, some three hundred thousand participants attended these training "development seminars" where they learned basic self-governance skills. Actual planning processes have involved more than a hundred thousand volunteers to develop village projects and more than twenty-five thousand to combine these projects into village-level plans. This sheer increase in village planning and project formulation far outstripped the central state government's ability to assess the quality of the plans or reject poor ones, much less provide feedback to improve them. To augment official capacities, some five thousand vol-unteers, many of them retired professionals, were enlisted into "Voluntary Technical Corps" that reviewed projects and plans.

Given the newness of the reform, its scale, and the paucity of resources available to evaluate it, it is unsurprising that we have only limited knowledge of its outcomes. In terms of both participatory process and technical effectiveness, progress thus far has been promis-ing but incomplete. While some villages produced what appear to be thoughtful plans with high levels of direct popular participation, many others failed to produce any plans at all. Of those plans that were sub-mitted, many were poorly integrated and had poor credit and financing schemes, and the projects within them were sometimes ill-conceived or simply mimicked bureaucratic boilerplate. On the dimensions of democratic process, participation in existing village governance struc-tures increased dramatically after the 1996 reform, but still only amounts to some 10 percent of the population. More optimistically, village-level empowerment has spawned the creation of grassroots neighborhood groups in hundreds of villages. Similar to the dynamic in Porto Alegre's participatory budgeting program, these groups articu-late very local needs and interests to village bodies.

II The Principles and Institutional Design of Empowered Participatory Governance

Though each of these experiments differs from the others in its ambition, scope, and concrete aims, they all share surprising similarities in their motivating principles and institutional design features. They may have enough in common to warrant describing them as instances of a novel, but broadly applicable, model of deliberative democratic practice that can be expanded both horizontally – into other policy areas and other regions – and vertically – into higher and lower levels of institutional and social life. We assert that they do, and name that model Empowered Participatory Governance (EPG).

EPG attempts to advance three currents in social science and democratic theory. First, it takes many of its normative commitments from analyses of practices and values of communication, public justification, and deliberation.[16] It extends the application of deliberation from abstract questions over value conflicts and principles of justice to very concrete matters such as street paving, school improvement, and habitat management. It also locates deliberation empirically, in specific organizations and practices, in order to marshal social experience to deepen understanding of practical deliberation and explore strategies to improve its quality. The recent body of work on civic engagement and secondary associations offers a second point of departure for EPG.[17] This family of scholarship attempts to understand, and by doing so demonstrate, the importance of civic life and non-governmental organizations to vigorous democracy. EPG builds upon this insight by exploring whether the reorganization of formal state institutions can stimulate democratic engagement in civil society, and so form a virtuous circle of reciprocal reinforcement. Finally, EPG is part of a broader collaboration to discover and imagine democratic institutions that are at once more participatory and effective than the familiar configuration of political representation and bureaucratic administration.[18] EPG adds considerable understanding of the institutions, practices, and effects of citizen participation to that investigation.

We thus begin, tentatively and abstractly, to sketch EPG by laying out three general principles that are fundamental to all these experiments: (1) a focus on specific, tangible problems, (2) involvement of ordinary people affected by these problems and officials close to them, and (3) the deliberative development of solutions to these problems. In the reform contexts examined here, three institutional design features seem to stabilize and deepen the practice of these basic principles: (1) the devolution of public decision authority to empowered local units,

[margin annotations: EPG: 1. values - delib. etc; 2. democ → civic life; 3. new democ. instits.]

(2) the creation of formal linkages of responsibility, resource distribution, and communication that connect these units to each other and to superordinate, centralized authorities, (3) the use and generation of new state institutions to support and guide these decentered problem-solving efforts. Finally, we discuss some crucial background conditions necessary for these institutional designs to contribute to the realization of democratic values.

Three Principles of Empowered Participatory Governance

First Principle: Practical Orientation

The first distinctive characteristic of the cases above is that they all develop governance structures geared to quite concrete concerns. These experiments, though often linked to social movements and political parties, differ from both in that they focus on practical problems such as providing public safety, training workers, caring for habitats, or constructing sensible municipal budgets. If these experiments make headway on these issues, then they offer a potential retort to widespread doubts about the efficacy of state action. More importantly, they would deliver goods to sectors of society that are often most grievously denied them. This practical focus also creates situations in which actors accustomed to competing with one another for power or resources might begin to cooperate and build more congenial relations. Conversely, it may also distract agents from more important, broader conflicts (e.g. redistributive taxation or property rights) by concentrating their attention on a constrained set of relatively narrow issues.

Second Principle: Bottom-Up Participation

All of the reforms mentioned establish new channels for those most directly affected by targeted problems – typically ordinary citizens and officials in the field – to apply their knowledge, intelligence, and interest to the formulation of solutions. We offer two general justifications for this turn away from the commitment that complex technical problems are best solved by experts trained to the task. First, effective solutions to certain kinds of novel and fluid public problems may require the variety of experience and knowledge offered more by diverse, relatively more open minded, citizens and field operatives, than by distant and narrowly trained experts. In Chicago school governance and policing, for example, we will see that bottom-up neighborhood councils invented effective solutions that police officials acting autonomously would never have developed. Second, direct participation of grassroots operators increases accountability and reduces the length of the chain of

agency that accompanies political parties and their bureaucratic apparatus. In developing areas like Porto Alegre, Brazil, and Kerala, India,
one of the main accomplishments of enlarged participation has been to
plug fiscal leaks from patronage payoffs and loosen the grip of traditional political elites.

This is not to say that technical experts are irrelevant to empowered
participatory governance. Experts do play important roles in decision-
making, but do not enjoy exclusive power to make important decisions.
Their task, in different ways in the various cases, is to facilitate popular
deliberative decision-making and to leverage synergies between professional and citizen insights rather than to pre-empt popular input.
Whether these gains from participation outweigh the potential costs of
reduced expert power is an empirical matter that other contributions to
this volume treat extensively.

Third Principle: Deliberative Solution Generation

Deliberation is the third distinctive value of empowered participatory
governance. In deliberative decision-making, participants listen to each
other's positions and generate group choices after due consideration.[19]
In contemplating and arguing for what the group should do, participants ought to persuade one another by offering reasons that others
can accept. Such reasons might take forms like: we should do X
because it is the "right thing to do," "it is the fair way to go forward,"
"we did Y last time and it didn't work," or "it is the best thing for the
group as a whole." This ideal does not require participants to be altruistic or to converge upon a consensus of value, strategy, or perspective.
Real-world deliberations are often characterized by heated conflict,
winners, and losers. The important feature of genuine deliberation is
that participants find reasons that they can accept in collective actions,
not necessarily ones that they completely endorse or find maximally
advantageous.

A deliberative decision process such as the formulation of school
improvement plans in Chicago or village plans in Kerala might proceed
first with the construction of an agenda: parties offer proposals about
what the group's priorities should be. They might then justify these
proposals in terms of their capacity to advance common interests (e.g.
building an effective school) or deliver social justice under severe
resource constraints (e.g. beneficiary selection in rural development
projects). After a full vetting of various proposals and the considerations backing them, participants might then, if remaining disputes
made it necessary, vote to select a group choice. In casting an authentic
deliberative ballot, however, each participant does not vote for the

option that best advances his own self-interest, but rather for the choice that seems most reasonable. Choices will be fair if groups adopt reasonable proposals rather than those that garner the greatest self-interested support or political influence. Similarly, participants then reason about the strategies that will best advance that group agenda and should adopt that set which seems prospectively most promising. These results, of course, depend upon participants following the procedures and norms of deliberation. The extent to which they do so depends upon both individual motives and institutional parameters.

One danger of participatory and discussion-based decision-making is that some participants will use their power to manipulate and enhance positions motivated by particularistic interests. To qualify as *deliberative* decision processes, however, earnest arguments and justifications must constitute the central kind of reasoning through which problem-solving actually takes place. While it may sometimes be difficult for a casual outside observer to distinguish between genuine deliberation and disingenuous posturing, the difference is nevertheless fundamental and generally apparent to participants.

While empowered participatory governance shares this focus on persuasion and reason-giving with all accounts of deliberation, its practical focus departs from many treatments that depict discourse as the proffering of reasons to advance pre-given principles, proposals, values, or policies. In these experiments, deliberation almost always involves continuous joint planning, problem-solving, and strategizing. Participants in EPG usually enter these discursive arenas to formulate together such means and ends. They participate not exclusively to press pre-formed agendas or visions, but rather they expect that strategies and solutions will be articulated and forged through *deliberation* and *planning* with the other participants. Though they often have little in common, indeed often have histories of animosity, participants in these settings are united in their ignorance of how best to improve the general situation that brings them together. In the village planning efforts of Kerala or habitat conservation planning, for example, initial steps of decision often involve assaying existing circumstances. It is no surprise that participants often form or transform their preferences and opinions in light of that undertaking. If they entered such processes confident in a particular course of action, some other strategy (such as management decree or partisan attempts to ascend to the commanding heights) might be more attractive than deliberative engagement.[20]

Empowered participatory decision-making can be contrasted with three more familiar methods of social choice: *command and control* by experts, *aggregative voting*, and *strategic negotiation*. In the first

familiar mode, power is vested in managers, bureaucrats, or other spe-
cialists entrusted to advance the public's interest and presumed to be
capable of doing so by dint of their training, knowledge, and normative
commitments. While such experts may engage in deliberative practices
among themselves, their discussions are insulated from popular participation. By contrast, in empowered participatory governance, experts
and bureaucrats are engaged in deliberation directly with citizens.

Aggregation is a second familiar method of social decision-making in
which a group's choice results from combining the preferences of the
individual participants that make it up. Voting – over issues, proposals,
or candidates – is perhaps the most common procedure of aggregative
social choice. In voting, participants begin by ranking alternatives
according to their desires. Then an algorithm such as majority rule
selects a single option for the whole group. Again, a main difference
between aggregative and deliberative voting is that in the former individuals simply vote according to their own self-interest, without necessarily considering the reasonableness, fairness, or acceptability of that
option to others. Without delving into the familiar merits or problems[21]
with aggregative voting, the shift to deliberative decision in some of
the empowered participatory governance experiments responded to
failings in aggregative mechanisms that preceded them. Sometimes, as
in Porto Alegre, these shortcomings lay in the failure of electoral mechanisms to effectively respect electors' desires due to problems like
patronage and corruption. In other instances, for example the formulation of school improvement or habitat conservation plans, complexity
and uncertainty often prevent participants from forming clear preferences that can be easily aggregated.

Strategic bargaining and negotiation[22] is a third contrasting method
of social choice. As with aggregation but distinct from deliberation or
most varieties of command, parties in strategic bargaining use
decision-making procedures to advance their own unfettered self-
interest backed by the resources and power they bring to the table. By
comparison, voting procedures typically attempt to equalize such
power differentials through provisions like "one person one vote."
Collective bargaining between large unions and employers captures
this difference; each brings different sources of authority and force to
the encounter, and each uses them to secure the best (not necessarily the
fairest) deal for its side. Unlike purely deliberative interactions, parties
typically do so through the use of threats, differential power, misrepre-
sentation and "strategic talk."[23]

These four modes of decision – deliberation, command, aggregation, and strategic negotiation – are ideal types. Actual processes, not

least those involving principles of empowered participatory governance, often contain elements of each. We privilege deliberation in EPG, however, as a value and norm that motivates parties and informs institutional design because of its distinctive benefits in these political and policy contexts. The case studies in the rest of this volume explore the extent to which the reality of decision practices vindicates this commitment.

Three Design Properties

Since these principles are in themselves quite attractive, the pressing question is whether feasible institutional configurations or realistic social conditions would measurably advance them in practice. The cases explored in this collection suggest that reforms advancing these principles in deep and sustainable ways often exhibit three institutional design properties. Since the empirical study of alternative institutional designs is too immature to reveal whether these features are necessary (they are certainly not sufficient) to deliberative democratic arrangements, we offer them as observations and hypotheses about design features that contribute to institutions that advance, stabilize, and deepen democratic values.

First Design Property: Devolution
Since empowered participatory governance targets problems and solicits participation localized in both issue and geographic space, its institutional reality requires the commensurate reorganization of the state apparatus. It entails the administrative and political devolution of power to local action units – such as neighborhood councils, personnel in individual workplaces, and delineated natural habitats – charged with devising and implementing solutions and held accountable to performance criteria. The bodies in the reforms below are not merely advisory, but rather creatures of a transformed state endowed with substantial public authority.

This devolution departs profoundly from centralizing progressive strategies, and for that reason many on the Left may find it problematic. Just as the participatory dimensions of these reforms constitute a turn away from authorized expertise, delegating to local units the power of task conception as well as execution stems from skepticism about the possibility that democratic centralism can consistently generate effective solutions. So, for example, the Chicago cases offer neighborhood governance of policing and public education as supple alternatives to conventional centralized solutions such as more stringent penalties and

3 design properties: devolution; centralised supervision & coord; state-centred, not voluntaristic. (& so, need to challenge centre)

ARCHON FUNG AND ERIK OLIN WRIGHT   21

more police on the street for public safety issues, and national testing, school finance reform, implementing the one best curriculum, racial desegregation, vouchers, and privatization for educational problems. Habitat conservation planning gives up the centralized and uniform standard of development prohibition under the Endangered Species Act in favor of a regime in which local stakeholders produce highly tailored habitat management plans that advance both development and species protection. Rather than allocating funds and staff to pave, electrify, and build sewers according to uniform criteria or centralized judgement, Porto Alegre's participatory budgeting system invites neighborhood residents and associations into the direct, repeated process of establishing, implementing, and monitoring these priorities.

Second Design Property: Centralized Supervision and Coordination

Though they enjoy substantial power and discretion, local units do not operate as autonomous, atomized sites of decision-making in empowered participatory governance. Instead, each case features linkages of accountability and communication that connect local units to superordinate bodies. These central offices can reinforce the quality of local democratic deliberation and problem-solving in a variety of ways: coordinating and distributing resources, solving problems that local units cannot address by themselves, rectifying pathological or incompetent decision-making in failing groups, and diffusing innovations and learning across boundaries. The Indian panchayat systems and participatory budgeting in Porto Alegre feed relevant village and neighborhood decisions to higher levels of government. Both of the Chicago neighborhood governance reforms establish centralized capacities for benchmarking the performance of comparable units (schools, police beats) against one another and for holding them accountable to minimum procedural and substantive standards. The U.S. Fish and Wildlife Service attempts to supervise some 380 habitat conservation plans through centralized monitoring, information pooling, and permit and performance tracking.

Unlike New Left political models in which concerns for liberation lead to demands for *autonomous* decentralization, empowered participatory governance suggests new forms of *coordinated* decentralization. Driven by the pragmatic imperative to find solutions that work, these new models reject both democratic centralism and strict decentralization as unworkable. The rigidity of the former leads it too often to disrespect local circumstance and intelligence and as a result it has a hard time learning from experience. Uncoordinated decentralization,

on the other hand, isolates citizens into small units, surely a foolhardy
measure for those who do not know how to solve a problem but suspect
that others, somewhere else, do. Thus these reforms attempt to construct connections that spread information between local units and
hold them accountable.

Third Design Property: State-Centered, Not Voluntaristic
A third design characteristic of these experiments is that they colonize
state power and transform formal governance institutions. Many spon-
taneous activist efforts in areas like neighborhood revitalization,[24]
environmental activism,[25] local economic development, and worker
health and safety seek to influence state outcomes through outside
pressure. In doing so, the most successful of these efforts do advance
EPG's principles of practicality, participation, and perhaps even deliberation in civic or political organizations. But they leave intact the basic
institutions of state governance. By contrast, EPG reforms attempt to
remake official institutions along these principles. This formal route
potentially harnesses the power and resources of the state to deliberation and popular participation thus making these practices more
durable and widely accessible.

These experiments generally seek to transform the mechanisms of
state power into permanently mobilized deliberative-democratic,
grassroots forms. Such transformations happen as often as not in close
cooperation with state agents. These experiments are thus *less*
"radical" than most varieties of activist self-help in that their central
activity is not "fighting the power." But they are *more* radical in that
they have larger reform scopes, are authorized by state or corporate
bodies to make substantial decisions, and, most crucially, try to change
the central procedures of power rather than merely attempting occasionally to shift the vector of its exercise. Whereas parties, social movement organizations, and interest groups often set their goals through
internal deliberative processes and then fight for corporate or political
power to implement those goals, these experiments reconstitute decision processes within state institutions. When this reorganization is
successful, participants have the luxury of taking some exercise of
authority for granted; they need not spend the bulk of their energy
fighting for power (or against it).

By implication, these transformations attempt to institutionalize the
ongoing participation of ordinary citizens, most often in their role as
consumers of public goods, in the direct determination of what those
goods are and how they should be best provided. This perpetual
participation stands in contrast, for example, to the relatively brief

democratic moments in both outcome-oriented, campaign-based social movements and electoral competitions in ordinary politics in which leaders or elites mobilize popular participation for specific outcomes. If popular pressure becomes sufficient to implement some favored policy or elected candidate, the moment of broad participation usually ends; subsequent legislation, policy-making, and implementation then occurs in the largely isolated state sphere.

Enabling Conditions

A host of background conditions can facilitate or impede the progress of empowered participatory governance. Literacy is an obvious example. Kerala's high literacy rates compared to those of other Indian states, and in particular female literacy, certainly facilitate the participatory democratic experiment there. Most fundamentally, perhaps, the likelihood that these institutional designs will generate desired effects depends significantly upon the balances of power between actors engaged in EPG, and in particular the configurations of non-deliberative power that constitute the terrain upon which structured deliberation inside EPG occurs. Participants will be much more likely to engage in earnest deliberation when alternatives to it – such as strategic domination or exit from the process altogether – are made less attractive by roughly balanced power. When individuals cannot dominate others to secure their first-best preference, they are often more willing to deliberate. It is important to note that this background condition does not require absolute equality. The participants in the experiments below enjoy vastly different resources, levels of expertise, education, status, and numerical support. Sometimes, however, they are on a par sufficient for deliberative cooperation to be attractive.[26]

At least three paths lead to power balances sufficient for deliberation. The first comes from self-conscious institutional design efforts. When administrators or legislators endow parents with the power to fire school principals or popular councils with authority for reviewing village budgets, they put citizens and local experts on a more equal footing. Second, historical accidents, not intended to establish deliberation or participation at all, sometimes also perform this equalization function. The Endangered Species Act in the United States, for example, threatens to impose costs on private property owners that can induce them to cooperate with environmentalists. Finally, groups such as community organizations, labor unions, and advocacy groups often check the tendencies of both officials and groups of citizens to commandeer ostensibly deliberative processes to advance their own narrow ends.

To recap, our experiments seem to share three political principles, three design characteristics, and one primary background condition:

- First, each experiment addresses a specific area of practical public concern.
- Second, this decision-making relies upon the empowered involvement of ordinary citizens and officials in the field.
- Third, each experiment attempts to solve those problems through processes of reasoned deliberation.

In terms of their institutional properties,

- These experiments devolve decision and implementation power to local action units.
- Local action units are not autonomous, but rather recombinant and linked to each other and to supervening levels of the state in order to allocate resources, solve common and cross-border problems, and diffuse innovations and learning.
- The experiments colonize and transform existing state institutions. The administrative bureaucracies charged with solving these problems are restructured into deliberative groups. The power of these groups to implement the outcomes of their deliberations, therefore, comes from the authorization of these state bodies.

And finally, in terms of background enabling conditions,

- There is a rough equality of power, for the purposes of deliberative decision-making, between participants.

III Institutional Objectives: Consequences for Effectiveness, Equity, and Participation

The procedural features of institutions designed according to the principles specified above may be desirable in themselves; we often consider deliberation and participation as important independent values. However, scholars, practitioners, and casual observers will judge these experiments by their consequences as much as by the quality of their processes. In this section, we describe how institutions following the design principles above might advance three especially important qualities of state action: its effectiveness, equity, and broadly participatory character. Whether institutions designed according to the principles of

Outcomes: effective problem-solving
equity
quality of deep partic.

ARCHON FUNG AND ERIK OLIN WRIGHT   25

EPG can advance these values or will instead yield a host of negative and unintended consequences must be settled primarily through empirical examination. We offer a set of optimistic expectations that might guide those investigations.

Effective Problem-Solving

Perhaps the most important, institutional objective of these deliberative democratic experiments is to advance public ends – such as effective schools, safe neighborhoods, protecting endangered species, and sensible urban budget allocations – more effectively than alternative institutional arrangements. If they cannot produce such outcomes, then they are not very attractive reform projects. If they perform well, on the other hand, then this flavor of radical democracy has the potential to gain widespread popular and even elite support. Why, then, might we expect these deliberative democratic institutions to produce effective outcomes?

First, these experiments convene and empower individuals, close to the points of action, who possess intimate knowledge about relevant situations. Second, in many problem contexts, these individuals, whether they are citizens or officials at the street level, may also know how best to improve the situation. Third, the deliberative process that regulates these groups' decision-making is likely to generate superior solutions compared to hierarchical or less reflective aggregation procedures (such as voting) because all participants have opportunities to offer useful information and to consider alternative solutions more deeply. Beyond this, participation and deliberation can heighten participants' commitment to implement decisions that are more legitimate than those imposed externally. Fourth, these experiments shorten the feedback loop – the distance and time between decisions, action, effect, observation, and reconsideration – in public action and so create a nimble style of collective activity that can recognize and respond to erroneous or ineffective strategies. Finally, each of these experiments spawns numerous component groups, each operating with substantial autonomy but not in isolation. This proliferation of command points allows multiple strategies, techniques, and priorities to be pursued simultaneously in order more rapidly to discover and diffuse those that prove themselves to be most effective. The learning capacity of the system as a whole, therefore, may be enhanced by the combination of decentralized empowered deliberation and centralized coordination and feedback.

Equity

In addition to making public action more effective, three features may enhance the capacity of these experiments to generate fair and equitable outcomes. First, these goals are well served by these experiments if they deliver effective public action to those who do not generally enjoy this good. Since most of the experiments concentrate on problems of disadvantaged people – ghetto residents in Chicago and Milwaukee, those from poor neighborhoods in Porto Alegre, Brazil, low status villagers in India – sheer effectiveness is an important component of social justice.

A second source of equity and fairness stems from the inclusion of disadvantaged individuals – residents and workers – who are often excluded from public decisions. A classic justification for democratic rule over paternalist or otherwise exclusive modes is that a decision is more likely to treat those affected by it fairly when they exercise input. These experiments push this notion quite far by attempting to devise procedures whereby those most affected by these decisions exercise unmediated input while avoiding the paralysis or foolishness that sometimes results from such efforts.

These experiments' deliberative procedures offer a third way to advance equity and fairness. Unlike strategic bargaining (in which outcomes are determined by the powers that parties bring to negotiations), hierarchical command (in which outcomes are determined according to the judgement of the highly placed), markets (in which money mediates outcomes), or aggregative voting (in which outcomes are determined according to the quantity of mobilized supporters), these experiments establish groups that ostensibly make decisions according to the rules of deliberation. Parties make proposals and then justify them with reasons that the other parties in the group can support. A procedural norm of these groups is that they generate and adopt proposals that enjoy broad consensus support, though strict consensus is never a requirement. Groups select measures that upon reflection win the deepest and widest appeal. In the ideal, such procedures are regulated according to the lights of reason rather than money, power, numbers, or status. Since the idea of fairness is infused in the practice of reasonable discussion, truly deliberative decision-making should tend toward more equitable outcomes than those regulated by power, status, money, or numbers. There will no doubt be some distance between this lofty deliberative ideal and the actual practices of these experiments, but the experiments should move decision-making closer to this ideal than existing alternatives.

Broad and Deep Participation

Beyond achieving effective and fair public outcomes, these experiments also attempt to advance the venerable democratic value of engaging ordinary citizens in sustained and meaningful participation. They rely upon popular engagement as a central productive resource. Such engagement can provide local information about the prospective wisdom of various policies, retrospective data on their effects that in turn drive feedback learning, and additional energy for strategy execution. The experiments invite and attempt to sustain high levels of lay engagement in two main ways. First, they establish additional channels of voice over issues about which potential participants care deeply, such as the quality of their schools and of their living spaces and the disposition of public resources devoted to local public goods. The experiments increase participation, then, by adding important channels for participation to the conventional avenues of political voice such as voting, joining pressure groups, and contacting officials. Second, they offer a distinct inducement to participation: the real prospect of exercising state power.[27] With most other forms of political participation, the relationship between, say, one's vote or letter to a representative and a public decision is tenuous at best. In these experiments, however, participants exercise influence over state strategies. This input often yields quite palpable responses. Often, the priorities and proposals of lay participants are adopted immediately or in modified form. Even in cases where one's proposals are rejected through deliberative processes, one at least knows why.

The quality of participation – as gauged by the degree to which participants' opinions and proposals are informed and the quality of their interactions with one another – might also be higher under these experiments in deliberative public action than under more conventional political forms such as voting, interest group competition, or social movements. Following John Stuart Mill's comment that the success of democratic arrangements can be measured in two ways, by the quality of its decisions and the quality of citizens it produces,[28] we say that the character of participation, quite apart from its level (as measured by voting turnout, for example) is an independent desiderata of democratic politics. Modern critics from both the Left and the Right seem to be unified in their low opinion of the political capacities of mass publics. Explanations from the Left include the rise of the "culture industry" and the concomitant decline of autonomous "public spheres" in civil societies where a competent public opinion might be formed. The political Right agrees with this diagnosis, but recommends elite democracy and techno-bureaucratic administration as a solution that does not require healing the public body. Against the background of this alarming diagnosis and even more alarming cure, concern for the public wisdom of private individuals is even more urgent than in Mill's time.

Individuals' capacities to deliberate, and make public decisions, atrophy when left unused, and participation in these experiments exercises those capacities more intensely than conventional democratic channels. In national or local elections, for example, the massive amounts of information sold to them from many vantage points tempt even engaged, well-educated citizens to throw their hands up in frustrated confusion or to focus on more easily understood dimensions of character, personality, or party identity. These experiments reduce expertise-based barriers to engaged participation and thus encourage participants to develop and deploy their pragmatic political capabilities. First, they allow casual, non-professional, participants to master specific areas of knowledge necessary to make good decisions by shrinking – through decentralization – decision scopes to narrow functional and geographic areas. Some of our experiments doubly focus decisions – for example, safety in a neighborhood – and so participants may master materials necessary to making high-quality decisions. Other cases, such as deliberative planning bodies in Kerala and Porto Alegre's participatory budget, have broader scope, but nevertheless retain the pragmatic, problem-centered concerns that enable ordinary citizens to engage in the decision-making process. Furthermore, citizens have incentives to develop their capacities and master the information necessary to making good decisions because they must live with the consequences of poor ones – these experiments institute "direct democracy" in the sense that these groups' decisions are often directly implemented by relevant state agencies. Again, this contrasts with most forms of political voice such as voting or letter writing, where the consequences of one's decisions are statistically negligible.

Beyond the proximate scope and effect of participation, these experiments also encourage the development of political wisdom in ordinary citizens by grounding competency upon everyday, situated experiences rather than simply data mediated through popular press, television, or "book-learning." Following Dewey and contemporary theorists of education and cognition, we expect that many, perhaps most, individuals develop skills and competencies more easily when those skills are integrated with actual experiences and observable effects. Since these experiments rely upon practical knowledge of, say, local needs or school operation, and provide opportunities for its repeated application and correction, individuals develop political capacities in intimate relation to other regions of their professional and private lives. Many participants will find it easier (not to mention more useful) to acquire this kind of "situated" political wisdom and capacity compared to the more free-standing varieties of political knowledge required for, say, voting. Finally, each of these experiments contributes to the political development of individuals by providing specialized, para-professional training. Leading reformers in each of our experiments realized, or learned through disappointment, that most non-professionals lack the capacities to participate effectively in functionally specific and empowered groups. Rather than retrenching into technocratic profes-sionalization, however, some have established procedures to impart the necessary foundational capacities to participants who lack them. For example, the Chicago local school governance reform requires parents and community participants to receive training in democratic process, school budgeting and finance, strategic planning, principal hiring, and other specific skills. These experiments not only consist of fora for honing and practicing deliberative-democratic skills, but also literally establish schools of democracy to develop participants' political and technical capacities.

IV An Agenda for Exploring Empowered Participatory Governance

Thus far, we have sketched the outlines of a model of radical democracy that aims to solve practical public problems through deliberative action, laid out the practical and ethical advantages of institutions built along that model, and offered brief sketches of real-world examples that embody these principles. The chapters in Part II of this book explore these cases in some detail, inquiring whether these abstract principles accurately characterize them, whether the experiments in fact yield the benefits that we have attributed to deliberative democ-racy, and whether these advantages must be purchased at some as yet unspecified price. Before we move to that very concrete discussion, however, we conclude this introduction by laying out three sets of criti-cal questions to guide these investigations. First, to what extent do these experiments conform to the theoretical model we have elaborated for the institutional design and effects of EPG? Second, what are the most damning flaws in our model? Finally, what is its scope – is it limited to the few idiosyncratic cases that we have laid out, or are the principles and design features more broadly applicable?

The Relationship of the Cases to the Model

Even if the normative principles of this proposed model offer an attractive guide for feasible institutional innovation, the specific experiments we have described may not in fact conform to it. Six critical dimensions of fit are:

1   How genuinely *deliberative* are the actual decision-making processes?
2   How effectively are decisions translated into action?
3   To what extent are the deliberative bodies able to effectively monitor the implementation of their decisions?
4   To what extent do these reforms incorporate recombinant measures that coordinate the actions of local units and diffuse innovations among them?
5   To what extent do the deliberative processes constitute "schools for democracy"?
6   Are the actual outcomes of the entire process more desirable than those of prior institutional arrangements?

1 Deliberation

Because many benefits of our model rest on the notion of deliberation, the first question goes to the degree to which decision-making processes within these experiments are genuinely deliberative. Equitable decisions depend upon parties agreeing to that which is fair rather than pushing for as much as they can get. Effectiveness relies upon individuals remaining open to new information and proposals rather than doggedly advancing preformulated ones. And learning at individual and group levels depends on people being able to alter their opinions and even their preferences. Though deliberation is seldom deployed as a descriptive characteristic of organizations in social science, its practice is completely familiar in public and private life – where we often discuss issues and resolve conflict not by pushing for as much as we can get, but rather by doing what seems reasonable and fair. Does this generous characterization of individual and group behavior accurately describe how participants make decisions in real-world cases, or is their interaction better characterized by the more familiar mechanisms of rational interest aggregation – command, bargaining, log-rolling, and threatening? In situations characterized by substantial differences of interest or opinion, particularly from ideological sources, deliberation may break down into either gridlock or power-based conflict resolution. Is the model's scope therefore limited to environments of low conflict or minimal inequality? In more contentious situations, do deliberative efforts generally lead to co-optation as one side softens its demands to get along or adapts to unjust conditions? If so, then the symbiotic relationship between deliberation and empowerment suggested above can become a trade-off.

2 Action

Collective decisions that are made in a deliberative, egalitarian and democratic manner may yet fail to be translated into action. Those who make the decision may lack the capacity or will to implement it. For example, Chicago community policing groups often ask patrol officers to perform various tasks. In such cases, weak accountability mechanisms of publicity and deliberation may be insufficient for the group to compel the action of its own members. In other cases, implementation may depend upon the obedience of others over whom the group has formal authority – such as the staff under a local school council. Such situations encounter familiar principal-agent dilemmas. In still other instances, implementation may rely upon bodies whose relations with primary deliberative groups are even less structured. In Porto Alegre's participatory budgeting system, for example, the deliberations of regional assemblies are passed on to a city-wide body whose budget must then be approved by the mayor. These budgetary decisions must then filter back down the municipal apparatus before, say, a sewer main gets built or a street paved. It is therefore important to know the extent to which decisions from deliberative processes are effectively translated into real social action.

3 Monitoring

Implementation requires more than turning an initial decision into action; it also demands mechanisms of ongoing monitoring and accountability. To what extent are these deliberative groups capable of monitoring the implementation of their decisions and holding responsible parties accountable? Most democratic processes are front-loaded in the sense that popular participation focusses on deciding a policy question (as in a referendum) or selecting a candidate (as in an election) rather than on monitoring implementation of the decision or the platform. These democratic experiments, by contrast, aim for more sustained levels of participation over time. Democracy here means participation beyond the point of decision, to popular implementation, monitoring of that implementation, and disciplined review of its effects. Popular participation throughout the entire cycle of public action, it is hoped, will increase the accountability of public power and the public's capacity to learn from past successes and failures. It remains to be seen, however, whether participants in these experiments can sustain involvement over time with sufficient intensity to become effective monitors of the decisions they make; as in conventional democratic processes, moments leading up to decision are no doubt more exciting and visible than the long periods of execution that follow.

4 Centralized Coordination and Power

While it is fairly clear that all of the experimental reforms decentralize power, the coordinating centralized mechanisms of accountability and learning theorized as the second design principle of EPG are less obvious. Under its pragmatic devolution, local units are by themselves unable to solve coordination and cross-border problems and would thus benefit from information-sharing connections to other units in the system. The fashion and degree to which the experiments reviewed above construct institutions to execute these functions vary widely. The empirical studies will, in more exploratory fashion, examine the extent to which these reforms construct recombinant linkages and establish how well those mechanisms work in practice.

5 Schools of Democracy

For deliberative democracy to succeed in real-world settings, it must engage individuals with little experience and few skills of participation. The fifth question asks whether these experiments actually function as schools of democracy by increasing the deliberative capacities and dispositions of those who participate in them. While many standard treatments of political institutions take the preferences and capacities of individuals who act with them as fixed, these democratic experiments treat both of these dimensions of their participation as objects of transformation. By exercising capacities of argument, planning, and evaluation, through practice individuals might become better deliberators. By seeing that cooperation mediated through reasonable deliberation yields benefits not accessible through adversarial methods, participants might increase their disposition to be reasonable and to transform narrowly self-interested preferences accordingly. Both of these hypotheses about the development of individuals as citizens in these democratic experiments require closer examination of actors' actual behavior.

6 Outcomes

For many potential critics and supporters, the most important question will be one of outcomes. Do these deliberative institutions produce strategies or effects more desirable than those of the institutions they supplant? One prime justification for reallocating public power to these decentralized and deliberative groups is that they devise public action strategies and solutions that are superior to those of command-and-control bureaucracies, by virtue of superior knowledge of local conditions, greater learning capacities, and improved accountability. A central topic of empirical investigation, then, is whether these experiments have in practice managed to generate more innovative solutions.

Criticisms of the Model

Beyond these questions that address whether the principles of our model of deliberative democracy accurately describe the experiments we examine, a second set of questions focusses pointedly upon criticisms that have been raised against proposals for associative, deliberative governance. The empirical materials can illuminate six critical concerns about EPG:

1   The democratic character of processes and outcomes may be vulnerable to serious problems of power and domination inside deliberative arenas by powerful factions or elites.
2   External actors and institutional contexts may impose severe limitations on the scope of deliberative decision and action. In particular, powerful participants may engage in "forum-shopping" strategies in which they utilize deliberative institutions only when it suits them.
3   These special-purpose political institutions may fall prey to rent-seeking and capture by well-informed or interested parties.
4   The devolutionary elements of EPG may balkanize the polity and political decision-making.
5   Empowered participation may demand unrealistically high levels of popular commitment, especially in contemporary climates of civic and political disengagement.
6   Finally, these experiments may enjoy initial successes but may be difficult to sustain over the long term.

1 Deliberation into Domination

Perhaps the most serious potential weakness of these experiments is that they may pay insufficient attention to the fact that participants in these processes usually face each other from unequal positions of power. These inequalities can stem from material differences and the class backgrounds of participants, from the knowledge and information gulfs that separate experts from laypersons, or from personal capacities for deliberation and persuasion associated with educational and occupational advantages.

When deliberation aims to generate positive sum solutions in which nearly all participants reap benefits from cooperation (outcome points that lie closer to pareto frontiers), such power differentials may not result in unfair decisions. However, serious projects that seek to enhance social justice and equity cannot limit themselves to just these "win–win" situations. Therefore our model would not be a very interesting one, it might be argued, if it did not apply to contested areas of public action or if its application to those areas systematically disadvantaged weaker participants. Perhaps too optimistically, deliberation requires the strong as well as the weak to submit to its norms; they ought to refrain from opportunistically pressing their interests even when power allows them to do so.[29] One set of questions that must be answered, then, concerns whether deliberative arenas enable the powerful to dominate the weak. Consider four mechanisms that might transform fair deliberation into domination.

One lamentable fact of all contemporary democracies is that citizens who are advantaged in terms of their wealth, education, income, or membership in dominant racial and ethnic groups participate more frequently and effectively than those who are less well off. These experiments demand intensive forms of political engagement that may further aggravate these status and wealth participation biases. If those who participate are generally better-off citizens, then resulting public action is unlikely to be fair. As in other channels of popular voice, the question of "who participates" remains a vital one in deliberative democracy.

Second, even if both strong and weak are well represented, the strong may nevertheless use tools at their disposal – material resources, information asymmetries, rhetorical capacities – to advance collective decisions that unreasonably favor their interests. While many other models of public decision-making such as electoral and interest-group politics expect such behavior, empowered participation is more normatively demanding, and so perhaps more empirically suspect.

Third, beyond unfair representation and direct force, powerful participants may seek to improperly and unreasonably exclude issues that threaten their interests from the scope of deliberative action. By limiting discussion to narrow areas of either mutual gain or inconsequence, the powerful may protect their status quo advantages without resorting to blatantly non-deliberative maneuvers. Nevertheless, constraining the agenda in this way obviously violates the norms of open deliberation and, if found to be a common phenomenon in the cases, would indicate a failure of the model.[30]

Finally, and ultimately perhaps most seriously, deliberative democracy may disarm secondary associations by obliging them to "behave responsibly" and discouraging radicalism and militancy.[31] After all, deliberation requires reasonableness, and so commitment to deliberative processes might be thought to require abstinence from vigorous methods of challenging power. That is, not only will the practices internal to the association bracket challenges to privilege, but in order to maintain their credibility to "the powers that be" the associations will strive to marginalize such challenges from the political arena altogether. If the popular associations engaged in these experiments fail to enforce these political parameters – if the deliberative apparatuses become sites of genuine challenge to the power and privileges of dominant classes and elites – then this criticism predicts that priveleged elites will seek to dismantle deliberative bodies.

2 Forum-Shopping and External Power

Even if deliberative norms prevail and diverse participants cooperate to develop and implement fair collective actions, the powerful (or the weak) may turn to measures outside of these new democratic institutions to defend and advance their interests. The institutions of EPG operate in a complex web of more conventional arrangements that include interest groups and politicians contesting one another in agencies, legislatures, and courts. When participants cannot get what they want in deliberative settings – perhaps because what they want is unreasonable – they may press their interests in more favorable venues. In the context of public education, for example, a parent who cannot secure special privileges for his child in the local school council may try to use the central school system office to overrule local deliberations. Real estate development interests in the city of Porto Alegre have bypassed the participatory budgeting system in favor of more friendly planning agencies when they anticipated neighborhood opposition. Engaging in such forum-shopping to overturn or avoid unfavorable deliberative decisions clearly violates deliberative norms that ground the experiments we are examining and, if widespread, will certainly poison the mutual confidence necessary for open discussion and cooperative collective action among diverse parties.

Aside from the possibility of defection, parties constituted outside of these deliberative bodies may not recognize their authority and resist their decisions. Driven by understandable jealousies, we might expect officials firmly ensconced in pre-existing power structures – elected politicians, senior bureaucrats, those controlling traditional interest groups – to use their substantial authority and resources to overrule unfavorable deliberative decisions. At the extreme, they might try to end these experiments or contain them in some seedling form. So, for example, environmental groups have sometimes viewed cooperative habitat management efforts as ceding too much ground to development or agricultural interests and fought locally deliberative decisions through litigious and legislative methods.[32] The Chicago school reforms empowered local governance councils by authorizing them to hire and fire their principals, and thereby removed the job tenure privileges that had been enjoyed by these school leaders. The association of principals fought back by arguing that the school reform's functional electoral structure violated the Constitutional mandate of one vote per adult citizen. Locally dominant left-wing political parties sustain both the Indian village governance reforms and Porto Alegre's participatory budget. Officials there have claimed credit for the success of these experiments and subsequently based their political fortunes upon the continuation of these experiments. Conventional politicians and bureaucrats thus became the handmaidens of deliberative-democratic transformation by mobilizing elite and popular support for the expansion and reproduction of these experiments. Without such political foundations, it is easy to imagine that these systems of popular deliberative action would be quickly overturned by the social and political elites that they often act against.

3 Rent-seeking versus Public Goods

We have hypothesized that these experiments produce public goods that benefit even those who choose not to participate directly. Sound urban budgeting would benefit all of Porto Alegre's residents, not just those who take part in the formal institutions of participatory budgeting. Similarly, most neighborhood residents enjoy the good of public safety and all students and their parents benefit from effective schools. Potentially, however, rent-seeking participants might reverse this flow of benefits by capturing these deliberative apparatuses to advance private or factional agendas. The system of participatory budgeting could be re-absorbed into old-school clientelist politics in which party bosses control discussion and resulting budget recommendations. Small factions of neighborhood residents or parents might use public powers created by the community policing and school governance reforms to benefit themselves by, for example, protecting just a few blocks or establishing special school programs for the sake of just their own children.

Some of these new institutions attempt to stem rent-seeking through centralized transparency and accountability measures. They link decentralized local bodies to one another and to centralized authorities in order to make the varied performance of deliberative action widely known and therefore more accountable. All habitat conservation plans, for example, must be reviewed by U.S. Department of Interior authorities in Washington, D.C. and summaries of those plans are publicly available in a centralized data warehouse. Similarly, the decentralized plans of police beats and schools in Chicago are reviewed and aggregated by higher bodies, as are the neighborhood budget priorities of Porto Alegre and panchayat decisions in India. In most of these cases, the capacity of accountability and transparency mechanisms to check self-interested behavior is simply not known. Accordingly, one critical question is the extent to which the institutions in these experiments can be perverted into rent-seeking vehicles and the efficacy of efforts to check this tendency.

4 Balkanization of Politics

In a further pitfall, these experiments may exacerbate the balkanization of a polity that should be unified. Prominent democratic theorists such as Rousseau and Madison worried that the division of the body politic into contending groups would weaken the polity as a whole because individuals would advance their factional interests rather than common good. In the extreme, such division might create conditions in which one faction dominated the rest. Or, divided political institutions and social factions might each be quite capable of solving its own particular problems, yet the system as a whole would be incapable of addressing large-scale concerns or formulating encompassing agendas. From this critical perspective, these experiments might aggravate the problem of faction by constituting and empowering hundreds of groups, each focussed on a narrow issue within cramped geographic boundaries. A proponent might respond that these channels of participation add some public component to lives that would otherwise be fully dominated by private, or even more particular, concerns and that therefore the net effect of these institutions is to broaden the horizons of citizens, not to narrow them. Both of these contending perspectives remain hypothetical, however, absent accounts of particular individuals and the relationship of these experiments to the political institutions that supposedly foster greater political commonality.

5 Apathy

While these four pathologies result from energetic but ill-constrained political engagement, a fifth criticism begins with the common observation that the mass of citizens are politically disengaged and ignorant, not fervid. From this perspective, empowered participation demands far too much in terms of the depth and level of participation from ordinary citizens, and the knowledge, patience, and wisdom that they are expected to possess or in short order acquire. It may be that the citizens in contemporary capitalist societies are generally too consumed with private life to put forth the time, energy, and commitment that these deliberative experiments require. Or, symptoms of apathy may result from institutional design rather than individual preference. These deliberative channels ask citizens to generate public goods which are broadly shared, and so many will be tempted to free-ride on the efforts of others. The cases discussed here will offer some evidence that begins to adjudicate these questions about citizen apathy by examining the quantity and character of participation.

6 Stability and Sustainability

A final concern focusses upon the stability of these experiments through time. They may begin in a burst of popular enthusiasm and goodwill but then succumb to forces that prevent these auspicious beginnings from taking root and growing into stable forms of sustained participation. For example, one might expect that the practical demands of these institutions might press participants eventually to abandon time-consuming deliberative decision-making in favor of oligarchic or technocratic forms. Even if one concedes that empowered participation generates innovations not available to hierarchical organizations, the returns from these gains may diminish over time. After participants have plucked the "low-hanging fruit," these forms might again ossify into the very bureaucracies that they sought to replace. Or, ordinary citizens may find the reality of participation increasingly burdensome and less rewarding than they had imagined, and engagement may consequently dim from exhaustion and disillusionment. Though most of the reforms considered here are young, some of them have a history sufficient to begin to ask whether their initial successes have given way to anti-deliberative tendencies.

Is EPG Generalizable?

A final and crucial question about this endeavor goes to its scope. Are the democratic principles and design features of EPG generally applicable? Or, is it limited to just a few settings such as those already mentioned? Since answering that question requires much more empirical research than is presently available, we can only offer a few speculative remarks.

The diversity of cases – across policy areas, levels of economic development, and political cultures – discussed in this volume suggests that EPG would usefully contribute to a large class of problem-solving situations. In the most general terms, those contexts are ones in which current arrangements – whether organized according to expert command, market exchange, or perhaps informally – are failing and in which popular engagement would improve matters by increasing accountability and capacity or by bringing more information to bear. Arguably, this is a large class indeed, and recent work has documented the emergence and operation of similar reforms in areas such as the treatment of addiction[33] and environmental regulation.[34]

In a variety of institutional settings, however, empowered participatory governance may not be helpful. It is not a universal reform strategy. In many areas of public life, conventional systems of guardianship, delegation, and political representation work well enough, or could be improved so as to be optimal. To take one small example, injecting more parental power and participation in already well functioning wealthy suburban school systems might lead to conflict and wasted energy that serves neither parents, students, nor educators in the long term. EPG would also be inappropriate where current institutions perform unsatisfactorily, but where direct participation would add little to problem-solving efforts. Sometimes, public policy might be naturally centralized, and so not admit of broad participation. At other times, policy areas may be so technically complex that they preclude constructive lay engagement. But perhaps the burden of proof lies on those who would oppose more participatory measures. After all, many of the areas of public life already subject to EPG reforms might have seemed, until quite recently, too daunting for ordinary citizens to contemplate: the formulation of municipal budgets, management of schools, habitat conservation, and the challenge of economic development.

V Prelude

"Democracy" is one of the most potent political symbols in the world today. The United States justifies much of its foreign policy and military interventions under the banner of restoring or protecting democracy. Masses in the streets in South Africa and Poland precipitated historic transformations of regimes in the name of democracy. And yet, just at the historical moment when an unprecedented proportion of the world's governments are becoming at least nominally democratic, public confidence in the capacity of democratic institutions to solve problems and represent the aspirations of ordinary citizens has declined in those countries with the longest democratic experience.

We believe that this decline in confidence in the democratic affirmative state does not reflect an actual exhaustion of democratic potential but rather the political triumph of antistatist neoliberalism. While ultimately a revitalization of democratic institutions on a wide scale requires political mobilization, that challenge also requires new visions for how democratic institutions can advance urgent social goals.

In the next part of this book, we will examine in considerable detail the empirical record of several experiments that manifest such visions. Each chapter consists of an extended essay written by a scholar closely associated with the experiment, laying out the experiment's institutional details and addressing the questions we have raised. These case studies are followed in Part III of the book by a series of critical and comparative commentaries, some by people intimately familiar with the empirical cases and others from those whose interest begins from political theory. We hope that the framework of EPG and the investigations that follow will help elaborate these visions and contribute to the project of participatory democratic regeneration.

Notes

* Respectively Assistant Professor of Public Policy at the John F. Kennedy School of Government, Harvard University and Vilas Professor of Sociology at the University of Wisconsin, Madison. We wish to thank all of the participants of the *Real Utopias V: Experiments in Empowered Deliberative Democracy* conference, held in Madison, WI (January 2000) for valuable comments on a previous version of this chapter. We would also like to thank our many friends and collaborators in this ongoing endeavor to discover more democratic governance forms, especially Joshua Cohen, Bradley Karkkainen, Jane Mansbridge, Joel Rogers, Dara O'Rourke, and Charles Sabel.

1. Karl Polanyi, *The Great Transformation*, New York: Rinehart & Co. (1944). The phrase appears originally in William Blake's *Jerusalem: The Emanation of the Giant Albion* (1804).

2. These four cases were presented at the conference in the *Real Utopias Project* held at the University of Wisconsin, Madison, in January 2000.

3. The Chicago School Reform Act, P.A. 85-1418, affects only schools in the city of Chicago, which is its own school district.

4. Bradley C. Karkkainen, Charles Sabel, and Archon Fung, *Beyond Backyard Environmentalism*, ed. Joshua Cohen and Joel Rogers, foreword by Hunter Lovins and Amory Lovins, Boston: Beacon Press (2000).

5. In 1999, almost 1,200 species were on the federal endangered species list, but only 120 of those had a designated "critical area" of habitat necessary to trigger strict protection. See Thomas F. Darin, "Designating Critical Habitat under the Endangered Species Act: Habitat Protection Versus Agency Discretion," *Harvard Environmental Law Review*. vol. 24, no. 1 (2000), pp. 209–35.

6. *Federal Register*, vol. 64, no. 45 (March 9, 1999), pp. 11,485–90.

7. Peter Kareiva *et al.*, *Using Science in Habitat Conservation Plans*, University of California, Santa Barbara: National Center for Ecological Analysis and Synthesis (1998).

8. See Boaventura de Sousa Santos, "Participatory Budgeting in Porto Allegre: Toward a Redistributive Democracy," *Politics and Society*, vol. 26, no. 4 (Dec. 1998), pp. 461–510.

9. Ibid.

10. Much in the account that follows has been drawn from G.K. Lieten, *Development, Devolution, and Democracy: Village Discourse in West Bengal*, New Delhi: Sage Publications (1996).

11. Ibid., p. 50.

12. Maitreesh Ghatak and Maitreya Ghatak, "Grassroots Democracy: A Case Study of the Operation of the Panchayat System in West Bengal, India" (Manuscript, 2000).

13. The panchayat system consists of three aggregated layers. The lowest level is an elected body called the Gram Panchayat, which typically covers some ten to twelve villages totaling ten thousand residents. The responsibilities of GPs have changed through time, but typically now include: the administration of public health, drainage and sanitation; supply of safe drinking water; maintenance of public utilities; primary education; agricultural development; irrigation; land reform; poverty alleviation; rural industrialization; electrification; and housing provision. The second tier is called the Panchayat Samity, and governs a unit of area that usually consists of ten GPs. Above this still is a district governance body called the Zilla Parishad, which aggregates and coordinates the panchayat samity-level plans.

14. See T.M. Thomas Isaac with Richard Franke, *Local Democracy and Development: People's Campaign for Decentralized Planning in Kerala*, New Delhi: Left World Press (2000).

15. Ibid.

16. Two especially relevant theorists of deliberation for the purposes here are Jürgen Habermas and Joshua Cohen.

17. See, for example, Robert Putnam, *Bowling Alone: The Collapse and Revival of American Community*, New York: Simon and Schuster (2000); Theda Skocpol and Morris P. Fiorina, eds., *Civic Engagement in American Democracy*, Washington, DC: Brookings Institution Press (1999), pp. 1–23; Joshua Cohen and Joel Rogers, *Associations and Democracy*, ed. Erik Olin Wright, London: Verso (1995); Paul Hirst, *Associative Democracy: New Forms of Economic and Social Governance*, Cambridge: Polity Press (1994).

18. See Joshua Cohen and Charles Sabel, "Directly-Deliberative Polyarchy," *European Law Journal*, vol. 3, no. 4 (December 1997), pp. 313–42; Michael C. Dorf and Charles Sabel, "Drug Treatment Courts and Emergent Experimentalist Government," *Vanderbilt Law Review*, vol. 53, no. 3 (April 2000); Archon Fung, "Street Level Democracy: A Theory of Popular Pragmatic Deliberation and Its Practice in Chicago School Reform and Community Policing, 1988–1997," Ph.D. dissertation, MIT Department of Political Science (1999).

19. This account of deliberation as reason-giving draws on recent treatments in democratic theory, especially various works of Joshua Cohen. See, for example, his "Procedure and Substance in Deliberative Democracy," in Selya Benhabib, ed., *Democracy and Difference: Contesting the Boundaries of the Political*, Princeton: Princeton University Press (1996), pp. 95–109.

20. Deliberative processes can affect the understanding individuals have both of their interests and of the optimal strategies for satisfying those interests. In general it would be expected that when people enter such deliberative processes they have a better sense of their basic goals than they do of the best means for accomplishing their goals, and thus much of the deliberative process concerns problem-solving discussions over alternative courses of action. Still, because interests are complex and often quite vague, and because individuals often define their interests over variable sets of other actors, deliberative practices can also affect how people understand the interests themselves. For a discussion of modes of interest transformation through deliberation, see Jane

Mansbridge, "A Deliberative Theory of Interest Representation," in *The Politics of Interests: Interest Groups Transformed*, Boulder, CO: Westview Press (1992), pp. 32–57.

21. The most famous of these is of course the problem of incoherence. See William Riker, *Liberalism against Populism: A Confrontation between the Theory of Democracy and the Theory of Social Choice*, Prospect, IL: Waveland Press (1982).

22. For the limited purposes of this discussion, we use negotiation and strategic bargaining interchangeably. Negotiations and strategic bargaining can, of course, also involve deliberation among the parties involved. The issue here, then, is the difference between such *deliberative* bargaining and *strategic* bargaining that is intended to give maximum advantage to one's own interests.

23. See, for example, David Austen-Smith, "Strategic Models of Talk in Political Decision Making," *International Political Science Review*, vol. 13, no. 1 (1992), pp. 45–58.

24. See, for instance, Harry Boyte's *Backyard Revolution: Understanding the New Citizen's Movement*, Philadelphia: Temple University Press (1980) and Peter Medoff and Holly Sklar's *Streets of Hope: The Fall and Rise of an Urban Neighborhood*, Boston, MA: South End Press (1994). For one prominent concrete example discussed from the perspective of its leader, see Ernesto Cortes, Jr., "Reweaving the Social Fabric," *The Boston Review*, vol. 19, nos. 3 and 4 (June–Sept. 1994), pp. 12–14, on the activities of the Industrial Areas Foundation (IAF) group Communities Organized for Public Service (COPS) in San Antonio, Texas.

25. Andrew Szasz, *Ecopopulism: Toxic Waste and the Movement for Environmental Justice*, Minneapolis: University of Minnesota Press (1994).

26. The range of equality here is perhaps akin to Rousseau's, when he claims that laws of democracy should create circumstances such that "no citizen shall ever be wealthy enough to buy another, and none poor enough to be forced to sell himself." J.-J. Rousseau, *Social Contract*, trans. Donald A. Cress, Cambridge: Hackett Publishing (1987), Book II, Chapter 11.

27. One classic problem of political science is explaining why people vote at all, given the complete absence of effect associated with a single vote. For an attempt to explain this apparently irrational behavior from the rational choice perspective, see William Riker and Peter Ordeshook, "A Theory of the Calculus of Voting," *American Political Science Review*, vol. 62, no. 1 (March 1968), pp. 25–42.

28. John Stuart Mill, *Considerations on Representative Government*, ed. with an Introduction by Currin V. Shields, Indianapolis: Bobbs-Merrill (1958, originally published 1861), Chapter 2.

29. For a variation on this critique, see Lynn M. Sanders, "Against Deliberation," *Political Theory*, vol. 25, no. 3 (June 1997), pp. 347–76.

30. For a classic statement of this dynamic, see Peter Bachrach and Morton Baratz, "Two Faces of Power," *American Political Science Review*, vol. 56, no. 4 (Dec. 1962), pp. 947–52.

31. See Szasz, *Ecopopulism*.

32. See Mark Sagoff, "The View from Quincy Library: Civic Engagement in Environmental Problem Solving," in Robert K. Fullinwider, ed., *Civil Society, Democracy, and Civic Renewal*, New York: Rowman Littlefield (1999) and Louis Jacobson, "Local Timber Collaboration Stalls in National Arena," *Planning*, vol. 61, no. 11 (Nov. 1998), pp. 22–3.

33. See Dorf and Sabel, "Drug Treatment Courts."

34. See Karkkainen, Sabel, and Fung, *Beyond Backyard Environmentalism*.

PART II

Case Studies

Participation, Activism, and Politics: The Porto Alegre Experiment
Gianpaolo Baiocchi[*]

The experiment in participatory governance in Porto Alegre, Brazil stands apart from many other similar attempts to institute civic governance in Brazil and Latin America. Its breadth and scope distinguish it from other efforts, past and present, that simply do not involve as many persons or, more commonly, do not devolve as much decision-making power to popular mandate. Its central institutional feature of utilizing neighborhood-based deliberation also sets it apart from participatory governance schemes that rely on organized civil society through sectoral interfaces, for example by calling upon teachers to consult on education policy. It is also unusual because it has served the Workers' Party (*Partido dos Trabalhadores*, PT) well, securing for it three uninterrupted terms at the helm of municipal government and, recently, largely as a result of the successes in Porto Alegre, a term at state government. Its record on good governance also stands in contrast to many well-known electoral and institutional failures of leftist municipal administrations: São Paulo, Fortaleza, and Florianópolis in Brazil, or Caracas in Venezuela, as well as a number of much more limited participatory experiments in Montevideo, Uruguay and Córdoba, Argentina.[1]

Despite the recent attention paid to Porto Alegre's innovative institutions, as well as a general interest in "participatory governance,"[2] little of this work explicitly addresses the theory of deliberative democracy – a body of thought that straddles normative and practical concerns of democratic governance.[3] Deliberative democratic accounts vary in the attention they give to institutional arrangements, and here I will focus on the account of Empowered Participatory Governance of Fung and Wright. EPG develops an institutional model that would guarantee fairness and efficiency within a deliberative framework.[4] Deliberative democratic theory refers to a body of political thought that seeks to develop a substantive version of democracy based on public justification. More than "discussion-based" democracy, it calls for the deliberation of citizens as reasonable equals in the legitimate exercise of authority. It offers a way of transforming the preferences and intentions of citizens to enhance the possibilities for social cooperation.[5]

The empowered participatory governance proposal is an extension, and further iteration, of these accounts. What distinguishes this intervention from many others is its concern with institutional arrangements. A central feature of "real utopian thinking" is that it places affirmative responsibility on institutional design to bring real-world institutions closer to normative "utopian" ideals. The empowered participatory governance proposal is an ideal-typical design proposal for deliberative decision-making and pragmatic problem-solving among participants over specific common goods, and is in principle applicable to a wide range of situations. It centers on reforms that devolve decision-making to local units that are supported, but not directed, by a central body. These units are in turn empowered to enact their decisions. This model aims to foster redistributive and efficient decision-making that is deliberative and democratic and superior to command-and-control structures in several dimensions.

A number of empirical questions arise in light of existing experiments that more or less meet the model's criteria. For example, can deliberative democracy ever be fair, or will those who are more powerful or well resourced dominate? While answers to these questions will not doom or "prove" the model, they raise issues about institutional features – which ones work and which ones bring us closer to normative ideals – that together with comparative and theoretical work can help to advance the theoretical and practical agenda of democratic reform. I will use the Porto Alegre experiment to raise three broad, central problems in the theoretical model: the problem of inequality, the problem of uneven civil society development, and the problem of politics. Based on a number of indicators about the Porto Alegre experiment collected between 1997 and 2000, I examine the implications of these problems and their solutions in this case, and offer extensions to the EPG model.

Each of the "problems" for the model is in reality an extension of the "real-world" question inspired by the call to utopian thinking: what are the difficulties encountered in the implementation of this design? The "problem" of inequality is not that persons are unequal, but that differences between them may hinder fair deliberation. Are participatory meetings dominated by certain citizens, for example? The "civil society problem" concerns the impact of EPG upon autonomous civil society and how participatory institutions should "interface" with secondary associations that have uneven capacities. Do EPG fora empty out civil society or privilege areas rich with secondary associations? The "politics" problem is the question of whether such experiments thrive only in certain political contexts. When do EPG proposals call forth opposition from the powerful? What institutional features might account for their durability in the face of uncertainty?

In this spirit, then, I offer three critical reinterpretations. After a very brief discussion of the institutions of the participatory governance in Porto Alegre, I argue in section II that the experiment offers a successful resolution of the problems of deliberation among unequals through its didactic functions. In the following section, I argue that the experiment also offers a hopeful example of how this relationship might work in a way that fosters new associations in unorganized areas of civil society. Finally, the very success of the participatory experiment necessarily poses the question of the context under which it has thrived. Here I argue that we should not forget legitimacy-enhancing features that, in a democratic context, foster its reproduction. These three types of concern should occupy a more central place within the EPG proposal.

I Background: Institutions of Participatory Governance

When the Popular Front, an electoral alliance headed by the PT, achieved victory in Porto Alegre in 1989 there was little agreement as to what, exactly, the "PT way" of governing[6] would look like, beyond a broad agreement on democratizing and decentralizing the administration, reversing municipal priorities toward the poor, and increasing popular participation in decision-making. Attending to a longstanding demand of The Union of Neighborhood Associations of Porto Alegre (UAMPA), which already in its 1985 congress called for a participatory structure involving the municipal budget, PT administrators developed a set of institutions that extended popular control over municipal budgeting priorities.

Developing participatory institutions while managing a city of the size of Porto Alegre posed a number of difficulties for administrators. The city of Porto Alegre, the capital of the industrialized and relatively wealthy state of Rio Grande do Sul, stands at the center of a metropolitan area of almost three million persons. And although the city of

1.3 million enjoys high social and economic indicators, with its life expectancy (72.6 years) and literacy rates (90 percent) well above national average, it is also highly segregated economically.[7] Almost a third of its population lives in irregular housing: slums and invaded areas. These slums fan outward from the city center, with the poorest districts generally the farthest from downtown, and generate geographically distinct economic and social zones throughout the city. This socio-geographic configuration poses distinctive obstacles to drawing representative popular participation.

The *Orçamento Participativo* (OP), or the "Participatory Budget" (henceforth PB) has evolved over the years into a two-tiered structure of fora where citizens participate as individuals and as representatives of various civil society groups (neighborhood associations, cultural groups, special interest groups) throughout a yearly cycle. They deliberate and decide on projects for specific districts and on municipal investment priorities, and then monitor the outcome of these projects. The process begins in March of each year with regional assemblies in each of the city's sixteen districts. These large meetings, with occasional participation of upwards of a thousand persons, accomplish two goals. First, they elect delegates to represent specific neighborhoods in successive rounds of deliberations. Second, participants review the previous year's projects and budget. The mayor and staff attend these meetings to reply to citizens' concerns about projects in the district. The number of delegates allocated to each neighborhood increases with attendees according to a diminishing marginal formula.[8] Neighborhood associations or groups are responsible for electing their own delegates.

In subsequent months, these delegates meet in each of the districts on a weekly or bimonthly basis to learn about the technical issues involved in demanding projects as well as to deliberate the district's needs. The number of participants varies, but forty to sixty persons regularly attend in most districts. In a parallel structure of thematic sessions, delegates deliberate projects that affect the city as a whole rather than those that concern specific neighborhoods. At both of these kinds of meetings, representatives from each of the municipal government's departments attend to address issues that touch specific departmental competencies. These smaller Intermediary Meetings come to a close when, at a Second Plenary Meeting, regional delegates vote to ratify the district's demands and priorities and elect councilors to serve on the Municipal Council of the Budget.

This council is a smaller forum of representatives. It is composed of a portion of representatives from each of the districts and thematic meetings. Its main function is to reconcile the demands from each district with available resources and to propose and approve a municipal budget in conjunction with members of the administration. Its forty-two members meet biweekly with representatives of municipal government over several months. Councilors – two per district and two per each of the five thematic areas – maintain links with organizations and individuals in their districts during this phase. In addition to developing a city budget, this group amends the scope and rules governing the process itself. In recent years, procedural changes have included increasing the scope of areas covered by the PB, broadening the powers of the Municipal Council of the Budget to cover personnel expenditures of the administration, and changing the criteria for assessing how resources are to be allocated to each of the districts.[9] The steps in this annual process are depicted in Figure 2.1.[10]

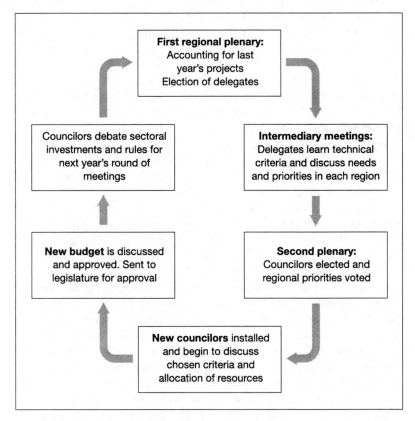

Figure 2.1 Annual Cycle of Participatory Budgeting

The Porto Alegre experiment meets the criteria of the empowered participatory governance proposal in a number of interesting ways. First, the process creates direct deliberation between citizens at the local level and devolves substantial amounts of decision-making power to these local settings. These citizens are involved in pragmatic problem-solving, and in monitoring and implementing solutions achieved. These deliberative processes occur continuously over the years, and thus provide opportunities for participants to learn from mistakes. These local units, though vested with substantial decision-making power, do not function completely autonomously from other units or from central monitoring units. Rather, central agencies offer supervision and support of local units but respect their decision-making power. In this case, support comes from the administration in the form of regional agents who act as non-voting facilitators.[11]

The Porto Alegre experiment also shows how complex management of a whole city can occur through combinations of direct and representative democracy. The higher tier of the participatory structures, the Municipal Council of the Budget, brings together representatives of each of the districts. They deliberate on the rules of the process as a whole as well as on broad investment priorities; they also act as intermediaries between municipal government and regional activists, bringing the demands from districts to central government, and justifying government actions to regional activists.[12] Participatory governance has expanded beyond participatory budgeting meetings to new fora that now include social service and health provisions, local school policy, and human rights. And the PB itself has grown to include investments in education, culture, health, social services, and sports.

As part of a joint strategy to make urban improvements in the lowest-income areas while "cleaning up" public finances, the participatory budget has improved the quality of governance. The percentage of the public budget available for investment increased to nearly 20 percent in 1994 from 2 percent in 1989. The legitimacy of public decisions from the PB has also made possible additional public finance improvements such as property tax increases and higher tax collection rates.[13] The proportion of municipal expenses in service provision to expenses in administration has also improved.[14] Of the hundreds of projects approved, investment in the poorer residential districts of the city has exceeded investment in wealthier areas as a result of these public policies. Each year, the majority of the twenty to twenty-five kilometers of new pavement has gone to the city's poorer peripheries. Today, 98 percent of all residences in the city have running water, up from 75 percent in 1988; sewage coverage has risen to 98 percent from

46 percent.[15] In the years between 1992 and 1995, the housing department (DEMHAB) offered housing assistance to 28,862 families,
against 1,714 for the comparable period of 1986–88; and the number
of functioning public municipal schools today is 86 against 29 in
1988.[16] Similarly, these investments have been redistributive; districts
with higher levels of poverty have received significantly greater shares
of investment.

The PB has enjoyed increasing levels of popular engagement over the
years, although participation rates have recently stabilized. Despite
potential barriers posed by their technical and time-consuming discussions, large numbers of participants representing broad segments of the
population have attended. Estimated yearly attendance at the PB, generated by a measure of participants in first-round meetings, is shown in
Figure 2.2. An analysis of participation per district, not reported here,
shows that while for the first year presence of associative networks was
a predictor of participation, for every year after that district-level
poverty, and not a strong civil society, predicts participation.[17]

A survey fielded by myself in conjunction with CIDADE, a local
NGO, revealed that the socio-economic profile of the average participant at the first meeting of the year in 1998 fell below the city's average

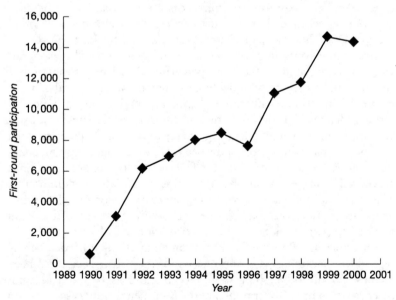

Figure 2.2 Participation Trends: First-Round Participatory Budget
Meetings, 1990–2000

in terms of education and income. Over half of participants have household earnings of four minimum wages or below, and over half lack education beyond the eighth grade.[18] On the other end of the scale, better-off citizens are underrepresented, as roughly a third come from households earning five minimum wages or more, against the 55 percent of the city's residents generally who do so.[19]

The Porto Alegre PB is a successful instance of empowered participatory governance. As a set of institutions it has achieved efficient and redistributive decision-making within a deliberative framework that has also attracted broad-based participation from poorer strata of Porto Alegre's citizenry. Nonetheless, its very success raises three important issues for the model: inequality within meetings, the issue of civil society interfaces and civic impact, and whether that success requires particular political conditions.

II Deliberation and the Problem of Inequality

One of the main concerns of the critics of deliberative democracy is that its fora are likely to reproduce inequalities in society at large. Since this project addresses local priorities and needs in service provision and investments in urban infrastructure, it is not surprising that the poor are well represented. But do they participate as effectively as other groups? Does their participation yield similar benefits for them? Deliberative settings in which citizens meet to debate formally as equals could be dominated by the more powerful. Criticisms of the "public sphere" might also apply to deliberative democratic proposals. In one poignant objection, deliberative democracy may create a fiction of rational deliberation that is in reality elite rule. More sinisterly, exercises of justification could lend legitimacy to certain inequalities, or to the political party in control of the project. Despite significant inequalities among citizens, the didactic features of the experiment have succeeded in large part in offsetting these potentials for domination. This confirms the expectations of democratic theorists who, while assuming that persons may come to deliberative settings with certain inequalities, expect that over time participation will offset them.

For critics like Bourdieu, deliberation and participatory democracy reproduce hierarchies. On the one hand, they reproduce class hierarchies; on the other, they reproduce hierarchies of political competence of "experts" over non-experts. Bourdieu denounces the fiction of "linguistic communism" – that the ability to speak is equally distributed to all.[20] Because language is a *medium* (as opposed to only an *instrument*) of power, utterances between speakers are always expressions of *relations of power between them*. The competence to speak embodies difference and inequality. A privileged class habitus imparts the technical ability to speak *and* the standing to make certain statements. This competence is a *statutory ability*, meaning that "not all linguistic utterances are equally acceptable and not all locutors equal."[21] Linguistic competence is not a simple technical ability, but certain interlocutors are not allowed certain speech acts. Bourdieu gives the example of the farmer who did not run for mayor of his township: "But I don't know how to speak!"[22]

There is also the theoretical expectation that relatively technical discussions and time pressures on poorer people pose obstacles to participation. As Jane Mansbridge writes of townhall participants:

> These patterns imply that the psychic costs of participation are greater and the benefits fewer for lower status citizens. In contacting town officials, for instance, they feel more defensive beforehand and less likely to get results afterward. In speaking at meetings they feel more subject to ridicule and are less likely to convince anyone. Each act of participation not only costs them more but also usually produces less.[23]

While ethnographic and life-history evidence would be crucial to account for the full effect of deep inequalities in these meetings, it is possible here to deploy survey and participation evidence to consider some of these effects. The survey, discussed above, was administered at meetings in all districts of the city.[24] Figure 2.3 shows the results as a comparison of the proportion of participants by gender, income, and education against city-wide proportions at each tier of the process.

There is some stratification at the higher tiers of the process, with participation by women and persons of low education falling off, while low income does not seem to affect election. Women are just over 50 percent of general participants, though they make up only 35 percent of councilors.[25] Low-educated persons[26] are just over 60 percent of general participants, but constitute only 18 percent of councilors. Persons of low income[27] make up 33 percent of general participants, and 34 percent of councilors. The best estimate of race[28] of participants also suggests that there is no evidence of lack of parity on racial grounds.[29] Education appears to have the most pronounced effect, and particularly so at the highest tier.

There is no evidence, however, that lack of education or gender pose insurmountable barriers to effective participation, or that this stratification results from masculinist prejudice or prejudice against

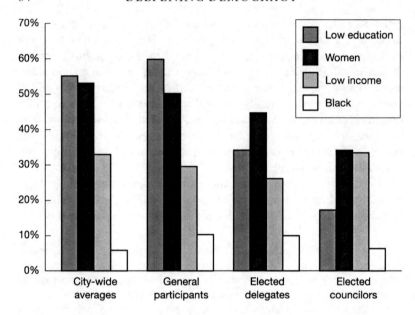

Figure 2.3 Proportion of Low Education, Women, Low Income, and Black Participants against City-Wide Averages, 1998

less-educated speech. Ethnographic evidence from district-level meetings did not show any pattern of women or the less educated speaking less often or conceding authority to educated men.[30] Interviews among participants also revealed that they did not perceive such defects. Common perceptions among activists were like the ones offered by an old-time community activist, who was asked if low education among the poor was a problem for the PB:

> No. I think it helps the OP, because it begins from below. It is not the suits[31] who come here and tell us what to do. It is us. I am a humble person. I have participated since the beginning. And like me, there are many more poor people like me who are there with me, debating or helping in whatever way possible. And so I think the OP is enriching in this way, because it makes people talk, even the poorest one. It has not let the suits take over.

A survey question about how often a person spoke at meetings painted a similar picture. Responses to the question: "Do you speak at meetings?" (Always, almost always, sometimes, never) showed that there was parity between the poor and non-poor, and between the less educated and the rest. It also found, however, that women reported

speaking less often than men.[32] However, the number of years of participation in the PB also turns out to offset this pattern significantly; years
of participation in the process are a powerful predictor of whether
persons will speak. Once we consider only persons with a certain
number of years of experience, we also find that there is no significant
difference between men and women reporting participation, or
between persons with or without formal schooling.[33]

Statistical analysis of election figures shows a similar pattern. When
we consider several significant intervening variables – as years of experience, number of ties in civil society, being on the board of directors of
a neighborhood association, and being retired or self-employed –
neither gender nor education nor poverty significantly affected a
person's chances of election.[34] Each additional year of experience
increased chances by 25 percent, and each additional tie in civil society
increased the odds by 55 percent. Being retired increases the odds by
over 200 percent, and being self-employed by over 80 percent.[35] These
results together suggest that experience offsets education and gender
disadvantages, and that education effects stem from a person's likelihood of being elected to a position in civil society and do not directly
result from what counts within PB meetings.[36] This evidence also
strongly suggests that the availability of time and women's "second
and third shifts" of household responsibilities account for many, if not
all, of these differences, particularly with respect to gender. Opinions
such as these are typical:

> Men are always flying about. To be a councilor you have to be able to go to
> many meetings, in the evenings, and in many different places. So even if you
> don't have a job outside, you still have to take care of the house. So I'd say
> this is more difficult for women.[37]

> It's difficult, but we always find time somehow, because I work, get home
> and then I feed the children, then I go to meetings. Sometimes my sister gives
> me a hand, sometimes the neighbor helps, but it's difficult.[38]

This analysis of inequality within participatory budgeting yields
several insights. First, lack of highly educated speech does not pose a
high barrier. Bourdieu's farmer, who did not "know how to speak,"
might have found in the institutions of participatory governance in
Porto Alegre a place where his type of speech might have been valued.
Certainly there are other standards for valued speech, but these do not
correlate with class or education. It is also clear that *outcomes* of participatory decision-making also do not reflect domination. This
domination would be evident if outcomes were systematically distorted

in the direction of the distribution of investments toward more power-ful citizens. If the more powerful had indeed been able to manipulate outcomes there would not be rules that privileged "regional need" over number of participants, for instance.[39] It is also clear that the hetero-geneity of persons has not derailed deliberation.[40]

This experience highlights the importance of the didactic component of PB meetings. From the perspective of individuals, the institutional design includes many meetings devoted to learning procedures and rules, as well as more specific technical criteria for municipal projects. Persons acquire specific competencies related to budgeting, but also acquire skills in debating and mobilizing resources for collective goals. And the evidence suggests there are fair opportunities for advancement for newcomers.[41] One participant with only a few years of schooling, elected councilor early on in the process, discussed his experience as a less-educated person:

> I had to learn about the process as the meetings took place. The first time I participated I was unsure, because there were persons there with college degrees, and we don't have it, so we had to wait for the others to suggest an idea first, and then enter the discussion. And there were things from City Hall in the technical areas, we used to "float." But with time, we started to learn.[42]

An explicit part of the design of the PB is a didactic component inspired by the "popular education" methodologies of Paulo Freire and the Ecclesiastic Base Communities.[43] As is clear from early materials of the administration, the ideas of popular educators of urban social move-ments were an important source of inspiration in how to run meetings and how to develop norms of dialogue that were respectful of different types of speech.[44] Meeting facilitators are always aware of their func-tion as partially didactic. One of these facilitators discussed her functions:

> Another task [. . .] is to preserve and help diffuse certain values. The partici-patory budget demands the construction of cooperation and solidarity, otherwise the logic of competition and "taking advantage" becomes estab-lished, creating processes of exclusion. Therefore, negotiations inspired in a solidaristic practice must be a constant in the pedagogical actions of facilitators.[45]

This didactic component is one of the salient features of the PB and alerts us to the fact that while persons may "naturally" learn from attending deliberative meetings, intentional design features make the learning more or less available to all. The evidence here both confirms the best expectations of deliberative democratic theory – that vast segments of participants are able to learn to participate effectively – and points to the importance of a self-conscious strategy to impart that learning. That this does not fully offset inequalities suggests that more institutional intervention is needed, though perhaps in novel ways that change time commitments necessary for effective participation. On the whole, however, the profile of the highest tier of participants in budget meetings shows that this institution is a tremendous advance over traditional democratic forms in Brazil.[46]

III Interfaces with Civil Society

Interviews showed that as persons became deeply involved in negotiations and became acquainted with other persons in the district involved in similar problems, they established lasting bonds with activists of other parts of their district and developed solidarities. This collective learning lies at the root of the transformations in civil society in Porto Alegre. Many associations in civil society have emerged since the inception of the PB. In this section, I develop a second extension to the EPG proposal around the issue of interfaces with civil society.

   One of the vexing issues for the model of empowered participatory governance is the relationship between deliberative democratic fora and civil society. Autonomous institutions of civil society are generally positively valued as the repositories of democratic practices and impulses in society; organizations in civil society might also have the best information and access to certain problems that the participatory scheme is designed to address. Relying on organized civil society in an institutional design might, for example, inadvertently favor citizens who are represented by formal and established organizations against citizens who do not enjoy such representation. It might also inadvertently reproduce and harden "movement oligarchies" by giving leaders of such organizations – that may not meet our normative democratic standards – additional legitimacy and political capital. There are also a number of negative expectations about the impact of participatory fora on civil society. If participatory fora run parallel to – coexist with – civil society, they may empty out fora of civil society by providing more efficient (and state-backed) channels for addressing collective problems. If participatory fora interface directly with civil society, might they co-opt movements? Or might local decision-making fora "balkanize" political life?[47] Cohen briefly addresses another possibility altogether, that deliberative democratic institutions might foster new forms of solidarity and help construct civil society:

> Notice, however that both the inclusion of nontraditional stakeholders and the development of deliberative arenas suggests a new possibility: that of constructing new bases of solidarity through a process of defining and addressing common concerns. [. . .] In short, these efforts – which could have very wide scope – have the potential to create new deliberative arenas outside formal politics that might work as schools of "deliberative democracy" in a special way.[48]

The Porto Alegre experiment has operated as a "school of deliberative democracy" rather than co-opting or hollowing out civil society. Participatory governance in Porto Alegre has, in fact, fostered new and more interconnected institutions within civil society. It has renewed leadership in civil society and "scaled up" activism from neighborhoods to municipal and district levels. Here I briefly explore the institutional features of participatory budgeting that account for these changes.

One of the most obvious transformations of civil society has been the rapid rise of new associations throughout the city. Although precise figures are difficult to establish, estimates for the number of neighborhood associations are shown in Table 2.1.[49] The table gives very general estimates of the trends in the transformation of civil society in Porto Alegre.

Table 2.1 The Development of Civil Society in Porto Alegre, 1986–98

Year	Neighborhood associations[a]	Cooperatives[b]	Regional popular councils[c]
1986	240		
1988	300		3
1990	380		5
1994	450	11	8
1996	500	32	11
1998	540	51	11

[a] Functioning neighborhood associations, estimated from unpublished documents from UAMPA, The Union of Neighborhood Associations of Porto Alegre, from CRC, the Center for Community Relations of the Municipality of Porto Alegre, and Baierle, *A explosão.*
[b] Estimated number of housing cooperatives from interviews.
[c] Popular councils are district-level voluntary entities that coordinate neighborhood associations.

The rise in the number of associations has been dramatic, and follows the increasing success of the PB throughout the years. By my conservative method[50] of estimation, associational density has almost doubled. Neighborhood associations are not the only type of organization in civil society. A number of other types of entity, such as Samba schools, religious and cultural groups, soccer clubs, mothers' clubs, social movements, professional organizations, and unions are part of civil society. In regional settings, many of these other entities revolve or center around the neighborhood association. There is also a limit to the number of neighborhood associations, which can help prevent an inflation in the measure due to credentialing. My survey of associational life in three of the city's districts found that 80 percent of associations held meetings at least once a month, and that over half had meetings more than once a month.

Popular Councils measure the interconnectedness of associational life. The creation of functioning popular councils was an innovation in civil society during this period. From Table 2.1 we see that the number of regional popular councils today is much greater than before, and almost all function with greater regularity. Popular councils are autonomous institutions that hold regular regional meetings on a weekly or bimonthly basis for representatives of neighborhood associations as well as independent citizens wishing to discuss the district's problems. The founding statutes of one of these councils, in the Partenon district, states that its purposes are:

1. To obtain and share information about the municipal administration . . .
2. To monitor public institutions . . .
3. To decide upon questions referent to our district, to the city, the state, and the country.
4. To create proposals to the public administration.
5. To define proper policies in the areas of transportation, social service delivery . . .
6. To participate in the planning of the city, state, and country.
7. To foster and support popular organizations.[51]

While popular councils do not exercise power over neighborhood associations, or over the PB, they often coordinate activities between neighborhood associations (to make sure a fund-raiser will not overlap with a cultural event in a nearby neighborhood), settle disputes among them and, more importantly, deploy collective resources to solve regional problems. Often popular councils act as intermediaries between associations and municipal government, approaching the government with the moral mandate of forty or fifty active associations. The founding statutes above show how popular councils have political goals such as sharing governance and scrutinizing public administration.

This picture contrasts with the situation in 1988. While much of the city had little associative activity, neighborhood associations and oppositional social movements were active in five or six of the sixteen districts into which the city is today divided. There was a functioning umbrella group for neighborhood associations, UAMPA, which according to a 1988 count, had approximately 150 associations registered. Today, associational life has grown more dense throughout the city. The segregated geography of Porto Alegre means that these changes have occurred most dramatically in the city's peripheries, areas with the least prior organization. The poorest districts of the city have felt the greatest impact.

An activist in the poorest district of the city, Nordeste, who has followed the process closely, accounted for these changes:

> New leaders appear with new ideas every year and they are hard workers and full of good intentions. Our district has benefited a lot. Many of the new vilas now have developed associations to fight through the participatory budget, and old ones are reopening to go and make their demands in the participatory budget. Every year two or three new associations appear.[52]

Activists describe a common pattern of neighborhood association development that begins with collective mobilization around common demands. Sometimes there already is a registered, but inactive, association for the area. Nonetheless, one or more concerned persons will begin to attend PB meetings and eventually mobilize a number of concerned neighbors who then attend as an ad hoc group that later becomes a more permanent association:

> We began by attending the participatory budget meeting. There used to be an association here, but it was more social and less interested in the problems of our side of the vila. So we went with a different name, and today we are registered as an association. We were able to get part of the street paved but we are still going to go back because there is a lot we still need.[53]

A smaller survey I conducted among "key activists" (n = 104) – regular participants in a regional forum – in three districts of the city shows that most participate in a number of different fora. On average, activists participate in two to three meetings per week, and are regular attendees in three to four different fora. There were regional differences, but 44 percent of activists participated regularly in a forum with a regional or municipal focus other than the PB or regional popular council. Almost all activists reported participating regularly in their local neighborhood association – which suggests that there are significant ties between local, regional, and municipal settings.

A number of respondents echoed that this indeed was an important process for developing more permanent networks of activists. For example, one woman described her trajectory from initial involvement in the Forum of Cooperatives to becoming an elected delegate and councilor, and the way the PB has helped foster enduring bonds:

> After starting to participate in the Forum of Cooperatives, I started to become involved with community leaders and wound up being elected as a Delegate of the Participatory Budget. At first, I did not understand much, but with time I started to get it. I got a group together from our cooperative to come on a regular basis. I then was elected to the Council. There it was where I really learned what is a movement, what a community leader does. It was an incredible learning experience in becoming a community leader.[54]

And a number of municipal mobilizations have resulted. The hunger campaigns in 1991 and the Human Rights Municipal Conference of 1997 drew activists from all districts as regular participants. A kind of city-wide solidarity emerged from participatory governance. Some of these municipal initiatives such as the human rights conference are sponsored by City Hall, but they have been peopled and organized by community leaders from participatory fora. Participants in the process often recounted that civil society had changed in these directions – toward municipal and regional focus – and they often thought that the process had compelled them to broaden their own horizons and see themselves as activists for a larger collective:

> As delegate and councilor you learn about the district, meet new persons, become a person who has to respond not only to your association, but also to the district as a whole and the city as a whole. I participated in the two congresses to decide the *Plano Diretor* [municipal planning priorities] and since I have worried about the city as a whole. After a year, I learned not to look only at the district, but that you have to look at the city as a whole.[55]

Consider the institutional features (and their alternatives) of participatory governance in Porto Alegre that account for these changes. One of the most salient features is its manner of recognizing participants and collectives. In the late 1980s, leftists in Brazil debated how leftist governments should interact with civil society. In São Paulo, for example, after the PT victory in 1989, some held that popular councils should be consultative and others argued that they should be deliberative. If popular councils were consultative, they would be part of the government's organizational structure, and if they were deliberative they would remain as autonomous associations inserted into municipal government.[56] In Porto Alegre, an early vision of interaction with organized civil society – presidents of neighborhood associations, for instance – gave way to a "laissez faire" relationship to civil society.

A hallmark of the PB is that anyone can in principle participate in deliberations. At meetings of the PB where organizations are counted, participants are asked which organization they represent in order to tally votes, but the deliberative processes do not discriminate between "actually existing" neighborhood associations and a momentary association of persons who decide to call themselves a "street commission." Some leaders of the neighborhood movement felt "slighted," but the practice reduces the advantages of prior organization. It has created a system that actually fosters the creation of new associations, as well as the creation of parallel organizations to counter unresponsive ones.

But participatory institutions here address issues that were already central to civil society concerns. For instance, in Porto Alegre in 1989, many neighborhood associations contested the poor quality of urban infrastructure and services. Municipal government might also have created deliberative channels to address environmental issues or the cultural policy of city government, both of which have since become part of participatory governance. Both would have no doubt attracted activists, but would not have attracted the attention of civil society as the PB did, and would not have reshaped it. Because significant proportions of the activities of neighborhood associations went to securing urban services and the PB offered a completely novel way of achieving those goals, civil society evolved even as it transformed its relations with municipal government. As an interviewee reiterated:

> Before you had to go to the *vereador's* (councilperson) office when you had to get something done, you had to go and sit in his waiting area, sometimes for more than a whole day. When you saw him you told him why you needed this street or materials for the (neighborhood) association building. It was always an exchange. Or you would bring a petition with lots of signatures to DEMHAB to show you had respect in the community. Today it is different. This brought big changes to the associations, because it was what we mostly used to do.[57]

Importantly, the PB has also made some of the principal tasks of neighborhood associations much easier. As another interviewee states,

Before the participatory budget, the associations used to work by themselves. Each one would write up its demands and go to the government. Today, 90 percent of the business of associations is through the participatory budget. All our main demands are through the participatory budget. And even complaints are through the participatory budget, because of the councilors. Councilors can speak directly with the government. Sometimes a president will take a month to get an audition from the government and a councilor will get it in a week.[58]

There is no direct incentive to create an association, as mentioned earlier, since formal existence is not a requisite for participation. But the calculus for forming an association has changed. For example, participants were asked if they used to participate more or less in civil society prior to the PB. While 10.2 percent of respondents did indeed participate less, 26.7 percent participated the same (in addition to now participating in the OP) and 26.7 percent participated more.[59]

While not part of the stated goals of the PB, its institutions provide a number of indirect "subsidies" for civil society. As mentioned earlier, the PB has individual didactic effects. But the PB also recruits activists into associations of civil society, and provides political education for most new activists today. In my smaller survey, of the 104 activists, approximately half had their start in associative life through the PB. Of activists with less than five years' experience, the vast majority had their start in the PB. Another "subsidy" that it provides is the regional forum in which activists meet other activists, share information and learning, and coordinate mobilization across districts. Observers of the process, such as Gildo Lima, one of the architects of the participatory structures in the first administration, argue that civil society has indeed become less locally focussed as a result of the PB, and that a new form of mobilization has emerged:

This type of mass mobilization campaign has become rapid, dynamic, and has established a frequent "network of conversations." While I don't speak to my neighbor who lives in front of my apartment, [. . .] in this network the guy who lives here speaks with the guy who lives on the other side, and the one who lives really far away, every week because of this process. Many people do not realize that we have created the capacity for dialogue every week as a result of the participatory budget.[60]

In the case of the PB, unlike the Associative Democracy proposal of Cohen and Rogers,[61] there are no institutional checks on associations for standards of democracy. And while this design has succeeded in fostering new associations, there is no assurance of the "internal quality"

of these organizations. While architects and managers of the PB in
Porto Alegre are well aware that certain neighborhood associations
may leave something to be desired in terms of certain procedural standards, City Hall has nevertheless refrained from interfering in these
popular organizations. The experience of political repression, or of
state-controlled labor unions and neighborhood associations in Brazil's
recent past, accounts for this reluctance to interfere. But an additional
feature functions as a potential check: just as the PB will recognize any
association, the door is always open for parallel groups to lay claim as
associations also. The PB allows for persons to associate informally and
to represent a district or a neighborhood, whether or not it is officially
in existence. If a recognized association is not sufficiently responsive to
persons in a community, members may "secede" through the PB and
eventually become dominant by earning respect by achieving goals in
the PB.

IV The Context of Participatory Reform

A final issue for the model of empowered participatory governance is
the enabling context of participatory reforms. Many of the other
Workers' Party administrations that were elected in 1988 and 1992,
such as that of São Paulo (1989–92), failed and so discredited the
municipal branch of the party. Other municipal administrations who
experimented with comprehensive participatory reforms, like the Florianópolis administration (1992–96) in the state of Santa Catarina,
under the Popular Socialist Party (PPS) did not achieve re-election.
While it is beyond the scope of this chapter to discuss in detail what
background conditions perhaps made Porto Alegre different from
some of these other cities, here I discuss "what went right" and suggest
that the EPG model ought more fully to consider governance outcomes
as a condition for the reproduction of deliberative institutions in competitive democratic arenas. More specifically, I suggest the issues of
institutional capacity to deliver results for participation enable deliberative democracy to enhance the legitimacy of governance and
sometimes extend that capacity.

One key to the generation of these positive civic outcomes was that
the reforms delivered public goods promptly to convince skeptical and
time-pressed residents that participation is worthwhile. The experiment would have failed as a participatory institution if it had not
produced tangible material improvements.[62] Students of urban politics
in Latin America have pointed to "bounded rationality" problems of

the poor in terms of democratic participation.[63] Participation may not make much sense for poor persons save for an assurance of timely returns. In highly fragmented social contexts, or where persons are not accustomed to civic engagement, the equation may be even more stark. In addition, effective deliberative governance may generate practical opposition as its redistributive consequences become evident.

Part of the explanation for the success is that "good governance" has always been central to the PT's agenda. From this commitment, it has made significant resources available to the PB. With decentralization reforms codified in Brazil's 1988 Constitution, cities gained new ways of raising revenue through vehicle, sales, and services taxes. Porto Alegre has been a relative winner by virtue of being a capital city in a wealthy state, and has raised enough revenues to keep pace with the increased fiscal burdens placed by the devolution of social services while carrying out new investments. The Porto Alegre administration, with yearly revenues today well over US$150 per person, has the capacity to offer many more returns than some of the municipal governments around Porto Alegre. For example, the commuter cities of Viamão and Alvorada have elected PT mayors but, with per capita revenues at a fraction of Porto Alegre levels, have failed to draw sustained attendance in participatory meetings.[64]

But these successes stem from the way in which participatory governance in Porto Alegre enhances the legitimacy of government decisions; this has in turn extended the capacities of municipal government. After the first year's budget was drawn up through the PB in Porto Alegre, the next legal step was to have it approved by the municipal legislative. While a majority of the city council was hostile to the PB and the Workers' Party, the submitted budget was approved without alterations. Popular pressure protected the autonomy of the process; participants from meetings personally went to the office of councilpersons to exert pressure. Despite a negative media campaign, they succeeded in guaranteeing the budget's approval.[65] The element of public justification from deliberations over the budget makes it difficult for politicians in the context of a democracy to oppose something that is a result of the "public will." Today, although the PT has not achieved a majority in the municipal legislature, the budget has been approved every year without major alterations.

There are other ways in which the legitimacy of the municipal government has extended its capacities. Genro argues that the PB has generated public support for raising land-use taxes; these new taxes were largely responsible for the revenues available for public investment through the PB.[66] And as has been pointed out, increased compliance with taxation has also increased revenues; though it is difficult to establish the degree to which this results from the PB, the increased legitimacy of the administration's policies no doubt help account for it. The continued ability of the municipal government to secure financing for projects also comes from public scrutiny of several thousand citizens over public funds.[67]

In fact, the success of the Porto Alegre experiment comes from its legitimacy-enhancing aspects rather than from "exceptional features" of the city's history. While Porto Alegre has a unique history of left-populism dating back to the 1930s, the Workers' Party came to play a part in municipal politics in opposition to the left-populist party, the PDT, winning the 1988 municipal election in large part as a protest against the PDT's failures of governance.[68] Other cities in Brazil, like São Paulo, where the PT did not re-elect its administration, possessed comparable, if not stronger, community movements and supportive unions. One of the key problems of many early PT administrations was their inability to give voice to organized social movements within the administration without succumbing to the charge of privileging "special interests" and without becoming embroiled in interfaction disputes between social movements within the party.[69] The PT administration in São Paulo, for instance, came under attack for giving "special privilege" to social movements sympathetic to the party without considering "the whole city's interests." Without a broad-based participatory system that drew participants from outside organized movement sectors, the municipal government was open to the charge of "left patronage."[70] And without a clear system of rules for negotiating competing interests, the administration in time also came under attack from segments of the Party that accused the administration of "class treason" for attending to the interests of business in certain decisions.[71]

Enhancing the legitimacy of government may not, by itself, always assure the reproduction of EPG institutions. But in the case of participatory budgeting, both of these types of problem – charges of patronage, and attacks from segments of the base of support of the party for not giving enough resources – are averted in an open, and transparent, participatory system like Porto Alegre's. In fact, PT administrations have become more successful in gaining re-election as the open style of participatory reform of the PB has become the standard for municipal governance. PT municipal governments with Porto Alegre-style participatory budgeting systems were re-elected more often in 1996 than in 1992, and the PT has continued to gain municipal administrations on the basis of the well-known success of participatory budgeting in delivering effective governance.

V Conclusion: On the Fertile Grounds for Utopias

The model of empowered participatory governance offers a set of institutional designs intended to solve many of the problems of both command-and-control institutions and inefficient New Left proposals. Deliberative decision-making that is sufficiently empowered in the correct way holds promise for efficient, redistributive, and fair decision-making. The Porto Alegre experiment I have described seems to both fit the model and confirm its optimistic expectations: high numbers of participants from several strata of Porto Alegre's society have come together to share in a governance structure that has been efficient and highly redistributive. I raised three issues that I believe are important across the range of EPG cases by extending the "real-world question" to a range of situations that ought to be difficulties for the PB.

I have suggested that despite the strong inequalities of urban Brazil, participation of the poor and uneducated is present and that the wealthy and educated do not dominate. The institutional feature of relevance is the didactic component that appears to offset these tendencies. The lesson is that participatory institutions should include mechanisms to deal with inequalities specific to their settings, and that we should reframe "the problem of inequality" as a problem of contexts rather than as a problem of persons. The difficulty with lack of education or of the poverty of participants is not that these are in themselves barriers to deliberating or collective problem-solving. Persons across all walks of life are effective problem-solvers and discussants in their own affairs. The difficulty involves establishing settings in which certain types of speech are not more valued than others, and in which opportunities for learning are broadly available. The data also showed lack of parity on gender dimensions; however, this may have more to do with the availability of time and schedules of meetings than deliberative competence per se. It is also clear that the participation of women in the higher tiers of the PB represents a significant advance over traditional democratic institutions. The proportion of women in the city council in Porto Alegre has never been above 10 percent, compared to over a third of the Council of the Budget.

I also discussed the impact of institutions on civil society. The remarkably positive impact of the reforms here stems from the type of interface with civil society and the incentive structures to participation. The PB supports civil society in a number of indirect ways, creating a "network of conversation," training activists, and making the task of neighborhood associations easier. This impact is not trivial; an organized and intermeshed civil society can help sustain a participatory experiment such as this one by sharing in its responsibilities in ways that individual citizens cannot. A survey question about how persons came to find out about budget meetings showed that among poorer persons, face-to-face interactions, through neighborhood associations and popular councils, was the main channel. A survey of the sixteen regions showed that popular councils supported budget meetings directly and indirectly through advertising them, recruiting new participants, and running meetings. The impact on civil society may be more appropriately described as a set of "synergies" than simply as a one-way support.

I also explored the enabling context for these reforms, the "politics" that make it possible, and pointed to legitimacy-enhancing features of participatory reforms that may extend the capacities of government to carry them out. The ability to satisfy participants' expectations is, in the context of strong need and a competitive electoral democracy, crucial to the survival and reproduction of the institution.

Another sense in which its "politics" are important is related to the origins of this utopian experiment. One question left for further research and reflection concerns the role of motivating political visions. In this case, the *raison d'état* driving Porto Alegre's participatory experiment was a radical democratic vision of popular municipal control and the inversion of government priorities away from downtown and toward the peripheries. For many PT administrators, participatory reforms are part of a broader transformative project. An early debate in terms of progressive administrations was whether municipal governments should function with the goal of most efficient and democratic delivery of services, or play a role in a larger culturally transformative project. One prominent PT intellectual, Jorge Bittar, writes in an official publication that:

> The inversion of priorities and popular participation are necessary, but not sufficient, components for a transformative project. An alternative project of local power must consider actions on two levels: at the municipal political power and in local society [. . .] the clash with the values that sustain local hegemony at the local level becomes a conflict that must cross all of our actions.[72]

Writings from the early days of the process document lofty objectives for a popular administration, as when the PT candidate for mayor Olivio Dutra wrote that popular councils would "restore the historical legacy of the working classes in giving form and content to democracy."[73] Early activists within these reforms were guided by visions of radical democracy borne of the Ecclesiastical Base Communities, of labor and urban movements, and of activism within socialist parties. These "true believers" helped establish popular deliberation early in the various districts.[74] One of the more experienced activists described his concern for new persons in terms that tell of an activist calling:

> The most important thing is that more and more persons come. Those who come for the first time are welcome, we have a lot of patience for them, there is no problem, we let them make demands during technical meetings, they can speak their mind and their anxieties. We have patience for it because we were like that once. And if he has an issue, we set up a meeting for him, and create a commission to accompany him. You have the responsibility of not abandoning him, of staying with him. That is the most important thing.[75]

As Cohen writes, deliberative democracy is at its best a process whereby participants reconsider and reconstruct their preferences.[76] The question we can ask is if it makes a difference if deliberation takes place not just under the aegis of rationality and problem-solving and with the goal of reforming government, but also under the aegis of empowerment of the poor and social justice, and with a goal of social transformation and rupture, visions borne of social movement activism and oppositional politics.

At the time of writing (2001), the PB appears to have become fully consolidated. In its fourth term, the administration concentrated on increasing the quality of the meetings rather than increasing the numbers of participants. Civil society activists have become concerned, in fact, with whether the PB has become too successful and whether civil society has become too oriented toward it.[77] The PB has been extended to state-level government, with ex-Porto Alegre Mayor Olívio Dutra as governor of the state since 1999, and a number of experiments with variants of participatory budgeting currently ongoing in over a hundred PT-controlled cities in Brazil. This large and decentralized experiment in empowered participatory governance, in a variety of diverse settings, will show whether variants of PB-style participatory reforms are robust enough to guarantee successes in a wide variety of contexts, or whether local variations more suited to local conditions will generate other novel forms. In either case, the legacy of this experiment should be watched with interest by students of participatory governance and deliberative democracy.

Appendix 1: Statistics

I analyzed a representative sample of PB participants drawn from first plenary meetings in March and April of 1998. Respondents were randomly selected from participants at each regional and thematic meeting and were asked to answer a questionnaire. If the person had difficulty in answering the questionnaire in written format, an interviewer would complete the questionnaire. The sample of participants was roughly 10 percent of the total number of participants. The survey was designed and applied by myself, members of an NGO, CIDADE, in Porto Alegre, and municipal government employees. For this analysis, the models were restricted to variables of interest. Independent variables of interest included Female, an indicator variable that assumed 1 for female; Poor, an indicator dummy variable for income up to two minimum wages; Low Ed, an indicator variable for education up to the 8th grade. Important intervening variables were the indicator variables Retired and Self Employed based on self-reporting; Experience was a count of years of participation in the OP; Ties was the number of ties in civil society, and Directorate, was an indicator variable of whether the person had been elected to a directory position.

Logistic Coefficients Predicting the Likelihood of Election to Delegate Position in the OP, 1998

Independent variables	Model 1	Model 2
Female	−0.53 (0.20)**	−0.48 (0.26)
Poor (1)	0.004 (0.23)	0.10 (0.28)
Low Ed (1)	−0.50 (0.21)*	−0.21 (0.26)
Years	—	0.23 (0.04)***
Ties	—	0.44 (0.09)***
Directorate	—	0.82 (0.26)**
Retired	—	1.18 (0.31)***
Autonomous	—	0.59 (0.28)*
Constant	−1.64 (0.11)***	−2.11 (0.27)***
Chi-Squared	13.95**	141.91***
−2L.L.	683.53	473.33

Note: numbers in parentheses indicate standard error.

  * $p < 0.05$
 ** $p < 0.01$
*** $p < 0.001$

Appendix 2: Weights and Criteria for Allocating Resources

Once municipal priorities for the year's budget are established by the Municipal Council of the Budget, specific investments are divided among the city's districts according to three criteria:[78]

1. Lack of the specific public service
    Up to 25% of district's population: 1
    26 to 50%: 2
    51 to 75%: 3
    76 to 100%: 4
2. Total population of the district, in thousands:
    Up to 49,999: 1
    50 to 99,999: 2
    100 to 199,999: 3
    above 200,000: 4
3. How the district prioritized the specific service
    Fourth or below: 1
    Third: 2
    Second: 3
    First: 4

Appendix 3: Development of Participatory Structures in Porto Alegre, 1983–98

1983	City-Wide Organization of Neighborhood Associations founded
1986–89	Failed attempts at City Hall participatory structures
1987	First Popular Councils developed throughout the city
1988	First Health Councils developed
1989	PT victory, participatory budget announced
1990	First rounds of participatory budget meetings, in five regions
1991	Direct voting for Tutelary Council introduced Number of regional meetings increased to 16
1992	Number of participants in participatory budget takes off
1992–95	Participatory structures widened to include municipal councils on housing, social assistance, child and family services, and technology

1993   City-Wide Congress to debate directives
          Municipal Health Council
1994   Direct voting for municipal school directors introduced
          Theme-oriented meetings introduced
1995   City-wide Forum of Child and Adolescent Services
1996   Human Rights Council instituted
          Municipal Councils on human rights, environment
1997   City-Wide Forum of Cooperatives
          Participatory planning of schools
1998   Human Rights Conference
          Second City-Wide Congress, Health Congress
2000   Thematic meetings expanded to six areas

Notes

* Assistant Professor of Sociology at the University of Pittsburgh. This work would not have been possible without the generosity of CIDADE, in Porto Alegre, the *Prefeitura* of Porto Alegre, and the participants of the OP, or the participants in the Real Utopias conference.

1. For similar experiments in Brazil, see Gianpaolo Baiocchi, ed., *Radicals in Power: Experiments in Urban Democracy in Brazil*, forthcoming: Zed Press; William Nylen, "Popular Participation in Brazil's Workers' Party: Democratizing Democracy in Municipal Politics," *The Political Chronicle*, vol. 8, no. 2 (1998), pp. 1–9; Ivo Lesbaupin, *Prefeituras do povo e para o povo*, São Paulo, Brazil: Edições Loyola (1996); Lucio Kowarick and Andre Singer, "The Workers' Party in Sao Paulo," in Lucio Kowarick, ed., *Social Struggles and the City*, New York: Monthly Review Press (1994); Sonia Alvarez, "Deepening Democracy: Popular Movement Networks, Constitutional Reform, and Radical Urban Regimes in Contemporary Brazil," in Robert Fisher and Joseph Kling, eds., *Mobilizing the Community*, Newbury Park: Sage Publications (1993). For other examples from Latin America, see Gerd Schonwalder, "Local Politics and the Peruvian Left," *Latin American Perspectives*, vol. 33, no. 2 (1998); Marta Harnecker, *Frente amplio: los desafios de un izquierda legal. Segunda parte: los hitos mas importantes de su historia* (Montevideo: Ediciones La Republica, 1991).

2. "Participation in government" has witnessed an explosion of interest from various quarters and perspectives, particularly in the context of the decentralization of government. For some representative positions see Benjamin Barber, "Three Challenges to Reinventing Democracy," in Paul Hirst and Sunil Khilnani, eds., *Reinventing Democracy*, Cambridge, MA: Blackwell (1998); John Keane, "The Philadelphia Model," in Takasi Inoguchi, Edward Newman, and John Keane, eds., *The Changing Nature of Democracy*, Tokyo: United Nations University Press (1998); Peter Evans, "Government Action, Social Capital and Development: Reviewing the Evidence on Synergy," *World Development*, vol. 24, no. 6 (1996).

3. For the city of Porto Alegre, see Rebecca N. Abers, *Inventing Local Democracy: Grassroots Politics in Brazil*, Boulder, CO: Lynne Rider Publishers (2001); Gianpaolo Baiocchi, "Militance and Citizenship: The Workers' Party, Civil Society, and Participatory Governance in Porto Alegre, Brazil," Ph.D. dissertation, University of Wisconsin (2001); Luciano Fedozzi, *Orçamento participativo: reflexoes sobre a experiencia de Porto Alegre*, Porto Alegre: Tomo Editorial (1997); José Utzig, "Notas sobre of governo

do PT em Porto Alegre," *Novos estudos cebrap*, no. 45 (1996), pp. 209–22; Sergio Baierle, *A explosao da experiencia; a emergencia de um novo principio etico-politico em Porto Alegre*, unpublished MA dissertation, UNICAMP (1991).

4. Fung and Wright's proposal stands alongside Cohen and Rogers's proposal of associational democracy as the most institutional accounts of deliberative democracy. Other theorists certainly pay attention to institutional conditions and arrangements, but do not engage in the thorough analysis of institutional design characteristic of the EPG proposal. See also Joshua Cohen and Joel Rogers, *Associations and Democracy*, London: Verso (1992).

5. Joshua Cohen, "Procedure and Substance in Deliberative Democracy," in Seyla Benhabib, ed., *Democracy and Difference: Contesting the Boundaries of the Political*, Princeton, NJ: Princeton University Press (1996).

6. The phrase, "*o modo petista de governar*" has since become part of the lexicon of political discussions about governance. See Jorge Bittar, *O modo petista de governar*, São Paulo, Brazil (1992).

7. See Tanya Barcellos, *Segregação urbana e mortalidade infantil em Porto Alegre*, Porto Alegre: F.E.E. (1986); Prefeitura Municipal de Porto Alegre, *Regioes do orçamento participativo de Porto Alegre – Alguns Indicadores Sociais*, Porto Alegre: Fundaçao de Educaçao Social e Comunitaria (1999).

8. The number of delegates for a district is determined as follows: for the first 100 persons, one delegate for every 10 persons; for the next 150 persons, one for 20; for the next 150, one for 30; for each additional 40 persons after that, one delegate. To cite an example, a district that had 520 persons in attendance would have 26 delegates. An association with 47 members in attendance would have two delegates (9 percent of the delegates). See Leonardo Avritzer, "Public Deliberation at the Local Level: Participatory Budgeting in Brazil," paper presented at the *Experiments in Deliberative Democracy* Conference, Madison, WI, January 2000.

9. Resources are allocated to each district based on a system of weights that considers the district's population, its need for the service, and its chosen priorities. I describe this system of weights in the appendix.

10. Adapted from CIDADE, "Ciclo do orcamento participativo," in *De olho no orcamento*, Porto Alegre: CIDADE (1995).

11. In practice, these fora also function as a space for community demands and problems in general to be aired, for information to be divulged about the functioning of government, and as a regular meeting place for activists of a district. My own research showed that meetings were often "taken over" by activists who make use of this regular forum to discuss issues beyond budgeting matters. See Baiocchi, "Militance and Citizenship."

12. As has been noted, councilors fulfill functions that would in other cities be associated with the official municipal legislative, though councilors are subject to immediate recall and have term limits of two years.

13. Tarso Genro and Ubiratan de Souza, *Orçamento participativo: a experiencia de Porto Alegre*, Porto Alegre: Fundacao Perseu Abramo (1997), discuss the increase in the property tax in the first tenure of the PT administration. This is also discussed by Utzig, who describes the reforms undertaken by the administration to modernize fiscal procedures: José Utzig, "Notas," pp. 215–20.

14. This is a measure of the overall efficiency of the administrative apparatus. Though national-level changes, as making municipal governments responsible for the provision of health services, complicate this comparison, all evidence points to increased efficiency. Of course, it is impossible, without suitable comparisons, to determine what portion of that increased efficiency is due to the OP and what portion is due to simply the fact that an outside political party has come into power.

15. Prefeitura Municipal de Porto Alegre, *Anuario estatistico*, Porto Alegre: GAPLAN (1997).

16. Regina Pozzobon, *Porto Alegre: os desafios da gestao democratica*, São Paulo: Instituto Polis (1998).

17. This figure, based on published numbers of municipal government, is the best available estimate of the actual number of participants from a figure of attendees at first-round meetings. On the one hand, persons at these first-round meetings are not the actual participants throughout the year, and as many as 15 percent of participants at district-level meetings also come to thematic meetings. But, on the other hand, much higher estimates of participation exist based on extrapolations of informal meetings that go on throughout the year, but there is no way precisely to assess its magnitude.

18. A "minimum wage" is a convenient unit to measure income in Brazil with currency fluctuations. As of January 2001 it is fluctuating at near US$60 per month, and "poverty" is often informally set at a household income of two minimum wages.

19. Pozzbon, *Os Desafios*, pp. 3–9.

20. Pierre Bourdieu, *Language and Symbolic Power*, Cambridge: Polity (1991).

21. Ibid., p. 146.

22. Ibid., p. 147.

23. Jane Mansbridge, *Beyond Adversary Democracy*, Chicago: University of Chicago Press (1980), p. 103.

24. Survey results are published in CIDADE, "Orçamento participativo – quem e a populacao que participa e que pensa do processo," Porto Alegre: Centro de Assessoria e Estudos Urbanos (unpublished report, 1999). See the statistical appendix of this essay for details.

25. 1998 Survey data. Women are 53 percent of the city's residents, and persons with low education are 55 percent of the city's residents.

26. The count of persons with education up to the eighth grade.

27. Persons with a household income of up to two "minimum-wages" per month, which comes to aproximately US$124 (November 1999).

28. It was not possible to include the question of race on the 1998 survey. Nonetheless, using other estimators for the race of participants strongly suggests that "race" by itself does not prevent participation or the achievement of elected positions, though the question certainly merits further inquiry. The general participant data comes from an existing earlier survey (1996), but which does not permit any tests as a result of the numerically small sample. The data on councilors and delegates comes from my own count of councilors and a sample of delegates. Here I considered specifically the category "black" (*negro*) which, as per the conventions of the Brazilian census, is based on self-identification. "Blacks" make up approximately 5 percent of the city's population, and persons of mixed descent (*pardos* – "browns") make up approximately 10 percent. For a discussion of race in this part of Brazil see Ilka Boaventura Leite, *Negros no sul do Brasil*, Ilha de Santa Catarina, SC: Letras Contemporaneas (1996). A survey fielded in 2000 by CIDADE did include the race question, but its results are not available at the time of writing.

29. These apparently surprising results are consonant with the available literature on race relations and urban poverty in Brazil. This process draws persons from the city's urban periphery, which is where non-whites tend to live, but which is also relatively integrated. Observers of the community-based "neighborhood movement" have pointed to the fact that its leadership is also relatively integrated. Ney dos Santos Oliveira, "Favelas and Ghettos: Race and Class in Rio de Janeiro and New York City," *Latin American Perspectives*, vol. 23, no. 4 (1996), pp. 71–89; Peggy Lovell, "Race, Gender, and Development in Brazil," *Latin American Research Review*, vol. 29, no. 3 (1994), pp. 7–35; Edward Telles, "Residential Segregation and Skin Color in Brazil," *American Sociological Review*, vol. 57, no. 2 (1992), pp. 186–97.

30. This was based on a year and a half of attendance of meetings between 1997 and 1999 in three of the city's districts. What did emerge was that there was an informal gendered division of labor among activists around types of issue for which women and men were suited. This does not mean, however, that women were prevented from effective participation.

31. *Colarinho-branco*, literally, the "white-collars."

32. The logistic coefficient predicting participation (model not reported here) based

solely on gender gives the odds at 28.33 percent lower, with a standard error of 0.09. and Chi-Squared of 13.75, statistically significant at p < 0.001.

33. Once we consider years of experience, gender ceases to be a significant predictor.

34. It should be noted, for example, that analyses, not shown here, that considered education in number of years, or income in terms of tiers, found that the highest levels of education and income negatively affected chances of election.

35. See the logistic models reported in the appendix.

36. Being elected to a directorate of a neighborhood association, for instance, is associated with education. Another result that suggests that this interpretation is correct is that conditional logistic regressions (not reported here) that estimate chances of election to councilor from the pool of delegates do not show any factor other than experience to be significant. Static data cannot be any more conclusive, however, since we cannot control for factors that may cause persons to be long-term participants.

37. Adriana, interview, May 1999. N.b. participants' names here are pseudonyms.

38. Marina, interview, June 1998.

39. The system of weights has changed over the years. "Popular mobilization" was an original criterion that was changed in favor a system that considers "needs" in the system of weights. These criteria are always in debate and revision by councilors. The current system, which considers need, followed by the district's priorities and population, clearly advantages a few of the city's districts in distribution of resources every year. The poorest district, Nordeste, for example, always takes resources regardless of the results of deliberation. For a discussion of the emergence and transformation of these principles, see Genro and Souza, *Orçamento*, chapter 1.

40. Although no standards exist against which to judge these outcomes, through the PB citizens have been able to decide upon more projects and on the allocation of more resources each year, deciding upon more than several hundred projects over the last few years.

41. The income level of two minimum wages against which I have tested for parity is less than a third of the city's median household income of 6.4 minimum wages, and the education level of eighth grade is well below the city's average. See Pozzobon, *Os Desafios*, pp. 3–9.

42. Gilberto, interview, 1997.

43. Paolo Friere, *Pedagogy of the Oppressed*, trans. Myra Bergman Ramos, New York: Herder and Herder (1970).

44. See, for instance, the discussion in Sergio Baierle, *A explosao da experiencia*.

45. Eunínce de Andrade Araújo, cited in Genro and Souza, *Orçamento*, p. 30.

46. If we compare the profile of city council-persons with the councilors of the budget meetings, we find that there are much greater proportions of women, of poorer persons, of the less educated, and of blacks involved in budget meetings. For instance, the average percentage of women in city councils since democratization has been less than 10 percent, and the percentage of poor persons or persons without formal education has been close to zero.

47. Fung and Wright, Introduction to this volume, p. 37.

48. Cohen, "Procedure," pp. 112–13.

49. One of the main reasons it is difficult to establish how many active associations existed at any one point in time is that there are many more groups "in law" than in practice. For this reason listings of officially registered organizations, which I do not use here, do not help assess activity in civil society.

50. There are at least twice as many associations officially registered with City Hall. I counted associations that either paid dues to the union of neighborhood associations or appeared listed with participants in the PB meetings.

51. Conselho Popular do Partenon, *Regimento interno*, Porto Alegre (1992), p. 1.

52. Fernando, interview, 1998.

53. Marilia, interview, 1997.

54. Maria, interview, 1999.

55. Antonio, interview, 1997.

56. In São Paulo, the deliberative vision of mayor Erundina won. Popular power was "instituted" as a fourth branch of government, after the legislative, executive, and judiciary. See Kowarick and Singer, "The Workers' Party."

57. Nelsa, interview, 1988.

58. Antonio, interview, 1997.

59. Survey data, 1998. These results are also reported in CIDADE, *Orçamento*.

60. Gildo Lima, interview, 1999.

61. Cohen and Rogers, *Associations and Democracy*.

62. One survey question, "Do you think the population really decides on the results of the Participatory Budget?," showed significant association with "Has your district or thematic area received benefits?" Positive answers to the perceived popular control and positive answers to having received benefits were very clearly linked. Crosstabulations of "population really decides" and "received benefits" show that positive answers to perceived popular control and receiving benefits were very clearly linked (Spearman correlation = 0.247. Chi-Squared = 47.161; Degrees of freedom = 1; $p < 0.001$.) An analysis of district-level participation for the first few years over time also shows that it was responsive to investment.

63. Henry Dietz, *Urban Poverty, Political Participation and the State*, Pittsburgh, PA: University of Pittsburgh Press (1998).

64. Marcelo Kunrath, in personal conversation, May 1999. On the other hand, there are PT administrations that have reported success in developing participatory schemas based on the Porto Alegre model in small towns with similar revenues as those of Viamão; this suggests that a combination of factors may offset the revenue constraint. See Nylen, *Participation*.

65. Gildo Lima, interview, May 1999. See also Abers, *Inventing Local Democracy*. For a comparison of PT cities in Brazil see Baiocchi, *Radicals in Power*.

66. Genro and Souza, *Orçamento*, p. 26. See also the discussion in Guilherme Cassel and João Verle, "A politica tributaria e de saneamento financeiro da administração popular," in Carlos Henrique Horn, ed., *Porto Alegre: o desafio da mudanca*, Porto Alegre: Ortiz (1994), p. 45.

67. Luciano Brunnet, in personal conversation.

68. Baierle, *A explosão*.

69. Some of these difficulties, which led in some cases to splits in the Party, are discussed in Margaret Keck, *The Worker's Party and Democratization in Brazil*, New Haven: Yale University Press (1992).

70. Kowarick and Singer, "The Workers' Party," pp. 240–47.

71. Ibid., p. 249.

72. Bittar, *O modo*, p. 8.

73. Arno Agostin Filho, "A experiencia do orçamento participativo na administração popular da prefeitura municipal de Porto Alegre," in Carlos Henrique Horn, ed., *Porto Alegre: o desafio da mudanca*, Porto Alegre: Editora Ortiz (1994) p. 50.

74. Based upon interview accounts of the development of the PB in various districts of the city.

75. Nino, interview, 1999.

76. Cohen, "Procedure."

77. Interviews.

78. Genro and Souza, *Orçamento*, p. 95.

3

Democracy and Development: Decentralized Planning in Kerala
*T.M. Thomas Isaac and Patrick Heller**

I Introduction

By any conventional measure India's democracy is a vibrant one. A competitive and robust party system complements its diverse, vocal, and autonomous civil society. But if Indian democracy has been rightfully celebrated for its ability to weather conflict, and its toleration and pluralism, the effectiveness of its democratic institutions are increasingly in doubt. Over a half century of almost uninterrupted democratic rule has done little to reduce the political, social, and economic exclusion of India's popular classes.[1]

Fung and Wright's exploration of Empowered Participatory Governance (EPG) begins with the assertion that the institutions of liberal democracy – representative democracy and techno-bureaucratic administration – are limited in their ability to address the challenges of just and equitable development. Nowhere is this more palpably the case than in India. On the one hand, representative structures have been dominated by elite interests. A fiercely competitive political party system grafted onto a highly unequal and fragmented social structure has privileged narrow and opportunistic interest politics over more encompassing forms of representation. In the absence of programmatic political formations (the Communist Party of India-Marxist – CPM – is an exception) oligarchical parties built on clientelistic networks have reduced politics to a frantic, zero-sum scramble for public resources that Bardhan has aptly described as "equal-opportunity plundering by all interest groups."[2]

On the other hand, state structures born at the intersection of an imperial bureaucracy, Soviet-inspired visions of planned revolution and Brahmanical social supremacy have produced a caricature of the command-and-control state. If the significant bureaucratic capacities of the Indian state have allowed for a degree of rule-bound and predictable administration that approaches the Weberian ideal-type, the state's monopolistic appropriation of planning and developmental functions has led at least one commentator to characterize state elites as "resource omnivores."[3] The developmental failures of the Indian state are all too well documented[4] and bear tragic testimony to the shortcomings of insulated, top-down, and unaccountable decision-making. The resulting crisis of Indian democracy has become so acute that across the political spectrum a consensus has emerged for promoting more decentralized and democratic forms of governance. However, the obstacles to such reforms remain significant. With the exception of Kerala, few states have decisively implemented the 1993 Constitutional mandates to increase local government power.

When the Left Democratic Front (LDF) coalition returned to power in Kerala in 1996, the CPM-led[5] government moved swiftly to fulfill one of its most important campaign pledges by launching the "People's Campaign for Decentralized Planning" (the Campaign). Though the Campaign is only in its fifth year, it has already empowered local government to a far greater degree than in any other Indian state. It has made significant progress along the three axes that James Manor[6] has identified as necessary components of any genuine and meaningful effort at democratic decentralization. First, there has been administrative decentralization. All local governments – municipalities and the three rural tiers of district, block, and Grama Panchayats (the all-India term for village councils) – have been given new functions and powers of decision-making and officials from many line departments have been brought under the authority of locally elected bodies. Second, there has been fiscal decentralization: 40 percent of all developmental expenditures have been allocated directly to LSGIs (Local Self-Governing Institutions). Third, there has been decentralization of political power. Elected local representatives now have the authority to design, fund, and implement a full range of development policies and projects.

But the Campaign represents far more than a simple devolution of governance powers to lower-level elected bodies. Its political and institutional design reflects its socially transformative ambition – similar to that in Porto Alegre – to compensate for the deficits of representative structures and bureaucratic decision-making. It stands out as a bold experiment in Empowered Participatory Governance (EPG) for these reasons. The first is the sheer scope and scale of the experiment. The decentralization of a wide range of developmental responsibilities to 1,214 elected local governments (encompassing municipalities, district, block, and village panchayats) represents a profound reconfiguration of the state and its relationship to society. By fortifying local governments, the Campaign has the potential to transform dramatically the everyday practice of democracy for Kerala's thirty-one million inhabitants.

Second, the nested design of the Campaign's core institutions – Grama Sabhas (ward-level assemblies), development seminars, task forces, and local governments – represent a deliberate attempt to broaden avenues for citizen participation. In every year since 1997, local governments in Kerala have formulated and implemented their own development plans. These plans take shape through a multi-stage process of iterated deliberation between elected representatives, local and higher-level government officials, civil society experts and activists, and ordinary citizens (see Table 3.1). The process begins in open local assemblies, called grama sabhas, in which participants discuss and identify development priorities. Development seminars formed by the grama sabhas are then tasked with developing more elaborate assessments of local problems and needs. The development seminars give way to multi-stakeholder task forces that design specific projects for various development sectors. These projects are in turn submitted to local elected bodies (municipal councils called panchayats) that formulate and set budgets for local plans. Final plans are presented back to grama sabhas for discussion. These local plans are then integrated into higher-level plans (blocks and districts) during which all projects are vetted for technical and fiscal viability.

The whole process closely conforms to three core institutional design principles of EPG. First, by devolving planning and implementation functions to local arenas, the Campaign has for the first time in India meaningfully empowered local governments and communities to address practical problems. The entire planning cycle – which begins with the collection of local data and ends with the formulation of a comprehensive local plan that consists of hundreds of projects – is an extended exercise in practical problem-solving. Second, both the institutional and political character of the Campaign has been centrally concerned with promoting bottom-up participation. The devolution of authority and resources to LSGIs has significantly reduced the transaction costs of participation, and the knowledge–capacity gap that has traditionally excluded ordinary citizens from playing an effective role in governance has been considerably narrowed by mass training programs, the active mobilization of civil society expertise, and concerted efforts to empower historically marginalized groups – women, adivasis ("tribals"), and dalits ("untouchables").

Third, the participatory institutions of the Campaign are self-

consciously deliberative – based on inclusive and reason-based decision-making – and directly empowered because they tie project choice
and formulation to actual implementation. At a broader level, the
Campaign is a historically significant attempt to dismantle entrenched
forms of bureaucratic domination and patronage politics by reinvigo-
rating Kerala's tradition of direct and mobilized democracy.

Background: the Struggle for Democratization

While the CPM's return to power in 1996 provided a critical opening,
the Kerala State Planning Board formulated, designed, and drove the
Campaign for Democratic Decentralization. In doing so, the Board has
relied on a stock of practical knowledge, ideas, and experiences drawn
from twenty-five years of local-level experiments conducted by NGOs,
most notably the Kerala Sastra Sahitya Parishad (KSSP) – the People's
Science Movement. Moreover, the KSSP has played an active role
within the SPB and at the grassroots level in implementing the Campaign. The historical and political circumstances under which this
synergy of state, political party, and civil society has evolved has been
explored elsewhere.[7] This chapter describes and evaluates the key institutions and processes of the Campaign. It is informed primarily by the
direct involvement of one of the authors – T.M. Thomas Isaac, who
was a member of the SPB during the first five years of the Campaign as
well as a long time activist in the KSSP – and by research conducted by
both authors.

As an institutional reform program, the Campaign was specifically
designed to nurture and facilitate greater direct participation by citizens in authoritative decision-making and was predicated on two basic
principles. The first was that local government institutions should be
transformed from simple service delivery conduits for national and
state schemes into fully fledged governing institutions with functional,
financial, and administrative autonomy. Devolution of functions and
resources should be based on the principle of subsidiarity: what can
best be done and decided at local level should be done there.[8]

The second principle was that traditional representative structures
should be complemented by more direct forms of democracy. Popular
participation would make elected representatives continuously rather
than just periodically accountable to the citizens and would introduce
transparency into bureaucratic operations. Increasing levels of direct
and informed participation required both mobilizing citizens and creating institutions that enable ordinary citizens to play an active role in
the selection, design, and implementation of local development plans.

The Campaign's designers (mostly the members of the SPB and key department heads) also realized from the outset that the instrumentalities of the state would be inadequate, both politically and practically, for advancing these two principles. Given the inertia of existing institutions and the power of vested interests, legislation alone could never sustain such profound changes. The success of Kerala's land reforms in the 1970s – widely recognized as having been the most far-reaching and equity-enhancing in the sub-continent – was made possible by a powerful peasant movement. A highly successful mass literacy campaign in 1991 also pointed to the importance of mobilizing popular initiative. Building on these lessons, and the recognition that Kerala has an impressive reservoir of capacity in non-state entities, the strategic emphasis from the outset was to conduct the reforms as a campaign that would mobilize civil society actors.

In the rest of this section we outline four key concepts that have informed the strategy of creating synergies between state intervention and mobilization. In Section II, we present a detailed discussion of the Campaign's institutional design and how it has sought to reconcile the democratic objectives of extensive participation and effective deliberation with the need for technical competency and inter-level coordination in the formulation and implementation of development plans. Section III critically evaluates the success of these mechanisms in achieving the objectives of democratic decentralization.

Reversing the Sequence of Decentralization Reforms

Democratic decentralization requires changes in administrative structures, in the allocation of functions and powers, and in the control of resources. Each of these three reforms depends on the other and so they should be pursued simultaneously. In the technocratic model advocated by multi-lateral development agencies, decentralization has been seen as an exercise in incremental institution-building informed primarily by public administration and managerial sciences.[9] Advocates of this model typically argue that certain sequenced preconditions, defined by a clear demarcation of functions among the various levels, must be met before genuine authoritative decision-making power can be successfully devolved: administrative support structures must be created, new organizational procedures should be in place, government staff have to be redeployed, a new information base has to be developed, and new personnel – both voluntary and official – have to be trained. The devolution of financial resources must be carefully calibrated to match the absorptive capacity of these nascent institutions.

A major difficulty with this linear model of decentralization is its assumption that the task of transforming the very mode in which government works can be achieved through a prescribed process that introduces a discrete set of technically and managerially rational solutions. The world is seen as largely frictionless and apolitical. But successful and sustainable democratic decentralization has been the exception to the rule, frustrated more often than not by bureaucratic inertia – most notably the resistance of powerful line departments – and vested political interests. Kerala certainly has its share of entrenched bureaucratic fiefdoms and political formations with stakes in the status quo. Yet, in the short history of the Campaign, devolution has already gone far beyond formal laws and executive orders.

Reform in Kerala reversed this linear prescription by first devolving fiscal control and then building local institutions. Since 1997, LSGIs have controlled between 35 and 40 percent of the annual developmental budget. During 1997–98, the total resources devolved (the "grant-in-aid") amounted to Rs. 10,250 million and, in 1998–99, Rs. 11,780 million, sums that do not include funds from centrally sponsored schemes and institutional loans to local governments. Before 1996–97, LSGIs received approximately Rs. 200 million in untied funds. There is little doubt that the administrative capacity and the management experience of the newly elected local government representatives was hardly up to the task of accommodating such large-scale transfers. But devolving fiscal resources and control – even while the immense task of building a new regulatory environment and administrative capacity was only getting under way – has had two critical strategic effects. First, because local governments now enjoy significant budgetary discretion, local planning exercises have a tangible and immediate character. This, as we shall see, has attracted high levels of participation. Second, shifting budgetary authority to lower levels has limited the ability of patronage politicians and top-down line departments to dominate or derail the process.

Planning as an Instrument of Social Mobilization

The second distinctive feature of the decentralization experiment in Kerala is the central role accorded to the planning function of the LSGIs. As a statutory precondition for receiving the grant-in-aid from the government, LSGIs must prepare comprehensive area plans. The planning process, as prescribed by the SPB, includes holding grama sabhas (ward-level assemblies), and convening sectoral task forces in which non-official experts and volunteers directly prepare reports, formulate projects, and draft sectoral plans. The various stages of plan preparation constitute new participatory spaces in which citizens, elected representatives, and officials deliberate and prioritize developmental goals and projects.

In order to ensure transparency and participation without compromising the technical requirements of planning, the planning process is divided into discrete phases with distinct objectives, key activities, and associated training programs. Though modifications to the sequence have been made every year, the basic model inaugurated in 1997 (Table 3.1) remains the same.

A critical component of the Campaign has been an elaborate training program that has become one of the largest non-formal education programs ever undertaken in India. In the first year, in seven rounds of training at state, district, and local level, some fifteen thousand elected representatives, twenty-five thousand officials and seventy-five thousand volunteers were given training. About six hundred state-level trainees – called Key Resource Persons – received nearly twenty days of training. Some twelve thousand district-level trainees – District Resource Persons – received ten days of training and at the local level more than a hundred thousand persons received at least five days of training. All the elected representatives were expected to participate in the training program at one level or another. Each round of training focussed on specific planning activities. Separate handbooks and guides, amounting to nearly four thousand pages of documentation, were prepared and distributed for each round.

Building Civic Engagement

Following Putnam's seminal analysis,[10] it is now widely accepted that a robust civil society – defined in terms of its "norms of reciprocity and networks of civic engagement" and embodied in different types of civic institutions – enhances the effectiveness of democratic institutions. Putnam's understanding of the contribution that associational life can make to deepening democracy is, however, informed by an essentialist interpretation that construes civic-minded behavior as deeply engraved in culture and history. It is, as Skocpol and Fiorina have argued,[11] a social-psychological view that leaves little room for the role of conflict in building democratic capacities. Critics have moreover pointed out that the forms of civic life that contribute to securing developmental goods (i.e. social capital) are in fact politically constructed[12] and that associational life is in large part artifactual, the product of institutional environments, shifting social relations, and state interventions.[13]

Table 3.1 Phases of the People's Campaign in its Inaugural Year, 1997–98

Phase	Period	Objective	Activities	Mass participation
1. Grama sabha	Aug.– Oct. 1997	Identify the "felt needs" of the people	Grama sabha in rural areas and ward conventions in urban areas	2 million persons attended grama sabhas
2. Development seminar	Oct.– Dec. 1997	Assessment of the resources and problems of the area and formulation of a local development strategy	Participatory studies: preparation of development reports, organization of development seminars	300,000 delegates attended seminars
3. Task forces	Nov. 97– Mar. 1998	Preparation of projects	Meetings of task forces	100,000 volunteers in task forces
4. Plans of grass-root tiers – municipalities and panchayats	March– June 1998	Formulation of plan of grass-root tiers	Plan formulation and meetings of elected representatives	25,000 volunteers in formulation of plan document
5. Plans of higher tiers – blocks and districts	April– July 1998	Formulation of plans of higher tiers	Plan formulation meeting of elected representatives	5,000 volunteers in formulation of plan documents
6. Volunteer technical corps	May– Oct. 1998	Appraisal and approval of plans	Meetings of expert committees	5,000 volunteer technical experts worked in the Appraisal Committees

Kerala's contemporary history fully illustrates this mutability of civil society.

Many observers have noted that Kerala boasts a vibrant and robust associational life, marked not only by the activism of citizens, but also by a proliferation of NGOs and community-based organizations and the highest rates of unionization in the country. Indeed, Kerala's celebrated achievements in the area of social development have been ascribed to high levels of public action marked both by state intervention and civic activism.[14] Yet in the early part of the twentieth century, Kerala was anything but fertile ground for civic republicanism. Kerala's caste system was generally considered to have been the most rigid and severe in the subcontinent and its agrarian economy was marked by pronounced land inequality and the deeply rooted labor-repressive institutions. Contemporary civil society in Kerala certainly did not, as such, rise from deep civic traditions (as Putnam argues for Northern Italy). Instead, the birth of a vibrant and effective democracy in Kerala must be located in its political history of conflict and social mobilization, the interplay of these dynamics with the process of state-building and the resulting transformation of social structure.[15] Kerala's class-centered mobilizations emphasized distributive demands and built associational ties across caste and communal divisions. Social reforms including the building of a modest but effective welfare state, land reforms, and labor market policies have all eroded the hold of patron–client relations and strengthened associational autonomy.

But if Kerala's long history of social mobilization has directly contributed to the vibrancy of its civil society, it has also created conditions that limit the capacity for civic action. Class-based redistributive conflicts had two notable effects. First, Kerala's political landscape has polarized into two highly mobilized left and right wing formations that have systematically politicized civil society organizations. Thus schools, cooperatives, shopfloors, and local institutions have all become objects of fierce political competition. This pervasive politicization has made it increasingly difficult to separate the provision of public services and goods from narrow political–organizational imperatives. Second, much as in the case of European social democratic states, redistributive demands expanded the size and role of the state and the power of bureaucratic structures. Though large-scale interventions in education, health, and social protection directly contributed to Kerala's social development, the growth of the bureaucracy has severely circumscribed the scope for civil society initiative. Because the bureaucratic development process is top-heavy and more responsive to highly organized rent-seeking interests than popular forces, ordinary citizens retain an interest in government programs only inasmuch as they concern narrow, individual returns. As the politics of pork replaced the politics of community improvement, Kerala's strong traditions of popular grass-roots development action eroded.

The Campaign grows directly from a critique of these corrosive effects. On the one hand, the centralized, command-and-control state is no longer capable of driving Kerala's development. Thus the supporters of the Campaign have been very vocal in arguing that the existing political climate of sectarian and partisan division has become an obstacle to development and that a key objective of the Campaign – much as in the case of participatory budgeting in Porto Alegre – is to break the hold of clientelistic politics. On the other hand, civil society initiatives require more avenues and opportunities for engagement with public authorities. Emerging as it has from within a party that has a long history of popular mobilization, and in particular a key group of activists and officials with close ties to a mass-based civil society organization with a track record of community participation (the KSSP), the Campaign's political project has been to create new spaces for associational life by promoting local democratic institutions.

In conceptualizing planning as an instrument of social mobilization, the Campaign has sought to deepen democracy along three different axes. First, devolving planning and authoritative decision-making to local arenas constitutes a more integrated approach to development that directly challenges the hold of hierarchical line departments and their extensive powers. Second, providing visible and substantive incentives for participation and emphasizing deliberative processes may reinvigorate civic action and loosen the grip of partisan patronage politics. Third, by fundamentally transforming the mode and channels of decision-making, the Campaign has created new political configurations and public policy networks. Thus elected local representatives whose functions were previously mostly ceremonial have now been brought directly into positions of authoritative decision-making, including authority over local administrative officials. Similarly, NGOs and Community-Based Organizations (CBOs) have been offered new opportunities for engaging directly in development and there has been a concerted effort to create new linkages between professionals and academic institutions and communities in order to bring expertise (especially during the transitional phase in which the bureaucracy has been less than cooperative) to the grass roots. This later development parallels the dynamic blurring of state–society relations marked by the emergence of new associational networks that Chalmers et al. have identified as the defining characteristic of revitalized civil societies in Latin America.[16]

In short, the objective of the People's Campaign for Decentralized Planning has not been simply to draw up a plan from below. The very process of planning has been conceived as a means to fundamentally transform the character and scope of participation and the nature of interest mediation. Such a transformation cannot be secured through government directives or institutional design alone. It requires creativity and integration with the logic of social movements.[17]

Institutionalization

Fung and Wright[18] argue that one of the greatest challenges of promoting EPG is to develop institutional forms that are robust enough to withstand efforts by traditional interest groups to either subvert or circumvent deliberative processes. In Kerala's highly volatile political climate, in which the two political fronts have historically more or less alternated in their control of state power, this problem is particularly acute. Governments formed by the Congress Party have a track record of reversing decentralization reforms, most notably by packing newly created local institutions with political appointees.

The Campaign has addressed this challenge of institutionalization by encouraging popular involvement as a counterweight to entrenched officialdom. High levels of participation have already yielded significant payoffs as some opposition parties – and most interestingly the conservative Muslim League – have expressed their support for the Campaign. The Campaign's localized planning structures have created spaces in which new political alliances and commitments have been forged. By replacing the conventional systems of vertical accountability to political parties and bureaucracies with horizontal forms of cooperation and autonomous sources of authority, the Campaign's locally integrated planning structures have provided local politicians and officials with a direct stake in the new system.

Political uncertainty has also underscored the need to institutionalize the Campaign through the passage of appropriate legislation. Thus the LDF government comprehensively amended the existing Kerala Panchayathi Raj Act of 1994 and the Kerala Municipality Act of 1994 to secure the autonomy and accountability of LSGIs. New laws concerning the transparency of administration and access to information have also been passed. Moreover, hundreds of government orders creating new accounting systems, devolving authority to local officials and establishing new procedures for reporting have engraved many of the Campaign's design features into the everyday workings of government.

But in India's highly fluid electoral environment, regime support for radical experiments can be fleeting. In May 2001, in keeping with a pattern of defeat of incumbent parties that has long been the norm in Kerala, the LDF was ousted from power by a Congress Party-led coalition. Most observers concur that the CPM's defeat was not a judgement about the Campaign.[19] At the time of writing (November 2001), it is too early to evaluate the impact of this change in government on the Campaign. In contrast to 1991, when the UDF returned to power and immediately scuttled a much less ambitious experiment in decentralization (one that had focussed on the district level), the new government has declared its commitment to the Campaign and to addressing its weaknesses. Two factors have pre-empted a frontal assault on the Campaign. One is its popularity at the grass-roots level. The Campaign had succeeded in building supportive bipartisan local coalitions that favor decentralization. Eroding the autonomy and authority of LSGIs will be difficult, therefore, not only because it would require significant legislative efforts, but also because such efforts would alienate the Congress Party's own rank and file. The second is the prestige that the Campaign had gained in national and international circles. In addition to significant media attention, the Campaign has attracted the attention of officials from other Indian states and even figured in the remarks made by the President of India (who is from the Congress Party) in his 2000 Independence Day national address.

II Participatory Plan Formulation and Implementation

Planning in India has historically been a highly insulated and top-down affair. In keeping with their high-modernist impulses, state planners have generally been skeptical of mass participation in the planning process.[20] In general, area planning has occurred at the level of districts, which encompass hundreds and even thousands of panchayats but do not have elected governance bodies. The modal pattern has been for teams of experts to draw up district- or block-level plans in consultation with groups of key informants such as officials, "progressive" farmers, representatives of cooperatives, local self-governments, and so on. Participation was carefully controlled from above. The Report of the Working Group on Block Level Planning expressed characteristic scepticism regarding direct public participation:

> First, we should be clear as to who we do have in mind when we talk of the people: their representative political institutions such as the district and taluka panchayats or class organizations where they exist (khedut mandals or trade unions), political or caste leaders or target groups. It is well known that the public is not a harmonious entity; it really comprises groups with conflicting interests. If we wish to plan for the weak, the plan may have to be imposed from above and cannot be a product from below in which "the below" is dominated by the rich and the strong.

Second, people can make a contribution to planning only if they are presented with a well-articulated and feasible framework of approaches, objectives, measures, and alternatives. If, however, they are asked to indicate their needs in a vacuum, they are bound to put up a charter of demands, which will be far beyond the capacities of the government.[21]

A number of model block- and district-level plans were prepared during the 1970s by voluntary agencies and professional bodies that have provided important methodological experience in local-level planning. By the early 1980s some form of district planning machinery existed in most states, but the planning process was anything but participatory. It was described by the Report of the Working Group on District Planning (Government of India 1984) as follows:

Usually, after the state budget is voted in the assembly, the different heads of departments are requested to make a district-wise break up of the outlays provided in the plan budget. This is then communicated to the districts, either by sectoral departments or by the planning department of the state. This usually takes four to five months after the commencement of the financial year. After this communication is received, the district attempts to incorporate a write up for the district-wise outlay and a document called "district plan" emerges in this manner, which is *purely an aggregation of departmental schemes* [our emphasis].

District planning was decoupled from budgetary discretion, and as such devoid of any authoritative decision-making. The major departure from this pattern took place in Karnataka and West Bengal where conscious attempts were made to link the district planning process to local self-governments. The Karnataka experiment was remarkable for the autonomy given to district panchayats in plan preparation and the involvement of lower panchayats and grama sabhas through a consultative process. However, it disintegrated after the state's ruling coalition was defeated in 1990. The West Bengal experiment has proved to be more enduring. West Bengal created a tradition of local democracy by organizing elections for local bodies at regular five-year intervals. Though the scope of powers of these bodies has grown, planning processes have remained centered around the district with lower-tier local bodies and grama sabhas playing only consultative roles. In contrast to Kerala, line departments of the state government continue to dominate the planning and implementation of schemes and programs that were supposedly transferred to local bodies.

This brief discussion of the theory and practice of decentralized planning in India provides a point of comparison with the decentralized planning procedures adopted in Kerala. The focus of decentralized planning is not the district but different tiers of local self-governments, the most important being the grass-roots tier – the grama panchayat or municipality.[22] Under the Campaign, the planning process begins at the lowest level of democratic representation, the grama panchayats and municipalities. Block- and-district level panchayats come into play only after local governments have prepared their plans, and then only to ensure regional coordination. There are 990 grama panchayats, 58 municipalities,[23] 152 blocks, and 14 districts in Kerala. The councils for each of these levels of local government are directly elected in a first-past-the-post constituency system. At the block and district levels, the democratic character of planning is ensured through the involvement of elected officials and a range of citizen committees. At the municipal and grama panchayat level, the planning process is driven by direct mass participation.

Autonomous decision-making power was granted to local govern-ments by providing untied "grants-in-aid." The heavy hand of bureau-cratic tradition has been blunted by continuous, mass, non-official participation in every phase of plan preparation and implementation. In building continuous deliberative structures, the Campaign has tackled two micro-level design challenges. The first was to create insti-tutional forms that can correct for the asymmetries of power among local agents. The second was to make local participation effective by creating space for grass-roots intervention and deliberation without sacrificing the technical and economic requirements of planning.

The Grama Sabhas

Grama sabhas, assemblies of ward- or panchayat-based residents, rep-resent the key deliberative moment in the planning process. By law, these meetings had to be held at least twice during the initial years of the Campaign. In later years, amendments to enabling laws required four meetings in each panchayat per year. The first grama sabha serves as an open forum in which residents identify local development prob-lems, generate priorities and form subsector development seminars in which specific proposals take shape. In the second grama sabha, plans approved by the elected panchayat council are presented to the public and departures from the original grama sabha proposals are explained. Beneficiaries for particular projects are also selected at the grama sabhas.

Rousseau notwithstanding, there is nothing spontaneously democ-ratic about a general assembly, especially in a society as inflected with complex and durable inequalities as India's. The Campaign's architects and activists devoted substantial time and energy to enhancing the deliberative quality of these large meetings. An obvious innovation, but one that nonetheless required significant organizational effort, was to adopt a small-group approach. In each grama sabha, after an introductory general body meeting (usually of several hundred people), participants are divided into smaller groups, each dealing with a particular development sector, to discuss issues and problems in depth. This small-group arrangement made it possible for ordinary people, particularly women, to be able to participate in the discussions. A second innovation was to create a semi-formal discussion format and provide a trained facilitator for each group. Working with a basic template of questions and useful planning concepts, locally recruited facilitators encouraged participants to list and analyze local problems based upon their real-life experiences.

Local Information-Gathering

Asymmetries of information are a key source of domination in nominally deliberative institutions. Even in Kerala's social climate of highly politicized and highly literate citizens,[24] durable social and status inequalities and official prerogative has severely skewed access to useful information. Moreover, though available planning data are a source of significant power, they are often inaccurate or maladapted to the requirements of local development. Taking much of its inspiration from the KSSP – which since its foundation in 1962 has been dedicated to "bringing science to the people" – the Campaign has taken local information-gathering as a first critical step in the planning process.

After a first round of grama sabhas, panchayats in the first year of the Campaign were required to make formal assessments of the natural and human resources of their localities. The idea was to promote effective integration of planning and resource optimization by actually comparing expressed needs with local assets. With assistance from specially trained resource persons and using techniques developed by the Campaign, a series of participatory studies was undertaken in every grama panchayat and municipality. These included the collection and organization of data available from various local-level offices, identifying and mapping local eco-zones using transect walk techniques, a review of ongoing schemes to be prepared by each local department, a social audit, and a review of local history. The widespread refusal of departments to cooperate often hampered local planning and inter-local coordination. Though the quality of data varied dramatically between localities, the exercise itself helped many individuals develop useful skills and, importantly, incorporated local knowledge into official development planning.

Development Reports and Seminars

The outcome of these data collection exercises was a "development report" prepared according to guidelines set down by the SPB. With a five-year strategic outlook, the reports serve as the basis of annual planning. Running on average seventy-five to a hundred pages, reports provide a comprehensive overview of local development. They include a chapter on local social history intended to underscore the role that social mobilization can play in meeting development challenges. The body of each report consists of 12 chapters assessing the current status of various sectors such as agriculture, energy, health, and drinking water, a review of ongoing schemes and problems and a list of recommendations. An assessment by the SPB revealed that the majority of the reports were of higher quality than any other existing department planning documents and offered by far the best benchmarks for local development.

Because the recommendations of development reports can differ from the demands raised in grama sabhas and because demands from different wards had to be integrated into area-wide perspectives, the reports were submitted to development seminars. The majority of delegates to the seminars were elected from the subject groups of the grama sabhas with, in principle, equal representation for men and women. Local-level government officials and other relevant experts were asked to participate. On average, development seminars had 231 delegates, with officials accounting for 13.8 percent, SC/STs (Scheduled Castes and Scheduled Tribes – the official designation for "untouchables" and tribal groups) for 10.5 percent and women for only 22.1 percent.[25] Extensive preparation went into the organization of the seminars including the distribution of the development report to all delegates and widespread publicity in the form of leaflets, festivals, jathas (marches), and exhibitions. The seminars were given a very high profile, with a member of the legislative assembly or a state minister inaugurating half of the seminars. A major proportion of the seminar time was devoted to sector-wise group discussions in order to facilitate in-depth analysis of the development reports and to propose amendments. The recommendations of the different groups were then presented to a plenary session for ratification.

Task Forces and Preparation of Projects

At the conclusion of development seminars in the first year of the Campaign, task forces of around ten persons each were constituted to prepare the project proposals on the basis of the recommendations of the seminar. In subsequent years, task forces became the starting point of the planning process in which development seminars were convened at a later stage to review the work of task forces. A key challenge of EPG is that experts, rather than simply deliberating among themselves, should also engage in direct deliberation with citizens.[26] The work of task forces in fact goes beyond simply leveling the playing field by guaranteeing that the process of project design is informed by experts but led by citizens. Each development seminar was composed of twelve task forces, one for each development sector. Delegates selected from the development seminars were ordinary citizens, though many have undergone specialized training through the Campaign. The chairperson of each task force was an elected ward councilor. This ensured that the work of the task force would be directly represented in subsequent deliberations of the panchayat or municipal council. In order to secure the relevant expertise as well as coordination with state structures, the convenor of the task force was an officer from the concerned line department.

The sustainability of a participatory institution is in large part determined by its demonstrated capacity for effective problem-solving. In order to ensure a degree of quality control and effective monitoring, task forces are required to prepare detailed project proposals in accordance with a set of criteria and standards established by the SPB. Thus all project proposals must include a definition of objectives (as far as possible in quantitative or measurable terms), criteria for beneficiaries or areas, a time frame, an organizational overview of the role of implementing agencies, a financial analysis including identification of funding sources, a social and environmental impact review, and details of the proposed monitoring mechanisms.

Plan Documents and Coordination

The fourth and final stage of the local planning process is marked by the prioritization and integration of projects prepared by various task forces into a plan document for each panchayat. The final form of the local plan is the legal prerogative of the elected council which must formally vote to approve the plan. There are, however, a number of formal and informal mechanisms to ensure that elected representatives abide by the recommendations and projects generated by the various participatory processes. The approved plan must conform to a detailed reporting format that lays out the general strategy and objectives of the plan as well as sectoral and redistributive criteria. Authorized projects must be specifically linked to the strategic statement and the full text of the proposed project must be listed in a separate appendix. This process not only guarantees accountability, but its sheer complexity ensures that the council – which has limited administrative support – has no practical alternative to building on the work of task forces. The fact that ward councilors participate actively at every level of the participatory process, from attendance at grama sabhas and training seminars to chairing the task forces, also ensures integration between participatory processes and the council's final deliberations.

Since the beginning of the Campaign, plan allocations have been separately indicated in the state budget, with broad guidelines regarding sectoral allocations to be made by the local body. These guidelines are both of a functional (sectoral) and redistributive character and are designed to coordinate and integrate local allocations with state-wide objectives. For example, to shift public investments away from Kerala's traditional strengths in social services and infrastructure, the SPB mandates that 40–50 percent of plan allocations must be directed to productive sectors such as agriculture. On the redistributive front, local governments are required to spend not less than 10 percent on projects targeted to women, and to proportionally direct funds to projects for scheduled caste and scheduled tribe portions of their population.

Block and district panchayats start the preparation of their annual plans only after grama panchayats have drafted their plans. The sequential ordering is intended to ensure that the plans of the various tiers are integrated and the plans of the higher tiers complement, rather than duplicate or overrule, those of the lower tiers. A matrix-based analytical tool has been developed to assist blocks and districts in integrating the analysis and programs of the grama panchayats into their own plans. Blocks have also been tasked with integrating into their plans the different centrally sponsored poverty alleviation schemes that have traditionally been implemented at the block level. There has been strong resistance to this move from both bureaucrats and elected representatives. This comes in part from genuine problems in maintaining separate guidelines for centrally sponsored programs, but also from fear of losing significant decision-making powers.

Plan Appraisal

In the first year of the Campaign, a sample review of the projects prepared by the local bodies revealed that a significant proportion had to be modified to ensure their technical soundness and viability before they could be approved for implementation. In all, more than a hundred thousand projects had to be evaluated. The object of evaluation was to rectify the technical and financial weaknesses in the proposals. This monumental task had to be undertaken within a span of three to four months. The official machinery lacked the capacity and will to accomplish this task.

The SPB responded to this problem by launching the Voluntary Technical Corps (VTC). Retired technical experts and professionals were encouraged to volunteer to help appraise the projects and plans of the local bodies. A professional or postgraduate degree or officer-level experience in a development sector was the minimum qualification for VTC membership. A volunteer expert committed herself/himself to spending at least one day a week giving technical assistance to the panchayats. District-level conventions were arranged for the experts who formally offered to join the VTC. More than four thousand technical experts enrolled in the VTC.

Expert Committees were then formed at block (BLEC), municipal (MLEC), and corporation (CLEC) levels, drawing from the VTC members and certain categories of mandatory officers. Each expert committee had a non-official as its chairperson and the block panchayat secretary or officer from the Town Planning Department as its convenor. The expert committees functioned through subject committees with membership confined to those who had expertise in the particular field. A non-official expert acted as the chairperson and a senior officer from the related department was appointed as the convenor of the subject committee.

The expert committees acted both as advisory arms of the District Planning Committees, helping to appraise the plans and projects, and as advisors to local planners. The committees were not empowered to modify priorities set by the local bodies. They were tasked only with providing technical and financial advice, appraising projects, and suggesting modifications. The district planning committees approved plans on the recommendations of these expert committees.

The formation of expert committees in the course of the Campaign's first year was an important organizational innovation which helped to debureaucratize the project approval process. Without this extra-bureaucratic expertise, line departments would have paralyzed local planning through inertia and outright resistance.

Financial Procedures

In Kerala's traditional system, development planning was the arbitrary and patronage-driven domain of elected representatives and implementation was the prerogative of the bureaucracy. A key rationale for making the decision-making process more participatory was to ensure the involvement of the beneficiaries and the public at large in project implementation. As Fung and Wright note,[27] "direct participation of grassroots operators increases accountability and reduces the length of the chain of agency that accompanies political parties and their bureaucratic apparatus." Popular involvement increases problem-solving efficiency through better and more rapid feedback and increases accountability by multiplying the points of scrutiny. The Campaign has developed a wide range of new fora and rules to maximize participation and transparency.

The Campaign's financial procedures for regulating the flow of grant-in-aid funds to local bodies and to specific projects has been designed to maximize effective monitoring. To begin with, officers can be held more directly responsible for financial flows because they have become directly responsible to locally elected councils. Financial allotments to local bodies are released in four installments annually. All funds must be specifically tied to approved panchayat projects or state schemes. They are held in special accounts that are managed by the implementing officer. Actual disbursement of funds requires co-authorization from the head of the elected body.

The creation of democratically accountable beneficiary committees has also been an important innovation. Instead of implementing public works through contractors, local bodies were encouraged to form committees of project beneficiaries to undertake the task. The objective was to break the ties of collusion between contractors, politicians, and government engineers that have historically been the most important source of corruption in Kerala. Doing so, however, required creating beneficiary committees that were sufficiently autonomous and empowered to resist capture by rent-seeking interests. Toward this end, officially ratified local market rates were adopted for estimation of cost of works so that the beneficiary committees could execute the work in a transparent manner and maintain credible financial records. A second step was to shift effective authority for the technical sanction of projects from department officials to block- or municipal- and district-level expert committees. Department officials continue to convene subject committees and grant technical sanction. However, they now make decisions in their capacity as members of a committee of peers rather than as officials in a departmental hierarchy. A third procedural innovation has been to shift responsibility for examining finished work and authorizing payment from official to non-official engineering experts from the VTC.

Beneficiary Selection

A major change introduced by the Campaign was in its procedure for selecting beneficiaries of development projects. Beneficiaries are individuals who receive direct benefits from projects, such as houses, irrigation systems, or construction-work opportunities. In the past, beneficiary selection has been little more than a concerted exercise in patronage that has enjoyed the tacit collusion of all political parties. Campaign rules call for grama panchayats to publicize the criteria for beneficiary eligibility and prioritization. Notices listing the projects and criteria must be prominently displayed in public places as well as printed and circulated. Applications must be printed in Malayalam and made freely available. The rules also provide for a system for verifying statements made in the applications. Verification can be conducted by designated officers or by a committee appointed by the panchayat. Finally, the list of applicants must be presented to the grama sabha with sector subject groups tasked with processing applications.

The responsibility for consolidating and finalizing the priority list of beneficiaries received from each grama sabha rests with the panchayat. The final priority list must be created on the basis of clearly stated norms. Members of the public and the local press can attend the proceedings of this final selection. The draft list must be exhibited prominently. All public objections must be given consideration and reasons for rejection stated.

III Critically Assessing the Campaign

So far we have discussed the history and formal institutional design of the Campaign. How have these new structures actually worked on the ground? Most critically, has the planning process been deliberative? Have local projects been effectively implemented and integrated with higher levels of planning? Given the sheer complexity and scale of the project, the inevitable teething problems, and the absence of cumulative data, it is still too early to reach definitive judgement. The institutional learning that has already taken place does, however, hold some important lessons for our understanding of EPG. Furthermore, several robust trends have already emerged.

Financial Resources

As we noted in the introductory section, the decision in 1996 to earmark 35–40 percent of plan funds for local self-governments kick-started the Campaign. The most important achievement of the Campaign to date has been sustaining the political will to maintain and increase the scale of devolution in subsequent years, despite very severe financial constraints faced by the state government. Consequently, local governments have enjoyed a continuous and substantial flow of financial resources.

The redistributive character of this resource devolution has improved significantly since the start of the program. In the first year, financial devolution was based on a straight per capita formula that did not take levels of interregional poverty and development into account. However, what was lost in policy was gained in politics. With its simplicity, this formula resisted political manipulation and criticism from partisan opponents. Moreover, the formula effectively corrected the highly skewed patterns of patronage-driven allocation of the past (in which underdeveloped northern Kerala was consistently short-changed) and so did have a de facto redistributive effect. In subsequent years, the devolution formula has progressively incorporated additional weights for poverty and underdevelopment.

A major weakness of local-level plans has been their weak credit linkages. Both commercial and cooperative banks have by and large been unwilling to link official credit planning to the local planning projects. Resources from voluntary labor, donations, and beneficiary contributions have fallen short of anticipated levels. However, a number of panchayats did successfully mobilize substantial resources from these sources, indicating their as yet untapped potential.

Plan Formulation

For the first time in India, grama panchayats and municipalities throughout an entire state have prepared local area plans. This is itself an important milestone. Given the sheer enormity of the task and the absence of local capacity, plan preparation in the first year ran six months over schedule. However, the dramatic returns of learning-by-doing have been reflected in the steadily increasing proportion of promptly completed plans.

A major objective of decentralized planning has been to match local needs to actual public expenditures. A rationalization of resource allocation based on more direct, informed, and deliberated inputs into decision-making processes is a critical gain for both fairness and efficiency from decentralized planning. Because of the empirical difficulties of comparing pre- and post-Campaign expenditures patterns (there are no subdistrict figures available for the pre-Campaign period) a definitive assessment must await more intensive research efforts. However, three important general trends are already apparent. First, the investment priorities in the plans prepared by the local bodies (after decentralization) differ significantly from priorities in prior district plans. Local bodies have accorded much greater priority to basic needs such as housing, drinking water, and sanitation. In the productive sectors, there has been a discernible shift toward animal husbandry, garden crops, and minor irrigation. Both these shifts have significant redistributive implications. Second, in contrast to past patterns, investment priorities in special plans prepared for scheduled castes and tribals differed significantly from the overall investment patterns. The low income, asset, and skill position of these marginalized communities has been taken into account. Third, in contrast to the one-size-fits-all logic of the past, there are significant interregional differences in the investment priorities of local bodies.

The most glaring weakness of the plan preparation in the first year was the quality of the proposed projects. Many of the projects proved to be little more than modified versions of standardized department schemes. There was often little consideration of forward and backward linkages and fully integrated plans were rare. The reflex to mechanically allocate funds on a ward basis proved tenacious, particularly among the higher tiers (blocks and districts). Beginning with the second year, measures were adopted to improve the quality of projects and programs. The most important measure has been to introduce subject-specific training programs for task force members. In the second year, the training program consisted of a series of locally organized stopgap measures that produced limited results. In the third year, the training program was formalized into a state-wide program linked to specialized institutions such as the Kerala Agricultural University, the Institute of Management in Government, the KSSP's Integrated Rural Technology Centre, COSTFORD (a low-cost housing NGO training institute), and NGOs involved in watershed management. These specialized training programs, coupled with the greater involvement of VTC members in the task forces, improve the quality of project design.

The spatial integration of projects on a watershed basis was a key planning goal of the Campaign. In practice however, block panchayats lacked the technical expertise and support to plan at this level. In the third year, the SPB launched a scheme to assist block panchayats in mapping all the micro-watersheds in the state and in preparing master plans for them. Administrators hope that this program will improve local spatial plans, raise awareness of ecological issues, and introduce the concept of sustainability into the planning process.

Physical Achievements

A major criticism of the Campaign has been that the attention paid to process and participation has come at the expense of actual project implementation as measured by physical achievements (the process–product trade-off). The logic of this criticism is misplaced inasmuch as it fails to recognize that the quality of participation is "an independent desiderata of democratic politics."[28] To focus on financial targets and expenditures, as many of the Campaign's critics have done, reflects a narrow technocratic understanding of development. But even if EPG institutions can be justified on the grounds of extending citizenship alone, their long-term viability, especially under the circumstances of the liberalization of the national economy, will rely on their capacity to provide tangible developmental goods.

At this stage, an accurate appraisal of physical achievements is complicated by practical problems of monitoring and aggregating existing data. Physical results, particularly in productive sectors such as industry and agriculture, require time to materialize. And even in the case of social and infrastructural sectors, the task of measuring the quality of project implementation is virtually impossible given the absence of a local data gathering system.[29]

However, the most readily measured physical achievements of the first two years of decentralized planning are impressive. From 1997 to 1999, 98,494 houses have been built, 240,307 sanitary latrines constructed, 50,162 wells dug, 17,489 public taps provided, and 16,563 ponds cleaned. A total of 2,800,179 individual beneficiaries received support from the plan for seedlings and fertilizers. 8,000 kilometers of roads were built. These figures far outpace public construction from previous comparable periods.[30]

Because the pace of delivery has surpassed expectations, the state government has taken steps to encourage institutional financial loans to the local bodies to provide additional resources. For the first time in Kerala (or any state in India), the government has set a target date (2003) for delivering shelter, sanitary latrines, and drinking water (within two hundred meters) to all households in the state. The universalization of pre-primary education, improvement in the quality of education and health care centers, and completion of rural electrification have also become imaginable. Tangible achievements such as these could play a critical role in sustaining and stabilizing the process of democratic decentralization.

Recombination

Effective decentralized planning must by definition be integrated. This is critical not only to optimize resource allocation, reduce duplication, and ensure sustainability, but also, as Fung and Wright argue, to capture and diffuse the innovations generated in decentralized units. The comparative advantage of "decentralized coordination" lies in increasing the "learning capacity of the system as a whole by the combination of decentralized empowered deliberation and centralized coordination and feedback."[31] This coordination has been one of the most daunting challenges faced by the Campaign.

In the first year, a number of factors contributed to weak coordination between the plans of the different tiers of local bodies and that of the state government. First, the functions of the local bodies were listed in the law by subject rather than by activity. This resulted in considerable overlap. Second, the decentralizing logic of the Campaign was a global one. Negotiation of schematic or activity-wise demarcation of functions would have been difficult and time-consuming due to resistance from line departments. LSGIs were instead granted full autonomy to formulate any project within their capabilities. The devolution of discretionary budgeting authority introduced a de facto functional division of labor between the state government and LSGIs. During the first year of the decentralized planning, most departments insisted on continuing their traditional schemes and there was considerable duplication between the state department programs and those of the LSGIs. This created considerable strain on the overstretched financial resources of state departments and most have gradually withdrawn their schemes that overlap LSGI projects. Thus village roads and minor irrigation have virtually disappeared from the state government's plan. And though all piped water supply schemes are by law the monopoly of the Kerala Water Authority, the Authority no longer undertakes small-scale projects.

Though prescribed planning procedures called for higher tiers to take the priorities and programs of lower tiers into account, in actual practice there was little coordination in the first year (in no small part because of a shortage of time). More detailed guidelines were issued in the second year, but problems persisted. In the third year, the format and logic of district-level planning was significantly revised. New procedures emphasized the district's role in (1) providing a macro-perspective for sustainable development of the district, (2) improving integration by consolidating lower-level plans and identifying gaps and duplications, and (3) providing a long-term strategic vision for future annual plans.

In the first two years, the planning process only provided feedback from below. In the absence of coordination from above, integration between the programs of different tiers was inadequate and insufficient attention was given to the spatial dimension of the planning process. District plans are now conceived of as providing the primary source of feedback from above. The intention is that this feedback should not take the form of instructions or commands, but of guidelines evolved in a participatory manner by the local bodies in the district. This in turn will allow for local plans at every level to be prepared with simultaneous feedback from both above and below.

Quality of Deliberation

The Campaign has created numerous opportunities for ordinary citizens to actively participate in the different phases of plan formulation and implementation. But how many citizens have made use of these opportunities? Were the discussions manipulated by locally dominant groups? Were the fora merely a means to legitimize decisions made by the elites?

Every ordinary citizen, irrespective of his or her membership in political or non-political social formations, has the right and opportunity to intervene in the planning process by participating in the grama sabhas. One of the greatest achievements of the Campaign has been to demonstrate that popular assemblies can function effectively. In the year before the Campaign, grama sabhas were called after the formation of the new local bodies, but a majority failed to actually convene. In the first grama sabhas of the Campaign in August–September 1996, over two million people participated with an average of 180 persons per grama sabha, representing 11.4 percent of the voting population and roughly one of every four households. Though participation rates have dropped slightly in subsequent years (possibly because the number of annual grama sabhas was increased from two to four), these popular assemblies have become an essential feature of Kerala's political landscape.

There are, however, significant limitations to the deliberative character of grama sabhas. To begin with, they are too large and unwieldy for meaningful deliberation. Due to Kerala's dispersed settlement pattern, grama sabha participants must travel significant distances and meetings cannot run more than two or three hours. This does not allow for serious discussion of the large number of complex issues that are normally included in the agenda of the grama sabha.[32] Participation across socio-economic groups has been uneven. Middle-class participation has been low, and most participants have been from lower classes that are the targeted beneficiaries of most development projects. In the first year the participation of scheduled castes and scheduled tribes was below their population share and women constituted a disappointing 25 percent. In subsequent years, the percentages have increased, but participation remains uneven.

The formation of Neighborhood Groups (NHGs) consisting of forty to fifty families has been a response from below – often initiated by KSSP activists – to the limitations of the grama sabhas. Though not formally required, NHGs have been formed in around two hundred panchayats. One study found that, in one hundred panchayats,[33] NHGs function as mini-grama sabhas that discuss local issues and priorities, review plan implementation, and select beneficiaries. NHG representatives often constitute a Ward Committee which in many cases becomes the de facto executive committee of the grama sabhas. NHGs have also taken up other activities such as conflict resolution, after-school educational programs, health clinics, cultural activities, thrift schemes, and project implementation. There is currently a campaign being led by the KSSP to extend NHGs to the entire state and institutionalize what is in effect a new layer of grass-roots democracy. The crowding-in effect that the Campaign appears to be having on associational life in Kerala is also manifest in the proliferation of a variety of self-help groups, particularly women's micro-credit schemes.[34]

Corruption and Nepotism

One of the most important criticisms of decentralization is that it often does little more than devolve corruption. Indeed, funneling substantial funds to localities, without proper safeguards, inevitably fuels rent-seeking behavior and possibly community conflict. The media and opposition parties in Kerala have raised serious allegations of nepotism in beneficiary selection and corruption in the implementation of projects. Critics allege that a substantial number of beneficiary committees are led by nominees of contractors (so-called *benami* committees).

State investigating agencies have also pointed to widespread irregularities in the first year's plan implementation.[35]

In its own evaluation the State Planning Board concluded that irregularities during the first annual plan resulted more from inexperience and haste than corruption. For example, when local bodies in the first year found it difficult to absorb and properly distribute funds, many transferred the funds to non-plan accounts or deposited the money with government or quasi-government agencies such as electricity boards or the Kerala Water Authority so that they could claim full utilization before the spending deadline. Even though regulations were bent and even broken, there was little leakage as such. Irregular expenditures that were identified by the government were disallowed and new rules have substantially curtailed such improprieties.

There is little doubt that many beneficiary committees have fallen prey to vested interests. But there is also little doubt that the traditional nexus of corruption between contractor, engineer, and politician has been decisively broken in a large number of local bodies. For example, in the district of Kannur – a CPM stronghold – one investigation revealed that beneficiary committees have been carefully constituted and run according to the Campaign's criteria of transparency and democratic accountability. Strengthening the capacity and accountability of beneficiary committees remains one of the most important priorities of the Campaign, and a number of important reforms have already been introduced.[36] Despite some leakage of funds, most observers agree that the multiplication of checks and balances and the increased scrutiny associated with citizen participation is a dramatic improvement over the routinized plunder that characterized the traditional system.

Institutional fine-tuning and increased community experience have visibly improved the beneficiary selection process. During the first year, complaints about the selection process were registered in a majority of local bodies. The volume of registered complaints is in itself indicative of the increased transparency of the system. The traditional system was entirely based on patronage. Complaints were rare simply because the information was accessible only to the patrons and their clients. The rules for beneficiary selection have been modified in every year of the Campaign. By the third year, less than a fifth of panchayats registered complaints.

Promoting Equity

As much as the Campaign has been concerned with the efficacy of deliberative institutions, it has also, in keeping with Kerala's long history of redistributive struggles, promoted the strategic goal of building equitable forms of participation and reducing substantive inequality. Gender justice in particular has been declared to be one of the major objectives of the Campaign. We have already noted efforts to increase participation of women in grama sabhas, and the extension of neighborhood groups and self-help organizations are clearly strengthening the associational capacities of women. Two other important strategies have been efforts to build on the constitutional provision for one-third reserved representation of women in LSGIs and the introduction of a special Women Component Plan amounting to 10 percent of the plan outlay. What has been the experience so far?

The Kerala experience certainly bears out the importance of affirmative action ("reservations" in the Indian context) in representative structures and indeed suggests that the principle should be extended to higher levels of government. But affirmative action alone is insufficient. An in-depth study of elected representatives in Kerala revealed that while elected women representatives are better educated than their male counterparts (a social fact that is unique to Kerala in the Indian context), the women were on average younger, much less politically experienced, and less knowledgeable about rules, regulations, and administrative issues. Women representatives have moreover had to bear a triple burden of public office, income-earning activities, and domestic duties. From its outset, the Campaign has run an in-depth and continuous capacity-building program for women representatives. The training program, which has evolved significantly to adapt to new challenges, has yielded impressive results. A self-assessment survey of elected women representatives shows that their administrative knowledge and management skills, as well as the ability to officiate at public functions and interact effectively with their constituencies, have improved significantly over the last three years.[37]

The WCP for the first year failed to meet its targets, both in terms of overall allocation and the relevance of projects. In part, this failure stemmed from insufficient representation of women among trained resource persons. This problem has been directly addressed in subsequent rounds of training. As women activists and representatives have started to play a more proactive and informed role in the Campaign, the effectiveness, content, and scope of the WCP has improved. First, more than the statutory minimum requirement of 10 percent of the plan grant-in-aid was earmarked for the WCP in all districts. Second, an undue emphasis on credit and beneficiary contribution in development projects for women was reduced and more realistic patterns of project financing were adopted during the second year. Third, the quality of projects improved. The tendency to include the general sector projects in the WCP on the basis of notional (indirect) benefits to women has declined and the number of projects that specifically address the gender status of women has significantly increased.

The fear that the interests of scheduled castes and scheduled tribes are more readily subverted at the local level, where severe caste inequality persists, has often been raised by SC/ST leaders. How have SC/STs fared under decentralized planning in Kerala?

The Special Component Plan (SCP) and Tribal Sub-Plan (TSP) in Kerala have been formulated and implemented in a decentralized manner since the mid 1980s. But this decentralization lacked real participation by any elected representatives, let alone members of the community. Under the Campaign, 75 to 80 percent of the SCP and TSP funds were devolved to LSGIs, taken from the coffers of the state bureaucracy.

The first visible effect has been a significant increase in the funds actually earmarked and spent for scheduled castes and scheduled tribes. Careful disaggregation shows that a substantial part of the SCP and the TSP have always been calculated on the basis of notional flows, i.e. by including general schemes that encompass, rather than target, SC and ST communities. The Campaign abolished this accounting method. As a result, the SPB estimates that real resources for the weaker sections have increased by 30 to 40 percent as compared to the pre-Campaign period. The SPB plan appraisal also revealed that fears that local bodies would divert funds were misplaced. Except in rare instances, local bodies have fully accounted for grants-in-aid from the SCP and the TSP. And even though it was permissible to allocate up to 30 percent of the grant-in-aid from the SCP and the TSP for infrastructure projects such as roads and bridges, actual expenditure under this heading was less than 20 percent. Local bodies emphasized projects that could be specifically targeted for individual beneficiaries from SC and ST communities such as housing, latrines, and income-producing animals.

IV Conclusion

The Campaign represents a watershed in the post-Independence history of Kerala. It has made the very nature and institutions of the state itself an object of contestation, with the goal of deepening and widening democracy. With every local plan formulated and every project implemented, the new institutions and procedures of decentralized participation deepen their roots. Because this in turn strengthens civil society and brings previously excluded or marginalized actors into the political arena, this democratic deepening may well become self-sustaining. But because the Campaign's mobilized mode will become increasingly difficult to sustain as local planning becomes routinized, sustaining the integrity and efficacy of deliberative institutions will require institutionalizing the authority and resource base of local governments. Many of the laws and regulations to accomplish this institutionalization have already been passed. But these gains may unravel quickly if the new institutions fail to deliver. And sustainable delivery rests first on maintaining adequate levels of financial devolution and second on successfully reforming the bureaucracy. Both factors in turn rest on features of the political environment.

With the return of Congress to power, the Campaign has lost political leadership and significant state support. Already, despite its public declarations of support for the Campaign, the government has weakened the institutional moorings of the Campaign by promoting parallel structures. Thus it has split the panchayat department into two separate entities, introduced new regulatory authorities that are outside of the Campaign's integrated structures, and has pledged to provide members of the legislative assembly with funds for local development that in effect bypass panchayats. The government has also undermined the Campaign's formal and informal support structures by demobilizing trained resource persons, providing only minimal training programs, and freezing the redeployment of department officials to the local level.

But even if the Campaign now finds itself settling into a less energized equilibrium, it nevertheless represents a dramatic advance over the pre-Campaign period. Local government plays a far greater role in development than anywhere else in India. Five years of experimentation with decentralized planning in Kerala has created new sources of democratic authority and generated lessons that are certain to have a lasting impact. Politically, the most important lesson has been that decentralization and people's participation can and do work. Even if only a small proportion of panchayats have approximated the ideal of local planning, the demonstration effect of what is possible has had profound reverberations. Very concretely, these hundreds of points of experimentation have brought countless innovations to project design and implementation. These in turn have been energetically diffused through training programs in which panchayats teach each other. Once impervious and all-powerful, the bureaucracy has in hundreds of local communities been displaced by the collective efforts of ordinary citizens. Ordinary citizens who have never been afforded an opportunity to effectively engage the state outside of campaign-oriented social movements now routinely deliberate and cooperate with elected representatives and local officials in deciding how to spend large sums of money. And a generalized discontent and even cynical despair about politics has in part been replaced by an open, articulate, and relentless attack on patronage politics and by the beginnings, through everyday participatory practices, of a new kind of transformative politics. At a very minimum, this is reflected in the new-found respect that political parties have for civil society.

The second broad lesson is that there are no blueprints, and that any successful reform effort of this scope and depth will of necessity consist of learning-by-doing. Being confident about the normative desirability of EPG institutions thus also implies being comfortable with the notion that making EPG institutions work is a process of trial and error that requires continuous feedback and institutional fine-tuning. The required flexibility certainly calls for particular kinds of institutions built most notably on the principles of coordinated decentralization. Kerala's experience, however, suggests that such institutions themselves are most likely to emerge from dynamic political reform networks that span state and society and from the creative and even mischievous logic of social movements.

Notes

* Respectively Professor of Economics, Centre for Development Studies (Thiruvananthapuram, Kerala, India) and Member of the Legislative Assembly (Kerala, India) and Associate Professor of Sociology at Brown University.

1. See Patrick Heller, "Degrees of Democracy: Some Comparative Lessons from India," *World Politics*, vol. 52 (July 2000), pp. 484–519.

2. Pranab Bardhan, "Sharing the Spoils: Group Equity, Development, and Democracy," unpublished paper, University of California, Berkeley (1997), p. 16.

3. Madhav Gadgil and Ramachandra Guha, *This Fissured Land: An Ecological History of India*, Delhi: Oxford University Press (1992).

4. Jean Drèze and Amartya Sen, *India: Economic Development and Social Opportunity*, Delhi: Oxford University Press (1995).

5. The Communist Party of India was unified until 1965 when it split into the CPI and the CPM. The CPM has emerged as the much larger of the two communist parties, and is the dominant partner of the Left Democratic Fronts that have come to power in Kerala and West Bengal.

6. James Manor, *The Political Economy of Decentralization*, Washington, DC: The World Bank (1999).

7. The origins of the Campaign are treated at length in Thomas Isaac, with Richard Franke, *Local Democracy and Development: People's Campaign for Decentralized Planning in Kerala*, New Delhi: Left World Press (2000). For a detailed examination of the interplay of political parties and social movements in shaping institutional reforms

see Patrick Heller, "Moving the State: The Politics of Decentralization in Kerala, South Africa and Porto Alegre," *Politics and Society*, vol. 29, no. 1 (2001), pp. 131–63.

8. The basic principles of local self-government – autonomy, subsidiarity, role clarity, complementarity, uniformity, people's participation, accountability, and transparency – were first formulated by the Committee on Decentralization of Power (popularly known as Sen Committee, after its late chairperson Dr. Satyabrata Sen) appointed by the Government of Kerala.

9. For a critique of the technocratic vision see Bardhan, "The State against Society: The Great Divide in Social Science Discourse," in Sugata Bose and Ayecha Jalal, eds., *Nationalism, Democracy, and Development*, New York: Oxford University Press, pp. 184–95, and Heller, "Moving the State." For an excellent case study see James Ferguson, *The Anti-Politics Machine: "Development," Depoliticization and Bureaucratic Power in Lesotho*, New York: Cambridge University Press (1994).

10. Robert D. Putnam, *Making Democracy Work, Civic Traditions in Modern Italy*, Princeton: Princeton University Press (1993).

11. Theda Skocpol and Morris P. Fiorina, eds., *Civic Engagement in American Democracy*, Washington, DC: Brookings Institution Press (1999).

12. Peter Evans, "Government Action, Social Capital and Development: Reviewing the Evidence on Synergy," *World Development*, vol. 24, no. 6 (1996), pp. 1119–32.

13. Joshua Cohen and Joel Rogers, *Associations and Democracy*, New York and London: Verso (1995).

14. Drèze and Sen, *India*.

15. Patrick Heller, *The Labor of Development: Workers in the Transformation of Capitalism in Kerala, India*, Ithaca: Cornell University Press (1999).

16. Chalmers *et al.*, "The Associative Network: Emerging Patterns of Popular Representation," in Douglas Chalmers, Carlos M. Vilas, and Katherine Roberts Hite, eds., *The New Politics of Inequality in Latin America*, New York: Oxford University Press (1997).

17. T.M. Thomas Isaac, The Socio-Economic and Political Context of People's Planning Campaign, National Workshop on Decentralised Governance, Organised by Kerala Institute of Local Administration and Swiss Agency for Development and Co-operation, Thrissur (1999a); Andrew Szasz, "Progress through Mischief: The Social Movement Alternative to Secondary Associations," in Erik O. Wright, ed., *Associations and Democracy*, London: Verso (1995).

18. Introduction to this volume.

19. A variety of factors contributed to CPM's defeat despite the People's Campaign. There was a consolidation of all casteist and communal groups and parties around the Congress Party-led opposition. The organizational problems within the Left-front including splits in some of its minor constituents also contributed to the electoral setback. The second set of factors are related to the omissions and commissions of the state government including a near paralyzing fiscal crisis of the government on the eve of the elections, a botched reform initiative in education, and a series of high-profile corruption scandals and embarrassing controversies. A third factor was the severe economic crisis that the state economy has been plunged into due to a sharp decline in prices of rubber, coconut, and other commercial crops that are the basis of Kerala's agricultural economy. The collapse of commodity prices was a direct result of trade liberalization and the national government's WTO agreement. The incumbent party in power in Kerala was, however, made to pay the price.

20. Government of India, *Guidelines for the Formulation of District Plans*, New Delhi: Planning Commission (1969); Government of India, *Report of the Working Group on Block Level Planning*, New Delhi: Planning Commission (1978); Government of India, *Report of the Working Group on District Planning*, New Delhi: Planning Commission (1984).

21. Government of India, *Report of the Working Group on District Planning*.

22. Village panchayats have an average population of ten to fifteen thousand and are broken down into ten to twelve wards each represented by a single councilor. In Kerala's highly competitive party system, most panchayats have multiple-party representation.

23. The grama, block, and district levels under the Indian constitution represent a continuous set of structures and are all referred to as panchayats. Municipalities stand alone.

24. At 93 percent, Kerala's literacy rate is almost twice the national average. The information returns of Kerala's high literacy are reflected in the fact that it boasts more daily newspapers (twenty-seven at last count) than any other Indian state, despite being among the smallest.

25. Tabulated from evaluation forms collected from development seminars, 1996.

26. Fung and Wright, Introduction to this volume, pp. 16–18.

27. Introduction to this volume, pp. 16–17.

28. Fung and Wright, Introduction to this volume, p. 27.

29. The Kerala Information Mission has been set up to rectify this situation. The mission's goal is to network the local bodies, train the personnel and generate software for effective plan monitoring and service provisioning by the local bodies. By mid 2001 the Mission plans to have installed a computer in all panchayats with links to all other panchayats and to the State Planning Board.

30. All figures are from the SPB.

31. Fung and Wright, Introduction to this volume, p. 25.

32. A number of steps have been initiated to strengthen the grama sabhas. The minimum number of legally required grama sabhas meetings in a year has been raised from two to four. The quorum has also been raised from fifty to a hundred or 10 percent of the voters. An official coordinator for each grama sabha is now appointed and made responsible for keeping records.

33. T.M. Thomas Isaac, "Janakeeyasoothranavum Ayalkoottangalum – Anubhavangalum Padangalum" [People's Planning and Neighbourhood groups – Lessons from Experience], in *Ayalkootta Sangamam* [Neighborhood Groups] vol. I, Kerala State Planning Board, Thiruvananthapuram (1999c).

34. T.N. Seema and Vanitha Mukherjee, "Gender Governance and Citizenship in Decentralized Planning," paper presented at the International Conference on Democratic Decentralization, Thiruvananthapuram, May 23–27, 2000; B. Manjula, "Voices from the Spiral of Silence: A Case Study of Samatha Self-Help Groups of Ulloor," paper presented at the International Conference on Democratic Decentralization, Thiruvananthapuram, May 23–27, 2000.

35. T.M. Thomas Isaac, "Gunabhokthra Samithikalude Anubhava Padangal" [People's Planning and Beneficiary Committees – Lessons from Experience], in *Gunabhokthra Samithikalum Janakeeyasoothranavum* [People's Planning and Beneficiary Committees] Kerala State Planning Board, Thiruvananthapuram (1999d).

36. The reforms include new standards of transparency, a new training program and the creation of a Technical Audit Team.

37. T.M. Thomas Isaac *et al.*, "Gender and Decentralised Planning – The Experience of People's Campaign" (unpublished working paper), Center for Development Studies, Thiruvananthapuram (1999).

4

Deliberative Democracy, Chicago Style: Grass-roots Governance in Policing and Public Education
Archon Fung[*]

I The Emergence of Accountable Autonomy

The city of Chicago hardly seems fertile ground for deliberative democratic institutions to take root and bear fruit. Although its history and environs have many contradictory strands – a tradition of machine politics, insular administrative bureaucracies installed in reaction to political manipulations, a vibrant tradition of neighborhood activism, and an extreme socio-economic inequality typical of urban areas in the United States – none is particularly friendly to a politics of fairness and reason.[1]

It is altogether surprising, then, that two recent institutional reforms have remade Chicago's public school and police systems into the most formally participatory and deliberative departments of their kind in the United States. Consider the basic features of these organizations. The Chicago Public Schools (CPS) consists of some 540 elementary schools and high schools. Since 1988, each of these has been governed by its own elected Local School Council (LSC). LSCs are elected every two years. Each consists of six parents, two community representatives, two teachers, the school's principal, and an additional non-voting student for high schools. They enjoy substantial powers and responsibilities such as hiring and firing principals of their schools, spending discretionary funds, and developing and implementing strategic plans for school improvement that address issues such as curriculum, instruction, physical design, and administrative operation. While individual schools thus gain wide latitude in determining their own affairs, they are by no means isolated from the larger city-wide system. District offices and city headquarters at the Chicago Board of Education support the governance and improvement efforts of individual schools by training LSC members and others in, for example, techniques of principal selection, school budgeting, curriculum design, and strategic planning. They also hold individual schools accountable for producing good educational outcomes first by monitoring performance across schools and then by making the system more transparent. The Board publicizes various dimensions of school operations such as test scores, student-body demographics, funding levels, and attendance and graduation rates. Schools that perform poorly are subject to disciplinary mechanisms such as increased scrutiny, active intervention to modify sub-par elements of a school's plan or its personnel, or complete "reconstitution" and receivership for cases of extreme failure.

The Chicago Police Department (CPD) implemented an architecturally similar reform in 1995. Disillusioned with the evident failure of classic policing strategies, the Department embarked on a major reorganization designed to encourage officers to actively identify and address sources of crime and disorder in their patrol areas. Unlike most other American cities that embraced problem-oriented policing,[2] however, the CPD reforms presumed that problem-solving efforts would work best with deep citizen involvement. On this view, residents often possess superior knowledge of problems in their neighborhoods and might have different priorities even when both were equally well informed. Therefore police–resident partnerships might better identify and act upon critical problems than police acting alone. Partnerships might also be more effective because police and neighborhood residents have different capacities and resources. Finally, more than a few public safety and police-reform activists thought that bringing citizens closer to sworn officers would enable them to monitor police activities better and hold the police more accountable for doing their jobs.

These sentiments were institutionalized into a distinctive form of community policing that, like the LSC reforms, creates a kind of neighborhood governance over public safety measures. Now, in each of Chicago's 279 police beats, patrol officers and their sergeants meet regularly with residents to identify which public safety problems (e.g. a crack house) constitute the neighborhood's most urgent priorities, to develop strategies involving both police and civilian action to deal with those problems, to report back on the emergence of new problems and the success or failure of past strategies, and to develop new approaches if initial plans prove disappointing. Like the LSC reforms, neighborhood residents and officers do not operate autonomously from higher, more central authorities or broader publics. Departments in the Mayor's Office and CPD provide training to both police and residents in the procedures and techniques of successful problem-solving and also deploy community organizers to mobilize resident participation in the ongoing effort. These teams must also document their problem-solving activities and outcomes for review by managers and supervisors.[3]

This chapter attempts to understand the form, potential, and implications of these reforms for the values of empowered deliberation. It does so by casting their deep structure as one of *accountable autonomy*. Though the parts of this term may seem to be in tension, the following analysis will show that either alone is insufficient and that together they offer a deliberative institutional form that can generate fair and effective public outcomes.

In Chicago LSCs and beat meetings, groups of citizens and street-level public servants (teachers, principals, and police officers) are autonomous in the sense that they set and implement, through deliberative processes, specific ends and means toward broad public aims such as school improvement and public safety. In contrast with command-and-control arrangements under which these public servants would follow the instructions of superiors, this autonomy affords greater voice to citizen-users, perhaps deploys more information in problem-solving, and allows those closest to concrete public problems to innovate and utilize their ingenuity.

Many theorists and political observers have correctly warned of localism's dangers. Foremost among these dangers are domination or capture by powerful factions or persons in small groups, the paralysis of local groups due to conflictual deadlock, and their lack of capacity and sophistication.[4] Circumstances of pervasive inequality and conflict, describing many Chicago neighborhoods, further compound these difficulties. These problems might well overwhelm the benefits to autonomy understood as pure neighborhood decentralization. The Chicago reforms, however, do not leave neighborhoods to their own devices. As mentioned, the central offices of the CPS and CPD support local actors by providing training, resources, and various kinds of coordination. When effective action requires these additional capacities, external supports enhance local autonomy. More importantly, central managers also monitor the deliberative processes and performance outcomes of local groups. When they detect shortfalls in local process or performance, they can intervene and even apply sanctions. Thus neighborhoods are subject to mechanisms of accountability that attempt both to check the tendencies of autonomy to degenerate into license and to assure that limited devolution advances broader public ends.

This structure of accountable autonomy, however, is an ideal type that the Chicago reforms only approximate imperfectly. The experience there falls short of the promise of empowered participatory governance. While some beats and school councils draw substantial citizen engagement, others elicit little. Some groups have coalesced into deliberative, effective, and innovative partnerships between residents and street-level bureaucrats, while others have degenerated into conflict or inactivity. Centralized efforts to find and bolster flagging local efforts often succeed admirably, but these interventions are sometimes as problematic as the situations they attempt to rectify. Throughout, both the CPD and CPS have thus far failed to leverage local innovations into broader improvements through the diffusion of "best practices." Though a few official programs and informal efforts at this kind of learning have taken place, the efforts are neither widespread nor systematic.

Nevertheless, these Chicago experiences provide opportunities to interrogate the theory, practice, and promise of Empowered Participatory Governance. Conceptually, the institutional architecture is a touchstone from which to generate a grounded account of *practical* deliberation that has been for the most part ignored in the abstractions of contemporary political theorists of deliberation. Empirically, the Chicago experiments provide a rich opportunity to examine how one variant of deliberative democracy plays out under quite diverse urban conditions. The harsh political and socio-economic climate in which these institutions operate also throws several pitfalls of deliberative democracy into sharp relief.

Part II begins this exploration by describing the neighborhood foundations of accountable autonomy in the Chicago reforms. Part III then shows how central authorities in the CPS and CPD have partially reinvented themselves to support, monitor, and discipline decentralized deliberations to both bolster autonomy and provide accountability. Part IV describes levels and biases of participation in the Chicago experience thus far. Part V uses two neighborhood-level case studies to illustrate the vulnerabilities and benefits of accountable autonomy. Part VI concludes by reflecting upon two critical, but still very open, questions: the effectiveness of this reform strategy compared to conventional alternatives and its political stability.

II Participatory Devolution: the Kernel of Autonomy

Far from being the result of masterful design, these institutions arose haphazardly – themselves the result of fitful informal deliberations – as reformers inside city offices and activists outside them groped toward more effective ways of organizing their police departments and schools. This process began in the late 1980s, when both agencies came under mounting criticism for their ineffectiveness and unresponsiveness. Though the CPD and CPS had withstood many such attacks throughout their histories without fundamental reorganization, this round of skirmishes was different. Conservative forces failed to rebuff demands for change, and consequently the agencies – though independently and through very different paths – were deeply reconfigured. Both moved decisively away from centralized command by devolving authority to school staffs, parents, police beat officers, and neighborhood residents.

In the Chicago schools, reform resulted from a pitched battle that pitted a diverse social movement – composed of parent organizations, "good government" civic groups, educational reform activists, and a coalition of business groups – against traditional school insiders such as the Chicago Teacher's Union and the Board of Education. Two proximate events – media fallout from a blistering 1987 evaluation in which then Secretary of Education William Bennett called Chicago's school system "the worst in the nation" and a grinding teachers' strike that delayed the opening of classes for four weeks – crystallized long-standing sentiments against the CPS into concrete and well-supported proposals for reform.[5] Though they varied in their particulars, most reformers blamed the large organizations that traditionally controlled the Chicago schools – the Board and the Union – for poor school performance. The old guard seemed beyond the pale of reform: so long as they controlled the schools, reformers thought, the system would remain among the nation's worst.

Education reformers eventually took their battle to the Illinois Assembly in Springfield, and there won a decisive victory. For better or worse, reformers got almost everything they asked for when the Assembly passed the 1988 Chicago School Reform Act. The law created the decentralized school governance arrangements described above. These bodies enjoy considerable powers. LSCs are responsible for hiring, firing, evaluating, and determining the job definitions of the principals of each school. They also approve school budgets. LSCs also develop a required document called the School Improvement Plan. Improvement plans are three-year, long-term plans that articulate improvement goals (attendance, graduation rates, achievement levels, school environment) and steps necessary to reach those goals for each school. The principal has primary responsibility for implementing the plan, while the council is charged with monitoring its progress. Finally, reform legislation shifted control of "Chapter 1" funds, discretionary state monies allocated to schools on the basis of economic disadvantage, to LSCs. This reform package made CPS the most decentralized and participatory urban educational system in the United States.

Through a very different path, the Chicago Police Department recently adopted strikingly similar organizational reforms under its "Chicago Alternative Policing Strategy." At the end of the 1980s, police forces and chiefs in many U.S. cities were engaged in self-reflective doubt about whether their two traditional methods – preventative patrols that demonstrate presence through marked vehicles and rapid response to "911" calls for emergency service – could address the diverse and severe crime and disorder problems they faced.[6] Typically, the reforms they proposed fell under the broad rubric of "community policing." They called for officers to use their initiative and ingenuity to tackle particular problems of crime and disorder, and for them to operate closer to citizens and sometimes to build partnerships with community groups. In Chicago, two extradepartmental forces supplemented these professional internal impulses and shaped the eventual course of reform.

Leaders from a sophisticated city-wide public safety organization called the Chicago Alliance for Neighborhood Safety had used their policy expertise and position as a community voice to advance a community-centered vision of community policing. From the Alliance's perspective, based upon its experience as advocate, police policy analyst, watchdog, and neighborhood organizing entity, other cities had largely excluded citizens from their reforms, and so they amounted more to policing of the community than in partnership with it. Alliance activists thought that citizens ought to be full partners in community policing because they could provide important local knowledge, generate distinctive resources, and, most importantly, monitor police officers and hold them accountable. The second important force was City Hall. Mayor Richard M. Daley and his staff seized on community policing as a good government issue to demonstrate the city's innovative spirit and commitment to fighting crime. Interest from the Mayor's Office increased the pace of community policing reform.

Without the street heat and legislative pressure that drove school reform, these discussions at the intersection of professional, political, and civic interests led quietly to the formulation of a participatory variant of community policing that was piloted in five of the city's twenty-five police districts beginning in 1993 and then expanded to the entire city in 1995. Its basic outlines resemble the central features of the 1988 school devolution. Recognizing the need to address situated issues with focussed and contextualized attention, police officers were organized into some 279 neighborhood-sized "beat teams" that would, in addition to their ordinary patrol and response duties, familiarize themselves with specific neighborhoods and their idiosyncratic problems. Presuming that neighborhood residents possessed detailed knowledge of these problems, resources for addressing them, and strong motivations to do so, the reform created channels for resident participation. Specifically, open "community beat meetings" would be held in each beat every month for the officers serving that area and its residents to jointly engage in problem identification and resolution efforts.

Thus the CPS and CPD both reorganized themselves through radically devolutionary measures that set in place three central planks of participatory local autonomy in police and school governance.

First, the reforms created opportunities for ordinary citizens to participate continuously and directly in the micro-governance of two important institutions of urban life: schools and police. Parents and community members who desire formal authority and are willing to devote substantial energies to school governance can run for election to one of the six parent or two community seats on each school's LSC. Those with less intense interests can attend and voice their views at their LSC's regular, typically monthly, meetings. By contrast, the community policing program has no formal governance councils. Instead, it requires police officers in each beat to attend open meetings (usually held monthly) with residents to engage in joint problem-solving on neighborhood issues of crime and disorder. Before these reforms, residents relied upon attenuated, less regular, and undoubtedly less effective methods to influence the decisions of these local institutions such as voting for their city council representative, contacting their offices about specific concerns and relying on the efficacy of subsequent constituent service efforts, or directly contacting police or school officials to lodge complaints or raise suggestions. These channels of participation increase citizens' and officials' knowledge of each other and allow citizens to hold officials accountable through continuous scrutiny of their priorities and actions.

Second, participation under this devolution instituted deliberative

decision procedures. In most forms of political action, such as aldermanic elections and informal contacting, citizens express their preferences for this policy or that candidate or occasionally register a
complaint. In LSC governance, by contrast, deliberation occurs in the
process of constructing, approving, and implementing school improvement plans. Under the 1988 legislation, each LSC is required periodically to submit a plan that lays out their three-year goals and steps to
achieve them. Those involved – usually led by the principal but drawn
from a school's staff and parental and community ranks – first develop
an educational vision or mission statement for the school, analyze their
present strengths and weaknesses, then construct curricular, instructional capacity, and physical plant strategies to advance their mission
statement, and finally allocate staff and financial resources to implement and monitor the progress of those strategies. The outcomes then
feed back into subsequent LSC deliberations and plan revisions.

Deliberation in community policing beat meetings is structured
according to a similar problem-solving process. Police and residents
begin by using a "brainstorming" process to generate a comprehensive
list of crime and safety problems in their neighborhood. They then
agree to focus on two or three listed items as priority issues, then pool
information and perspectives to develop analyses of these problems.
From these analyses, they construct strategies and a division of labor to
implement these strategies. The success of the strategies is assessed in
subsequent meetings. Groups typically try to develop additional strategies to address stubborn problems or take on new problems after
resolving old ones. This short feedback loop between planning, implementation, and assessment increases both the practical capabilities and
the problem-solving success of residents and police officers in each
beat.

Third, these devolutions establish an element of empowerment: the
expectation that citizens' participation and deliberation will directly
affect public action. Ordinary channels of political influence and public
discussion are less empowered in this regard. When one participates in
deliberation in the public sphere of mass media as a spectator or even as
an author, votes for a candidate to represent one's views, or even serves
on advisory committees, there is but a thin connection between one's
views and official actions. In such processes, a citizen's views must be
aggregated with those of many other voters, weakened by considering
them across multiple-issue spaces, filtered up through the ranks of
political representation, and then once again diluted by administrative
discretion as interpreted down the chain of bureaucratic command.
The Chicago reforms increase citizen power over public affairs on at

least two dimensions. First, since citizens join with "street-level" public officials such as teachers, principals, and police officers to analyze localized problems and develop plans to respond to them, citizens expect their input to shape directly the subsequent official priorities and actions. Second, even if particular contributions are not incorporated into interim plans, they will at least have been publicly considered against other proposals and reasons.

III A New Center: Building Capacity and Imposing Accountability

Compared to hierarchical bureaucratic forms, these devolutions in police and school organization increase the scope for citizen participation and deliberation. From their inception, however, even reformers who viewed bureaucracies as hopelessly ineffective and unresponsive recognized the dangers inherent in decentralization and sought to remake central authority to mitigate them. Additional early experience with these new institutions of neighborhood governance revealed more pitfalls that in turn required further reconfiguration of administrative centers to support their action units in the neighborhoods. Building on this insight, the CPS and CPD central offices have moved away from attempting to direct local level operations to supporting and monitoring the self-directed governance efforts of their neighborhood units. Accountable autonomy requires that the center both support the capacity of schools and beats to act autonomously through various supports and hold them accountable through monitoring, sanctioning, and intervention.

Support: Training, Mobilization, and Institutional Intervention

From the outset, advocates of police and school decentralization recognized that many citizens would find constructive engagement with professionals difficult. They therefore urged that training programs be developed and provided on a city-wide basis. As it turned out, professionals would undergo exactly the same training as lay citizens, for the difficulties associated with deliberative problem-solving were new to both. Since there was no body of off-the-shelf expertise or experts in deliberative local governance, training was necessarily a bootstrapping process. In community policing, activists and officers from the police academy developed a group problem-solving method and hands-on curriculum based on their early experiences with informal community–police partnerships. Under a US$2.9 million contract, the city hired the Chicago Alliance for Neighborhood Safety to teach this curriculum to residents and officers. The Alliance dispatched teams of community organizers, civilian trainers, and experienced police officers to each of the city's beats.[7] Over the three or four months that they spent in each beat, teams taught deliberative problem-solving by leading residents and beat officers through practical reasoning processes. By the end of the period, residents had learned the process by applying it themselves. In many cases, they could see progress on a real-world problem that they had selected as part of the training exercise. In the two years of the Joint Community–Police Training Project, organizers estimate that they trained some twelve thousand residents and several hundred police officers. In a move that was controversial because this effort was generally regarded as successful, the city terminated the Alliance contract in 1997 in favor of conducting training and mobilization activities from within city departments.

School reformers also saw that LSC members might be initially bewildered by their new governance duties, and so developed their own series of training programs. During the first few years, groups within the CPS and non-profit community organizations like the Chicago Association of Local School Councils and the Beverly Improvement Association provided training on an ad hoc basis to schools and LSC members who sought it out. In response to the perception that many LSCs were failing, the Illinois legislature in 1995 passed a second major school reform law, this one focussed on school accountability. One of its provisions was that all new LSC members must undergo three days, or eighteen hours, of training or be removed from office. Training focussed on basic school governance issues such as principal selection and contract terms, school budgeting, LSC member responsibilities, teamwork, and school improvement planning. This program resembled community policing efforts in that training was centrally coordinated by a University of Illinois group, but was initially provided by experienced practitioners from community and school reform organizations as well as school system employees. Like the policing training program, the CPS brought the program in-house in 1998, preventing outside, mostly community-based, organizations from providing basic training.[8]

Just as the creation of opportunities for direct self-governance does not imply that citizens will possess capacities necessary to utilize them, neither does it mean that they will actually participate. Some may not know about the opportunities, others may know but not care to join. In a second area of support, then, centralized efforts also attempted to boost awareness and participation in deliberative governance. Community policing outreach has employed both mass media and community organizing techniques. Between 1997 and 2000, the city spent US$1.6 million annually on media efforts to advertise and educate residents about participation opportunities in community policing.[9] Partially as a result of these television and radio spots, billboards, and a weekly cable television program called CrimeWatch, approximately 79 percent of Chicago's adults knew about the program in 1998.[10] These efforts have been supplemented by time-tested community organizing methods. First provided as part of the training program and then later managed from the Mayor's Office, the program deployed between thirty and sixty community organizers that publicized beat meetings and partnership possibilities by visiting churches, neighborhood associations, and individual residences.

In contrast to continuous outreach in community policing, mobilization for local school governance has focussed on the biannual LSC elections and been funded primarily through private sources rather than from city coffers. In the first year of elections, 1989, charitable foundations donated some US$750,000 to community organizations to recruit LSC candidates. But this sum dropped to US$318,000 and US$215,000 for the 1991 and 1993 elections respectively.[11] In 1996, community organizations received only US$216,000 in private donations to recruit and train LSC candidates.[12] Though causality is of course difficult to establish, many associate declines in both the number of LSC candidates and voter turnout (discussed below) to this decrease in funding for outreach.

Central authorities can also help local units through institutional interventions that make the external legal, political, and administrative environment more conducive to local deliberative problem-solving. Local experience often reveals the most urgent and fruitful subjects for centralized intervention. Many LSCs proposed restructuring their school day to allow more time for teachers to collaborate and plan classes. The collective bargaining agreement between the CTU and Board of Education, however, established precise work rules that prohibited local modification. In the next round of negotiations, the Board performed its facilitative role by building into the collective agreement a waiver option through which schools could modify the work day if their teachers supported the alterations.

In another example, community policing groups often faced the drug houses that had become foci of street violence and other disturbances. Although acting separately, dozens of police–resident groups converged upon a workable strategy. Residents would try to persuade a landlord to clean up his property by evicting tenants who dealt drugs, by reporting criminal activity on the property to police, by screening out potentially problematic tenants, and by upgrading the property's condition. If a landlord responded to these entreaties, his cooperation with residents might eliminate the problem. If the landlord refused to cooperate, residents would begin to build a legal case that could be used in housing court to seize the property and thereby eliminate the drug house. The Illinois nuisance abatement law was an important instrument in this strategy. According to that statute, a court may act against a drug house by "restraining all persons . . . from using the building for a period of one year" if it establishes that "nuisance was maintained with the intentional, knowing, reckless or negligent permission of the owner."[13]

Officials in the police department and Mayor's Office took note of this strategy and secured two institutional changes that increased its effectiveness. First, a 1996 city ordinance enacted a stricter version of the Illinois nuisance abatement law.[14] This ordinance imposed the burden of monitoring illegal activities on the property owner and created a fine for allowing a nuisance to occur. Furthermore, whereas the Illinois law requires the illegal activity to occur inside the premises,[15] the new law only requires a geographic nexus between the problem property and the nuisance.

Second, the city's Law Department created a Drug and Gang House Enforcement Section that helped community policing groups utilize this law. They send staff lawyers to community beat meetings to provide expertise in the formulation and implementation of problem-solving strategies.[16] If residents identify a drug house as a priority problem, the lawyer will deploy the Law Department's resources to help them. According to the Section's supervising attorney, the office uses the strategy of persuading first and prosecuting second described above, but now backed by the power of the city.[17] They first send city inspectors to document all code violations in addition to the nuisance. They then invite the landlord to a meeting whose goal is to secure voluntary compliance with the law. If the landlord does not respond to an initial letter, rejects voluntary compliance, or does not show up to the meeting, corporation council pursues measures in administrative court. It asks for fines, and then for criminal contempt charges that can result in 180 days' imprisonment. These two background measures, then, increase the autonomy of beat groups by using state power to strengthen strategies invented by communities themselves.

Accountability: Monitoring, Adjudicating, Intervening, and Learning

Beyond providing these supports, central authorities can also enhance the public accountability and deliberative quality of police and school governance by monitoring, publicizing, and, when necessary, intervening in local activities. Though this design of democracy gives local schools and neighborhood beats power to construct their own plans of action, it does not grant license to refuse to plan either by unreflectively continuing old habits or by doing nothing at all. Due to capriciousness or incapacity, the processes of some local units may unfairly exclude some citizens, be controlled by powerful and self-interested local individuals, or fail to address priority problems. Local units subject to these various kinds of "deliberative breakdown" will be often unable to restore the integrity of their internal democratic process. It falls to centralized powers to ensure that local actors are deliberating effectively by constructing appropriate incentives and monitoring routines.

To assure that localities fulfill their minimal obligation to engage in structured problem-solving, both the CPS and CPD require LSCs and beat groups respectively to document their deliberative processes and consequent actions. As mentioned above, each LSC must prepare and submit annual school improvement plans that follow uniform CPS guidelines that prescribe the form, but not the content, of their deliberations. Similarly, community policing groups must submit both long-term and monthly reports to document their deliberations and strategies. The officers in each beat, frequently working with residents, must prepare detailed reports called beat profiles that describe available resources, local institutions, demographics, and persistent problems. In addition to this baseline information, they must document their problem-solving deliberations, including descriptions of priority targets, strategies to address them, justifications of those strategies, actions taken, and observable results for their district supervisors in "beat plans." Both the CPS and CPD supervisors review school improvement and beat plans and return facially unsatisfactory plans – e.g. those with missing plan elements – to local actors to help assure that the stages of structured deliberation have been followed.

Such reporting offers a basic but imperfect indicator of the quality of deliberation. Two additional methods offer more accurate assessments: inspection and complaint. Inspectors from central offices visit local units both to learn from those that seem most inventive and to identify those that are performing poorly. The CPS plans to establish a quality assurance agency that dispatches teams of educational experts – including consultants, master teachers and principals, and agency officials –

to individual schools. Over the course of several days, the review team would observe classes, interview staff and students, and review planning documents in order to develop performance assessments.[18] The CPD has instituted a more hierarchical process in which top staff under the police superintendent meet with each of the twenty-five district commanders to review local police performance. District commanders report on the activities of their individual beats, and in particular on whether they have developed and implemented beat-level problem-solving effectively.

But such inspections are costly and difficult to execute. Passive means that rely upon citizen complaints can also detect procedural breakdowns. When participants to local deliberation notice violations of deliberative norms (for example principals who disregard parent input or police officers who refuse to implement actions set out in beat plans), they can lodge complaints with higher authorities (such as district commanders or regional school staff). Ideally, these complaints would then trigger active official scrutiny, and if necessary direct intervention. Though this dynamic occurs informally, on an ad hoc basis, neither the CPS nor CPD has implemented official citizen complaint systems and procedures.

Other measures also attempt to assess the outcomes of local problem-solving. Centralized performance evaluation provides important tools both for external supervision and local intervention. In formulating their school plans, for example, LSC members often use trends in standardized test scores to identify weak instructional or curricular areas. By comparing their methods with those of similarly situated but better-performing schools, LSCs sometimes discover promising school improvement strategies. Careful monitoring of outcomes can also alert central authorities to laggards that deserve disciplinary intervention and leaders that merit praise.

Developing and applying outcome measures that can realize the potential benefits of monitoring is, however, no simple matter. The difficulty lies in constructing measures that accurately reflect the impact of local strategies but that do not punish schools for conditions beyond their control. Though current tools fall short in this regard, both the CPS and CPD leaderships seem satisfied with traditional metrics such as standardized test scores and crime rates. Status quo metrics may enjoy favor because they are familiar and seem objective. The primary tool to assess student achievement in math, reading, writing, science, and social studies in Chicago, for example, is the Iowa Test of Basic Skills (ITBS) which has been published continuously since 1942 and is used by school districts across the nation. Similarly, crime statistics for the city of Chicago have been gathered at both the municipal and federal level (by the FBI Uniform Crime Reports) for more than fifty years and reflect obvious dimensions of public safety such as murder, rape, robbery, and assault. Altering these metrics would require new administrative machinery and probably spark intense political conflict akin to the current battles over standardized testing.[19]

Nevertheless, some reformers have offered performance metrics that are useful not only for comparing and assessing general conditions, but also potentially for judging and improving the success of local governance efforts. Education researchers at the Consortium on Chicago School Research have developed a metric to measure the productivity of a school, or grade within a school, that attempts to capture academic gains that result from programming.[20] They propose the following two-step method of calculating the productivity of a grade within a single school. First, consider only the subset of children who attended that grade for the entire year. Second, subtract the scores of that subset for a test administered at the beginning of the year from year-end test scores. This method discounts students who attend classes for only part of the year. It also controls for differences in the preparation of students before their enrollment in a grade. Annual productivity gains (or losses) that result from school-specific factors can then be measured by subtracting a school's productivity in one year from that of the preceding year. Such a system allows central office administrators, LSC members, and the public at large to more accurately gauge school governance efforts.

Generally, the construction and application of performance metrics, like the practices whose performance is measured, is a complex matter that itself ought to be the subject of participatory deliberation and open-minded transformation. Venerable metrics like test scores and crime rates were designed to track broad changes in the academic abilities of students and safety of neighborhoods. They may perform reasonably in that regard, though many doubt even that. However, they were not designed, and are much too crude, to determine which particular educational or policing activities are more effective than others. Incremental steps, like the school productivity measures developed by the Chicago Consortium, seem to offer straightforward gains. But even these ought to be viewed as the beginning of a deliberative process to develop ever more useful metrics for assessing and thus enhancing school improvement and problem-solving strategies.

Central authorities can use existing or improved metrics as tools of accountability to identify local bodies that are laggards or leaders in deliberative governance. They can intervene to improve the performance of laggards through support or discipline. Conversely, they can publicize leaders, study their sources of success, and reward them as incentives to spur groups. The CPS and, to a lesser extent, the CPD central offices have begun to implement comparative programs of this kind. In 1995, a series of reforms led from the center by Mayor Daley and his long-time associate and newly appointed CEO of Schools, Paul Vallas, sought to increase LSC and school accountability by disciplining laggards.[21] One of its central provisions created an "academic probation" status that marked schools in which less than 15 percent of the students score at or above national norms on standardized reading tests. This program placed 109 schools on academic probation status – designating them for centralized assistance and scrutiny – in 1996, its first year of operation.

Far from re-establishing centralized direction over these schools, the probation program attempted to improve the quality of each school's deliberative planning and problem-solving processes. First, the center provided additional educational resources by requiring each school to form a partnership with outside educational experts in the private or university sector. Second, they dispatched an intervention team, led by a probation manager assigned to the school, to work with staff and parents to review and improve their school improvement plan by conducting an external review, use that report as the basis of LSC discussions to develop a Corrective Action Plan, and incorporate changes into successive improvement plans. Finally, the Office of Accountability assigned a probation manager to monitor implementation of the new plan. Though the program has been in operation only a short time, experience so far suggests that staff and parents at probation schools, while at first wary of heavy-handed CPS intervention, have generally experienced the program as a sometimes painful, but collaborative and essentially self-directed, project in enhancing their own capabilities.[22]

The center–locality collaboration in Chicago's community policing and school governance reforms differs from devolution in several ways. First, the current institutional structure is neither centralized nor de-centralized. Although local officials and ordinary citizens enjoy much more power and voice than under the previous, more top-down, arrangements, they remain dependent on central offices for various kinds of support and accountable to those offices for both process integrity and performance outcomes. Second, the role of central power shifts fundamentally from that of directing local units (in the previous, hierarchical system) to that of *supporting* local units in their own problem-solving endeavors and *holding them accountable* to the norms

of deliberation and achievement of demanding but feasible public outcomes. Third, support and accountability from the center advance the
three democratic goals of participation, deliberation, and empowerment that justify local autonomy in the first place. Each of these central
functions involves complex dilemmas with no obvious solutions.
Therefore the same principles that motivate the deliberative transformation of school and police governance also apply to the design of
the central institutions. Even when practices like standardized testing
are entrenched and enjoy wide support, alternatives might do better.
Since the advantages of competing proposals are difficult to assess
a priori (e.g. should support services be provided by a city agency or
community-based organizations?), institutions should open spaces for
competing proposals rather than advancing only the most politically
expedient or administratively convenient proposal. Centralized interventions, themselves formulated through deliberation, could then
further enhance the deliberative, participatory, and empowered character of otherwise isolated local actors. Although neither the CPS
nor CPD has achieved such a fully deliberative transformation, many
essential elements are in place in both these institutions.

We turn now to the performance of these institutions in light of
general concerns about the demands and potential pathologies of
empowered participatory governance.[23]

IV Who Participates?

These reforms aim to involve citizens more intensively in decision-
making areas from which they were previously excluded. The first
operational question, therefore, is who, if anyone, utilizes these new
forms? Since participation in these local bodies requires much more
time, knowledge, and energy from citizens than voting or contacting
officials, engagement levels may be so low that school officials and
police officers end up deliberating with one another rather than with
those they serve. Since those who have less generally participate less,[24]
this concern is especially pressing in poor neighborhoods. Relatedly,
biases in participation may amount even to systematic exclusion.

This section examines levels of and socio-economic biases in participation. It then reflects on the implications of this dimension of the
Chicago reform experience for empowered participatory governance.

Overall Participation

To answer the question of how many citizens participate in Chicago's deliberative governance institutions, we rely on official CPS election statistics and beat meeting attendance records gathered by CPD beat officers and compiled by researchers at the Institute for Policy Research at Northwestern University. These records show that community policing and school governance exhibit a similar pattern of aggregate participation: generally, a community beat or LSC meeting draws between ten and twenty participants. The regular participants in LSC meetings are the elected representatives themselves, but meetings also draw interested parents or community members with no official position. Community policing offers no formal positions for residents and so attendance is always fully voluntary.

Beat meeting participation data shows that, on average, between five and six thousand residents attend beat meetings each month.[25] Since there are 279 beats and most meet monthly, between seventeen and twenty-one residents generally attend each meeting in addition to five or six beat officers. This number, while a small percentage of the four to six thousand adults who live typically in a beat, is more than enough for problem-solving planning and implementation. Although this structure of community beat meetings has existed only since 1995 and so trajectories are difficult to discern, there seems to be a slight upward trend in meeting attendance. This trend offers some preliminary evidence against the concern that the demands of participatory democracy may result in civic exhaustion and declining rates of participation.[26]

Participation in school governance exhibits comparable levels.[27] In terms of both candidacy and turnout, participation was very high in the first year of reform (1989) and then dropped off to a lower, but relatively stable, level in successive elections. In the last three elections, the ratio of candidates to positions has been less than 1.5 in all three categories, which means that more than half of the seats are uncontested. Accordingly, LSC service resembles volunteerism more than competitive selection. Furthermore, since the ratio is substantially greater than unity, few LSCs have empty seats. The number of citizens who actually engage in deliberation is much smaller than the number affected (roughly four thousand residents live in the area served by a school). However, there are usually enough members to engage in school improvement planning. Furthermore, the levels of participation are for the most part stable.

Socio-Economic Bias

Who are these people who spend precious evenings discussing crime and schooling, and some portion of their days doing what they promised to do in those discussions? Two general patterns emerge in both school and police governance. Surprisingly, those in low-income neighborhoods participate as much or more than people from wealthier ones. Within any given neighborhood, however, the more advantaged – homeowners and those with more income and education – participate at disproportionately greater rates. This pattern confirms the well-grounded intuition that resources and other advantages influence citizens' abilities to participate.[28]

Engagement patterns in community policing are especially striking. There, contravening most empirical social science findings, residents from poor neighborhoods participate at *greater* rates than those from wealthy ones. The best predictor of neighborhood beat meeting attendance rate is the personal crime rate of the neighborhood, which tends to vary inversely with household income.[29] In a regression analysis for predictors of beat meeting attendance rate[30] that includes: (1) the percentage of beat residents that are African-American, (2) percentage Hispanic, (3) percentage of adults that have college degrees, (4) median household income, (5) personal crime rate, and (6) percentage of residences that are owned by their occupants, the only statistically significant factor in this regression – and the one with the most substantial coefficient – is personal crime rate.[31] According to this model, an increase of 40 crimes per 1,000 residents (mean personal crime rate in Chicago was 84 crimes per 1,000 residents in 1996) corresponds to an increase in beat meeting attendance of 8 persons per 10,000 adults, or some 4 persons per meeting in a medium-sized beat. The same predicted increase requires, according to this regression, an increase in neighborhood mean household income of US$20,000 (almost doubling the average neighborhood median household income of US$24,000). Interestingly, the effect of percent college educated on beat meeting attendance is small, but in the opposite of the expected direction; the regression model finds that the controlled effect of increasing the number of college graduates in a neighborhood weakly reduces beat meeting attendance.

Although participation patterns in local school council elections have been less well documented and the trends themselves more equivocal, the data also weigh against the expectation that those in less well off areas will also participate less. In their study of the 1991 LSC elections, the non-profit school reform organization Designs for Change analyzed the number of candidates standing for election to parent seats on local school councils according to student body characteristics of race, income, and ethnicity. They found that an average of nine parental candidates stood for election at any given school and that there was no substantial relationship between levels of parental candidacy and percentage of Hispanic students, or percentage of African-American students.[32] The study also found a slight positive correlation between the percentage of low-income students at a given school and the number of parental candidates standing for election in 1991.

Using data from the 1996 Chicago local school council elections,[33] I independently analyzed the relationships between school-level variables such as school size, percentage of students from low-income families at a particular school,[34] student mobility,[35] percentage of African-American students, and percentage of Hispanic students and two indicators of LSC participation: the number of parental candidates standing for election at each school[36] and the parent turnout at each election.[37] In the regression, only school size bore a statistically significant relationship with the number of parental candidates. In a regression treating parental turnout rate in LSC elections as the dependent variable, poverty, race, mobility, and ethnicity variables were statistically significant. The magnitude of the coefficient on low income is small, but in the expected direction; as the percentage of low income students at a school increases, parent turnout rate declines slightly. An increase of 25 percent in the portion of low-income students at a school corresponds to a decrease of 4.5 percent in the fraction of parents turning out to vote in an LSC election. Similarly, increases in student mobility (and thus decreases in school stability) produce small declines in parental turnout rates. The coefficients on race and ethnicity variables are also small, but in the opposite of the expected directions. Whereas previous studies have found that African-American and people of Hispanic backgrounds are somewhat less likely to vote than others,[38] higher proportions of black and Hispanic students in a school correlated with slightly higher parental turnout rates in the 1996 LSC elections.

While these data show that participation rates compared *across* neighborhoods do not exhibit straightforward biases against the worst off, the same cannot be said for participation patterns considered *within* neighborhoods. Available data suggest that those who serve on local school councils and attend community beat meetings tend to be better off than their neighbors. A survey of all local school council members conducted in 1995 and 1996 reveals that LSC members were substantially better educated and more employed than other adults in

Chicago. Thirty-one percent of LSC members surveyed had a bachelor's degree or higher, compared to only 19 percent of adults in Chicago. Predictably, schools in more wealthy areas had more educated LSC members, but "even in schools with virtually all low-income students, the educational level of LSC members is almost equal to that of the general Chicago population."[39] LSC members are also more likely to hold professional jobs, less likely to occupy unskilled positions or be unemployed, and more likely to be "home with children" than the other adults in Chicago.[40] A similar pattern appears in community beat meeting participation: homeowners and English speakers are more likely to know about beat meetings and attend them than are their less well off neighbors.[41] As with rates of overall participation, these biases sketch an equivocal portrait for the Chicago style of deliberative governance. Contrary to skeptical expectations that reforms demanding active participation will further disadvantage badly off areas, residents of poor neighborhoods participate at rates equal to or greater than those from wealthy ones. Nevertheless, better-off residents are generally disproportionately well represented within neighborhood meetings.

How Much Participation is Enough?

These results lead to no straightforward assessments, either positive or negative, regarding the operations of deliberative democracy as it actually exists in Chicago. On the one hand, the proportion of total adults who participate in these direct governance opportunities is much less than for conventional forms such as voting. If we judge desirability solely on the basis of how many people participate, then these experiments must be regarded as failures compared to voting. If we include additional desiderata – for example citizens' knowledge on issues about which they are asked to express opinions, the impact of those opinions on state action, and finally the effect of state action on social outcomes – then the current levels of participation exceed minima necessary for participatory problem-solving.

The eleven positions of LSCs are filled in the typical school and community policing beat meetings are on average attended by seventeen residents and six police officers. Meetings with much lower (say only two or three people) levels of average attendance would lead correctly to fundamental doubts about the viability of this variant of urban deliberative democracy. Very low participation would demonstrate lack of citizen interest, provide too few heads to generate information and effective solutions, and offer too few bodies to implement any resulting group decisions. On the other hand, much greater participation would also create difficulties. Neighborhood crises such as drive-by shootings or serial rapes, for example, often draw dozens of additional participants to community policing meetings. When fifty or a hundred people attend, it becomes extremely difficult to conduct structured, much less sustained and inclusive, problem-solving deliberations. If there is a magic number for a group that is small enough so that all of its members can contribute seriously to an ongoing discussion, and yet large enough to offer diverse views and ample energies, it is probably not so far from the actual numbers of people that actually participate in groups constituted by the Chicago reforms.

Whereas voting is an infrequent activity for which there are few repercussions for either not voting or making poor choices, participation in local school councils or community policing groups requires much more knowledge and commitment. In exchange, such participation offers a modicum of real decision power. Only those with an abiding concern in specific issues are likely to join these efforts. If these reforms were expanded to include other public problems such as the environment, social services, or employment – a possibility not developed here – the ideal of participation would not be one in which every citizen deliberates every issue, but in which everyone seriously deliberates something. Current institutional arrangements do not offer such diverse opportunities for empowered discursive engagement.

Patterns of participation with respect to time and socio-economic status also ease some serious concerns about the sustainability and fairness of these intensively deliberative governance institutions. Although both are relatively new, their short track records of eleven years for school governance and five for community policing indicate that participation levels have been for the most part stable. Signs of citizen exhaustion have not surfaced. Regarding fairness, these institutions offer substantial advantages over more familiar forms of political participation – such as voting, contacting officials, and interest-group activism – that display strong biases favoring the better off. Despite this surprising absence of conventional biases, these quantitative characteristics of participation leave many open questions. While enough people participate across many kinds of neighborhoods, their actions may not meet the demanding standards of deliberation. They may fall victim to pathologies such as domination, corruption, or incompetence. We turn now to these questions about the structure and quality of participation.

V Deliberation or Domination? Problem-Solving in Two Neighborhoods

Do the diverse citizens and street-level bureaucrats[42] who join in Chicago school and police governance actually engage in open deliberation and fair exchange about how best to advance public ends? Or are these decision processes more often characterized by the domination of officials over residents, more advantaged citizens over the less well off, or factional paralysis? No study has yet examined all of the beats and schools in Chicago to determine definitively whether these governance transformations have produced substantial domination and corruption. Yet less systematic evidence and observation affords some purchase on this critical set of issues. Except in one or two well-publicized instances,[43] the most blatant forms of theft and fraud have not surfaced in either the community policing or school governance reforms. At the other extreme, no informed observer would argue that school and police governance processes have been fully deliberative or domination-free.

This section offers two accounts of typical conflicts to show how a structure of accountable autonomy that connects central supervisors to locally autonomous groups can set deliberation on track and reap its fruits.[44]

Deadlock in Central School

Like many schools on the city's South Side, Central Elementary sits in a neighborhood that is 100 percent African-American and very poor. The median household income in 1990 was US$15,000. In addition to contending with the typical problems of poor inner city neighborhood schools, this one also suffered paralyzing conflicts, stemming from old feuds, among the parents, teachers, and the principal. Many dimensions of the school's operation – including academic performance, discipline, and the condition of the grounds – suffered from the ensuing collective inaction.

The most visible signs of decay came from the building itself. The rooms and halls were ill-kept and often dark. Though the building was overcrowded, failure to repair water damage rendered three classrooms unusable and so further increased class sizes. Insufficient resources cannot explain away this situation, as similarly funded schools elsewhere had superior physical plants. The school also suffered from chronic truancy rates. In 1996, 6 percent of its students missed more than 10 percent of the school days without excuse.[45] Teachers and other school staff complained that they were unable to discipline children who attended class. Many classes were loud and unruly, and children often roamed the halls without supervision. Central's students also scored poorly on standardized tests. In 1996, only 14.6 percent of students met or exceeded national reading norms according to the Iowa Test of Basic Skills (ITBS), and only 13.4 percent met or exceeded that test's math norms. By these measures, Central fell within the lowest decile of worst-performing Chicago schools in math and reading.

These difficulties were compounded, and in some measure caused, by bitter political conflict within the school. In 1994, the LSC faced the difficult choice of selecting a new principal. Like some University tenure decisions, discussions were heated and some say duplicitous. Years afterward, the parties to school governance – active parents, community members, teachers, and the principal herself – were still divided along the factions that formed during the principal selection decision. To some extent, these rifts reproduced themselves as older participants transmitted their biases to newer ones. However, many of those who joined in the 1994 decision were still active and bore hard feelings over the conflict. As a consequence, the energies of the LSC between 1994 and 1996 were consumed with bureaucratic infighting and attempts by all sides to build complex alliances. The principal sided with one section of the parent representatives against a stable section of community representatives who were joined by parts of the school staff and other parents. These conflicts destroyed staff morale and paralyzed school governance.

Poor student test performance triggered an accountability mechanism called probation whereby the CPS dispatched an expert "intervention team." Many at the school feared that these central office administrators would take back much of the autonomy given to its LSC under the 1988 law. To the surprise of LSC members, the next few months did not require them to give up power to external authorities. Instead, the probation team forced LSC members and others in the school community to break through their entrenched lines of conflict into more serious deliberations about strategies that might improve the school.

The intervention team conducted a review of the school that pointed out problems such as: LSC budgeting decisions, lack of teacher monitoring, ineffective use of school staff, poor instructional technique and classroom management, funded but vacant teacher positions, and poor physical plant. Although their report contained proposed solutions to these problems, the team made it clear that these were recommendations rather than orders. The LSC developed a corrective action plan after reflecting on this report and incorporating the perspectives and knowledge of its own members. The intervention team was widely respected and thus able to facilitate the LSC's deliberative planning effort and set their group process on track.

After six months, LSC members seemed to have transcended their histories of conflict. They began to behave cordially to one another and, more importantly, to deliberate about substantive school improvements rather than using meetings as occasions for political maneuvering. Substantively, the LSC reached consensus on a corrective action plan that included funds to make capital improvements to increase classroom space, fill shortages of instructional materials, extend the school's computer network, and to purchase additional equipment for the science lab. Whereas a discussion of indicators of school progress such as test scores would have likely drawn accusations and defensive responses only six months earlier, LSC members used the June meeting as an occasion for thoughtful reflection on the school's weak grades. Whereas the principal had been a highly controversial figure several months earlier, the group gained respect for her through several months of facilitated deliberation and the LSC voted unanimously to renew her contract.

From Laissez Faire Domination to Structured Deliberation in Traxton Beat

Consider now community policing in a neighborhood called Traxton, which also lies on Chicago's South Side, several miles distant from Central Elementary. This neighborhood is literally split in half by railroad tracks, with wealthy, mostly white, professionals living on its west side and lower middle class African-Americans on its east. It is only by administrative coincidence that these two groups lie in the same police beat, for their problems are very different. West-siders face occasional burglaries, illegal traffic and noise, loitering and drinking, and the like. East-siders, on the other hand, face armed robbery, occasional gunshots from houses or passing automobiles, and a house in the middle of their section where people come to buy narcotics. In one year, three people were shot to death within one block of this house.

Empirically informed critics[46] would not be surprised that community deliberations often led to an inequitable allocation of police resources. This group elected a beat facilitator each year. In 1996, the beat facilitator conducted meetings in a laissez faire, first-come, first-served, style in which residents raised problems as they came to mind. In this mode, wealthy and educated west-side residents dominated proceedings with their concerns. Their priorities included a potentially dangerous abandoned building, noise from late-night patrons of a nearby pancake house, street peddlers, and generally poor 911 response. Police, often in cooperation with west-side residents, were able to resolve most of these issues. Yet the concerns of east-side residents, often more serious, went for the most part unaddressed.

This pattern began to change in 1997 upon the election of a new beat facilitator; call her Emily Crenshaw. Unlike the previous facilitator, Crenshaw had worked for the Chicago Alliance for Neighborhood Safety as an official community policing trainer.[47] Schooled in the procedures and techniques of problem-solving, she had instructed many beat groups in those techniques. When she became Traxton's beat facilitator, she utilized her experience to impose recommended structure on previously unstructured discussions. She directed the group to produce a "beat plan," required according to recent CPD directives, that would describe and justify the neighborhoods' top safety issues.

Crenshaw facilitated discussions by first asking participants to generate a comprehensive list of candidate problems. West-side residents raised many of the same concerns as in previous meetings. This "brainstorming" space, however, allowed east-side residents to bring up many issues about which they had been previously silent. When it came time to designate priorities, participants from both sides of the beat easily reached consensus on an ordered list dominated by east-side problems: an alleged drug house on the east side, burglaries and armed robberies on an east-side commercial strip, and west-side residential burglaries. Once charged with ranking and discursively justifying an agenda of public safety problems, the better-off residents quickly agreed that the east-side house, around which shootings occurred and drugs were trafficked, topped the list and therefore deserved the lion's share of their attention and that of the police.

Having prioritized these problems, residents and police developed cooperative and effective strategies. Resident surveillance and police searches yielded arrests around the alleged drug house, court testimony from organized residents helped send some of those perpetrators to jail, and residents reported substantial reductions in criminal activity there. To address commercial burglaries, police increased their patrol visibility and worked with African-American storeowners to develop preventative measures and to enhance their own responsiveness. The proprietors report that thefts and robberies declined following these interventions. Due to their sporadic nature, residential burglaries are harder to address and progress against them is more difficult to assess. The group attempted to solve this third problem through plainclothes surveillance and resident education. Police apprehended one serial burglar, but the problem lingered.

Redux

These two experiences may seem to highlight the defects of deliberative decision-making. The "natural" course of autonomous discursive governance led to conflictual paralysis in Central Elementary and to domination by wealthy and well-educated residents in Traxton Beat. But both benefited from external forces – an intervention team in Central and community policing trainer/facilitator in Traxton – that set deliberation back on track.

The perspective of accountable autonomy suggests that these interventions ought to result from design rather than luck. Both interventions depended upon prior centralized initiatives: the CPS school probation program and the CPD training initiative. Yet not every troubled school or beat received external support. The probation team was assigned to Central Elementary as a result of its low standardized test scores, but many schools whose students test satisfactorily surely suffer similar governance challenges. It was even more a matter of chance that one of Traxton's community policing participants was an experienced CPD trainer, willing to serve as beat facilitator, and elected to that position. A full model of accountable autonomy would prescribe developing institutions to make these interventions deliberate priorities rather than leaving them in part to fortune.

Both cases also illustrate two other benefits of autonomous deliberative local action. In both, opposed factions possessing unequal resources nevertheless overcame differences of interest and perspective when their discussions were appropriately structured and facilitated. Participants in each case were able to subordinate at least some of their interests for the sake of reasonable norms. In both cases, the process led some participants to broaden and transform their prior interests. Subsequently, both groups devised and implemented creative strategies and plans that were probably more effective than what school officials and police would have accomplished on their own. In Traxton Beat, for example, residents contributed information, resources, and organized to act in ways that police could not have done.

VI Open Questions: the Effectiveness and Politics of Accountable Autonomy

Given the relative youth of these experiments and the constraints of a single chapter, this exploration into the actual and potential deliberative qualities of the Chicago community policing and school governance reforms necessarily raises more questions than it answers. By way of conclusion, consider two important and open issues: the overall effectiveness of these reforms in improving schools and beats and the political controversies surrounding these reforms.

First, scholars and citizens alike rightly wonder about the effectiveness of these reforms compared to other alternatives. In education, schools governed along the lines of accountable autonomy should ideally be compared to public school systems with small classrooms and well-trained teachers, high-stakes testing, charter schools, or fully privatized districts. Chicago-style community policing should ideally be compared to strictly professional problem oriented policing, enhanced managerialism, or privatized security. We can offer no such comparison of systematic alternatives at this point. Research on the Chicago reforms does indicate, however, that the reforms have achieved some gains compared to preceding arrangements.

Examination of test scores suggests that the effectiveness of Chicago schools has improved since the devolutionary reforms of 1988, but especially since the accountability amendments to those reforms in 1995. Anthony Bryk and his associates[48] developed the metric of school productivity, described above, to isolate the impact of school factors – such as teaching, curriculum, atmosphere – on student learning while discounting factors that cannot be controlled through site governance efforts such as the preparedness of children when they enter the school. Based upon this productivity analysis, Bryk and his team found that, from 1987 to 1997, the majority of schools have become more effective in educating students even though they have become increasingly disadvantaged and less well prepared:

> Chicago school reform has precipitated substantial improvements in achievement in a very large number of Chicago public elementary schools. The governance reforms of 1988 and 1995 have significantly advanced the learning opportunities afforded to literally hundreds of thousands of Chicago's children.[49]

A similar metric to measure the productivity of the public safety efforts of police and residents would be much more difficult to construct. On a more standard measure, however, the number of violent crimes has declined steadily since the city-wide community policing program began in 1995;[50] though not as dramatic as the much more publicized declines in New York City under Mayor Rudolph Giuliani's contrasting policing approach, declines in Chicago are in some areas comparable.

These gross trends offer no precise assessment of Chicago's reforms compared to other alternatives. Its approach is not at this time demonstrably better, but perhaps no worse, on aggregate performance measures than approaches based on more expert command or market mechanisms. Until more definitive assessments are available, then, the primary attraction of these reforms lies in their democratic quality. They create new channels of citizen voice, influence, and deliberation that are widely utilized in Chicago, especially by those who live in disadvantaged neighborhoods. According to surveys,[51] 14 percent of Chicagoans attended at least one beat meeting in 1997. By far the majority of people of color who are elected officials in Illinois serve on local school councils. This democratic experience, together with the conceptual arguments for the effectiveness of accountable autonomy offered above and the uncertain relative performance of other alternatives, favors keeping this institutional design in our repertoire of reform strategies.

Second, in a world where the politics and ideas of reform are dominated by the dichotomy between devolution – either as community control or the market – versus the centralization of expert managerialism, a hybrid model such as that just presented finds few predisposed supporters. In the case of Chicago school and police reform, the institutions that came to approximate accountable autonomy emerged fitfully from struggles between the neighborhoods and downtown. They began as a project in community control, developed in response to defects in the original reforms, and then changed again as central authorities reasserted a measure of control. Neighborhood and community participants fear that centralized power will infringe their autonomy while turning a blind eye to their own shortcomings. Conversely, many in the central offices of CPD and CPS worry that local autonomy will decay into paralysis or license. They are also oversensitive to criticisms from neighborhood and watchdog groups. If they could, many would impose commands that reach for effectiveness by short-circuiting local deliberation and reverse the 1988 CPS and 1995 CPD reforms.

At the moment, neither neighborhood nor center can impose its side of the dichotomy. The neighborhoods have tasted power, entrenched it in law or administrative rule, and are reluctant to cede it. But City Hall and the agency heads are strong in Chicago, and have eroded many local and independent prerogatives. Officials have already reduced the roles of independent groups in providing training and mobilization services. In school governance, some of the original latitude for local principal selection and instruction has been narrowed, while some police administrators are reducing opportunities for community participation by decreasing beat-meeting frequency.

Occasionally because of this conflict but more often in spite of it, many elements of accountable autonomy have emerged in the CPS and CPD reforms. Absent an entrenched model, conflict and randomness have limited the extent to which the complementary sides of this structure can contribute to fair and effective police and school governance. The commands of central officials sometimes overrule sensible and perhaps more effective local deliberation. But sometimes accountability measures are well justified. Deepening the institutionalization of accountable autonomy in the CPS and CPD requires moving from happenstance to a stable vision of reform. With a model of accountable autonomy before them, proponents of localism would recognize the contributions of central power and the necessity of external accountability mechanisms. Those accustomed to managing and commanding might see the limitations in their own foresight and capability and come to respect the knowledge and ingenuity of those who work and live in the neighborhoods. The experience of Chicago makes it clear that practical deliberative democracy at the local level requires a language that reaches beyond the simple antithesis between centralization and decentralization.

Notes

* I would like to thank Alan Altshuler, Joshua Cohen, David Hart, Jane Mansbridge, Charles Sabel, Lynn Sanders, Deborah Satz, Theda Skocpol, Craig Thomas, and Erik Olin Wright for their generous and invaluable feedback.

1. Among the many excellent books on the "blood and guts" of Chicago politics see William J. Grimshaw, *Bitter Fruit: Black Politics and the Chicago Machine, 1931–1991*, Chicago: University of Chicago Press (1992) and Milton L. Rakove, *Don't Make No Waves, Don't Back No Losers*, Bloomington: Indiana University Press (1975).

2. See, for example, Herman Goldstein, *Problem Oriented Policing*, Philadelphia, PA: Temple University Press (1992).

3. See Wesley G. Skogan and Susan M. Hartnett, *Community Policing: Chicago Style*, New York: Oxford University Press (1997).

4. For a discussion of the liabilities of small-group decision, see Jane Mansbridge, *Beyond Adversary Democracy*, Chicago: University of Chicago Press (1980) and John

Gastil, *Democracy in Small Groups: Participation, Decision Making, and Communication*, Philadelphia, PA: New Society Publishers (1993).

5. Chicago Tribune Staff, *Chicago Schools: "Worst in America": An Examination of the Public Schools that Failed Chicago*, Chicago: Chicago Tribune (1988).

6. See Malcolm K. Sparrow, Mark H. Moore, and David M. Kennedy, *Beyond 911: A New Era for Policing*, New York: Basic Books (1990) and Herman Goldstein, *Problem Oriented Policing*.

7. See Archon Fung, "Contract Expired: Is Chicago Poised to Take the Community out of Community Policing?" *Neighborhood Works* (March/April 1997), pp. 8–9.

8. Dan Scheid, "Board Bumps Reform Groups from LSC Training," *Catalyst: Voices of Chicago School Reform*, vol. 10, no. 1 (September 1998), pp. 1, 20–21; Alison Pflepsen, "LSCs Lose 182 Members Who Didn't Complete Training," *Catalyst: Voices of Chicago School Reform*, vol. 10, no. 8 (May 1999), pp. 24–25.

9. The Chicago Community Policing Evaluation Consortium, *Community Policing in Chicago, Years Five–Six: An Interim Report* (Evanston, IL: Institute for Policy Research, 1999), p. 18.

10. Ibid.

11. William S. McKersie, "Private Funding Down for LSC Elections," *Catalyst: Voices of Chicago School Reform*, vol. 7, no. 6 (March 1996), p. 15.

12. Dan Weissmann, Jennifer Randall, Lisa Lewis, and Jason Grotto, "Did Community Groups Have an Impact," *Catalyst: Voices of Chicago School Reform* vol. 7, no. 8 (May 1996), pp. 1, 25–26.

13. *Illinois Compiled Statutes*, Ch. 720, Sec. 37–4 (1996).

14. The ordinance described in this paragraph went into effect on November 11, 1996. See City Council of Chicago, "Amendments of Titles 8 and 13 of Municipal Code of Chicago Concerning Liability of Property Owners and Management for Unlawful Activities on Property," *Chicago City Council Journal* (July 31, 1996), pp. 27, 730–35.

15. The state statute was originally targeted against prostitution.

16. This program, called the "Corporation Council Program," is presently being tested in five "prototype" police districts. It began on November 1, 1996.

17. Telephone interview (February 27, 1997).

18. See Steven R. Strahler, "It's Back-to-School Time: Daley's Crisis Plan Begins to Take Shape," *Craine's Chicago Business* (April 10, 1995), p. 3.

19. See National Research Council, *High Stakes: Testing for Tracking, Promotion, and Graduation*, Washington, DC: National Academy Press (1999).

20. Details in this paragraph are taken from Anthony S. Bryk, Yeow Meng Thum, John Q. Easton, and Stuart Luppescu, *Academic Productivity of Chicago Public Elementary Schools: A Technical Report Sponsored by the Consortium on Chicago School Research*, Chicago: Consortium on Chicago School Research (March 1998).

21. For a more detailed account, see Archon Fung, "Street Level Democracy: A Theory of Popular Pragmatic Deliberation and Its Practice in Chicago School Reform and Community Policing, 1988–1997." Doctoral dissertation, Massachusetts Institute of Technology Department of Political Science (1999).

22. Elizabeth Druffin, "Spotlight Brings Focus: One School's Probation Story," in *Catalyst: Voices of Chicago School Reform*, vol. 9, no. 9 (June 1998), pp. 112–15; See also Fung, "Street Level Democracy," especially chapters 8 and 15.

23. Described in Fung and Wright's introduction to this volume.

24. See, for example, Sidney Verba and Norman Nie, *Participation in America: Political Democracy and Social Equality*, New York: Harper and Row (1972); Jack Nagel, *Participation*, New York: Prentice Hall (1987).

25. Chicago Community Policing Evaluation Consortium, *Community Policing in Chicago, Year Seven: An Interim Report*, Illinois Criminal Justice Authority (November 2000).

26. For an argument that high frequency of elections depresses participation, see Robert Jackman and Ross Miller, "Voter Turnout in the Industrial Democracies during the 1980s," *Comparative Political Studies*, vol. 27, no. 4 (January 1995), pp. 467–92.

27. See Catalyst Staff, "Local School Council Elections," *Catalyst: Voices of Chicago School Reform*, vol. 7, no. 8 (May 1996), p. 26; and Rosalind Rossi, "School Races Attract Few Candidates," *Chicago Sun Times* (April 6, 1998), p. 8.

28. See Sidney Verba, Kay Lehman Schlozman, and Henry E. Brady, *Voice and Equality: Civic Voluntarism in American Politics*, Cambridge, MA: Harvard University Press (1995).

29. See Chicago Community Policing Evaluation Consortium, *Community Policing in Chicago, Years Five–Six: An Interim Report*, Evanston, IL: Institute for Policy Research (1999).

30. This rate is given as attendees per meeting per 10,000 residents, with the attendance for each beat averaged over all available meeting data from January 1995 until May 1997. Crime rate is calculated from 1996 figures, and other remaining demographic data is drawn from the 1996 census.

31. When %home owners is removed from the list of regression variables, both %College Educated and Median Income become statistically significant at the 0.01 level, indicating multicolinearity between these variables.

32. Designs for Change, *The Untold Story: Candidate Participation in the 1991 Chicago Local School Council Elections*, Chicago: Designs for Change (October 1991), p. 7. The authors did not report full regression results, and so the correlation may have been statistically insignificant.

33. Candidate and turnout data were very kindly provided by Mr. Doug Dillon of Management Information Services at the Chicago Public Schools. Demographic information on schools was taken from Chicago Public Schools, Office of Accountability, *The Illinois State School Report Card Data Book for 1995–96: An Analysis of Student, School, District, and State Characteristics*, Chicago: Chicago Public Schools (1996).

34. A student is classified as "low income" just in case he or she is from a family receiving public aid, lives in an institution for neglected or delinquent children, is supported in a foster home with public funds, or is eligible to receive free or reduced-price lunches. In 1996, approximately four-fifths of Chicago students were "low-income," compared to less than one-fifth of the students in the state of Illinois. See ibid.

35. Student mobility at a school is defined as the number of students enrolling in a school or leaving that school during a single school year. Students may be counted more than once.

36. Recall that each LSC provides six positions for parent representatives.

37. Parent turnout is given as the percentage of parents eligible to vote in the election who actually vote.

38. See Steven J. Rosenstone and John Mark Hansen, *Mobilization, Participation, and Democracy*, New York: Macmillan (1993) and Verba, Schlozman, and Brady, *Voice and Equality*, p. 233.

39. This survey was sponsored by the Consortium on Chicago School Research and its results are reported in Susan Ryan, Anthony Bryk, *et al.*, *Charting Reform: LSCs – Local Leadership at Work*, Chicago: Consortium on Chicago School Research (December 1999), p. 6.

40. Ibid., p. 7.

41. Chicago Community Policing Evaluation Consortium, *Community Policing in Chicago, Years Five–Six*, pp. 28–9.

42. This term comes from Michael Lipsky, *Street-Level Bureaucracy: Dilemma of the Individual in the Public Services*, New York: Russell Sage Foundation (1980).

43. See Michael Martinez "Clement's Council Renews Principal War," *Chicago Tribune* (November 18, 1997).

44. These cases are described in much more detail in Fung, *Street Level Democracy*, chapters 13 and 15.

45. Chicago Public Schools, Office of Accountability, *The Illinois State School Report Card Data Book for 1995–96*. The Chicago-wide chronic truancy rate in that year was 4.7 percent.

46. See, for example, Lynn Sanders "Against Deliberation," *Political Theory*, vol. 25, no. 3 (June 1997), pp. 347–76 and Mansbridge, *Beyond Adversary Democracy*.

47. See discussion of JCPT in section 3 above.

48. Anthony Bryk, Yeow Meng Thum, John Q. Easton, and Stuart Luppescu, *Academic Productivity*.

49. Ibid., p. 44.

50. Source: Illinois State Police, Division of Administration, Crime Studies Section, *Crime in Illinois – 1998*, Springfield, IL: State of Illinois (April 1999).

51. Chicago Community Policing Evaluation Consortium, *Community Policing in Chicago, Years Five–Six*, p. 18.

5

Habitat Conservation Planning
Craig W. Thomas*

I Introduction

Habitat Conservation Plans (HCPs) have become the most controversial component of the U.S. Endangered Species Act (ESA). Some argue that HCPs undermine the purpose of the ESA by compromising species and habitat conservation for economic gain. Others counter that HCPs allow the ESA to work by avoiding prolonged political and legal conflicts over resource use. Some contend that HCPs are based on weak science. Others counter that they are based on the best science available. Some argue that HCPs increase public input into endangered species issues. Others respond that public participation is highly variable and not assured.

These debates result in part from the great variation that exists among HCPs. Given this variation, habitat conservation planning should not be viewed as a single example of the empowered participatory governance model, but rather as a range of examples that vary in terms of the model's six dimensions.[1] As of April 2002, there were 379 approved HCPs in some stage of implementation, covering roughly thirty million acres.[2] Many additional HCPs were in the planning stage. When viewed together, along with the federal guidelines, policies, and rules that govern how HCPs are prepared and implemented, it is possible to make some claims regarding how well the HCP experience fits these dimensions.

This chapter begins with a brief history of the HCP experience, and then evaluates habitat conservation planning according to the six dimensions and the six potential criticisms of empowered participatory governance. HCPs fit the model well in terms of empowerment. They fit less well in terms of participation. These are gross simplifications, however, because HCPs vary widely. Some departures from the model can be rectified through changes in federal policy, but it is not yet clear whether any HCP is now or ever will be an exemplar of the model.

II What Are Habitat Conservation Plans?

HCPs are a peculiar product of the U.S. legal system. They exist solely because of the federal Endangered Species Act. In the absence of a similar law, one cannot assume that HCPs would appear in other countries because individuals and organizations would lack the fundamental motivation to expend the significant time and financial resources required to complete and implement an HCP. They proliferate in the United States because, to paraphrase Don Corleone in *The Godfather*, the federal government makes an offer that some individuals and organizations cannot refuse. HCP participation is voluntary, but some actors face little choice given existing alternatives.

The ESA is sometimes called the pit bull of environmental laws because it has extraordinary teeth, particularly in federal courts. Among other effects, lawsuits filed or threatened under the ESA have foreclosed economic use of public and private resources, shaped urban growth patterns, and reoriented state and federal agency missions.[3] These outcomes occur because the ESA prohibits certain actions. By contrast, the National Environmental Policy Act (NEPA) is a procedural law. NEPA requires federal agencies to produce environmental impact statements that evaluate the environmental consequences of major federal activities, but NEPA does not specify whether or not a particular federal activity should be carried out and it does not apply directly to nonfederal actors. The ESA actually prohibits public and private actions that push species toward extinction.

The ESA has two types of prohibitions, the most powerful of which is tied directly to HCPs. This is the Section 9 prohibition on "take," which applies to all persons and organizations subject to U.S. jurisdictions. By contrast, the Section 7 "jeopardy" standard applies only to federal agencies, and is not tied directly to HCPs.[4] Section 9 prohibits any person or organization subject to U.S. jurisdictions from taking fish or wildlife species listed as endangered by the U.S. Fish and Wildlife Service (FWS), with "take" defined broadly in Section 3 to include "harass, harm, pursue, hunt, shoot, wound, kill, trap, capture, or collect, or to attempt to engage in any such conduct."[5]

The FWS subsequently expanded this definition of take by issuing a rule that defines "harm" to include "significant habitat modification or degradation where it actually kills or injures wildlife by significantly impairing essential behavioral patterns, including breeding, feeding or sheltering."[6] Therefore environmental activists can successfully sue a private landowner for altering the habitat of an endangered species (e.g. through logging, farming, or land development), and they can sue a local or state agency for either engaging in such activities or permitting them to occur. If a federal court rules in favor of the plaintiff, it can prohibit these activities, or fine and even jail those committing the offense. Property owners have felt sufficiently threatened by the Section 9 prohibition on take that they have attempted (so far unsuccessfully) to reverse the charges, claiming that the federal government is "taking" their private property without just compensation, and so violating the Fifth Amendment.

Prior to 1982, the ESA was unyielding with regard to endangered fish and wildlife species. As Steven Yaffee has argued, the ESA amounted to "prohibitive policy."[7] Only scientific research and conservation activities constituted permissible take for endangered animal species. This near-absolute ban posed economic, political, and ecological problems. Economically, if one knew about the presence of an endangered animal species, the ESA essentially implied an order to cease activities because they might cause take. Although the FWS lacked sufficient staff to monitor all such activities, environmentalists stood in the wings waiting to sue landowners and developers for such infringements, and to sue local and state agencies for permitting them to occur.

Politically, the prohibition on take was a time bomb because the ESA lacked a release mechanism to allow limited economic activity to occur within the habitat of a listed species. For this reason, economic interests lobbied hard to keep species off the list, which necessarily politicized the listing process.[8] Environmentalists also picked their fights carefully. They did not petition to list every species for which data supported a listing; instead they focussed on charismatic species, limiting the ability of property rights advocates to frame endangered species issues as pitting "rats against people" or "bugs against jobs."

Ecologically, the absolute prohibition on take was also not entirely sensible. Endangered species suffer from the cumulative impacts of many activities, not simply the few activities someone happens to notice. Therefore many ecologists argued that it would be more effective to preserve a species' habitat over the long run by acquiring property and adopting formal land-use restrictions than by blocking bulldozers at each site or punishing individuals after habitat is altered, perhaps irreparably. In other words, it would make more sense to develop and implement a plan to preserve habitat than to track individual activities eating away at the habitat on a site-by-site, project-by-project basis.

As the 1970s came to a close, economic, political, and ecological interests dovetailed when a novel idea emerged to preserve a butterfly habitat near San Francisco. Development creeping up the slope of San

Bruno Mountain had been a political issue for years, but it was framed in terms of open space and growth control, not species protection. The San Bruno conflict assumed a dramatically new form in 1975 when the FWS listed the mission blue butterfly as an endangered species and a local environmental group threatened legal action to stop residential and commercial development in the butterfly's habitat. In 1978, the FWS proposed listing an additional species, the callippe silverspot butterfly. Backed into a corner, the primary landowner and developer, Visitacion Associates, struck a deal with environmentalists, agreeing to set aside approximately 2,000 of its 3,500 acres on San Bruno Mountain as butterfly habitat and open space in return for being allowed to develop the remaining acres. The logic was simple. The developer would be allowed to take butterflies by building on part of the mountain because ecologists endorsed the HCP as a means for protecting sufficient habitat to maintain viable populations of both species. In other words, economic development would be allowed to destroy some of the habitat because credible scientists believed the HCP would preserve sufficient habitat to guarantee the long-term survival of both butterfly species.[9]

This agreement led to the first HCP. But it could not be implemented until Congress amended the ESA to authorize the FWS to issue a new kind of permit that would allow take. When Congress amended the ESA in 1982, new language authorized the FWS to issue permits to nonfederal actors who submitted satisfactory HCPs.[10] Taking endangered animal species for economic purposes was no longer prohibited absolutely. Take was now permitted under Section 10 if it was "incidental to, and not the purpose of, the carrying out of an otherwise lawful activity."[11] Hence the coveted permit to implement an HCP is known as an "incidental take permit." The 1982 ESA amendments established common ground between economic and environmental interests by allowing incidental take during the course of economic activities, while creating a mechanism to compel private actors and local and state agencies to preserve habitat for the long-term survival of endangered species. In other words, Section 10 reframed endangered species debates from "species *versus* jobs" to "species *and* jobs," thereby providing a legal mechanism to avoid political impasses.

In practice, HCPs must meet several basic conditions for applicants to receive incidental take permits. Specifically, they must provide detailed information about the likely impacts resulting from the proposed take; measures the applicant will undertake to monitor, minimize, and mitigate such impacts; available funding to undertake such measures; procedures to deal with unforeseen circumstances;

alternative actions considered by the applicant that would not result in take, and the reasons why such alternatives will not be used; and any additional measures the FWS requires as necessary or appropriate for purposes of the plan.[12] How applicants meet these conditions is left largely to them. Thus the ESA and FWS regulations essentially compel nonfederal actors to forego all use of certain natural resources, act illegally and risk enforcement, or prepare an HCP that meets the above criteria. This is a difficult deal to refuse.

Yet, unlike Don Corleone's offer, the federal government empowers applicants to determine the institutional design of their HCP. For example, applicants define the planning area, choose the number of species covered, decide who will participate, and select the policy tools for habitat protection. Thus they can write an HCP covering one acre or a million acres; they can focus on one species or dozens of species; they can submit HCPs individually or with multiple partners; they can request extensive public input or largely ignore it; and they can select from numerous policy tools to implement the plan, including development fees to acquire or restore habitat, dedication of land for habitat preserves, land-use controls, and market-based approaches such as habitat mitigation banks and tradeable development rights. Large HCPs typically establish preserve areas, within which few human uses are allowed, surrounded by buffer zones of less restricted use; but there are numerous ways to acquire, regulate, restore, monitor, enforce, or otherwise manage these areas. To a large extent, these methods are determined by the applicants, subject to FWS approval. Discretion empowers applicants to be creative, and to tailor solutions to local problems.

In sum, the 1982 ESA amendments empowered nonfederal actors to develop HCPs as a means for complying with the Section 9 prohibition on take. The stage was now set for a grand experiment in land-use planning. Yet HCPs did not immediately proliferate. The FWS issued only fourteen incidental take permits in the first decade following the 1982 amendments (1983–92) – one each in Texas and Florida, and twelve in California. HCPs diffused slowly during this period because the initial expertise was in California, and because the FWS did not distribute draft HCP guidelines until 1990. With the new guidelines, and with strong support from the Clinton administration after 1992, HCPs spread rapidly. By April 2002, 379 HCPs had been approved, with some HCPs covering much larger planning areas than their predecessors.[13]

In light of this explosive growth, an increasing number of observers have wondered whether HCPs adequately protect species, and whether the public is appropriately involved. Congress has also considered several bills to amend the ESA, and the Department of the Interior and FWS have experimented with new HCP policies. Yet these policies primarily provide economic assurances to applicants, not ecological assurances to species or democratic assurances to a broad range of stakeholders who may want to participate. In other words, the new policies are designed primarily to create incentives for applicants to complete HCPs.

One such incentive is embodied in the 1994 No Surprises Policy, which assures applicants that no additional land-use restrictions or financial compensation will be required with respect to species covered by an incidental take permit if unforeseen circumstances arise indicating that additional mitigation is needed.[14] Under the No Surprises Policy, the federal government, not the permit holder, assumes responsibility for implementing additional conservation measures that may become necessary as new knowledge and information arise. This means that the general public – not applicants – bears the risks associated with ineffective HCPs. This risk is magnified by the absence of federal programs to identify and buttress ineffective HCPs. With the guarantee that there will be no regulatory surprises forthcoming from the federal government, applicants have become much more certain about the future benefits that HCPs provide.

Fundamentally, applicants want to know what they can do within a given planning area. They are willing to spend substantial sums of money and devote years to developing and implementing an HCP because the incidental take permit provides them with great certainty about their ability to use natural resources in the future. Without a permit, the ESA's regulatory hammer looms, poised to foreclose any and all activities. With a permit, applicants know they can pursue activities specified in the HCP. Thus HCPs tend to occur where the Section 9 prohibition on take is enforced aggressively.[15] If the prohibition on take were not enforced by the FWS or citizen suits, then potential applicants would have no legal or economic incentive to prepare – let alone implement – HCPs.

While the No Surprises Policy is politically expedient and encourages growth in the number of HCPs, it is ecologically unsound because it reduces the incentive for participants to rethink HCPs during implementation. Adaptive management is more sensible because ecological knowledge and information are fluid.[16] As we learn more about species and their habitat requirements, HCPs should be revisited and redesigned.[17] After all, the ESA's purpose is to prevent extinctions. If new knowledge or information suggest that an HCP does not ensure the survival of listed species, then the HCP should be adapted to new circumstances or the permit withdrawn. Adaptive management also provides an opportunity for public participation and continued deliberation after incidental take permits have been issued.

In an attempt to reconcile this conflict, federal officials issued revised guidelines for the *Habitat Conservation Planning Handbook* in 2000.[18] Under the revised guidelines, adaptive management is now encouraged for HCPs that pose a significant risk to species due to data gaps when a permit is issued. While these new guidelines lack the legal authority of regulations, they do offer a mechanism through which monitoring and deliberation can occur during implementation.

III How Well Do HCPs Fit the Empowered Participatory Governance Model?

The previous section provided an overview of habitat conservation planning under the U.S. Endangered Species Act. This section evaluates the HCP experience according to the six dimensions of the empowered participatory governance model. Given that HCPs vary widely in many dimensions, some HCPs fit the model better than others. This section also considers the federal guidelines, policies, and rules that shape HCPs in relation to the model.

Deliberation

How genuinely deliberative are HCP decision-making processes? To be deliberative, participants must listen to and carefully consider each other's positions before making final decisions. Rather than simply voting or advocating preformed preferences, they must allow their preferred goals and strategies to evolve through collective deliberation. We should also consider how long deliberation occurs, how many actors are involved, and who these actors represent during both the planning and implementation phases.

These dimensions of deliberation vary widely during the planning phase. The best evidence in this regard was reported by a team of researchers who studied public participation in fifty-five large HCPs (i.e. those covering more than a thousand acres).[19] Within this sample, they surveyed the most recent FWS contacts for forty-five HCPs, and wrote in-depth case studies of fourteen HCPs. They found public participation varying widely from open, collaborative steering groups to closed-door processes in which the only opportunity for participation beyond the applicant and the FWS came during the notice-and-comment periods required under the ESA and NEPA. The latter indicates a narrow deliberative scope because little (if any) deliberation takes place during notice-and-comment periods, which occur after an HCP is virtually complete and the FWS is ready to issue an incidental take permit. Moreover, NEPA does not require federal agencies to incorporate public comments into planning documents, which means the FWS need not ask applicants to consider the merits of such comments – let alone deliberate with those submitting them – during notice-and-comment periods.

While the authors of this study do not use the language of deliberation, their conclusions nevertheless suggest that deliberation does occur in some HCPs. "In those cases where public participation resulted in substantive changes to the HCPs, public participation invariably began early in the process, and often included a committee with members of the public."[20] Yet such changes were relatively rare. Their survey of FWS staff "indicated that public participation resulted in significant substantive changes to only 3 out of 45 responding HCPs (7 percent)" while more than 75 percent of the sample reported that public participation led to "only minimal or moderate changes."[21] These findings clearly indicate that public participation should be required early in the planning process to expand the scope of deliberation. Unfortunately, the new HCP guidelines simply encourage public participation for large HCPs; they do not require it for any HCP or establish standards regarding who should participate.[22]

The number of participants and interests represented by them varies greatly across HCPs because applicants define the scope of participation. Some HCPs are submitted by a single applicant. The Simpson Timber Company, for example, submitted an HCP in 1992 covering 380,000 acres of private timberland in three California counties. With only one applicant, deliberation likely occurred only between the Simpson Timber Company and the FWS. By contrast, the *Coachella Valley Fringe-Toed Lizard Habitat Conservation Plan* was completed in 1985 by a steering committee composed of a wide spectrum of stakeholders, including representatives from local governments, state and federal agencies, an Indian tribe, and a non-profit environmental group. Presumably, deliberation is more prevalent within a multi-organizational committee than a single firm. Indeed, the literature on the Coachella Valley HCP suggests that deliberation was extensive, including actors not formally identified as members of the steering committee.[23]

That deliberation occurs in some HCPs is not surprising, given that

HCPs grow out of stalemates in the traditional form of environmental regulation, in which actors are unable to achieve their preferred outcomes. Developers, for example, prefer to build housing tracts, but doing so is illegal if it harms an endangered species, and they might be sued by environmental watchdogs for violating the Section 9 prohibition on take. This gives them an incentive to work with local governments to roll zoning plans into an HCP, so planned development is covered by an incidental take permit. Doing so requires deliberation among private and public actors, along with professional or academic ecologists, as to what percentage of the remaining habitat should be preserved, where it should be preserved, and how it should be managed.

Moreover, to avoid future lawsuits, applicants sometimes request public participation early in the planning process so completed HCPs will not be challenged during implementation. This choice is left to applicants, because the scope of deliberation is not driven directly by federal laws, rules, or guidelines. HCP guidelines instruct FWS staff to encourage participation, but applicants are not required to do so. Moreover, the FWS "regards HCPs as voluntary, applicant-driven processes where the applicants decide whether and how to involve outside stakeholders."[24] Hence there is no guarantee that deliberation will occur among more than a single applicant and the FWS. Where deliberation among many actors occurs, it is driven by other factors, particularly by patterns of private land ownership and public jurisdiction. Where habitat is shared among multiple owners, agencies, and political jurisdictions, species conservation becomes a collective-action problem, in which actors come together to share information and develop solutions to their common problem.[25] Hence broad participation in HCPs is more likely in areas with complex ownership patterns.[26]

Action

How effectively are decisions made during the planning process translated into action? There is little evidence upon which to answer this question because no one has systematically studied HCP implementation across multiple cases. For empirical evidence, we have to rely on the one known case study of HCP implementation, which focussed on the Coachella Valley HCP.[27]

Yet there are several economic and legal reasons to believe that HCPs are actually implemented. Applicants prepare HCPs because they want incidental take permits to use natural resources for economic or public purposes. This permit removes them from the shadow of the ESA's regulatory hammer. The FWS can revoke a permit if the applicants do not implement an HCP because implementation is a condition of the permit. Environmental activists also sit in the wings prepared to sue under the ESA's strong provisions when they see violations. In addition to legal incentives for applicants to implement HCPs, the FWS also assesses whether an HCP is likely to be implemented before issuing a permit. The ESA and federal guidelines stipulate that HCPs must identify funding to implement specific provisions in the plan designed to mitigate the impacts of incidental take.[28] The FWS may also require an implementation agreement, in which participants specify who is responsible for implementing specific parts of an HCP. In sum, financial feasibility is a condition of the permit, implementation is a condition of retaining the permit, and the FWS can require a signed implementation agreement to establish accountability.

We should not assume, however, that any HCP is fully implemented. Multi-partner HCPs tend to be thick documents because they stipulate a diverse range of actions that are allowed or required across multiple ownerships and jurisdictions. These HCPs contain numerous provisions, any one of which might be overlooked or found infeasible during implementation. In the Coachella Valley, for example, participants made a good-faith effort to translate the plan into action, but thirteen years after the FWS issued the permit the original plan was still not completely implemented in some respects; however, in other respects, such as enforcement, those implementing the HCP significantly exceeded requirements in the plan.[29]

In sum, there are strong legal and economic incentives for permit holders to implement their HCPs. Unfortunately, there are too few empirical studies of HCP implementation to make broad claims about the extent to which HCPs have been translated into action.

Monitoring

Monitoring is a crucial component of the empowered participatory governance model because it provides information about how well these experiments work. This information in turn indicates whether and how they should be revisited and redesigned in an ongoing deliberative process. In the environmental policy literature, this process of experimentation, monitoring, and redesign is called "adaptive management."[30] Without monitoring mechanisms in place, there is action without learning and accountability. Thus Fung and Wright ask in this volume: "To what extent are these deliberative groups capable of

monitoring the implementation of their decisions and holding responsible parties accountable?"[31] To this I would add a prior question: To
what extent are these groups willing to monitor implementation?
Deliberative groups may be technically, financially, and organization-
ally able to monitor implementation, but that does not mean that all
participants necessarily want to monitor, learn from, and redesign their
experiments. This is particularly the case with HCPs, because the very
thought of redesigning HCPs creates regulatory uncertainty in the
minds of applicants and permit holders, many of whom have significant financial investments at stake.

Indeed, monitoring has been a significant shortcoming for HCPs in
terms of fitting the model. The best evidence for this comes from a team
of scientists who evaluated the use of science in HCPs.[32] While twenty-
two of forty-three HCPs in their sample contained "a clear description
of a monitoring program," only seven contained monitoring programs
"sufficient for evaluating success."[33] On a more positive note, they
found monitoring to be closely correlated with adaptive management.
"In particular, 88% of the plans with provisions for adaptive management had clear monitoring plans, whereas less than 30% of the
remainder had clear monitoring plans."[34]

Two implications can be drawn from these data. First, relatively few
HCPs have been conceived in terms of adaptive management (i.e.
experimentation, learning, and redesign). Hence they do not include
sufficient monitoring programs to evaluate HCP effectiveness during
implementation. Given that adaptive management necessarily entails
monitoring, those HCPs conceived in terms of adaptive management
typically have clear monitoring programs. Second, we do not know
whether the monitoring programs found to be sufficient were actually
implemented, or whether HCPs with insufficient monitoring programs
were nevertheless implemented with modified programs sufficient for
evaluating HCP effectiveness.

Moreover, regardless of whether sufficient monitoring programs
exist in HCP implementation, it is crucial to know whether participants
want to learn from new information and are willing to revisit the plans
and deliberate anew. Some actors may be open to such reconsideration,
but others are not. During implementation of the Coachella Valley
HCP, monitoring by participants indicated that crucial habitat had
been overlooked in the original preserve design.[35] This oversight was
due primarily to limited information and estimated acquisition costs at
the time the plan was completed, not to political intrigue. Nevertheless,
many of the actors who developed or implemented the HCP preferred
not to reopen and redesign the original HCP. Instead, they sought to

protect the "missing" habitat through other institutional processes, such as local zoning, acquisition by land conservancies, and a new HCP they were developing for multiple species.[36]

The Coachella Valley experience offers intriguing lessons about HCP implementation. Habitat conservation planning is challenging, expensive, and time-consuming, particularly when it involves deliberation among multiple actors. Hence there is great inertia against reopening an HCP after the FWS issues a permit, regardless of applicant sincerity about implementing the plan. In the Coachella Valley, participants made a good-faith effort to implement the plan, discovered the plan was inadequate, and sought to address its shortcomings through other means. All of which suggests that we should not expect to see an HCP revised voluntarily due to monitoring because participants perceive the planning process to be very cumbersome. Instead, the lingering threat that the FWS will pull an incidental take permit provides an incentive for permit holders to fix HCP weaknesses through other planning processes. While this is a motivating threat, the FWS has never actually carried it out, in part because HCP implementation is not systematically monitored, and in part because FWS officials prefer to work with permittees to bring them into compliance when problems are discovered.[37]

Similarly, we should not expect the FWS – the only consistent HCP participant – to monitor implementation because the agency's Endangered Species Division is underfunded relative to its workload. Without additional funding, FWS staff are unable to monitor HCP implementation systematically. Given the agency's backlog on more pressing tasks under the ESA (such as listing species, mapping critical habitat, developing recovery plans, and reviewing draft HCPs), there is little reason to expect FWS staff to monitor HCP implementation. Moreover, neither the FWS nor the Department of the Interior have developed a public HCP library, let alone a transparent monitoring program through which centralized actors and citizens can learn whether and to what degree HCPs are being implemented. Given the dearth of centralized HCP monitoring within the federal government, we might wonder whether high-level federal officials are interested in learning from these experiments.

On the positive side, the FWS issued new guidelines on adaptive management in 2000.[38] These guidelines state that "an adaptive management strategy is essential for HCPs that would otherwise pose a significant risk to the species at the time the permit is issued due to significant data or information gaps."[39] Yet the guidelines also state that an adaptive management strategy is not needed for all HCPs. So it remains unclear which HCPs should have them or what constitutes a "significant" information gap. The guidelines also specify four components that should be included in adaptive management strategies: (1) identification of uncertainty and questions that need to be addressed to resolve it, (2) alternative implementation strategies, (3) a monitoring program that can detect information necessary to evaluate these strategies, and (4) feedback loops that link implementation and monitoring to appropriate changes in management.[40] These new guidelines are compatible with the No Surprises Policy because HCPs containing an adaptive management strategy "should clearly state the range of possible operating conservation program adjustments due to significant new information, risk, or uncertainty."[41] In other words, the adaptive management strategy would become part of the HCP and would be a condition of the permit; thus any adjustments within the stated range would not constitute a regulatory surprise. While these guidelines are not retroactive, they suggest that monitoring programs will likely become a more significant part of future HCPs.

Regardless of the extent to which monitoring programs are incorporated into HCPs as part of an adaptive management strategy, external monitoring is also necessary to ensure that participants are meeting their legal commitments and that HCPs are effective as designed. Thus far, systematic external monitoring has been virtually absent during HCP implementation. As already noted, the primary regulatory authority – the FWS – does not systematically monitor HCP implementation, and there is only one known case study of HCP implementation by academics. In sum, monitoring by participants will never be sufficient; HCPs must also be monitored by external evaluators, who are better situated to hold participants accountable for accomplishing the public regulatory goal of species protection.

Centralized Coordination and Power

In the empowered participatory governance model, local units (such as HCP planning committees) do not act autonomously. Instead, they learn from and coordinate their actions with other local units and with state structures. The key question for this dimension is: "To what extent do these experiments incorporate recombinant measures that coordinate the actions of local units, diffuse information and innovations among them, and follow centralized mechanisms that ensure accountability and learning?"

To answer that question, we should recall that some HCPs are submitted by a single applicant (such as a landowner or private firm). In such cases, applicants believe they own or manage enough habitat to determine their own destiny, and with it the destiny of relevant species. Because they do not perceive a collective-action problem, the only other actor with whom they coordinate is the FWS, which reviews their HCP. The term "habitat conservation plan" is a misnomer because HCPs need not cover a species' entire habitat. Neither the ESA nor FWS regulations require coordinated action. Instead, the specific time and location of coordination is determined by the desire of applicants to pool land, water, information, money, and other resources as a collective means to remove themselves from the threat of legal challenges under the ESA.[42] Hence horizontal coordination varies with the extent to which habitat sprawls across ownerships and jurisdictions.

In the Coachella Valley, for example, many HCPs could have emerged, instead of one coordinated HCP. Yet, rather than develop separate HCPs, nine cities and one county, along with developers, state and federal agencies, and other participants, jointly designed an HCP for the fringe-toed lizard that created a main preserve, two smaller preserves, and a fee area. In the fee area, developers could transform habitat by paying a mitigation fee of US$600 per acre to one of the ten local governments, which then forwarded the fees to a non-profit organization (The Nature Conservancy) that pooled the money to purchase the designated preserve lands. In this case, local governments and developers created a novel means for addressing the common problem they confronted on lands they individually owned, managed, or zoned.

But such coordination is certainly not ubiquitous. In Texas, for example, coordination proved difficult in the case of the golden-cheeked warbler. Rather than a single HCP for the warbler, there are roughly seventy HCPs – nearly one-fifth of all HCPs. Most of the warbler HCPs have a single applicant (typically a lot owner or developer), most are in Travis County (which includes Austin), and many cover fewer than five acres. The one exception is the Balcones Canyonlands HCP, which covers 633,000 acres and nine species, including the golden-cheeked warbler. Thus an important empirical question remains to be explained: Why were local governments and developers able to coordinate a single HCP in the Coachella Valley for the fringe-toed lizard but were unable to do so for the golden-cheeked warbler in Travis County? The precipitating factor was that Travis County voters failed to pass a US$50 million bond referendum to pay for the HCP, which led some landowners and developers to develop their own HCPs, but there are likely deeper reasons as well.

One possible explanation is based on size and complexity: the completed Balcones Canyonlands HCP covers nine times as many acres and species as the Coachella Valley HCP, thus suggesting a possible upper bound on the scale of coordinated outcomes. Indeed, participants in the Coachella Valley are now facing the more difficult task of developing a multi-species HCP to cover species and habitat not included in the original HCP for the fringe-toed lizard.

Another possible explanation is based on the slow diffusion of expertise. The Coachella Valley HCP was the second HCP and, like the first HCP on San Bruno Mountain, the innovations were locally developed, within California. One of the principal architects of the Coachella Valley HCP – Paul Selzer, an attorney initially hired by one of the developers – has since built a career by diffusing HCP innovations to neighboring areas, including the Clark County HCP for the desert tortoise near Las Vegas. Another architect of the early HCPs was FWS biologist Gail Kobetich, who worked for the agency's Pacific Region, which included California but not Texas. Because Kobetich, Selzer, and others were based in California, that is where the initial expertise (including deliberative skills) resided, which partially explains why twelve of the first fourteen HCPs emerged in that state.

HCPs did not diffuse widely until the FWS issued draft guidelines in 1990 that provided templates for those lacking expertise, and the Clinton administration provided additional incentives to garner further interest from potential applicants. Yet the role of central structures in the Clinton administration has largely been one of policy diffusion, not monitoring and accountability. HCP guidelines helped actors across the country learn about and copy experiments in California and other states, without having to hire or wait for experienced actors to appear on the scene. Interior Secretary Bruce Babbitt and his legal staff also roamed the country, spreading ideas and encouraging local actors to undertake HCPs through centrally administered incentives such as the No Surprises Policy.

Schools of Democracy

Do HCPs increase the deliberative capacities and dispositions of participants, thereby functioning as schools of democracy? This is an intriguing question, which has not been studied systematically. The public participation study cited earlier provides indirect evidence,[43] but there is no direct evidence of whether HCPs enhance the deliberative skills of participants. Nevertheless, the participation study is telling because the data and case studies indicate that participation varies widely, and that some participants consider the planning process to promote strategic rather than deliberative bargaining. A quote from one participant in the Balcones Canyonlands HCP illustrates this point:

> The public participation process is really not designed to help people develop a new or redirected self-interest. It . . . allows people who already have pre-conceived positions to continue to state and argue for those . . . It's a process designed to allow people to express pre-conceived or pre-established positions, not to adjust their positions based on new information. I don't think it's a dynamic or real iterative process; it's a real static process.[44]

The Balcones Canyonlands HCP suffered from diminished trust because it did not incorporate public participation, particularly from landowners, early in the planning process.[45] This may also help to explain why so many landowners chose to prepare their own HCPs for the golden-cheeked warbler, rather than participate in a multi-species plan that included the warbler, and in which their participation was not included from the beginning.

As suggested in previous sections, the extent of deliberation is enhanced by inviting public participation early, before significant decisions are made. Relying on notice-and-comment periods merely allows a relatively narrow range of participants to promulgate their decisions to the larger public. Adaptive management (with monitoring) can also enhance HCPs as schools of democracy by extending deliberation beyond the planning phase into implementation. For HCPs, therefore, the key to enhancing this dimension is to focus attention on other dimensions of the empowered participatory governance model – specifically, deliberation and monitoring.

Outcomes

Are HCP outcomes more desirable than those of prior institutional arrangements? This answer depends on who one asks and the criteria they believe most important. With regard to planning, scientists – particularly conservation biologists, who study the causal mechanisms of extinction – have not been entirely pleased. As a group, they have criticized the scientific standards and data underlying HCPs.[46] As individuals, they have also criticized the disjunction between scientific guidelines and planning details.

A prominent example of the latter occurred with Natural Communities Conservation Planning (NCCP), a multi-species program sponsored by the State of California for coastal sage scrub habitat in Southern California. As a program, NCCP is essentially an aggregation of HCPs. The FWS issues incidental take permits to subregional NCCP plans within the six thousand square mile NCCP region. In 1993, the NCCP Scientific Review Panel disbanded over conflicts between scientific guidelines and planning details. As two conservation biologists who served on this panel later stated: "Local implementation of these guidelines and fulfillment of the research agenda have been troublesome, but nevertheless, they represent a rare conscious and formal attempt to integrate science into the decision-making process."[47] This statement should make us wonder whether and to what extent HCPs benefit targeted species, given that conservation biologists have much to say about the appropriate design of habitat preserve systems.[48] But it is likely that scientists will never be satisfied with the HCP planning process because it is inherently political, not scientific.

The political nature of HCPs similarly leads some environmental interest groups to criticize HCP outcomes. The National Wildlife Federation, for example, commissioned the previously cited public participation study due to concerns about limited participation.[49] Defenders of Wildlife also published a critical study of HCPs, giving similar attention to public participation, but also focussing on the absence of an explicit legal mandate for HCPs to promote the recovery of species.[50] The Nature Conservancy, on the other hand, regularly provides financial and technical support to HCPs around the country.

This variation among environmental groups can be explained in two ways. First, some groups have successfully pursued litigation under the ESA, and accordingly worry that HCPs compromise their comparative advantage in court. By contrast, The Nature Conservancy never litigates; instead, it conducts on-the-ground conservation activities through real-estate transactions and technical advice on preserve design. Thus an environmental organization's perception of HCP outcomes likely depends upon its propensity to litigate, because HCPs are an alternative to litigation and top-down regulatory bureaucracy. Second, locally based environmentalists often have a social and economic stake in the communities where HCPs are developed. For them, HCPs allow for environmental protection, socio-economic welfare, and local participation. Therefore local environmentalists appear to be more open to a wider range of outcomes and strategies than national groups, particularly those who have traditionally relied on litigation.

It should also be noted that outcomes under the traditional alternative to HCPs – strict prohibition of take – have not been positive. For evidence, one need only review the small number of fish and wildlife species that have been de-listed because their populations recovered. In the U.S., there are only six such species – compared with seven that have been de-listed because they are now believed extinct, and 387 still on the endangered list as of July 2002.[51] Whether HCPs help species more than the strict prohibition on take, however, is unknown. Logically, one might presume that no take is better than some take; but strict prohibition on take does not prevent take, while HCPs proactively channel take in ways that (presumably) preserve habitat integrity. This remains largely a rhetorical debate, with thin evidence to sway neutral minds.

In sum, litigation is necessary to provide the fundamental incentive for applicants to develop HCPs, but that does not mean that litigation alone leads to socially preferred outcomes. Thus it is not clear whether HCPs improve upon traditional command-and-control implementation of the ESA in terms of species protection. HCPs provide a better opportunity for citizens to participate in a deliberative process, but there is great variation in the extent of deliberation and participation. Flexibility has also empowered some HCPs to be highly innovative. Hence every HCP has the potential to be a unique, innovative experiment in empowered participatory governance.

IV Criticisms of the Empowered Participatory Governance Model, as Viewed from the HCP Experience

This section evaluates HCPs by the six potential criticisms of empowered participatory governance, the first of which considers whether HCPs may evolve into fora for domination rather than deliberation.

Deliberation into Domination

One of the intriguing characteristics of HCPs is that the ESA can level the playing field by making actors relatively dependent upon one another, rather than independent and potentially dominating. The desire for certainty among permit applicants can be so strong that they actively seek to work with others to reduce uncertainty by warding off potential lawsuits over resource use. This mutual dependence increases their willingness to share information and resources, and decreases their potential dominance within deliberative arenas. One might argue that this moral character of HCPs is undermined by implicit or explicit threats to sue, but these threats constitute part of the background that brings actors to a common table.

In the Coachella Valley, for example, a few biologists brought developers to the table by threatening legal enforcement – even though they possessed no obvious political, financial, or legal resources of their own to pressure the FWS to enforce the ESA or to mount a successful lawsuit.[52] The mere threat of enforcement, which could halt development in the valley, was sufficient to bring developers to the table. Thus the ESA leveled the playing field, on which developers, with millions of dollars in assets at stake, would seemingly have the upper hand.

Unfortunately, this dynamic only applies within the deliberative arena, which can be relatively small and elitist. For most HCPs, participants are not typically ordinary citizens. Many are highly educated and informed.[53] Few ordinary citizens understand how the ESA works, or have time to devote themselves to a lengthy planning and implementation process. Thus one might argue that this deliberative arena excludes important parts of society. This concern may be assuaged where representation is broad, but single-applicant HCPs should give us pause to reflect, particularly when there is no public participation before notice-and-comment periods under the ESA and NEPA. In these cases, HCPs may be strategic mechanisms for newly empowered applicants to pursue their preferences, rather than experiments in empowered participatory governance. HCPs indeed empower applicants, but it would be hard to claim that single applicants deliberate in a democratic way, if they deliberate with anyone at all. To the extent that their use of natural resources perpetuates negative externalities for society, then such HCPs should be considered a means for continued domination by the economically privileged. In this respect, reforms would be needed to require – not simply encourage – broader public participation.

Forum-Shopping and External Power

Some HCP participants certainly forum-shop during the planning process. One might even argue that all permit applicants forum-shop: that they initiate and complete HCPs because they believe they can achieve better outcomes through this process than through the ESA's otherwise prohibitive regulatory framework. As a corollary, one might also hypothesize that those HCPs which collapse during the planning process fail because applicants pull out when the expected value of participating in some other forum exceeds that of participating in the HCP. This represents a strong view of self-interested behavior, but it likely applies to some applicants given their economic stake. If it did not apply, then we would not need legal assurances like the No Surprises Policy to keep permit applicants at the table.

Environmental groups similarly press their advantage outside the deliberative process when dissatisfied with HCPs. This usually takes the form of filing a lawsuit or whipping up a public relations frenzy against an HCP. In Southern California, Dan Silver became notorious in this regard, particularly with NCCP participants. Silver directs the Endangered Habitats League, a small non-profit organization representing dues-paying environmental groups. His reputation for leading participants to believe he was part of the deliberative process, and then pressing his advantage outside the deliberative arena when dissatisfied with impending outcomes, extended beyond the NCCP-related HCPs in which he participated.[54]

In sum, HCPs emerge due to forum-shopping by applicants, while forum-shopping by environmental activists has the potential to undermine existing HCPs. This is probably a good thing. After all, forum-shopping by environmentalists – particularly those that litigate – provides a lingering threat that keeps applicants at the discussion table and prompts them to implement HCPs in a responsible manner. This lingering threat levels the table, limiting the ability of applicants to dominate the deliberative process. Because the threat of lawsuits gives applicants the basic incentive to develop HCPs, forum-shopping by environmental activists before, during, and after planning is always a possibility. In short, forum-shopping is an inherent part of the process.

Rent-Seeking versus Public Goods

Unlike forum-shopping, it is difficult to put a positive spin on rent-seeking. If deliberative experiments fall prey to rent-seeking and capture by well-informed or interested parties, then empowerment becomes a means for self-aggrandizement. This is a common critique of HCPs, particularly single-applicant HCPs. According to this critique, the FWS allows applicants to pursue economic gain at the cost of species and habitat conservation, while requiring only minimal mitigation measures for species and habitat.[55]

We should certainly assume that HCP applicants attempt to better their position. After all, HCPs are voluntary. Applicants would not bother to prepare and implement an HCP unless they believed it to be in their advantage. The crucial question here is whether applicants – particularly single applicants – pursue or achieve outcomes that benefit primarily themselves, while providing few (if any) positive externalities for society. In deliberative HCPs with broad participation, participants typically design a preserve system with other social benefits in mind, such as where to zone open space and how to manage growth. In doing so, they also develop social capital, including skills for deliberative practice. When HCPs are prepared by single applicants, however, consideration of such positive externalities falls by the wayside. They become incidental to the HCP, rather than an integral part of it.

This problem can be addressed by encouraging or requiring broad participation early in the planning process, with transparency and accountability. Broad participation leads to wider discussion of positive and negative externalities. Transparency allows observers to monitor planning and implementation, and thereby to hold applicants accountable for rent-seeking behavior. Unfortunately, broad participation is currently only encouraged, and not required, by federal HCP guidelines. The FWS and Interior Department have done little to make the process transparent to the public. Anyone who has searched for an HCP – whether in draft or final form – understands the transparency problem. One can purchase copies from the federal government, but this is an expensive and time-consuming proposition. A web-based library would be ideal; but simply creating an accessible library of HCPs, incidental take permits, and implementation agreements would be a big improvement for now. Given the current role of centralized institutions as empowering agents, participation and transparency are problematic, which means that rent-seeking is always a possibility.

Balkanization of Politics

At first glance, one might presume that HCPs necessarily balkanize politics by focussing on a narrow issue (one or more endangered species) and a limited geographic space (some or all of the species' habitat). Indeed, more than a dozen of the golden-cheeked warbler HCPs in Texas cover less than two acres, which suggests extreme balkanization. Yet other HCPs cover tens of thousands of acres, with the Wisconsin HCP for the Karner blue butterfly topping out at seven million acres. Again, the key point to consider is variation. It is the large, multipartner HCPs that best approximate empowered participatory governance.

One might still argue that HCPs balkanize politics by focussing only on endangered species. Superficially, this is correct. Yet the desire for an incidental take permit among applicants is so great that HCPs have become the focal document for general planning purposes, particularly in urban areas, where habitat is directly affected by numerous issues, including physical infrastructure, pollution, open space, development patterns, and transportation. This has certainly been the case with NCCP, which covers a planning area of six thousand square miles in Southern California and fifty-nine local jurisdictions. In the Pacific

Northwest, salmon listings will likely further the trend toward aggregation because salmon HCPs will have to incorporate the waterways through cities, as well as the land-based activities that affect salmon, such as urban runoff, agriculture, and logging. Thus the potential for issue aggregation is great.

Even with respect to endangered species per se, balkanization is a moot issue because HCPs have not fragmented and factionalized something that was previously unified. Prior to the 1982 amendments to the ESA, the closest thing to HCPs were – and still are – the recovery plans mandated under Section 4 of the ESA, which the FWS prepares for listed species. These plans are supposed to identify the management responsibilities of agencies and other actors with jurisdiction over listed species. Yet the mandate to prepare recovery plans is not absolute, and the FWS failed to prepare recovery plans for 45 percent of listed species through 1992.[56] Moreover, recovery plans are merely advisory documents, not binding agreements like HCPs. Thus there was nothing to balkanize through decentralized empowerment.

To the contrary, HCPs arguably aggregate conservation efforts in certain situations. As previously noted, species conservation is a collective-action problem wherever habitat is shared among multiple owners, agencies, and political jurisdictions. Rather than preparing individual HCPs, applicants can lower their transaction costs by sharing information, pooling resources, and developing integrated solutions to the common problem they face. Though federal regulations do not require applicants to plan for a species' entire habitat or to coordinate with others when preparing an HCP, the FWS nevertheless encourages them to do so. This occurred with NCCP in Southern California, where FWS staff made it known that anyone choosing to develop their own HCP outside the NCCP process would have to demonstrate that their plan was compatible with subregional NCCP plans.[57]

Nevertheless, it is true that many HCPs focus on a narrow issue (species conservation) and a narrow geographic area (some or all of a species' habitat). Positive externalities may result from HCPs, particularly multi-partner HCPs. Some HCPs cover large planning areas, but the planning process itself is relatively focussed, particularly when public participation is limited, as it tends to be for single-applicant HCPs. Thus balkanization is more likely to be a problem whenever there is only one applicant, regardless of the size of the planning area; but we will not know the magnitude of the problem until researchers specifically study this issue.

Apathy

Citizen apathy is a serious problem for HCPs because planning and implementation occur over many years. For many potential participants, this is an unbearable commitment, unless it is part of their job description. Therefore most participants in large HCPs represent specific organizations, such as local planning agencies, state and federal agencies, environmental non-profits, and private firms. Ordinary citizens rarely participate for sustained periods. This is not a critique of public apathy per se, which is indeed a problem for the empowered participatory governance model. It is a realistic assessment of the extraordinary time demands required to produce an HCP – particularly a multi-partner HCP – regardless of whether the HCP is ever implemented, monitored, or redesigned. If the empowered participatory governance model requires participation by ordinary citizens, then HCPs will never become exemplars of the model without funding to support citizen participation. Such funding could come from the federal government, or it could be required of applicants as a condition of the incidental take permit. Both scenarios are unlikely, however, given that current FWS guidelines only encourage participation, but do not require it.

Stability and Sustainability

Growth in the number and size of HCPs during the 1990s suggests they are stable and sustainable. We might have wondered about future trends in the 1980s, but the current trend clearly suggests continued proliferation of HCPs in both number and geographic extent. There is also a compelling logic behind this trend. The pool of potential applicants will remain large so long as the FWS continues to list species, which seems likely given that listing decisions must be based on biological rather than political criteria. Moreover, human use of natural resources will undoubtedly continue. In this context, HCPs will likely thrive as the preferred means for nonfederal resource users to comply with the ESA's prohibition on take, particularly if the federal government continues to provide applicants with legal assurances such as the No Surprises Policy.

The important question is whether HCPs will thrive as experiments in empowered participatory governance. HCPs vary widely in how well they fit the model's dimensions. Rent-seeking, for example, is primarily a problem for single-applicant HCPs, which notably lack public participation. For this reason, it is probably best to remove single-applicant HCPs from consideration because they do not approximate the model in several dimensions. Instead, we should focus on multi-partner HCPs – particularly the institutional incentives that encourage applicants to submit them and to deliberate broadly during planning and implementation – so that they better approximate experiments in empowered participatory governance.

V Suggested Reforms

Some reforms seem obvious, if not politically feasible. An accessible library of HCPs and related documentation, including findings from monitoring programs and implementation evaluations, would enhance transparency and accountability. A web-based library would be particularly helpful for expanding public participation. This is a relatively easy reform because it simply requires gathering existing documentation and loading it onto a website. The FWS has been moving in this direction with the Environmental Conservation Online System (ECOS), which contains summary data for species and HCPs.[58] Summary data is certainly helpful, but ECOS does not yet include the text (in readable or searchable formats) of draft HCPs, final HCPs, incidental take permits, or implementation agreements – let alone monitoring reports, implementation evaluations, or the minutes from group meetings. Making these documents readily available would enhance accountability, participation, and deliberation, thereby reducing opportunities for rent-seeking by permit applicants.

More ambitious reforms would include required publication of periodic self-monitoring reports; federal funding for public participation, implementation evaluations, and adaptive management; and terminating the No Surprises Policy. Required publication of periodic self-monitoring reports – perhaps on the web library suggested above – would enhance accountability during implementation and allow broader participation in adaptive management. Federal funding for public meetings and implementation evaluations would expand the scope of deliberation and monitoring during planning and implementation. Federal funding of adaptive management is needed to cover the expense of fixing faulty HCPs, particularly those covered by assurances under the No Surprises Policy. Alternatively, the federal government could terminate the No Surprises Policy, which would encourage adaptive management in HCPs that do not include an adaptive management strategy, and in HCPs that include an insufficient adaptive management strategy.

Many of these reforms would increase uncertainty for applicants, which may reduce the number and size of HCPs in the future, but deliberation thrives on uncertainty. In a world of certainty, there is no reason to deliberate. The more certain people are about what they want and expect, the more likely they will conceal their preferences through strategic bargaining rather than allowing their preferences to change by revealing them through deliberation. The No Surprises Policy, for example, necessarily constricts the range of deliberation by creating legal certainty in an uncertain political and ecological environment. While the new guidelines on adaptive management expand the range of deliberation for HCPs covered by the No Surprises Policy, such regulatory assurances nevertheless restrict deliberation within a limited range.

Thus enhancing deliberation may be the most challenging problem for all HCPs. Even if federal guidelines, rules, or laws mandate increased public participation, we will not necessarily see more deliberation. Indeed, centralized directives cannot mandate deliberation per se, though they can readily change the incentives for deliberation by altering participant perceptions of uncertainty. This can be done, for example, by increasing the probability of enforcing the Section 9 prohibition on take (which would bring more applicants to the table) and by reducing regulatory assurances (which would keep them at the table during implementation).

Similarly, if participants view habitat as a zero-sum pie, then they will fight over the relative size of the pieces they want to preserve for species or consume in markets, which means the standard pluralist model of strategic bargaining with concealed preferences will likely prevail. From a scientific perspective, however, this is the wrong view. Information and knowledge about the relationship between species and habitats is constantly changing. Hence to view the habitat pie as fixed ignores the evolving nature of scientific knowledge and the accumulated information gleaned from monitoring programs and implementation evaluations. This is why adaptive management is crucial to environmental policy applications of the empowered participatory governance model. If HCPs are framed in terms of adaptive management, then monitoring, learning, and redesign can occur. Deliberation is feasible in this institutional framework because learning implies that individual preferences and strategies are not stable.

The fundamental weakness of the No Surprises Policy is that it constrains the range of adaptive management, thereby encouraging strategic bargaining in the short run, while constraining deliberative possibilities in the long run. In a world of limited regulatory surprises, the habitat pie is relatively constant and participants grind out rational-comprehensive plans. Even a devoted pluralist like Charles Lindblom understood that rational-comprehensive plans are technically infeasible.[59] Yet, forty years later, such plans are still promoted under the "no surprises" banner. Admittedly, fewer actors will participate in HCPs without such regulatory assurances. Yet those who do participate will be much more likely to do so in a deliberative manner. Moreover, the federal government can assuage their uncertainty by creating a federal program to subsidize adaptive management. By subsidizing adaptive management, regulatory surprises will not be so painful, and the burden of species conservation will be more widely distributed.

Notes

* Assistant Professor of Political Science at the University of Massachusetts, Amherst. I would like to thank Archon Fung, Bradley Karkkainen, Dara O'Rourke, Andrew Szasz, and Erik Olin Wright for helpful comments on earlier drafts, and Jennifer Balkcom, Alice Napoleon, and Jessica Rajotte Wozniak for research assistance.

1. Archon Fung and Erik Olin Wright, "Thinking about Empowered Participatory Governance," this volume.

2. Current HCP data, along with federal policies and guidelines, can be found on the U.S. Fish and Wildlife Service website, at http://endangered.fws.gov/hcp/.

3. See, for example, Craig W. Thomas, *Bureaucratic Landscapes: Interagency Cooperation and the Preservation of Biodiversity*, Cambridge, MA: MIT Press (2003); Steven L. Yaffee, *The Wisdom of the Spotted Owl: Policy Lessons for a New Century*, Washington, DC: Island Press (1994); Steven L. Yaffee, *Prohibitive Policy: Implementing the Federal Endangered Species Act*, Cambridge, MA: MIT Press (1982); and Timothy Beatley, *Habitat Conservation Planning: Endangered Species and Urban Growth*, Austin, TX: University of Texas Press (1994).

4. While both Section 7 and Section 9 address habitat modification, they do not provide the same incentives for actors to develop HCPs because Section 10 authorizes HCPs as a means for complying with the Section 9 prohibition on take, not the Section 7 jeopardy standard for federal agencies. Hence federal agencies do not have a strong legal incentive to participate in HCPs. The FWS is an exception because it reviews and approves HCPs, and must consult with itself under Section 7 when issuing HCP permits.

5. Sections 9(a)(1) and 3(18), Endangered Species Act of 1973, as amended. The Section 9 prohibition on take applies only to fish and wildlife species listed by the FWS as "endangered" (i.e. at imminent risk of extinction). It does not apply directly to plant species, or to species listed as "threatened" (i.e. likely to become endangered in the foreseeable future). Yet Section 9 does cover plant species indirectly because plants (such as old-growth forests) provide habitat for wildlife (such as spotted owls).

6. 50 CFR 17.3. This regulation was upheld by the Supreme Court in *Babbitt v. Sweet Home Chapter of Communities for a Great Oregon*, 515 U.S. 687 (1995).

7. Yaffee, *Prohibitive Policy*.

8. This occurred, and continues to occur, even though the ESA instructs the Secretary of the Interior to make listing decisions based "solely on the basis of the best scientific and commercial data available . . ." (Section 4(b)(1)(A)).

9. Beatley, *Habitat Conservation Planning*. For additional background on this first HCP, see Lindell L. Marsh and Robert D. Thornton, "San Bruno Mountain Habitat Conservation Plan," in David J. Brower and Daniel S. Carol, eds., *Managing Land-Use Conflicts: Case Studies in Special Area Management*, Durham, NC: Duke University

Press (1987). On the role of consensual ecological knowledge in habitat planning and management, see Craig W. Thomas, "Public Management as Interagency Cooperation: Testing Epistemic Community Theory at the Domestic Level," *Journal of Public Administration Research and Theory*, no. 7 (1997), pp. 221–46; and Thomas, *Bureaucratic Landscapes*.

10. The National Marine Fisheries Service (NMFS) reviews and approves HCPs for marine species, including anadromous fish. NMFS is relegated to footnotes in this chapter because most HCPs are land-based.

11. Section 10(a)(1)(B), Endangered Species Ac of 1973, as amended.

12. U.S. Fish and Wildlife Service and National Marine Fisheries Service, *Habitat Conservation Planning Handbook*, Washington, DC: U.S. Fish and Wildlife Service and National Marine Fisheries Service (1996), chapter 3, p. 10.

13. For current data on HCPs, see the Environmental Conservation Online System (ECOS), at http://ecos.fws.gov/.

14. The No Surprises Policy was introduced by the Clinton administration in 1994, and codified in 1998. During this interim period (1994–97), the policy was so popular that at least seventy-four HCPs were thought to contain assurances under the No Surprises Policy. See Steven L. Yaffee *et al.*, *Balancing Public Trust and Private Interest: Public Participation in Habitat Conservation Planning*, Ann Arbor: School of Natural Resources and Environment, University of Michigan (1998), chapter 2, p. 5. The No Surprises Policy was codified (50 CFR Parts 17 and 222) when the U.S. FWS and NMFS published the final "Habitat Conservation Plan Assurances ('No Surprises') Rules" *Federal Register*, vol. 63, no. 35 (1998), pp. 8, 859–73. All HCPs must now be consistent with this rule. More recently, the FWS has developed similar assurances through Safe Harbor and Candidate Conservation Agreements. See the final rule in U.S. Fish and Wildlife Service and National Marine Fisheries Service, "Safe Harbor Agreements and Candidate Conservation Agreements with Assurances," *Federal Register*, vol. 64, no. 116 (1999), pp. 32, 705–16.

15. Yaffee *et al.*, *Balancing Public Trust and Private Interest*, chapter 1, p. 1.

16. Kai N. Lee, *Compass and Gyroscope: Integrating Science and Politics for the Environment*, Washington, DC: Island Press (1993); C.S. Holling, *Adaptive Environmental Management and Assessment*, Chichester, NY: Wiley (1978).

17. Reed F. Noss, Michael A. O'Connell, and Dennis D. Murphy, *The Science of Conservation Planning: Habitat Conservation under the Endangered Species Act*, Washington, DC: Island Press (1997).

18. U.S. Fish and Wildlife Service and National Marine Fisheries Service, "Notice of Availability of a Final Addendum to the Handbook for Habitat Conservation Planning and Incidental Take Permitting Process," *Federal Register*, vol. 65, no. 106 (2000), pp. 35, 241–57.

19. Yaffee *et al.*, *Balancing Public Trust and Private Interest*.

20. Ibid., p. xv.

21. Ibid.

22. For example, the new HCP guidelines state: "for large-scale, regional, or exceptionally complex HCPs, the Services are increasingly encouraging applicants to use informational meetings and/or advisory committees. In addition, the minimum comment period for these HCPs is now 90 days, unless significant public participation occurs during HCP development." U.S. Fish and Wildlife Service and National Marine Fisheries Service, "Notice of Availability," pp. 35, 256.

23. See, for example, Michael J. Bean, Sarah G. Fitzgerald, and Michael A. O'Connell, *Reconciling Conflicts under the Endangered Species Act: The Habitat Conservation Planning Experience*, Washington, DC: World Wildlife Fund (1991), pp. 66–79; Timothy Beatley, "Balancing Urban Development and Endangered Species: The Coachella Valley Habitat Conservation Plan," *Environmental Management*, no. 16 (1992), pp. 7–19; Dwight Holing, "Lizard and the Links," *Audubon*, no. 89 (1987), pp. 39–49; Robert Thompson, "Coachella Valley Habitat Conservation Plan," in Judith Innes, Judith Gruber, Michael Neuman, and Robert Thompson, eds., *Coordinating*

Growth and Environmental Management through Consensus Building, Berkeley, CA: California Policy Seminar, University of California (1994).

24. Yaffee *et al.*, *Balancing Public Trust and Private Interest*, p. vi.

25. Thomas, *Bureaucratic Landscapes*.

26. Yaffee *et al.*, *Balancing Public Trust and Private Interest*, chapter 4, p. 21.

27. Part of this case study is reported in Charles Schweik and Craig W. Thomas, "Using Remote Sensing to Evaluate Environmental Institutional Decline: A Habitat Conservation Planning Example," *Social Science Quarterly*, vol. 83, no. 1 (2002), pp. 244–62. For the full case study, see Craig W. Thomas and Charles Schweik, "Regulatory Compliance under the Endangered Species Act: a Time-Series Analysis of Habitat Conservation Planning Using Remote-Sensing Data," paper presented at the *Association for Public Policy Analysis and Management (APPAM) Annual Research Conference*, Washington, DC (1999). This conference paper has been extensively revised and is available on request from the authors.

28. Section 10(a)(2)(A)(ii), Endangered Species Act of 1973, as amended; U.S. Fish and Wildlife Service and National Marine Fisheries Service, *Habitat Conservation Planning Handbook*, III-10.

29. Thomas and Schweik, "Regulatory Compliance."

30. Lee, *Compass and Gyroscope*; Holling, *Adaptive Environmental Management and Assessment*.

31. Fung and Wright, Introduction to this volume, p. 31

32. Peter Kareiva *et al.*, *Using Science in Habitat Conservation Plans*, Washington, DC: American Institute of Biological Sciences (1999).

33. Ibid., p. 40.

34. Ibid., p. 41.

35. During implementation, some participants wondered whether the Coachella Valley HCP protected the most important sand sources for the dunes in the preserve system. The preserve manager accordingly commissioned geological field studies, which indicated that the primary sand sources were inadequately protected. See Cameron Barrows, "An Ecological Model for the Protection of a Dune System," *Conservation Biology*, no. 10 (1996), pp. 888–91. Our subsequent analysis of remote-sensing data from Landsat satellites confirmed this finding and pinpointed the areas requiring additional protection. See Schweik and Thomas, "Using Remote Sensing." We accordingly gave them the processed data to aid in adaptive management.

36. Thomas and Schweik, "Regulatory Compliance."

37. Marjorie Nelson, Division of Endangered Species, U.S. Fish and Wildlife Service, personal communication, October 1, 1999.

38. U.S. Fish and Wildlife Service and National Marine Fisheries Service, "Notice of Availability."

39. Ibid., pp. 35, 252.

40. Ibid.

41. Ibid., pp. 35, 253.

42. Thomas, *Bureaucratic Landscapes*.

43. Yaffee *et al.*, *Balancing Public Trust and Private Interest*.

44. Ibid., chapter 3, p. 4.

45. Ibid., appendix A.

46. Kareiva *et al.*, *Using Science in Habitat Conservation Plans*.

47. Noss and Murphy, *The Science of Conservation Planning*, p. 58.

48. Reed F. Noss and Allen Y. Cooperrider, *Saving Nature's Legacy: Protecting and Restoring Biodiversity*, Washington, DC: Island Press (1994).

49. Yaffee *et al.*, *Balancing Public Trust and Private Interest*.

50. Laura C. Hood, *Frayed Safety Nets: Conservation Planning under the Endangered Species Act*, Washington, DC: Defenders of Wildlife (1998).

51. As of July 2002, the FWS had de-listed twelve fish and wildlife species due to recovery, but the habitat of six of those species is in other countries (i.e. Australia and Palau), which makes them irrelevant to the HCP experience. Plant species are not

included in this count because they are not covered by the Section 9 prohibition on take. For current data, see http://ecos.fws.gov/.

52. Bean and O'Connell, *Reconciling Conflicts*; Beatley, "Balancing Urban Development and Endangered Species"; Holing, "Lizard and the Links"; Thompson, "Coachella Valley Habitat Conservation Plan."

53. For example, the primary environmental protagonist in the Coachella Valley HCP during the planning phase was Allan Muth, Ph.D., director of the University of California's Deep Canyon Desert Research Center. To the west, in San Diego and Orange Counties, one of the primary environmental protagonists in several HCPs was Dan Silver, a former medical doctor. Given their academic credentials, these individuals cannot be considered "ordinary citizens."

54. Silver focussed primarily on HCPs associated with Natural Communities Conservation Planning (NCCP), but his reputation extended further than his geographically isolated participation. In the Coachella Valley, a representative of the Building Industry Association (BIA) pointed to Silver as an example of destructive forum-shopping – even though Silver and NCCP operated an hour or more to the west (Ed Kibbey, Executive Director, Building Industry Association of Southern California, personal communication, June 8, 1999). Silver justified such forum-shopping by claiming that it provides clout within these planning processes (Yaffee *et al.*, *Balancing Public Trust and Private Interest*, p. xvi, note 16). Yet forum-shopping during the planning process pushes HCPs toward traditional power-based bargaining, and away from deliberation.

55. This critique has some empirical merit. Scientists evaluating the use of science in HCPs found that 85 percent of the species in their sample were protected by mitigation procedures that addressed the primary threat to the species' continued existence; but for only 57 percent of the species did they rate proposed mitigation procedures as sufficient or better, while 43 percent of the species were covered by proposed mitigation procedures that were "significantly lacking" (25 percent), "inadequate" (13 percent), or "extremely poor" (5 percent). See Kareiva *et al.*, *Using Science in Habitat Conservation Plans*, p. 39.

56. Andrew A. Smith, Margaret A. Moote, and Cecil R. Schwalbe, "The Endangered Species Act at Twenty: An Analytical Survey of Federal Endangered Species Protection," *Natural Resources Journal*, vol. 33 (1993), pp. 1,027–1,075, 1051.

57. Thomas, *Bureaucratic Landscapes*, Chapter 6.

58. ECOS is maintained on the FWS website, at <http://ecos.fws.gov/.

59. Charles E. Lindblom, "The Science of Muddling Through," *Public Administration Review*, no. 19 (1959), pp. 79–88.

PART III
Commentaries

6

Practice–Thought–Practice
Jane Mansbridge*

The theory and cases presented here constitute a major step forward in the theory and practice of participatory democracy.

As sometimes happens with the most original forms of theory, this new theory derives from acute observation of practice. People who were actually engaged in trying to make democracy work tried first one form of practice and then another until they evolved a set of institutions that came closer to meeting their needs. Fung and Wright, with the theory advanced in this book, have schematized and brought to conscious articulation the understandings that evolved from this incremental evolution in practice. Their theory can now serve as a further guide to practice.

The individuals in the conference that inspired this book have already begun taking the next step, using the new theory as a guide for people who continue to be engaged in making the institutions of democracy work. The step as yet untaken would require repeating the original observation of practice. It would require asking what sense people make, in practice, of the new institutions that follow from the new theory, and revising the theory from their new experience. The old formula, "practice–thought–practice," works best if repeated over and over.

To aid in future observation and theory-making, I first sketch what I see as the origins of the original and important "recombinant" feature of Empowered Participatory Governance in theory and practice, and suggest some remaining problems. I then identify silences in the theory of deliberation, as exemplified in past work, in Fung and Wright's introduction, and in the case studies in this volume. Theory is usually silent when theorists fail to see what does not fit. Observations from practice give us clues on how to fill the silence – by expanding what we mean by deliberation to incorporate self-interest, emotion, conflict, inequality, and informal representation.

Each subsequent section of this chapter addresses one of these issues, suggesting questions that practitioners might want to ask themselves and that researchers might now address when they return to scrutinize the practice.

First, the chapter urges expanding the concept of deliberation to include a greater normative role for *self-interest*. As participants in deliberation, we cannot understand ourselves or others, or work out just resolutions to many conflicts, if we cannot formulate relatively accurately and express relatively well some conception of our own narrow self-interest. At the same time, we need to learn how to transform our interests in order to forge a common good. The normative, psychological, and institutional trick lies in finding ways to move in both, not necessarily contradictory, directions at once.

Second, the chapter urges expanding the concept of deliberation beyond reason-giving to encompass many interactions based in the *emotions*. It also urges designing institutions to provide non-destructive venues for certain expressions of emotion.

Third, the chapter urges expanding the normative aims of deliberation and deliberative institutions to make uncovering and expressing *conflict* a valued goal.

Fourth, it urges incorporating *inequalities* in our conception of legitimate deliberation. It suggests criteria for judging which inequalities among individuals and groups significantly undermine the normative legitimacy of the deliberative process and which can be ignored without great harm.

Finally it urges incorporating *informal representation* in our understanding of deliberative democracy. It suggests criteria by which one can judge the quality of the representation that those who engage in deliberation provide to those who are absent.

I Recombination

The original theory of participatory democracy simply devolved power to the lowest possible level. Our chant in the streets was "power to the people!" And we meant it. The Port Huron Statement, which brought the phrase "participatory democracy" into the language, was written by students who had never themselves had the experience of political power. It was written in the midst of an era, much like today, in which decisions that potentially involved global nuclear holocaust were being made by people whose names most citizens did not even know. In the words of C. Wright Mills, whose works inspired several Port Huron writers, the people "feel they live in a time of big decisions; they know they are not making any."[1] The Port Huron Statement called for a democracy in which citizens participated actively – a democracy that would "bring people out of isolation into community."[2]

The young political philosopher Arnold Kaufman, who coined the term "participatory democracy" and first enunciated its theory, stressed its positive effects on the citizens themselves. As he put it, wielding political power would improve the citizens' capacities for "thought, feeling and action."[3] As a young professor in the philosophy department at the University of Michigan, Kaufman worked with Tom Hayden and other students from Michigan who collectively wrote the Port Huron Statement. Kaufman himself was an acute observer of practice. Before he died prematurely in a plane crash only a few years later, his own experience with fledgling participatory democracies led him to formulate what he called the "paradox of participatory democracy." The paradox is that although participation in democracies helps people increase their capacities, those who have not yet had the experience of participation will sometimes not have sufficient capacity to bring off a successful democracy. What they need is precisely what, because of their need, they cannot get.[4]

Over the years other democrats have run into various versions of Kaufman's paradox. Urban reformers who instituted decentralization to increase the power of the people, for example, sometimes found that the newly decentralized units became so incompetent or corrupt as to alienate even those who exercised considerable power in them.[5] In 1988 the school reformers in Chicago explicitly tried to find solutions for problems like these, which had been raised by the school reform in New York and other places twenty years earlier.

The theory of "recombinant" participatory democracy thus emerged from many years of experiment and learning. Archon Fung's study of the newly decentralized school system in Chicago led him to articulate and name this new form of participatory structure – one in which participation at the grass roots works interactively with facilitative regulation, monitoring, and sanctioning at a higher level. In this model, the entity on the lower level experiments, innovates, draws from local knowledge, and engages local individuals in potentially transformative kinds of participation, while the entity on the higher level monitors for quality, sanctions when standards of quality are not met, and shares innovation among lower-level entities. The goal is to capture the positive features of local participation without some of the previously experienced drawbacks.

Once the theory is formulated explicitly and its elements articulated, we can see that the principles behind the theory have implicitly informed a great deal of federal practice, at least in the United States. In state–local relations in New England, for example, state governments require that towns hold their meetings at least once a year at a specified time. Some states require that certain items must appear on the "warning," or agenda, of the meeting. States or voluntary associations provide training for the town moderators. Outside New England, states set other procedural requirements that towns and cities must meet or face sanctions. In a parallel manner, the federal government monitors the state governments, holding them, for example, to certain requirements in the electoral process.

The temptations at the higher level are always to promote the interests of the whole even when they differ from the interests of the part, and to impose the vision – and sometimes, consciously or unconsciously, the interests – of the "experts" or of sectors that are more powerful at the higher level, suppressing the experimentation, vision, and interests of the local participants. The temptations at the lower level are to promote the interests of the part even when they differ from the interests of the whole, and to impose the vision – and sometimes, consciously or unconsciously, the interests – of the most active or most powerful at the local level, ignoring the needs of the less powerful, other locales, or the whole. Only trial and error will suggest ways to gain most of the benefits of recombination while avoiding its greatest costs. At the moment, the theory of recombinant participatory democracy produces a notable advance over the original theory of participatory democracy because it introduces an interaction between levels of government that can be synergistic, creative, and mutually reinforcing.

II Deliberation

The observation and theory of deliberation are also in their infancy. At the moment, we know relatively little about what makes for good deliberation in a democratic assembly. Informally and in the theory so far, we currently judge good deliberations on the basis, among other things, of the degree of mutual respect, recognition and acknowledgement among the participants, their openmindedness and willingness to listen, the consistency in their arguments and the accuracy of their facts, their "economy" in disagreement (seeking rationales that minimize the rejection of an opposing position and avoid affronting the deepest commitments of others), their capacity to bring to light most of the relevant considerations, their capacity to discover or forge common interests and values, and the space the deliberative arena itself provides for the expression of authentic feeling. As meta-criteria for judging deliberations, I suggest that deliberations should be as likely as possible to make the participants 1) aware of the implications of their own preferences and interests, the preferences and interests of others, and the interests of the polity as a whole, and 2) capable of transforming their interests in ways that they themselves, looking back on that transformation from a state of reflection and awareness, would approve.[6]

Some easily identifiable lacunae in current analyses of deliberation involve the relation between the common good and self-interest, the use of emotion, the handling of conflict, the appropriate stance toward inequalities, and the criteria by which to judge informal representation.

1 Incorporating Self-Interest

As Fung and Wright point out, the guiding norm in public deliberation, even in small groups, ought to be the overall good of the group. Most arguments should be made in those terms. Indeed, the arguments that carry the most weight will usually be made in those terms.

This issue is, however, not as open and shut as it appears either in Fung and Wright's theory or in the writings of most earlier democratic theorists.[7] A single focus on the common good tends to make the assertion of self-interest illegitimate. Yet recognizing and asserting self-interest helps advance distributive justice. Recognizing and asserting self-interest helps one figure out oneself what one wants. Recognizing and asserting self-interest helps in becoming understood (and respected) for what one wants and needs. Finally, recognizing and asserting self-interest helps unveil hegemonic understandings of the common good when those understandings have evolved to mask subtle forms of oppression.

Self-Interest and Distributive Justice

Whether or not the background circumstances are relatively just, participants should have – or develop during deliberation – a reasonably good sense of what their own self-interest (including the most narrow sense of that self-interest) is.

Even when the background conditions are relatively unjust and therefore the chances that the outcome will be substantively just are slim, the deliberations themselves can still be relatively good or bad. If, as I suggest later, we expand what we mean by deliberation to encompass the discussion of irreconcilable conflict as well as the search for a common good, then we can consider as a form of deliberation even the negotiations between two states, one of which has acquired its greater power relatively unjustly. In cases like these, and particularly when conceptions of justice themselves are contested and those conceptions coincide with material interests, it may not be possible to engage in a good-faith search for a common good that is acceptable to all. It is surely critical, in such cases, for all parties to have a solid sense of their own self-interest – including their most narrow and material interests.

The failure to reach consensus on a just or good outcome does not automatically mark a bad process of deliberation. A good deliberation will clarify both conflict and commonality, even if the final decision is to go to war. If, short of war, the participants can agree to a relatively legitimate procedural mechanism for settling the conflict, the deliberation can clarify the conflict and conclude in a form of decision, such as a majority vote, that does not produce a consensual outcome. Whether the outcome is war or a vote, we must judge separately from a normative perspective the quality of the *deliberation* (on criteria such as those listed earlier), the quality of the *decision procedure* (on criteria such as that it institutionalizes a legitimate allocation of power in the decision-rule), and the quality of the *outcome* (on criteria that derive from a standard of justice independent of the deliberative or decision-making procedure).[8]

When the background conditions are relatively just, communities can also face irreconcilable conflict. For example, they may need to distribute, relatively justly, scarce goods that many want. Many such cases are zero-sum, so that a good for me inevitably entails the loss of a good for you. A budget process with a fixed income often has this characteristic. To allocate zero-sum goods justly (that is, accounting for relevant considerations), a group needs to know what its different segments need. In this process, the different segments usually have to articulate what they need. It is not useful in this process to have norms that no individuals or groups should think about or articulate what they need in terms of their own self-interest.[9]

Consider a couple deciding whether to move to Chicago or Boston, when one member of the couple has a good job offer in Chicago and the other a good job offer in Boston. One or another city may be best for both members of the couple in the long run. If so, those arguments should be made and should carry great weight. But those arguments may not be dispositive. Then the norms of discussion should allow both individuals to recognize and articulate where their individual self-interest lies, in order to work out some fair arrangement. For example, if the couple moves to Boston, the one who has to turn down the job in Chicago might gain some offsetting good or accumulate "credit" for a future decision. Both individuals could agree on the fairness of the overall bargain even when their more proximate interests came in conflict.

If in such a deliberation neither member of the couple thinks it legitimate to recognize and articulate his or her self-interest, the two may end up making the decision entirely on the basis of a "common good" that does not encompass all of the issues involved. They may, for example, phrase the entire deliberation in terms of what is good for the children. In this case their discussions of what is good for the children will probably be freighted, at least unconsciously, with the other issues that have normatively been ruled off the table. Ideas about the "good of the children" will take on an intensity the basis of which the parents will not let themselves recognize. Although not articulating individual self-interest may produce a communal spirit, that spirit will come at the risk of future problems. It is also likely to result in injustice to the individual who accepts a loss without compensation or explicit acknowledgement.

To move from a dyadic to a slightly larger deliberation, consider an academic department to which the dean gives one new faculty position. In the discussion over where to allocate that position, the greatest weight should be given to arguments that allocating that position to one or another subfield in the department will promote the reputation or good functioning of the department as a whole. But it may not be obvious which allocation will be best for the department. When no greater good of this sort is clear, the good of the department may be best served by giving one subfield the position and either giving the others some other good or promising them the next available free position.

This kind of thinking and negotiation rightly constitutes much of the deliberative work of parliaments as well as couples and academic departments. It is likely to appear in participatory budget processes and to a lesser degree in all the cases discussed in this volume. It does not further our capacity for analysis, I believe, to exclude this kind of thinking from what we mean by "deliberation."

Creating a "deal" of this sort often involves expanding the scope of the decision-making either into more substantive areas or to a longer time horizon (e.g. adding future decisions into the mix). When the specific choices at hand have individually a zero-sum character, the deal produces an aggregate or composite "common good" rather than a unitary common good on which everyone can substantively agree.[10] The discussion of how to compensate in other areas or extend the trade-offs over time is a central feature of such a deliberation.

Other central features of such a deliberation include discussing the meaning and implications of the components of the possible deal and the intensity of preferences around each component. In these circumstances, deliberation promotes self-understanding, mutual understanding, and a useful understanding of the world only when individuals can try to understand not only what common interests can be forged, but also their own and others' self-interest. The individuals in the deliberation should use their talk to help find out 1) what they really want and need from each thing that they think they want, 2) what others really want and need, 3) what everyone's wants and needs imply for other things, 4) where the indissoluble conflicts lie between their wants or needs and those of others, and 5) what commonalities can be forged between their own wants or needs and those of others. It is not always easy to understand what one really wants even within the horizon of one's own narrow self-interest. It becomes harder as one expands the horizon of self-interest to encompass experiencing the good of others as one's own. Even in trying to figure out what *you* want, thinking alone can get you only so far. At some point you need your friends, at least as a sounding board and also for their shared experiences, emotional resonance, and analytic capacities. On issues appropriate to public discussion, you usually also need the thoughts of those who are not your intimate friends, even including the thoughts of those who stand to lose by your gains and gain by your losses.

In a dyadic negotiation, for example, each negotiator has an incentive to help the "opposing" negotiator find ways of satisfying his or her constituency's needs at less cost and more gain to the needs of the first negotiator's constituency than either had originally imagined. Assume that you need x and y, and come into the negotiation thinking that to satisfy these needs you need x^1 and y^1, which are costly to me. If I can show you correctly that x^2 and y^2 will satisfy your needs equally well or better at less cost to me, then we can settle for x^2 and y^2 and both be better off. In this interchange I have an incentive to work with you creatively to see if we can together come up with x^2 and y^2.

Discussions like this are often contrasted with "deliberation" and given a lower, or even negative, normative status. When Jürgen Habermas or Fung and Wright label these kinds of discussions "strategic" and their outcomes "bargains," they want to save the terms "communicative" and "deliberation" for discussions of a more unitary common good.[11] I contend, however, that a form of deal-making in which I work with you, for my own narrow self-interest, to help you find a form of your narrow self-interest that costs me less or gives me greater gain, is a process that – in a non-manipulative setting – can deepen your self-understanding, our mutual understanding, and our understanding of the world. It is thus an important and integral component of deliberation properly understood.

Greater awareness of self-interest also improves deliberation in instances of "the Abilene paradox," in which each member of a group goes along with a suggestion because he thinks it will help the others even though he does not want that outcome himself.[12] This paradox is one form of the larger phenomenon of "group-think" in which members of a group come to agree with what they perceive as a group consensus even though each of them harbors unexpressed doubts about the wisdom of that consensus.[13]

Finally and crucially, greater awareness of self-interest is absolutely required for good deliberation when a hegemonic definition of the common good makes less powerful members either unaware of their own interests or convinced that they ought to suppress those interests for the common good even when others are not doing their just share.

One critical normative issue is the degree of power that may legitimately be deployed in reaching a decision. To summarize a much longer discussion, power (the threat of sanction or the use of force) should ideally be absent in a deliberation, although influence (getting others to do something they would otherwise not do by making a good argument) should be present and may legitimately be very unequal. In practice, power can never be fully absent, but its absence remains a standard at which to aim. When deliberation cannot produce agreement on a substantive common good and the polity must craft a consensual democratic bargain, the goal is still absence of power. In majority rule, a legitimate outcome depends normatively on equal individual power – again a goal not fully achievable in practice but which serves as a standard at which to aim.[14]

Self-Interest in the Process of Personal Transformation

If, as I urge, we include in deliberation deals made to achieve distributive justice, we see why it is important in such deals for the parties concerned to be aware of their interests – including their most narrow, material self-interests – and to communicate those interests effectively to others. Indeed, deliberation ought to make people more aware of these interests and the ways they may conflict with those of others, as well as more aware of potential commonalities. Transformations ought to occur in the direction of recognizing conflict as well as in the direction of forging commonality.[15] Ideally, only *after* these considerations have been brought to light and to the table should one ask the participants to vote "not for the option that best advances his self-interest, but rather for the choice that seems most reasonable."[16]

Previous deliberative theorists, however, have focussed largely on the undeniably important process of forging more unitary forms of the common good. The practice evident in the cases presented in this book should allow theorists to go further than this in probing the norms of participatory transformation.

In Porto Alegre, for example, activists – at least from the poorer districts – seem to have articulated a major part of what they are doing in terms of local material group interest. One commented, for example, that his "district has benefited a lot" from the Participatory Budget,[17] and another that, "We were able to get part of the street paved but we are still going to go back because there is a lot we still need."[18] The first of these activists, described as being from "the poorest district of the city," revealingly reported that the districts develop associations "to *fight* through the Participatory Budget and . . . to go and make their *demands* in the Participatory Budget."[19] Although the subject of the "fight" that he envisioned is not clear from the short quotation, he probably had in mind a fight against the central government, seen as the holder of large amounts of money, and not against the other districts, which also had important needs in implicit conflict with his own. He may, however, have thought that because his district is the poorest, almost any amount allocated to it would be just even if other districts must thereby lose. Or he may have thought that the deliberation legitimately incorporated some sort of fight of all against all. We do not know whether the weapons he envisioned using in the fight are good arguments or the amassing of power through organization and votes, although we do know that he considered these fights and demands to be motivated by "good intentions."[20] Here we see little that relates to personal transformation. Returning to the practice enriched by theory, researchers might now ask the participants what transformations they have seen or experienced. What conception did they have before and after the deliberation of their own self-interest, their local group interests, the interests of other groups, the interests of the city as a whole, and the way all of these interact?

Three of the experiments reported in this volume – Porto Alegre, Kerala, and Chicago – employed "trainers" to help the citizens transform themselves in capacities not fully specified. Trainers could in theory help solve the paradox of participatory democracy that Kaufman identified. As Fung and Wright report, "Leading reformers in each of our experiments realized, or learned through disappointment, that most non-professionals lack the capacities to participate effectively in functionally-specific and empowered groups."[21] Returning to practice, it would be useful to find out precisely what capacities the non-professionals lacked and what the trainers who worked to improve the citizens' capacities in Porto Alegre, Kerala and Chicago thought they were doing. When the trainers give "training in democratic process,"[22] what do they think they are teaching? What did the citizens they trained think they were learning and why? What were the results of all this training in the deliberations themselves?

Based on their own observations of practice, democratic theorists have argued that democratic deliberation does and should transform "I" into "we."[23] Accordingly, one trainer in Porto Alegre comments explicitly that one function of the training

> is to preserve and help diffuse certain values. The participatory budget demands the construction of cooperation and solidarity, otherwise the logic of competition and "taking advantage" becomes established.[24]

We now want to ask: How does the trainer accomplish this task of constructing cooperation and solidarity? In what contexts does such a construction lead some people to fail to understand properly their own narrow self-interests? On reflection, when the trainers think through the goals and methods that they are teaching, do they have any hesitations or caveats they would like to introduce? What have they learned in practice? What do the citizens themselves think of this training? In the trainers' eyes (and other measures), do the groups trained in cooperation and solidarity engage in better deliberation than the untrained? What are the criteria for "better?" Did the citizens trained in cooperation and solidarity have more satisfying experiences or see themselves as better people after this training, or after the deliberations?[25]

Neither democratic theorists nor empirical political scientists or sociologists have much evidence on the actual, as opposed to the theoretical, effects of democratic transformations. These experiments provide one form of such evidence, in the form of retrospective and introspective reports. In Porto Alegre, for example, we read that participants "often" reported that the process "had compelled them to broaden their horizons."[26] One individual, who had the position of "delegate and councilor," reports that he or she became "a person who has to respond not only to your association but also to the district as a whole and the city as a whole." Since that time, the activist says, "I have worried about the city as a whole. I learned not to look only at the district, but that you have to look at the city as a whole."[27]

This transformation toward "largeness" of view, in the words of John Stuart Mill,[28] is one of the major positive transformations that Mill and later democratic theorists have predicted. In my own experience, transformations in this direction occur most often among those who have been in some way formally selected to be responsible for others. (The theory would predict, for example, such movement among those selected to be chair of a department.) Any such transformation undoubtedly also depends heavily on the norms that govern the interaction, including the norms inherent in the instructions given to those who are responsible for others. These norms and transformations are critical to promoting a just and efficient system of governance in which most citizens can rely on the basic goodwill and broader perspective of those to whom responsibility has been delegated. It would help to make explicit these norms and hopes for transformation. It would also help if citizens immersed in practice and researchers returning to it scrutinized these norms and any explicit training that promotes them for possibly imposing an understanding of the common good that implicitly benefits those with more power or follows the vision of "experts" in the field while marginalizing the experiences of the citizens themselves.

In Kerala, the organizers discovered that "there is nothing spontaneously democratic about a general assembly." They realized that they had to divide the assembly of several hundred people into small groups (it is not clear from the report how small), with a "semi-formal discussion format and provide a trained facilitator for each group."[29] This process took a great deal of time. It probably took money as well to organize "a hundred thousand volunteers" to facilitate these deliberations.[30] And it certainly took labor. Because in the first year "a significant proportion" of the local projects had technical and financial weaknesses,[31] retired technical experts and professionals were encouraged to volunteer to give the local groups technical assistance "at least one day a week."[32] The supply of voluntary labor, not surprisingly, fell short of what was needed.[33] In the third year of the project, a "statewide" training program was instituted to help task force members gain the technical information required to produce an effective local product. The resulting "elaborate training program . . . has become one of the largest non-formal education programs ever undertaken in India."[34] The personal transformations involved perhaps included only the accumulation of technical knowledge. But researchers returning to the field might investigate the degree to which lessons about deliberation were explicit or implicit in the more technical training, and particularly what the training for and by the facilitators implied about the relation between self-interest and solidarity.

These cases are better designed than any I know to elaborate and begin to test the theory that good deliberation can act as a school for democracy. As Fung and Wright point out, discovering whether and in what circumstances participants actually become "better deliberators" or "increase their disposition to be reasonable" will take "closer examination of actors' actual behavior."[35] We do not know at the moment how important or likely are the "independent desiderata"[36] of personal transformation and better deliberation. We do not even know exactly which transformations and deliberations are "better" and why. For now, simply recognizing that closer examination is required and gathering cases in which that closer examination can take place constitute major advances. We may now return to practice to ask, for example, whether the citizens themselves think that building solidarity is an important goal and, if so, what techniques develop reliable feelings of solidarity and what techniques build that solidarity with the whole at the expense of other values, such as recognition of one's own (or one's small group's) interest.

Even processes that at least one participant in one process thought were "really not designed to help people develop a new or redirected self-interest," such as the Habitat Conservation Planning process,[37] may have some transformative effects as a by-product.[38] Only attentive observation and questioning back in the field can bring to light the kinds of transformation these deliberations produce, if any, and the problems these transformations may entail – such as dampening an appropriate attention to self-interest.

Combining Self-Interest and the Common Good

Democratic theorists have not parsed out fully the appropriate relation in democracy between power motivated by narrow self-interest and power motivated by a concern for the common good. An easy way to handle this relation is simply to declare power motivated by narrow self-interest democratically illegitimate. Most theorists have taken this route, as have Fung and Wright, with their conclusion that a participant in EPG should vote (that is, exercise coercive power) not "for the option that best advances his self-interest, but rather for the choice that seems most reasonable."[39] This normative stance, however, makes illegitimate a good part of what goes on in the voting booth in most liberal democracies. The relatively recently forged theory of "adversary" democracy, by contrast, provides that when no common good can be forged and the choice devolves simply down to whose ox will be gored, I am normatively allowed to vote that his ox be chosen and he to vote that it be mine, so long as, in the long run, I win on some of these issues and he wins on some.[40]

In all existing liberal democracies some people vote on election day for what will benefit them, others vote for their view of the common good, and still others vote for some inchoate mixture of the two. As Brian Barry pointed out a while ago, this procedure mixes apples and oranges.[41] Barry suggested that in such circumstances everyone should vote his or her self-interest, so that the vote could become a rough gauge of which policy would bring the greatest good to the greatest number. His suggestion, based on what some people already think is the norm, did not catch on. Fung and Wright suggest, by contrast, that everyone should vote for the policy they think is "reasonable." Their suggestion, also based on what some people already think is the norm, is also unlikely to convince every voter. This difficult normative question is still open. No one has succeeded in making much normative sense of the mixed system that, as a consequence of these mixed norms, prevails in most Western democracies.

It is hard to find ways to count self-interested and non-self-interested votes in a common metric. It is equally hard to create good deliberations in which considerations of the good of the whole do not diminish appropriate considerations of self-interest and vice versa. It is particularly hard to create personal transformations in which participants' understandings of their selves and their interests become both more communal *and* more conflictual when appropriate. To develop a better understanding of each of these conundrums, we might usefully now return to practice to investigate what people think who are themselves engaged in an experiment in which the explicit instructions are to vote "not for the option that best advances your self-interest, but rather for the choice that seems most reasonable."

2 Incorporating Emotion

If emotional as well as rational commitments are required for people to experience the good of the whole even when their narrow self-interest conflicts with that good, then emotions must play a legitimate role in deliberation. Indeed, many theorists now agree that the simple equation of good deliberation with "reason" is false. Yet no one has fully parsed out what emotions a deliberation should discourage and encourage. Simply approving what psychologists call "positive" emotions and disapproving "negative" ones will not suffice, as we would expect most deliberations to be undermined by expressions of the "positive" joy felt in winning when someone else in the deliberation must lose, yet sometimes bolstered by "negative" anger directed at injustice. Participants in deliberation are often uncomfortable with the emotions used to express intensity of conviction or need, but few would want to exclude the emotions associated with altruism, group spirit, or self-sacrifice.

Judging the expression of emotion is further complicated by its role in challenging or reaffirming received statuses. Men, more educated participants, and anyone who takes the status quo position may find it easier than others to adopt a non-emotional style. Over time, the cultures and habitual practices of groups privileged in these ways may accustom their members to providing "reasons" for their actions, even when the actions are motivated by far more than the surface rationality that is adduced.[42] When this easy access to reason-giving seems to suppress other perspectives, and when emotional, sometimes angry, appeals are needed to draw attention to these perspectives, good deliberation requires developing and making explicit norms that allow "non-rational" forms of communication. Fung and Wright fail to ask how such forms of communication might count normatively as deliberation or might further the goals of deliberation in practice. In this they follow many earlier theorists and lay practitioners of deliberation, whose conceptions of a "deliberate" endeavor simply exclude most forms of emotional expression. Because in many cultures (particularly the Anglo-American) "reason" is associated with men and "emotion" derogatorily associated with women, feminist scholars have often been quickest to understand and explore the appropriate uses of emotion in deliberation.[43]

Over the course of our history, human beings have worked out many useful rules for "rational" discussion, including, for example, demands for logical consistency. We still need to work out some practical understandings for the appropriate use of emotions in deliberation. Returning to practice in a set of cases like this, which include differing national cultures and many differing subcultures, could further the inductive search for effective norms in the deliberative uses of emotion.

3 Incorporating Conflict

Good deliberation, as we have seen, requires trying to move toward consensus while retaining and refusing to downplay or suppress existing elements of genuine conflict, either in opinion or in interests.[44] This task is not easy. Future deliberators would benefit from understanding the practice of deliberating groups that have appropriately maintained both sides of this tension. In my experience, at least three factors contribute to a group's capacity to sustain the recognition, acceptance, and productive nurturing of conflict while searching for outcomes that will attract genuine consensus. These factors include cross-cutting cleavages, a mixture of relatively consensual and relatively conflictual issues on the agenda, and a membership whose experiences and personalities allow them to feel 1) equally at ease with both sharpening conflict and crafting compromise, and 2) equally at ease with both recognizing their own self-interest and experiencing the good of others as their own.

Groups with cross-cutting cleavages are probably more likely than groups with segmented interests to create a productive deliberative arena. Cross-cutting cleavages encourage individuals to ally first with one set of others and then with another set on different issues. This process allows each to see the others more in the round – as individuals (or groups) with recognizable weaknesses and strengths, forms of blindness and acuteness, and interests that both conflict and are congruent with their own. Cross-cutting cleavages also encourage informal consultation, because members of a group formed around one issue are likely to find in an opposing group friends or at least acquaintances with whom they are on working terms through alliances formed on another issue. Cross-cutting cleavages do not preclude the discussions within specific groups that help their members become more aware of their interests and their conflicts with other groups.[45] But cross-cutting patterns of interests tend to prevent those conflicts from becoming fatally entrenched through the familiar process of exaggerating similarities among the in-group and differences with the out-group.[46]

A second factor, collective decision-making on problems susceptible to solutions that are good for all, also adds an important leaven to problems in which important interests conflict. A town meeting that has discussed the question of the right materials for the new fire department building, resolving the issue when one participant tells of a sale on materials in the next town, creates in this small way a history of successful action and mutual respect on which it can draw when it reaches more divisive issues. In an academic department, when people work together on a problem to which they can come up with a successful solution – even a relatively small problem such as the timing of graduate examinations – they often acquire a mutual respect that serves them well when their interests clash on another issue.

Political theorists, however, sometimes divide the issues before a polity into two groups – "administrative" and "political." They consider "administrative" all the issues that require only investigation and consensual decision. They consider "political" only the issues derived from conflicting opinions or interests. This division may serve useful analytic purposes, but in practice, most productive politics mixes both. Moreover, more consensus arises in "politics" and more disagreement in "administration" than many accounts would have us believe. Most participants in the cases in this volume would find it strange to have only their more conflictual (or only their more consensual) issues demarcated as "political."

In my experience, productive deliberation requires mixing problems that begin with conflicts in opinion and interest with other problems that begin with open questions whose resolution is likely to produce consensus, mutual respect and a productive history. At least in the United States Congress, in state legislatures, in town meetings, and in department meetings – the only deliberative assemblies with which I am familiar – the dynamics of decision-making include both kinds of problems, not demarcated into two separate groups but intermingled in ways that I believe are healthy for deliberation and decision-making. Here, as with cross-cutting cleavages, it would be useful to have reports from practice, in a range of participatory democracies, on the degree to which successes in less conflictual areas lay the emotional and cognitive groundwork for successes in the more conflictual ones.

The kind of deliberation in which a group engages has much to do with the kind and degree of internal conflict it expects to face. The cases in this volume do not usually specify whether the deliberating group expected to end its decisions by a vote or by consensus, or how conflictual they expected the process to be. One would expect these dimensions to affect the kind of deliberation that ensued, as would whether or not the deliberation was expected to end in a binding decision that affected the participants directly or whether the result was advisory and more general. Future researchers might note the ways deliberations are affected by the expected decision rule, the likelihood of significant conflict, and the degree to which the deliberation produces a binding decision.

Finally, deliberation benefits greatly from many different individual capacities – to engage without fear in a process of making conflict more visible and clear; to think through and craft compromises acceptable to others; to probe and understand one's own self-interests; and to experience the good of others and the whole as one's own. Some individuals have the capacity to say what they think in a conflict in a way that does not leave lasting wounds. Others (particularly in a large group, where one has to screw up one's courage to speak) may not speak up at all until they "get mad," but then are not in full control of their words and phrase their thoughts in extreme language.[47]

Returning to practice, the trainers of the deliberative groups featured in this volume might have useful thoughts on what individual capacities facilitate good deliberation, how to build these individual capacities, and how to craft group norms that facilitate the building and expression of these capacities. The capacities and problems involved are likely to take very different forms in different cultures.

4 Incorporating Inequalities

Individual differences in the ability to articulate strong disagreement in ways that do not provoke enmity are only one example of the kinds of individual differences that produce inequalities in influence, and even power, in deliberative groups. Other differences not frequently noted include differences in fear of conflict, differences in fear of speaking, and differences in whether one is on the intense or diffuse side of a conflict.

In an adversary framework, inequalities are most serious when they coincide with differences in interest and produce inequalities of power. Because adversary democracies settle issues by, ideally, taking a vote in which each individual's interests carry equal weight, inequalities that might, for example, disproportionately prevent the carriers of one kind of interest from showing up for a vote undermine the normative legitimacy of the final decision.

In a deliberative framework, inequalities are most serious when they coincide with differences in perspective that would help in producing good solutions to communal problems. Because deliberations ideally take from each relevant perspective the insights necessary to solve a common problem, inequalities that prevent one or another perspective from emerging in the deliberation undermine the normative legitimacy and the practical usefulness of the final decision.

In a participatory framework that emphasizes individual growth and equal respect, any factor is important that either prevents individuals from taking advantage of the opportunities for participation that will help them develop their faculties or makes some individuals feel less respected than others.

Inequalities that have none of these consequences may be relatively safely ignored.

Fung and Wright thoughtfully enumerate many of the problems with inequality in deliberative democracies.[48] The cases suggest that training may provide some potential solutions. But training is not likely, for example, to overcome major differences in power outside (and usually therefore inside) the assembly. Nor is it likely to overcome deep individual differences such as fear of conflict or the ability to handle conflict. At least in the United States, many people avoid talking about and being involved in "politics" because they want to have friendly, non-conflictual relations with their neighbors. People in New England towns avoid going to town meetings because when you get involved in conflict, "you make a lot of enemies."[49] As a result, what looks like "apathy" is sometimes a conscious choice not to get involved in "a disagreeable situation." When training cannot eliminate inequalities such as these, it helps to have a theory – based in aggregative, deliberative, and participatory values – as to which inequalities produce the most serious problems for democracy.

For example, even with training, the perpetual and continuing entrance of untrained and unsocialized individuals into a deliberative process creates a source of frustration for many more seasoned participants. In Porto Alegre "one of the more experienced activists" described the patience required in terms "that tell of an activist calling:"

> Those who come for the first time are welcome, we have a lot of patience for them . . . we let them make demands during technical meetings, they can speak their mind and their anxieties. We have patience for it because we were like that once.[50]

These sentiments are fine from an experienced activist, committed ideologically to the process and to bringing in new people. One would not expect the average member of the group, who had made a huge effort in the way of childcare and other arrangements to get there that evening, to show such patience. Ongoing participatory democracies with complex questions to handle must find some way of restricting at least some of the "technical meetings" and often many others to those who already understand most of the issues.[51] The major inequalities that result require explicit justification. Future deliberators would benefit from knowing more about the techniques that present practitioners use to limit participation and the justifications they advance.

5 Incorporating Informal Representation

I suggest thinking of the individuals who do attend deliberative assemblies as informal representatives of those who do not attend. As with formal representation, these representatives ideally ought to meet the criterion for adversary democracy that conflicting interests be represented in proportion to their numbers in the population. They ought to meet the criterion for deliberative democracy that useful perspectives be represented in sufficient critical mass and internal variety to inform the deliberation on relevant issues. Finally, they ought to meet the participatory criteria that the arrangements of the polity give all citizens an opportunity to develop their faculties and that inequalities in participation do not generate, or map heavily onto, inequalities in respect. We must apply this three-part analysis to the cases at hand to understand whether these assemblies advance an acceptable form of informal representation or whether they reproduce and amplify harmful underlying inequalities.

If we think of those who attend the meetings as informal representatives of those who do not, normative issues familiar from the study of formal representation – such as transparency and accountability – become important.[52] Here too, however, we have much to learn. Transparency is not always good. When complex bargains must be struck, closed doors let negotiators speak freely, try out potential solutions that on reflection they may not want to stick with, and forge relationships out of the spotlight of publicity. Accountability is also problematic. Not everyone attending a meeting will want to see him or herself as the informal and accountable representative of those who do not attend. Attenders pay a cost in time, energy, and the emotional costs of interaction, even if they get many benefits back. They are likely to think that the people who fail to attend are shirkers, who "sit back and complain, but [do not] do anything about it."[53] It may be going too far to ask the attenders to change their behavior in order to represent more accurately the needs and desires of those who do not attend. In that case, the only answer is to structure the participatory assemblies to attract in some way more of those who would otherwise not attend (e.g. dividing the assembly into small groups, as in Kerala, to facilitate women's participation). Creating more formal representative arrangements may serve a similar purpose.

In some of the cases reported here, formal representation plays a role unforeseen or rejected in the original participatory vision. In Porto Alegre, some individuals "wound up being elected" as delegates of the participatory budget.[54] In Chicago, many members of the school boards were elected in a formal election. Community leaders who decide to enter and who survive this process do not usually have the same personality traits or skills as those who decide not to become active. Yet in the right circumstances the bodies to which they are elected can meet the adversary, deliberative, and participatory criteria for representation. The practice in these cases and the conclusions of both their elected and non-elected participants might illuminate when various forms of formal and informal representation best meet those criteria.

III Theory from Practice

The moment at which individuals are engaged, with good intentions, in a self-conscious experiment to deepen democracy is a moment when theorists can learn from their experiences. When activists and lay-people committed to the ideal of democracy put their lives on the line, create new institutions and try to make those institutions work, their struggles may teach both those who participate in them and the theorists who draw lessons from these experiments.

One kind of moment is particularly productive for theory. It is the moment when people insist more strongly than usual on putting an ideal into practice. Insisting on actualizing an ideal almost always puts strain on a system, because most systems have evolved incrementally to work on a less than ideal level. Pushing the ideal increases the pressure on the system, and that pressure often makes the underlying relations clearer, the way clenching your fist makes the veins stand out from the flesh.

In this volume Fung and Wright and their co-authors have seized the experimental moment, analyzed the patterns of democratic interaction, compared the practice to the ideal, and formulated an original theory of participatory democracy that reflects the lessons learned both recently and over the past thirty years. The next stage in practice and thought is in the hands of the people who are still putting parts of their everyday lives into the task. It is in the hands of future researchers, who can return to learn from the people immersed in the process. It is also in the hands of the readers of this volume – whether academic theorists, trainers and facilitators, participants in similar deliberations, students, or casual readers – whose own experiences and insights may help improve our still fledgling understanding of how to deliberate better. The issues need all the thought and practice they can get.

Notes

* Adams Professor of Political Leadership and Democratic Values at the John F. Kennedy School of Government, Harvard University.

1. C. Wright Mills, *The Power Elite*, New York: Oxford University Press (1959, originally 1956), p. 5.

2. "The Port Huron Statement," in Paul Jacobs and Saul Landau, eds., *The New Radicals*, New York: Random House (1966, originally published 1962), p. 156.

3. Arnold Kaufman, "Human Nature and Participatory Democracy," in Carl J. Fridrich, ed., *Responsibility: NOMOS III*, New York: Lieber-Atherton (1960), p. 277.

4. Arnold Kaufman, "Participatory Democracy: Ten Years Later," *La Table Ronde*, no. 251–252 (1968), pp. 216–28, reprinted in William E. Connolly, ed., *The Bias of Pluralism*, New York: Atherton Press (1971).

5. Learning through experience has also produced innovations in advocacy groups (Carmen Sirianni and Lewis Friedland, *Civic Innovation in America*, Berkeley: University of California Press (2001)) and in smaller and more radical forms of participatory democracy (see Jo Freeman, "The Origins of the Women's Liberation Movement," *American Journal of Sociology*, vol. 78 (1973), pp. 792–811; Jane Mansbridge, *Beyond Adversary Democracy*, Chicago: University of Chicago Press (1980); Stephanie Riger, "Challenges of Success: Stages of Growth in Feminist Organizations," *Feminist Studies*, vol. 20 (1994), pp. 275–301; Myra Marx Ferree and Patricia Yancey Martin, eds, *Feminist Organizations: Harvest of the New Political Women's Movement*, Philadelphia, PA: Temple University Press (1995); Robin Leidner, "Stretching the Boundaries of Liberalism: Democratic Innovation in a Feminist Organization," *Signs*, vol. 16 (1991), pp. 263–89; Robin Leidner, "Constituency, Accountability, and Deliberation: Reshaping Democracy in the National Women's Studies Association," *National Women's Studies Association Journal*, vol. 5 (1993), pp. 4–27; Carmen Sirianni, "Learning Pluralism: Democracy and Diversity in Feminist Organizations," in Ian Shapiro and John Chapman, eds., *Democratic Community: NOMOS XXXV*, New York: New York University Press (1993a); Carmen Sirianni, "Feminist Pluralism and Democratic Learning: the Politics of Citizenship in the National Women's Studies Association," *National Women's Studies Association Journal*, vol. 5 (1993b), pp. 367–84).

6. For these criteria, and other more problematic criteria such as publicity, accountability, freedom, equality, and aiming at a rationally motivated consensus, see Iris Marion Young, *Inclusion and Democracy*, Oxford: Oxford University Press (2000); Amy Gutmann and Dennis Thompson, *Democracy and Disagreement*, Cambridge, MA: Harvard University Press (1996) and other works cited in Jane Mansbridge, "On the Idea that Participation Makes Better Citizens," in Stephen L. Elkin and Karol E. Soltan, eds., *Citizen Competence and Democratic Institutions*, University Park: Pennsylvania State University Press (1999), pp. 221–7. For an early study of deliberation in practice, see Tali Mendelberg and John Oleske, "Race and Public Deliberation," *Political Communication*, vol. 17 (2000), pp. 169–91; for a summary of the psychological literature, Tali Mendelberg, "The Deliberative Citizen: Theory and Evidence," in Michael Delli Carpini, Leonie Huddy, and Robert Y. Shapiro, eds., *Research in Micropolitics, Volume 6*, New York, Elsevier Press (forthcoming).

7. E.g. Jürgen Habermas, *Theory of Communicative Action*, trans. Thomas McCarthy, Boston: Beacon Press (1984) and Joshua Cohen, "Deliberation and Democratic Legitimacy," in A. Hamlin and Phillip Petit, eds., *The Good Polity: Normative Analysis of the State*, Cambridge: Basil Blackwell (1989).

8. On the quality of deliberation see note 6 above and notes 43 and 44 below. On the legitimacy of procedures, see among others Charles Beitz, *Political Equality: An Essay in Democratic Theory*, Princeton: Princeton University Press (1989); Robert Dahl, *Democracy and its Critics*, New Haven: Yale University Press (1989); Mansbridge, *Beyond Adversary Democracy*. On the justice of outcomes, see among others John Rawls, *A Theory of Justice*, Cambridge, MA: Harvard University Press (1971).

9. In a direct parallel, Jon Elster, in "Selfishness and Altruism," in Jane Mansbridge, ed., *Beyond Self-Interest*, Chicago: University of Chicago Press (1990), p. 45, points out that self-interest is in one sense "more fundamental" than altruism. Logically, if no one had "first-order, selfish pleasures," altruists would have no one toward whom to direct their altruism.

10. James Buchanan and Gordon Tullock, *The Calculus of Consent: Logical Foundations of Constitutional Democracy*, Ann Arbor, Michigan: University of Michigan Press (1965), for example, recommend "sidepayments" to create consensus in zero-sum situations. See also Lani Guinier, *The Tyranny of the Majority: Fundamental Fairness in Representative Democracy*, New York: Free Press (1995) and Arend Lijphart, *Patterns of Democracy*, New Haven: Yale University Press (1999) for solutions such as taking turns or proportional outcomes.

11. Habermas, *Theory of Communicative Action*; Fung and Wright, Introduction to this volume, pp. 18–19.

12. Jerry Harvey, *The Abilene Paradox*, Lexington, MA: Lexington Books (1988), pp. 107–110.

13. Irving L. Janis, *Groupthink: Psychological Studies of Policy Decisions and Fiascos*, Boston: Houghton Mifflin (1982).

14. For the ideal of absence of power in deliberation, see e.g. Habermas, *Theory of Communicative Action*, p. 25. For the distinction between power and influence, see Stephen Lukes, *Power: A Radical View*, London: Macmillan (1974), drawing on Peter Bachrach and Morton Baratz, "Decisions and Non-Decisions: An Analytical Framework," *American Political Science Review*, 57 (1963), pp. 632–42. Lukes points out that influence applies in cases of common interest, power almost always in cases of conflicting interest. "Force" here refers to any form of constraint. It need not be intentional or noticed, and does not include "influence." For the legitimacy of unequal influence and majority rule, see Jack Knight and James Johnson, "Aggregation and Deliberation: On the Possibility of Democratic Legitimacy," *Political Theory*, no. 22 (1994), pp. 277–96, Jack Knight and James Johnson, "What Sort of Political Equality Does Democratic Deliberation Require?" in James Bohman and William Rehg, eds., *Deliberative Democracy*, Cambridge, MA: MIT Press (1968), and Mansbridge, *Beyond Adversary Democracy*.

15. Peter Bachrach, "Interest, Participation and Democratic Theory," in J. Roland Pennock and John W. Chapman, eds., *Participation in Politics: NOMOS XVI*, New York: Lieber-Atherton (1974).

16. Fung and Wright, Introduction to this volume, pp. 17–18. "Reasonable" is a less loaded and even more ambiguous word than "just." It is therefore probably more useful in a practical context in which both theorists and participants are engaged in an incremental search for the appropriate norms.

17. Baiocchi, this volume, p. 60.

18. Ibid.

19. Ibid.

20. Ibid.

21. Fung and Wright, Introduction to this volume, p. 29.

22. Ibid.

23. E.g. Benjamin Barber, *Strong Democracy*, Berkeley: University of California Press (1984).

24. Baiocchi, this volume, p. 56.

25. Research with Deliberative Opinion Polls is making major headway on this issue (see Robert C. Luskin and James Fishkin, "Does Deliberation Make Better Citizens?," paper presented at the meeting of the European Consortium for Political Research, Turin, Italy (March 22–27, 2002)). Yet in the immediate future no one is likely to get sufficient funding to mount a research design in the field with sufficient numbers of cases and a control group to measure actual transformations in citizen attitudes, character, or behavior as a result of participation in existing democratic institutions. Most participatory theorists since Tocqueville and many simple observers of events such as jury duty think that participation in collective decisions that affect oneself and others does increase, as Kaufman hoped, one's "powers of thought, feeling and action." But because these changes are relatively subtle, we are only just beginning (with the Deliberative Opinion Poll data) to be able to document them with the existing tools of social science (Mansbridge, "On the Idea that Participation Makes Better Citizens"). We can, however, measure relatively easily whether or not people think in a given instance that they have had a satisfying or transformative experience.

26. Baiocchi, this volume, p. 61.

27. Ibid.

28. John Stuart Mill, *Considerations on Representative Government*, ed. with an Introduction by Currin V. Shields, Indianapolis: Bobbs-Merrill (1958, originally published 1861), p. 53.

29. Thomas Isaac and Heller, this volume, p. 91.

30. Fung and Wright, Introduction to this volume, p. 14.

31. Thomas Isaac and Heller, this volume, p. 95.

32. Ibid.

33. Ibid., p. 98.

34. Ibid., p. 83.

35. Fung and Wright, Introduction to this volume, p. 32.

36. Ibid., p. 27; Thomas Isaac and Heller, this volume, p. 100.

37. Thomas, this volume, p. 159.

38. Jon Elster, in *Sour Grapes: Studies in the Subversion of Rationality*, Cambridge: Cambridge University Press (1983), pp. 91–100, rightly points out that improvements in citizen skills and character are a "by-product" of processes primarily designed to make good decisions. He is wrong, in my view, in discounting the value of that by-product on the grounds that it is not the central aim of the endeavor. Because participatory procedures have great costs as by-products as well as gains, a full analysis of their worth should take into consideration the probably important by-products of improved citizen skills and character, even though these cannot easily be measured.

39. Fung and Wright, Introduction to this volume, pp. 17–18.

40. When one group wins all the time, majority rule on the basis of self-interest cannot be legitimate, and must be replaced in adversary theory with some form of power-sharing or consensual bargain (Mansbridge, *Beyond Adversary Democracy*, pp. 265–8; Arend Lijphart, *Patterns of Democracy*, New Haven: Yale University Press (1999)).

41. Brian Barry, *Political Argument*, London: Routledge & Kegan Paul (1965), pp. 62–5.

42. Iris Marion Young, "Communication and the Other: Beyond Deliberative Democracy," in Seyla Benhabib, ed., *Democracy and Difference: Contesting the Boundaries of the Political*, Princeton: Princeton University Press (1996).

43. For problems with the traditional distinction between reason and emotion, see Amélie Oksenberg Rorty, "Varieties of Rationality, Varieties of Emotion," *Social Science Information*, vol. 24 (1985), pp. 343–53 and Martha Craven Nussbaum, "Emotions and Women's Capabilities," in Martha Craven Nussbaum and Jonathan Glover, eds., *Women, Culture, and Development*, Oxford: Oxford University Press (1995). For the association between the male/female and the reason/emotion dichotomies in twenty-eight cultures, see John E. Williams and Deborah L. Best, *Measuring Sex Stereotypes*, Beverly Hills, CA: Sage (1982), reanalyzed in Jane Mansbridge, "Feminism and Democratic Community," in John W. Chapman and Ian Shapiro, eds., *Democratic Community: NOMOS XXXV*, New York: New York University Press (1993). For more detailed discussions of the appropriate role for emotions in deliberation, see Lynn M. Sanders, "Against Deliberation," *Political Theory*, vol. 25 (1997), pp. 347–76; Iris Marion Young, "Communication and the Other: Beyond Deliberative Democracy," in Seyla Benhabib, ed., *Democracy and Difference: Contesting the Boundaries of the Political*, Princeton: Princeton University Press (1996); Iris Marion Young, *Inclusion and Democracy*, Oxford: Oxford University Press (2000); Jane Mansbridge, "A Deliberative Theory of Interest Representation," in Mark Petracca, ed., *The Politics of Interests: Interest Groups Transformed*, Boulder, CO: Westview Press (1992); Jane Mansbridge, "On the Contested Nature of the Public Good," in Walter W. Powell and Elisabeth S. Clemens, eds., *Private Action and the Public Good*, New Haven: Yale University Press (1998). Young in particular argues for the virtues of "greeting," or public acknowledgement; "rhetoric," in the non-manipulative sense; and "narrative," or storytelling. On emotion see also George E. Marcus, *The Sentimental Citizen: Emotion in Democratic Politics*, University Park: Pennsylvania State University Press (2002); Douglas Walton, *The Place of Emotion in Argument*, University Park: Pennsylvania State University Press (1992); Jon Elster, *Alchemies of the Mind: Rationality and the Emotions*, Cambridge: Cambridge University Press (1999a); Jon Elster, *Strong Feelings: Emotion, Addiction, and Human Behaviour*, Cambridge, MA: MIT Press (1999b); Michael Lewis and Jeanette Haviland-Jones, eds., *Handbook of Emotions*, New York: Guilford (2000).

44. On the importance of conflict, see in particular Iris Marion Young, *Inclusion and Democracy*, Oxford: Oxford University Press (2000), Jack Knight and James Johnson, "Aggregation and Deliberation: On the Possibility of Democratic Legitimacy"; on

retaining suppressible conflict, see Bonnie Honig, *Political Theory and the Displacement of Politics*, Ithaca: Cornell University Press (1993).

45. On the uses of "enclaves" of the like-minded, see Jane Mansbridge, "Using Power/Fighting Power: The Polity," in Seyla Benhabib, ed., *Democracy and Difference*, Princeton: Princeton University Press (1995) and Young, *Inclusion and Democracy*, p. 143.

46. John C. Turner, in *Rediscovering the Social Group: A Self-Categorization Theory*, Oxford: Basil Blackwell (1987), points out that the phenomenon of "meta-contrast" – highlighting similarities within the group and differences with outsiders – is inherent in the conceptual framing of a "group." He also shows that the more salient the self-categorization, the greater the "perceptual accentuation of intra-class similarities and inter-class differences" (ibid., p. 49). See also Marilynn B. Brewer and Rupert J. Brown, "Intergroup Relations," in D. Gilbert, S. Fiske, and G. Lindzey, eds., *Handbook of Social Psychology* (1998) and Michael C. Dawson, *Behind the Mule: Race and Class in American Politics*, Princeton: Princeton University Press (1994).

47. Mansbridge, *Beyond Adversary Democracy*.

48. See also Young, *Inclusion and Democracy*, especially "Democracy and Justice."

49. Mansbridge, *Beyond Adversary Democracy*, p. 64. More than a quarter of the people I interviewed of a random sample in a relatively typical small town suggested that the conflict they experienced in town meetings upset them. See also John R. Hibbing and Elizabeth Theiss-Morse, *Stealth Democracy: Americans' Beliefs about How Government Should Work*, Cambridge: Cambridge University Press (2002) for fears of conflict in U.S. democracy.

50. Baiocchi, this volume, p. 69.

51. On the disadvantages of repeating decisions when newcomers join a group, see essays in Patrick Coy, ed., *Conflicts and Consensus Decision-Making in Social Movements*, Volume 24/5 of *Research in Social Movements, Conflicts and Change*, Elsevier Science/JAI Press (forthcoming).

52. See Fung and Wright, Introduction to this volume, pp. 36–7.

53. Mansbridge, *Beyond Adversary Democracy*, p. 351, n. 2.

54. Baiocchi, this volume, p. 61.

7

Reflections on What Makes Empowered Participatory Governance Happen

Rebecca Neaera Abers*

The case study literature on experiments in direct citizen participation in governance is on the whole pessimistic. There are, loosely speaking, two basic critiques. The first is that such experiments typically are not "empowered" when the state initiates them. Since Selznick's study of citizen participation in the Tennessee Valley Authority,[1] numerous observers have noted that supposedly participatory fora tend to have little actual power, serving instead as spaces in which governments create the illusion of popular control while real decisions continue to be made elsewhere. Even when politicians in office are ideologically committed to promoting participatory decision-making, they often find practical and political limitations to doing so. Put simply, those accustomed to influencing decisions – political and economic elites, bureaucrats, and so on – resist losing control. Since they are powerful, they usually succeed.

The second critique is that such experiments are not actually "participatory." They do not bring "ordinary citizens" into the public sphere, but, rather, draw the same groups that normally have influence over decision-making. The poor are less likely to participate, not only because they lack time and resources, but also because they do not perceive participating in such fora as worthwhile. Instead, those with more money, stronger organizations, and more information tend to dominate.

Three of the four case studies presented in this volume (with the HCP case as an exception) are examples that apparently counter the pessimistic tone of this literature. Yet, with the exception of the article by

Why should govts delegate power?

Fung, the case studies provide little insight into how deliberative decision-making is politically possible. Here I believe we must return to the
two central critiques just mentioned: why would governments transfer
decision-making power to deliberative spaces in which "ordinary
people" have influence and why would those ordinary people, most of
whom have little political experience beyond the occasional vote, voluntarily subject themselves to time-consuming and often frustrating
deliberative processes?

While most of the studies in this volume touch on both of these questions, none answers both fully. Baiocchi discusses why the participatory
budget attracts women and the poor but does not satisfactorily explain
why the government would give so much power to them. Thomas Isaac
and Heller pay more attention to the politics of the participatory
process, noting that the reforms fit into a strategy for increasing political support for the CPM in Kerala, but do not explain what motivated
so many people to participate in the Campaign. Thomas's study clearly
shows how the lack of government commitment to promoting participation by "ordinary people" limits the likelihood that HCPs will actually exemplify EPG, but does not explore why, given the chance, such
people might actually want to participate. Fung goes most in depth in
analyzing both aspects, telling the "political history" of the Chicago
reforms and showing that neighborhoods and school zones with
greater problems and needs were best able to mobilize participation.
But he does not explain why the reforms became politically robust (why
did they last?), nor does he explore how people in needy neighborhoods
became convinced that their problems might be addressed through
participatory fora.

With these comments, I hope to contribute to the discussion of EPG
initiated in this volume, using my own research on the participatory
budget in Porto Alegre. I argue that the success of participatory institutions depends on a dual process of commitment-building. Unless both
state actors (ranging from politicians to bureaucrats) and ordinary
people are motivated to support, take part in, and respect EPG experiments, those policies are unlikely to become either empowered or
participatory.

I Participation as an Alternative Political Strategy

Case studies of participatory experiments suggest that even when governments have the "political will" to create participatory mechanisms
of decision-making, their efforts create political and practical burdens

that most governments cannot withstand. Politically, the attempt to transfer power to fora in which "ordinary people" have influence usually means taking power away from those that both have it and also possess the ability to resist such changes. In Brazil, a number of PT municipal administrations with participatory platforms faced devastating boycotts from the media and from economic groups that disapproved of the policies. The bureaucracy also usually resists handing over decisions to people they perceive as having no technical expertise. Practical problems also occur, especially when the government administration is inexperienced and under-funded: participatory decision-making requires money to organize the process and financial, operational and legal capacity to implement its results. In Brazil, participatory budget experiences were undermined in several cities run by the PT after the first round of discussions, when participants made colossal lists of investment demands that eclipsed financial resources.[2]

Porto Alegre avoided this fate because participatory decision-making functioned there as a political asset to the administration instead of operating as a "burden to be overcome." Not fully a result of political intentions, over the course of the first administration (1989–92) the participatory budget became a central part of the PT's strategy for re-election. Put simply, rather than attempting to compete on traditional grounds, where favor exchanges and pork barrel politics rally support, the Porto Alegre administration successfully built an alternative political coalition.

In the first place, the policy responded to the demands of neighborhood leaders who had traditionally relied on clientelist favor-exchange mechanisms by focussing initially on community-based infrastructure. Thus gaining the support of neighborhood leaders, a large portion of whom were linked to the populist–clientelist opposition party (the PDT), the administration gained bargaining power with the city assembly to pass critical tax legislation that increased city revenues. This, in turn, enabled the administration to continue to attend to the material demands of participants.

Second, a key sector of the economic elite – the construction companies – provided veiled support to the administration (also pressuring the city assembly to support property-tax increases) because they benefited from massive and unprecedented investments in public works. To acquire this support, the administration made a critical decision not to reject alternative proposals for construction often supported by the Left, such as working with local labor cooperatives.

Third, and possibly most importantly, the policy acquired the support of a middle class that wished for a government associated with social justice, transparency, and the battle against corruption. Certainly, the fact that the policy was initiated at a political moment when major national corruption scandals (such as the one that culminated in the impeachment of the nation's president in 1992) had mobilized huge street demonstrations throughout the country. The wave of popular optimism about eliminating corruption certainly benefited the administration.

The fact that the participatory budget gained international attention over the course of the second administration further increased its popularity among the middle class. The administration worked hard, and successfully, to build an image as an "international innovator," bringing famous intellectuals from around the world to highly publicized events. Symptomatically, expressions like "Porto Alegre: The Capital of Democracy" appeared on billboards, pamphlets, and the administration's Internet homepage, clearly targeting middle-class public opinion.

Fourth, and more subtly, the policy helped the government coordinate its actions and contributed to the PT's reputation for administrative competence. Here, centralization of all budget decisions by the Municipal Budget Council was essential. Traditionally, in Porto Alegre (as in most Brazilian cities), city agencies had a great deal of autonomy to use their budget allocations as they wished. To facilitate budget discussions with the Council, the administration created mechanisms to organize information and control agency spending. Perhaps surprisingly for a North American audience, it was in the context of the participatory budget that, for the first time, the administration created a municipal information system that tracked expenditures in all city agencies. A new Planning Office with direct ties to the mayor increased the authority of the Council to ensure that the agencies implemented its decisions. The result was that the participatory process, rather than complicating city governance, actually helped bring a highly fragmented administration under central control.

The administration would not have been able to increase its governance capacity through the participatory budget were it not for the program's eminent practicality. The administration began with decisions well within its administrative competence and with small-scale public works that required little external funding or technical capacity. Furthermore, the administration was able, over the course of its first terms, to significantly increase city revenues, partly as a result of Constitutional changes that increased transfers from the state and federal levels and partly as a result of the tax legislation mentioned above. Only after the policy gained momentum on this relatively simple and small foundation were large public works, and the non-capital components of the budget, included in the scope of the participatory budget.

These political successes brought re-election to the PT and legitimacy to participatory decision-making in Porto Alegre. These factors, in turn, allowed the government to create a number of "sectoral" participatory decision-making fora in areas such as housing, human rights, city planning, and so on. This process seems to be completely different from the "big-bang" dynamic described by Thomas Isaac and Heller in Kerala, in which a massive participatory campaign was inaugurated in a single year. In Porto Alegre, a city-wide system of participatory governance grew and expanded from a relatively modest endeavor that worked.

II Participation as Worth the Effort

Key to understanding why that relatively modest endeavor worked so well is that the community-based infrastructure of the participatory budget in its early form attracted participants. Baiocchi's study confirms my own research: the participatory budget drew the poor into the decision-making process. The participants were on average poorer and less formally educated than the population as a whole and poor regions of the city participated with more intensity than middle-class regions. In the first years of the policy, a few regions of the city that had strong histories of neighborhood organizing participated most intensely, but over time, impoverished regions with little prior history of civic organizing came to participate with greater intensity. In fact, the policy helped build new participatory civic associations in areas of the city previously dominated by clientelist-neighborhood politics.

My own explanation of this pattern supports Baiocchi's: the participatory budget addressed the needs that the urban poor prioritized even before the policy was initiated. Mobilizing participants, which is usually difficult where interests are diffuse (such as for environmental protection, economic planning, and the like) was relatively easy in Porto Alegre because the program initially focussed on local issues that were important to neighborhood residents. Just as in Chicago, where crime-ridden neighborhoods had no problem attracting participants, there was no need to convince poor Porto Alegre residents that basic sanitation, flood control, street pavement, bus service, schools, and health posts were important to their lives.

We must keep in mind, however, that the Porto Alegre poor had little access to information about government actions, that the electronic media made no effort to inform them, and that in general, the urban poor in Brazil are pessimistic (with good reason) about the will and capacity of governments to respond to their needs. How, then, did unorganized neighborhood residents know that participating in the budget assemblies might actually be worth it? Two factors help explain why the budget policy was successful at mobilizing neighborhoods that did not previously have strong civic associations.

The first is that the budget policy itself had a "demonstration effect." In the early years of the policy, the main participants and beneficiaries of the policies were historically organized neighborhood associations. As highly visible public works – such as paved roads – were built in these neighborhoods, residents of less organized neighborhoods recognized that participation actually yielded returns. This reflects again on the thematic focus of the policy: visible infrastructure projects that could be implemented within a year.

Second, the administration hired activists from neighborhood movements to help organize the process. When neighborhood residents came to the administration to demand infrastructure, they were connected with community workers who helped them call meetings to organize participation in the following year's budget process. In many cases, they visited neighborhoods that had not yet participated, sought out potential leaders and helped them organize from scratch. The literature on urban social movements has always noted the key importance of "external agents" for mobilizing groups with few resources and little access to information. In Porto Alegre, the government itself created a band of community organizers that played this role.

III From Self-Interest to Deliberation

It should be clear that my approach to participation attempts to connect institutional change to interests. It seems most likely that EPG will work when both government and participants are convinced that a participatory system will benefit their interests: to build political support on the one hand and to resolve perceived problems on the other. This leads me to conclude with some reflections about the link between self-interest and deliberation.

In their introductory chapter, Fung and Wright seem at times to distinguish quite harshly between deliberation and decision processes characterized by competition among interests. I would argue that deliberative processes are most successful, however, when they are initiated, at least, by self-interest. In the Porto Alegre example, people are not drawn into the process because they wish to deliberate, but because they wish to get infrastructure for their own neighborhoods, to improve their lives. Typically, new participants have almost no perception and little concern for other neighborhoods' needs. They mobilize their neighbors because the more people that go to the meetings, the more likely they will be able to win the prioritizing vote that determines which neighborhoods will benefit first. That is, the participatory budget has an extremely competitive component which is precisely what gives it its vitality: if it did not provide the prospective of providing returns to their specific needs or concerns, most people would not go to the meetings. The same, I am sure, is true for the other cases described in this volume.

Here the importance of participatory fora as civic learning spaces is critical. Through the participatory process itself, people begin to perceive the needs of others, develop some solidarity, and conceptualize their own interests more broadly. Forced to confront their needs with others, argument and reason come to the fore, although usually not totally replacing "strategic bargaining that is intended to give maximum advantage to one's own interests."[3] I doubt very much that purely deliberative processes ever occur in participatory fora, except where issues are not particularly contentious. Nevertheless, in the Porto Alegre fora I studied, deliberation became more and more common over time as participants gained experience with public debate. Competitive participation, I would argue, initiates a learning process from which deliberation results, and which leads to continued learning as participants develop their capacity to argue and reason. Or, put simply, to get deliberation, you need self-interest.

I highlight this fact because all too often idealistic designers of participatory processes fall into a trap. Requiring that decision-making result from reason and solidarity, rather than self-interests, usually means that very few "ordinary people" will be motivated to participate. Critics of the Porto Alegre participatory budget, for example, complain that the process focusses too much on the immediate and the local. Yet the portrait I just drew suggests that it is precisely this focus that attracts people into the budget fora. The real problem is not that in policy arenas where the interests of "ordinary people" are apparent, self-interest will dominate over deliberation. It is that ordinary people are much less likely to participate in policy arenas where interests are diffuse.

In Brazil, for example, there is a growing trend to create "Watershed Committees" that bring together government agencies, big water users, and civic groups to discuss water policy. One of the main difficulties these committees face is how to mobilize "ordinary people" who do not perceive water supply and water quality as major problems. Not surprisingly, the committees work best in places where pollution and scarcity have reached dramatic proportions, while in areas where there is great need for preventative measures to avoid such problems in the future, they face greater difficulty in getting the general public involved. These difficulties echo those described by Thomas in promoting participation around environmental protection.

I conclude, therefore, with the question of how the lessons of successful EPG experiments might be transferred to other decision-making arenas. The participatory budget and the Chicago reforms (and perhaps the Kerala campaign as well) worked with small-scale decisions of direct interest to local people which lay within the competence of local governments. But broad-based issues around which ordinary people only have diffuse interest and which are beyond the full capacity of local governments to resolve might also benefit from EPG (if it worked), since incorporating the knowledge and concerns of ordinary people and making government more transparent and accountable is needed in many policy arenas. One insight from the Porto Alegre experiment is the value of starting small. Participatory decision-making can gain legitimacy on the small scale and participants can learn about political life and broaden their interests to other spheres. However, bringing EPG to other spheres would probably require a redoubled effort to help "ordinary people" understand how the issues at hand were related to their everyday concerns and to convince governments that participation would yield political benefits for them.

Notes

* Associate Researcher, Núcleo de Pesquisa em Políticas Públicas, University of Brasília/National Science Foundation International Post-Doctoral Scholar.
1. Phillip Selznick, *T.V.A. and the Grassroots*, Berkeley: University of California Press (1949).
2. Rebecca N. Abers, "From Ideas to Practice: The Partido dos Trabalhadores and Participatory Governance in Brazil," *Latin American Perspectives*, vol. 91, no. 23 (1996), pp. 35–53.
3. Fung and Wright, Introduction to this volume, p. 42, note 22.

8

Toward Ecologically Sustainable Democracy?
Bradley C. Karkkainen[*]

Archon Fung and Erik Olin Wright sketch an appealing vision of a participatory democratic alternative to the familiar hierarchical, bureaucratic institutions that came to dominate the public sphere in the nineteenth and twentieth centuries. They see novel experiments in localized participatory governance emerging across highly varied domains of public decision-making. Accompanying this wave of devolution, they argue, are opportunities for democratic renewal.

Fung and Wright cite the emergence of Habitat Conservation Planning in the United States as a leading example of this thrust toward devolved and locally empowered participatory governance. As Craig Thomas correctly points out, however, Habitat Conservation Plans (HCPs) in practice often tend to be messy political compromises, seldom matching the highly idealized participatory and deliberative model Fung and Wright describe. Nonetheless, while we may quibble over the particulars, I shall argue that larger trends now reshaping environmental regulation and natural resource management in the United States are broadly congruent with the major themes sounded by Fung and Wright.

I The Policy Logic of HCPs

Habitat Conservation Plans (HCPs) allow landowners to escape the rigidities of a notoriously inflexible command-style rule, the "no-take" provision of the Endangered Species Act (ESA), by drawing up conservation-oriented land-use plans fitted to their own particularized circumstances. The HCP planning process thus establishes a new locus for policy-making within a regulatory program heretofore defined almost exclusively by centrally imposed, nationally uniform, categorical rules. In principle, this approach offers some distinct advantages. By localizing decision-making, it invites attention to a level of fine-grained, place-specific contextual detail that ordinarily lies beyond the resolution of generic rule-making. It thus can lead to better-informed policies fitted to the unique local circumstances of varied habitats and ecosystems, and avoid the problems of over- and under-inclusiveness that routinely attend categorical regulation. This approach also creates opportunities for local actors – landowners in the first instance, but other "stakeholders" as well – to draw upon their own problem-solving skills and knowledge of local conditions to propose tailored solutions to seemingly intractable and generic "economy versus environment" conflicts. In some cases, the results may be beneficial both to wildlife and to landowners.

A seminal example is the San Bruno Mountain HCP. In that case, the ESA's "no-take" rule would have prohibited modification of one of the last remaining fragments of habitat for the endangered mission blue butterfly, thwarting the landowner's plans to develop a suburban mountainside outside San Francisco. But the butterfly habitat was in a badly degraded condition, a situation the "no-take" rule would do nothing to address. A committee consisting of the landowner, a local environmental group, and federal, state, and local government officials was convened to search for a solution. Under the plan devised through this collaborative process, the landowner would scale back development to one portion of the tract, and transfer the remaining land to public ownership for permanent protection as butterfly habitat. The plan further called for upgrading the remaining butterfly habitat by removing invasive plants and replanting native species upon which the mission blue butterfly depends, with the work financed by development fees on the newly developed lands. From the perspective of the Fish and Wildlife Service, trading off a fraction of the protected acreage in exchange for qualitatively superior butterfly habitat and a long-term funding source for habitat management looked like a good bargain. Congress ultimately agreed, and amended the Endangered Species Act not only to authorize the San Bruno Mountain plan but also to permit similar incidental "takes" of listed species in exchange for site-specific HCPs promising conservation benefits. Out of a simple but innovative case of collaborative, location-specific problem-solving, the national HCP program was born.

What has the HCP program wrought in the years since its enactment? Is it, as Fung and Wright claim, the harbinger of a democratic transformation of environmental decision-making, until recently a largely top-down, expert-driven, rule-bound affair? Is it, as some of its environmentalist critics contend, a give-away program to accommodate landowners and real-estate developers at the expense of endangered species and protected habitats? Or is it, as some landowners and developers see it, a license for the federal government to engage in legalized extortion, forcing property owners to cede portions of their land to "national zoological use"[1] under threat of Endangered Species Act enforcement that could have devastating economic consequences?

The answer, I submit, lies somewhere between these various extremes, but also somewhere beyond them.

II Two Models of HCPs

Craig Thomas's thoughtful chapter in this volume provides a useful point of departure. Thomas offers a useful corrective to some of the more hyperbolic claims made by enthusiastic boosters of the HCP program, among whom I count not only Fung and Wright but also myself, among others.[2] Canvassing the entire HCP program, Thomas concludes that although HCPs empower local actors (principally landowners), they should be counted neither as "deliberative" nor as "democratic" because in most cases they involve limited public participation.

It is difficult to disagree with the particulars of Thomas's critique, which in his usual style is backed by careful research. But while not disputing the underlying facts, I would depart from his main interpretive conclusions. Like Fung and Wright and, indeed, most commentators on the HCP program, Thomas paints with too broad a brush. Although he acknowledges that HCPs come in many shapes and sizes, he, too, elects to characterize the program in sweeping generalities that do injustice to the most interesting and innovative elements embedded within it.

I submit that it is more useful and revealing to think of the HCP program as encompassing two distinct regulatory models, each serving its own distinctive purposes:

Type I: Bilateral Plans

In the first model, an HCP is a simple bilateral deal for a partial waiver from an otherwise applicable regulatory requirement. I will call this the "Type I" HCP. Arguably, this model is what Congress had in mind when it amended the Endangered Species Act in 1982 to permit the "incidental taking" of listed species in exchange for an approved HCP.[3] Type I HCPs are typically neither broadly participatory nor collaborative, nor is this required under the statute. In many cases, they are not even especially deliberative. Instead, they represent a compromise, "split-the-difference" outcome of self-interested bargaining by a single landowner with a Fish and Wildlife Service field agent, subject to veto by the field agent's regional supervisor. They are also typically narrow in scope and limited in geographical scale, aiming to mitigate harm to a single listed endangered or threatened species on a single parcel of land. Some Type I HCPs involve affirmative conservation efforts that produce a net benefit to the listed species, though this, too, is not required. In many cases, the goal is a more modest one: they permit economic activity to proceed in some portion of otherwise protected but often qualitatively marginal habitat if the resulting incidental harm to the listed species is judged to be minor, especially when balanced against the economic burden the landowner would otherwise incur. Type I HCPs, then, represent a kind of "safety valve" to mitigate the harshest economic consequences of an otherwise inflexible regulatory rule, and thereby to ameliorate political opposition to the endangered species program itself. However useful they may be as a device to introduce a measure of regulatory flexibility, Type I HCPs hardly portend the democratic transformation of environmental policy that Fung and Wright envision.

Type II: Multi-Party Adaptive Management Plans

In the second and more recent model, developed and enthusiastically promoted during Bruce Babbitt's tenure as Secretary of the Interior, HCPs are broadly collaborative and decidedly ambitious ecosystem conservation planning efforts at large regional landscape scales. These "Type II" HCPs aim well beyond the species-specific concerns of the Endangered Species Act itself and their simpler Type I cousins. Their goal is nothing short of proactive and scientifically informed management of entire communities of species (both listed and non-listed) and the ecosystems of which they are part.[4] At their most ambitious, they employ advanced techniques of biological monitoring and adaptive management, seeking to generate and continuously fine-tune affirmative conservation measures of a kind and at a level of attention to ecosystem-specific detail not achievable through centralized rulemaking. Not surprisingly, given their scale, sophistication, and ambition, Type II HCPs typically involve (indeed, require) participation by multiple parties, public and private, landowners and non-landowners alike, including various tiers and agencies of government, conservationists, independent scientists, and other interested citizens. Unlike Type I HCPs, they do not depend upon fixed, split-the-difference, bargained-for outcomes, but rather demand open-ended commitments by diverse parties to participate over the long haul in jointly exploring and continuously reassessing innovative solutions to complex problems. To that extent, they require a kind of practical deliberation and expansive openness to experimentation that is likely to be absent from the Type I model. The HCPs that emerged out of California's Natural Communities Conservation Planning (NCCP) process,[5] particularly those in the coastal sage scrub of San Diego, Orange, and Riverside Counties, most clearly fit this description,[6] though others, including some of the watershed-scale salmon habitat restoration plans now under development in the Pacific Northwest, approximate this model as well. Type II HCPs are self-consciously transformative, seeking to permanently alter the landscape of environmental regulation by reorienting it toward integrated environmental and natural resources management at ecosystem scales. With their proactive, multi-species, ecosystem-protective orientation, they arguably lie in a legal nether region, stretching and possibly exceeding the bounds of the narrower Type I HCP program Congress appeared to have had in mind when it amended the Endangered Species Act in 1982. Indeed, in crucial respects Type II HCPs appear to have more in common with other large, landscape-scale, collaborative initiatives in regional ecosystem management, like the Chesapeake Bay Program, the South Florida Ecosystem Restoration project, the Northwest Forest Plan, or the CALFED Bay-Delta program, than with their simpler, single-landowner, single-species Type I HCP cousins.

These are, of course, ideal types. Some HCPs may not fall squarely into either type, but instead embrace a mix of Type I and Type II features. For example, the San Bruno Mountain HCP, progenitor of the national program, looks in most respects like a Type I HCP, involving a single landowner, a single species, and a relatively small geographical scale (2,500 acres). Yet the San Bruno Mountain HCP was negotiated through a collaborative multi-party process, and thus embodies a key characteristic of Type II. Despite this minor classificatory complication, however, I believe the typology is a useful device to allow us to sort and analyze the differences among HCPs. Most will fall roughly into one of the two broad types, or lie somewhere on the continuum between them.

III Recent HCP Policy: Proliferation of Type I, Emergence of Type II

Bruce Babbitt's tenure as Interior Secretary saw a dramatic increase in both types of HCP; indeed, prior to this time, only a small handful of Type I HCPs had been negotiated. Type I HCPs are by far the more numerous, but because they usually involve small acreage, marginal habitat, and minimal harm to listed species, they tend to operate at the fringes of the endangered species program. There, one hopes, they will amount to little of ecological consequence, individually or in the aggregate – though this is far from certain.[7]

Although fewer in number, Type II HCPs tend to operate over much larger geographic scales, and implicate far more complex and far-reaching ecological and economic issues. They also lie much closer to the center of environmental policy as it emerged during the Clinton–Babbitt years.

There are some very simple and straightforward reasons for the comparative numerosity of the simpler Type I variant. If given the option, self-interested landowners would generally prefer to deal solely with an FWS field agent empowered to grant them partial exemption from the ESA "no-take" rule, than to collaborate with a broader, more diverse, and potentially more troublesome cast of participants, some of whom might be intent on seeking more ambitious conservation measures and affirmative ecological benefits. Parcel-specific planning is also, by its nature, a less complex, less information-intensive, and lower-stakes undertaking than the regional-scale coordination required for Type II HCPs. Moreover, since Type I HCPs typically involve small acreages and marginal habitat, they often attract less public attention and political controversy than the large regional HCPs. "Flying beneath the radar" of environmental politics, they can often be negotiated in relative obscurity, even secrecy, and in many cases on terms quite favorable to the landowner.

Large regional ecosystem-scale Type II HCPs, on the other hand, tend to attract a good deal of attention and controversy. Because they usually involve multiple parties, multiple species, and the full range of competing land uses within the region, they are politically, institutionally, and scientifically more complex, and farther-reaching in their economic and environmental implications. Consequently, both the initial negotiating process and ongoing governance arrangements may be messy, cumbersome, time-consuming, and resource-intensive. Numerous parties may seek to intervene, using a variety of legal and political leverage points to influence or upset the process.

Why, then, would anyone bother with a Type II HCP? For the Department of the Interior, the answer is straightforward: only through regional-scale land use planning and integrated management of all the parts of the ecosystem can we begin to move in the direction of proactive conservation of ecosystems and ecologically sustainable patterns of development. Indeed, it might be argued that a series of separate, parcel-specific deals is fundamentally incompatible with a policy that seeks integrated, holistic, coordinated, and ecologically sound management.

Nonetheless, parcel-specific deals – Type I HCPs – may also be attractive to the Department of the Interior for other reasons: they provide economic and political benefits, ease dissatisfaction among landowners, and reduce the intensity of opposition to the endangered species program and conservation initiatives more generally. Thus it appears that the Department of the Interior has reasons to favor both types of HCP.[8]

For landowners, the logic compelling participation in a Type II HCP is equally straightforward: sometimes they have no choice. As Secretary of the Interior, Bruce Babbitt was not shy about using the Endangered Species Act as a coercive "hammer" to force landowners, local governments, and others to engage in landscape-scale ecosystem planning and management when he believed it was necessary and he had the political and legal leverage to make it stick. Once again, Southern California provides the clearest case. Regional habitat conservation planning was triggered there by Babbitt's decision to list the California gnatcatcher, a small songbird native to the coastal sage scrub, as a threatened species. Listing would invoke the "no-take" provision and effectively bar adverse modification of the coastal sage scrub habitat upon which the gnatcatcher depends, thereby undercutting the prospects for future real estate development in one of the nation's fastest-growing regions. Babbitt seized on this threat as an opportunity to compel landowners and local governments to work out a comprehensive regional plan to curb and redirect real-estate development in ways that would be compatible with conservation of the remaining coastal sage scrub, an ecological goal that could not be achieved through piecemeal deal-making, one landowner at a time. In short, landowners and local governments faced an ultimatum – either they cooperated in working out a satisfactory, forward-looking regional conservation plan, or they accepted the potentially devastating economic consequences of Endangered Species Act enforcement.

IV Sorting out the HCP Commentary

Unfortunately, the popular and academic commentary has thus far not recognized the distinction I outline here between two markedly different models of HCP. The result is not only a great deal of confusion, but also much misdirected hostility toward the HCP program as a whole. By conflating two innovative regulatory programs – Type I and Type II HCPs – we make a hash of public discourse, effectively foreclose opportunities for informed, critical evaluation of either approach, hand everyone a reason to dislike HCPs, and undercut political support for innovative and attractive elements of the program, even in quarters where those innovations might be expected to garner the most sympathy.

Focussing on the perceived pathologies of the Type I model of bilateral backroom dealing between landowners and FWS field agents, some environmentalists warn that the HCP program represents a short-sighted, politically motivated, unprincipled, and cumulatively damaging erosion of our public commitments to endangered species protection, in favor of private landowner interests. Compounding the problem, in their view, is a process that appears to involve a dangerous lack of transparency and accountability. If the environmentalist critique were leveled against Type I HCPs, it might have considerable merit. But these concerns do not arise in precisely the same way in Type II HCPs, which tend to be much more visible, transparent (at least in the localities in which they are negotiated), open to participation by non-landowner parties, and less tilted in favor of landowner interests. This is not to say that all issues of transparency, accountability, procedural fairness, and adequacy of public participation have been resolved in Type II HCPs. These continue to be matters of critical importance, but in the large regional HCPs the crucial question is typically not *whether*, but rather *how* and *by whom* non-landowner viewpoints will be represented.

Landowners and the ideological champions of the primacy of private property rights, on the other hand, emphasize Bruce Babbitt's skillful use of the "hammer" of ESA listing to force Southern California politicians and landowners to the bargaining table in a Type II ecosystem planning process. They fear this portends the erosion of private property rights under the coercive hand of a distant, unaccountable, power-mad eco-bureaucracy, intent on using the Endangered Species Act to bludgeon concessions out of landowners. Although greatly exaggerated, this fear is not entirely without foundation. The Type II HCP process is neither well defined nor clearly constrained by statutory standards, procedural rules, or administrative precedent. Under such circumstances, concerns about the potential for overreaching by zealous government officials may be legitimate. A strong case can be made for the need to clarify and regularize the procedures that govern regional, multi-species HCP planning. Yet the landowner-property rights critique ignores the fact that most Type I HCPs are landowner-initiated and distinctly landowner-friendly in their terms. Whatever we might think about Type II HCPs, the HCP program as a whole cannot be characterized as an anti-landowner conspiracy. It is, perhaps by Clintonesque design, a mixed bag, pairing an aggressive pilot program for large-scale ecosystem protection (Type II) with an aggressively expanded version of a moderately pro-landowner program (Type I), apparently with the hope that the latter would afford the former some measure of political cover. In fact, however, the result has been to trim enthusiasm for all parts of the HCP program in virtually all quarters.

For their part, conservation biologists look across the landscape of the HCP program and register grave concern that only a fraction of HCPs employ independent scientific review and rigorous, science-based techniques like biological monitoring and adaptive management.[9] Careful reading of the scientific critique, however, reveals that sound scientific baselines, peer review, and scientifically defensible management techniques are emerging as the norm in the larger and more sophisticated Type II HCPs, those involving the largest acreages and the most ecologically sensitive lands. In these cases, such measures are likely to be economically and technically feasible, and because they are necessary elements of ecologically sound management, they arguably should be made mandatory for Type II HCPs. It should not be surprising, however, that single-landowner, small-scale Type I HCPs would not employ such sophisticated scientific methods, which most landowners would find technically challenging and prohibitively costly. Yet I do not undertake to defend the lack of scientific grounding for Type I HCPs. If neither the government nor the landowner can afford to base a Type I HCP on sound science, should we then proceed on the basis of willful scientific ignorance? Most in the scientific community, and many others as well, would answer that question in the negative, especially since it also appears that little attention is currently being paid to the cumulative ecological impacts of multiple small-scale HCPs.[10] This argues for a careful rethinking of Type I HCP policy.

Finally, the more radical devolutionaries among us – Fung and Wright, myself, and others – tend to seize upon the Type II model as emblematic of the emergence of a new era of enlightened environmen-

tal regulation, integrated ecosystem management, and localized participatory governance. If our exuberance were explicitly confined to Type
II HCPs, we might invite a serious debate on these points. By failing to
make that distinction clearly, however, we invite the rejoinder (here
made by Craig Thomas) that most HCPs do not fit this model, instead
representing nothing more than a series of modest bilateral deals,
tweaking the background "no-take" regulatory rule at the margins in a
mildly pro-landowner direction. Thomas is right, of course, as far as
his criticism goes. But if the Fung and Wright claim were properly
understood to be restricted to Type II HCPs, the Thomas response
would be seen as a non sequitur that does not really advance the
debate.

All these various commentators are right in some measure. But all
have contributed to the confusion surrounding the HCP program by
making exaggerated and misleading claims, conflating two quite distinct regulatory phenomena that march together under the common
banner of the HCP program.

It should be noted that proposed legislation circulating on Capitol
Hill, especially a bill introduced by Representative George Miller in the
106th Congress,[11] would go some distance toward clarifying the distinction between these two types of HCP, and regularizing procedures
appropriate to each. That bill would establish one set of standards and
procedures for small-scale HCPs, which need not be participatory or
collaborative under the Miller proposal. Large-scale, multi-party HCPs
would be governed by a different set of standards and procedures,
requiring the Secretary of the Interior to establish opportunities for
robust and diverse public participation.

V Are Type II HCPs an Example of Empowered Participatory Governance?

Fung and Wright argue that the "most advanced" HCPs "incorporat[e]
significant elements" of their model of empowered participatory governance.[12] Thomas replies that most HCPs do not fall into the empowered participatory governance model, or indeed come anywhere close
to it. But once we understand the HCP program as encompassing not
one regulatory model but two, Thomas's observation should hardly be
surprising or disturbing. Indeed, the more surprising result would be
that the Type I safety valve HCPs did fit the model, for they are non-
participatory almost by definition.

The more interesting question is not whether all, or even most,

HCPs fit the Fung–Wright model, but whether Type II HCPs as a group approximate the model; or, indeed, whether any of them do. If even a few Type II HCPs fit this model, then we might further inquire to what extent and under what conditions they do so, and on that basis we might experiment with replicating those conditions so as to expand the possibilities for democratic participation in other locales, or in other regulatory arenas. Yet there is not a sufficiently thick description of Type II HCP processes in either the Fung and Wright introductory chapter, or in the Thomas critique, or in the commentary on HCPs that has appeared elsewhere, to fairly answer those questions. We are left, then, with an intriguing and provocative assertion, and not much more. What is required is a much more thorough, detailed, on-the-ground examination of particular HCPs, and the nature of the processes of governance and public participation that occur there.

More fundamentally, however, this shortcoming in the academic debate is rooted in a crucial deficiency in the HCP program itself as it has developed to date. As Thomas correctly notes (and as my own research has found), precious little information is presently available to government officials or to other interested parties, including academics, about HCP processes or outcomes. The federal government does virtually no central monitoring, oversight, or coordination of the HCP program, and provides no central repository of HCP information. Consequently, although individual Type II HCPs may be highly visible in their own communities, the program as a whole lacks transparency, accountability, systematic pooling of information, benchmarking and diffusion of best practices, systemic learning, and opportunities for institutional self-improvement, whether it be with regard to the conditions of public participation or any other critical operational element. Under those circumstances, it is difficult to determine whether genuinely democratic and participatory governance practices have emerged. Moreover, even if such practices were to appear in some locales, these could be accidental and isolated developments; there is no documentary evidence suggesting that it is the goal of the HCP program to propagate such practices, nor is there any mechanism for doing so. In this regard, the HCP program differs markedly from the other examples of empowered participatory governance described by Fung and Wright and discussed elsewhere in this volume. In each of those cases, popular democratic participation appears to be an integral, deeply embedded, and consciously implanted element of the overall design of the program, not only as the preferred mechanism for implementing public policy reforms but also as a central goal in its own right.

The lack of any concerted, systematic effort on the part of the federal government to monitor, evaluate, learn, and diffuse the lessons derived from the successes and failures of disparate HCP experiments has consequences far beyond complicating our work as academics, of course. It reveals a deep limitation in the program's capacity to develop beyond its current stage. The need for an experimental approach to policy-making in the context of highly complex problems like ecosystem management is now widely appreciated, in both academic and policy circles. But experimentation without rigorous and systematic observation, analysis, and interpretation of the results is not really experimentation at all. It wastes opportunities to learn and to inform subsequent rounds of experimentation with new learning, invites policy drift, and sharply reduces the likelihood that successful models will be developed, refined, and replicated. Indeed, persistent refusal to learn from experimentation would threaten the intellectual and policy justifications for the very existence of an experimental Type II HCP program.

VI HCPs in a Larger Context: Collaborative Ecosystem Governance

Despite these programmatic deficiencies, the emergence of HCPs, and Type II HCPs in particular, is congruent with larger trends that are reshaping the face of environmental regulation and natural resource management in the United States and elsewhere. We are rapidly shifting from a model based on top-down, piecemeal, command-style regulation, toward a model based on locally or regionally tailored, broadly integrative, collaborative, and self-consciously experimental ecosystem governance arrangements.

This new model explicitly recognizes that ecosystems are complex dynamic systems that must be managed as systems, employing an integrated and holistic approach. It emphasizes the need for governance structures matched to the scale of the ecological resource to be managed, typically a scale that does not map well onto conventional political and administrative boundaries and therefore requires, at a minimum, a high degree of intergovernmental coordination. It grapples with complexity, acknowledging the need for continuous experimentation and dynamic adjustment in response to new learning. These challenges are typically addressed through hybrid public–private governance structures that feature broad pooling of information, expertise, and competencies; systematic monitoring of ecosystem conditions and the outcomes of policy measures; and collaborative problem-solving among parties representing diverse interests at multiple, nested spatial scales, from the immediately local (e.g. the landowner) to the national, international, or even global.

This new model can be discerned in such diverse areas as:

- the watershed approach to aquatic ecosystem management, as exemplified by the Chesapeake Bay and Great Lakes Programs, California's Bay-Delta Program, and literally hundreds of smaller collaborative watershed management initiatives;
- new directions in public lands management in places like the Everglades, the Greater Yellowstone ecosystem, and the old-growth national forests of the Pacific Northwest, in response to the recognition that protection of environmental values on public lands is often possible only through broader, ecosystem-scale collaborations; and
- regional collaborative efforts to protect coastal seas, estuaries, and other critical marine ecosystems.

Like Type II HCPs, these efforts are multi-party collaborations operating at more localized scales than conventional categorical, command-style, top-down regulation. Thus they involve many more local actors in the policy-making and implementation process, drawing upon local expertise and empowering parties previously shut out of any meaningful role in shaping environmental policy. Yet for all that, they do not appear to involve the kinds of large-scale, direct popular participation that Fung and Wright envision, and which can be discerned in their other examples of empowered participatory governance.

In part, this may be simply a question of scale. The Chicago, Porto Alegre, West Bengal, and Kerala reforms operate at the level of the urban neighborhood or village, typically comprising several thousand people. At that level, direct participation by large numbers of people is possible – though even in those cases, the skeptic might fairly question what fraction of the local population actually participates in governance activities, and by what mechanisms the views and interests of non-participants are represented. In contrast, collaborative ecosystem governance, whether through HCPs or any of the other initiatives outlined above, tends to operate over much larger geographic scales, in regions with much larger populations. The San Diego County Multiple Species Conservation Plan, for example, covers an area of nine hundred square miles in San Diego County – with three million residents, the second most populous county in California. The South Florida

Ecosystem Restoration initiative encompasses an area of eighteen thousand square miles, home to six million people. The Chesapeake Bay
Program is even larger, attempting to manage a sixty-four thousand
square-mile watershed with fifteen million residents. While policy-
making at these levels might be "local" in contrast to national rule-
making, it is not nearly so intimately local as the Kerala village or the
Chicago or Porto Alegre neighborhood, where presumably conditions
are conducive to direct, face-to-face popular participation. Nor is it
easy to translate ecosystem management to such immediately local
scales. The boundaries of ecosystem management are dictated by the
laws of ecology, which would divide territory into ecologically linked
bundles of interacting species and the common physical substrate upon
which they depend. Such boundaries typically do not map well onto
existing human institutions. Indeed, the driving ambition of ecosystem
management is to create new human institutions matched to the scales
of crucial ecological processes – which often extend far beyond the
bounds of the human village or neighborhood.

On the other hand, many of the better-developed regional ecosystem
governance projects have found it advantageous to operate at multiple
scales simultaneously, recognizing that ecological processes themselves
operate at multiple "nested" scales. Under this approach, one set of
region-wide institutions is responsible for overall planning and coordination, while more localized coordinating bodies are "nested" within
the regional framework, and vested with the responsibility to manage
particular habitat patches, tributaries, or other ecologically or hydro-
logically defined subareas. These local units often have a good deal of
discretion to devise locally tailored approaches and solutions, so long
as they are consonant with the broad goals and objectives set by the
regional plan. Activities at these more localized scales appear to
provide greater opportunities for public participation. Within the
regional coordinating framework of the Chesapeake Bay Program, for
example, citizens are involved in such localized activities as tributary-
based water quality monitoring, local habitat restoration projects, and
tributary-specific planning and management coordinated by "tributary
teams" and some three hundred watershed organizations active across
the region. Even at these local levels, however, most activities appear to
be organized across larger geographical scales and population bases
than the typical Kerala village or Porto Alegre urban neighborhood.
Moreover, although figures are not available, it appears that even in the
Chesapeake Bay region, a relatively small fraction of the total population participates directly in ecosystem management activities.
In contrast, the case studies of citizen participation in village-level

economic development in Kerala and participatory budgeting in Porto Allegre suggest (but do not document) significantly higher rates of direct popular participation.

Beyond questions of institutional scale and participation rates, regional ecosystem governance institutions appear to diverge from Fung and Wright's other examples of empowered participatory governance in another crucial respect. In contrast to the Chicago, Porto Alegre, West Bengal, and Kerala models, which apparently seek to mobilize direct and unmediated popular participation, regional ecosystem governance is conducted primarily through what I shall call "hybrid" institutions, comprising collaborative arrangements among government agencies, non-governmental organizations, and purely private entities, including business organizations. Intergovernmental and inter-agency coordination often lies at the core of these hybrid arrangements. The San Diego County MSCP, for example, describes itself as "a cooperative effort between the County of San Diego and 12 other local jurisdictions and agencies such as the U.S. Fish & Wildlife Service and California's Department of Fish & Game . . . working with various private landowners."[13] Similarly, the core institutions of the Chesapeake Bay Program and the Everglades restoration initiative are primarily intergovernmental and inter-agency arrangements, with various federal and state agencies in the most prominent roles.

Clearly non-governmental actors are also a significant force within some of these hybrid institutions, but it appears that citizen participation is only one strand in a more complex web of institutional reconfigurations and realignments in which traditional government agencies remain leading players. And even where it does occur, citizen participation is typically mediated through the citizen's affiliation with an issue-defined non-governmental organization, community group, business or property interest, or some other institutional vehicle. This institutional or interest-group affiliation is thought to confer the status of "stakeholder" on the individual participant, and becomes a badge entitling its bearer to participate in the inter-institutional collaborative process. Because such local institutions are often more than happy to welcome like-minded persons as new members, the entry barriers may be quite low in practice. Nonetheless, this model of local participation through intermediary institutions can be distinguished from the model of direct and unmediated popular participation that appears to be characteristic of the other cases in this volume.

What is the significance of this distinction? At this point, it is difficult to draw firm conclusions. Fung and Wright's analysis is a useful starting point, but only that. Unfortunately, they do not define what counts as "participation" in their model, and the notion upon which they implicitly rely appears vague and underdeveloped. This prevents them from identifying different kinds of participation and evaluating the implications of each. Future research on the nature and extent of popular participation and the roles of various kinds of intermediary organizations in collaborative ecosystem governance can make a valuable contribution toward clarifying, refining, extending, or revising Fung and Wright's analysis.

Nonetheless, at least in a general way, the emerging hybrid ecosystem governance institutions appear to exhibit many of the principles and design properties identified by Fung and Wright. These institutions are locally devolved (relative to the *status quo ante*), practically oriented, collaborative, and "deliberative" in the practical problem-solving sense of that term. Consistent with Fung and Wright's central claims, these institutions set out self-consciously to transform state power by reassembling and fusing its elements into new configurations that transcend established jurisdictional, territorial, and functional boundaries. In ecosystem governance, however, direct popular participation is not the only, or even the primary, mechanism by which this transformation is carried out.

VII Conclusion

In its broadest outlines if not in all its finest details, the Fung and Wright model of empowered participatory governance appears to capture many of the features of collaborative ecosystem governance as it is emerging in the United States. Some HCPs, specifically those I have characterized as Type II HCPs, are part of this larger trend. Yet there is much we do not yet understand about this new model of environmental regulation and natural resources management. Additional research is needed to identify its most important characteristics and enabling conditions, to draw critical distinctions and comparative lessons among experiments, and to learn from their successes and failures.

Notes

* Associate Professor, Columbia Law School.

1. See *Babbitt v. Sweet Home Chapter of Communities for a Greater Oregon*, U.S. (Scalia, J., dissenting), 515 U.S. 687 (1995).

2. See Bradley C. Karkkainen, Charles Sabel, and Archon Fung, *Beyond Backyard Environmentalism*, ed. Joshua Cohen and Joel Rogers, foreword by Hunter Lovins and

224   DEEPENING DEMOCRACY

Amory Lovins, Boston: Beacon Press (2000); Bradley C. Karkkainen, Archon Fung, and Charles F. Sabel, "After Backyard Environmentalism: Toward a Performance-Based Regime of Environmental Protection," *American Behavioral Scientist*, vol. 44 (2000), pp. 692–711.

3. See Endangered Species Act 16 U.S. Code, Chap. 35, Sec. 1531 et seq.

4. See George Frampton, "Environmental Law Faces the New Ecology: Ecosystem Management in the Clinton Administration," *Duke Environmental Law and Policy Journal*, vol. 7 (Fall 1996), pp. 39–48.

5. The Natural Communities Conservation Planning Act (NCCP) is a California state statute that prescribes a collaborative approach to landscape-scale conservation planning, aimed at protecting "natural communities" of plants and animals.

6. See, e.g., Marc J. Ebbin, "Is the Southern California Approach to Conservation Succeeding?" in *Ecology Law Quarterly*, no. 24 (1997), p. 695. The San Diego County Multiple species Conservation Plan (MSCP), for example, covers an area of some nine hundred square miles

7. Laura H. Watchman, Martha Groom, and John D. Perrine, "Science and Uncertainty in Habitat Conservation Planning," *American Scientist*, vol. 89 (2001), p. 351.

8. It remains to be seen, however, whether ambitious Type II HCPs of the kind launched in the Clinton–Babbitt administration will survive the present Bush presidency.

9. See Watchman *et al.*, "Science and Uncertainty" (in a study of forty-three HCPs involving 97 species, few were based on thorough baseline studies of population size, only 18 percent included biological monitoring sufficient to evaluate the success of the HCP, and only about a third included built-in adaptive management measures).

10. See ibid.

11. Endangered Species Recovery Act of 1999, H.R. 960, 106th Congress, introduced by Representative George Miller, March 3, 1999. The bill would create separate categories of "low effect, small scale plans" and "multiple landowner, multispecies conservation plans," subject to different procedures and standards. See ibid., §108. Miller has not reintroduced the bill in the 107th Congress.

12. Fung and Wright, Introduction to this volume, p. 10.

13. County of San Diego, Multiple Species Conservation Program, *Plan Summary* (1998). Available at http//www.co.sandiego.ca.us/cnty/cntydepts/landuse/planning/mscp/1_plansum/1_plsum.html (accessed on July 25, 2002).

9

Cycles of Reform in Porto Alegre and Madison
Rebecca S. Krantz*

At the end of their introduction to this volume, Fung and Wright speculate about whether their model of Empowered Participatory Governance (EPG) is "generalizable."[1] Experiences of participatory planning in Madison, Wisconsin, suggest that the generalizability of the EPG model can be aided by two reorientations. First, I argue that we can view EPG reforms as part of a larger trend toward participatory democratic innovation. Many of the innovations in this larger trend are similar to the EPG reforms, but are occurring in a more partial or gradual fashion than the exemplary cases described in this volume such as the participatory budget in Porto Alegre, Brazil. I will briefly outline a case from Madison to illustrate this trend. Second, similar to Baiocchi's argument,[2] I suggest that we treat both EPG reforms and their gradualist counterparts as interventions into larger state–civil society arrangements, and assess them according to their long-term effects on these systems. It is from this larger perspective and longer time-horizon that we can assess the extent to which more gradualist forms of participatory civic innovation might contribute to more widespread adoption of EPG. I will finally argue that if I am right that gradual or partial reforms are similar and related in important ways to the more radical EPG reforms, then evidence from Madison regarding constraints on deliberation due to institutional embeddedness in the state may also be relevant to the long-term success and diffusion of the EPG model.

I Wider Trends in Civic Innovation

In their recent book *Civic Innovation in America* (2001), Sirianni and Friedland document a long-term process of social learning and civic renewal enabling increasingly participatory forms of democratic citizenship in the United States. They argue that the activists and experiments of the 1960s and 1970s have matured, the activists learning from experience and the early experiments giving way to more sophisticated and strategic forms of participatory decision-making in areas such as urban development, environment, and health.[3] In many of these innovative settings, as with EPG, ordinary citizens and stakeholders deliberate about concrete problems, often in devolved local action units, sometimes mobilizing state power and resources to do so. Since this is a process of social learning, where experiences and practices are shared and modified over time and space, and since there is evidence elsewhere of cross-national influences in related phenomena like social movement repertoires,[4] it is reasonable to assume that the trend Sirianni and Friedland identify may extend beyond the U.S. Thus, although there may be only a small number of cases in the world today where all of the components of the EPG model are in evidence, there are many more settings where some aspects of EPG are in play and others are not, or where an EPG-like model is in the process of being implemented in a more gradual fashion.

Attention to such cases should help us assess the potential for the EPG model and its influence to become more widespread over time. Since the institutional design focus of the Real Utopias framework has a tendency to treat existing designs as *faits accomplis*, attention to cases where actors are in the process of working toward more empowered and participatory governance structures can help us address not only the question of whether EPG is generalizable, but also the time-honored question, "How can it be done?"

II Participatory Planning in Madison, Wisconsin

My research[5] explores one such "gradualist" case. In it, civic innovation has led to state-sponsored participatory deliberation over concrete local problems, but the level of empowerment to allocate resources and oversee implementation is limited. I will briefly describe characteristics of the area I studied and the history and institutional design of the reform before discussing the relevance of this case to the generalizability of EPG.

The Madison, Wisconsin metropolitan area has a population approaching a half million, is home to the state's capitol and a large university, and has a tradition of progressive politics and a relatively active citizenry.[6] The city's near east side, where my research is focussed, was traditionally a working-class and industrial area, on the other side of town from the University. It has had small pockets of both affluence and poverty, with wealthier homes concentrated along a lakeshore and the low-income ones in public housing developments. Even now, it is home to several active factories, an airport and military base, and a technical college. Some of the traditionally working-class areas have become middle class, and the areas closer to downtown have an increasing number of university students and professionals. Some of these areas have developed a reputation for being "progressive," "alternative," "artsy," or "gay- and lesbian-friendly." Largely white for many years, the population of Latino, Southeast Asian, and Black residents in the area increased substantially during the 1990s. The area's residents face issues such as skyrocketing property values, development pressures, an affordable housing shortage, traffic safety, factory emissions, poverty, race relations, crime, and small locally owned businesses being replaced by large chain stores.

One of the public deliberative spaces in which residents grapple with these issues is called a Neighborhood Steering Committee (NSC). An NSC is a city-government-sponsored public forum designed to increase citizen participation in urban planning decisions. NSCs are empowered to allocate federal community development funds to chosen projects, and they do so through participatory deliberation.

Madison's neighborhood steering committee program dates back to the 1970s. A city planner, Ellen,[7] explained to me that during this period, federal dollars were being diverted to state and local levels to encourage citizen participation. At the same time, the city was composing its first official land-use plan. Ellen said, "But the land use plan is general, it doesn't focus on specific neighborhoods. The central city neighborhoods came in and said this is so general, we want more detailed studies for our neighborhoods . . . It came from the neighborhoods."[8]

Out of this grass-roots effort, using federal funds, the city developed the neighborhood planning program. When the federal funding for citizen participation was cut by Reagan, Ellen reports, "the city felt it was important to keep it up." Currently, the program is supported by federal Community Development Block Grant (CDBG)[9] money as well as city funding.

Each year, one Census Tract[10] is selected by city staff based on CDBG eligibility requirements regarding low- to moderate-income populations, and on proximity to upcoming development or redevelopment projects. In this "concentration neighborhood," city staff members solicit citizen input by setting up an NSC that acts as a representative deliberative body.

The city staff solicit applications for membership on the committee using a variety of avenues of publicity and networking over two to three months to allow time for personal recruitment of underrepresented categories of people if necessary. The nomination forms include demographic information, which city staff use to select as representative a committee as possible. Since the concentration neighborhoods are supposed to be in areas with a majority of low- to moderate-income residents, they form a committee that has at least half low- to moderate-income representatives. They also seek variation by age, race, gender, length of time living in the neighborhood, geographic area of residence, and "old guard" membership of neighborhood associations versus those newly involved in neighborhood activities. One representative of area businesses is also appointed to the committee.[11]

The ten to fifteen committee appointees and other volunteers from the chosen census tract meet with city planners approximately biweekly for over a year to learn about, discuss, and set neighborhood priorities for land use, city and non-profit services, traffic circulation, safety, and business development. All meetings are open to the public, and several widely advertised public fora are held during the planning process to obtain further citizen input. A city staff team from fifteen different departments is charged with responding to recommendations coming from the committee and providing information on resources available to help implement its plans. The resulting Neighborhood Plan is then submitted to the city council (the local legislative body) for adoption. The committee is allotted between US$180,000 and US$200,000[12] of CDBG funding as seed money to begin to implement some of its eligible planning priorities. Other plan recommendations are taken into consideration in ongoing city and private development projects; when a developer applies for city approval for a plan, it is checked against the neighborhood plan and its chances of approval are considerably higher if the two are consistent.

Although this process contributes to making Madison's city planning process more participatory than most in the country,[13] the NSC program fails to meet several EPG criteria. Only one set of neighborhoods at a time participates in the process, the amount of money the committee has the power to allocate is relatively small, the group is temporary, and there is no formal structure to support long-term implementation. However, some leadership development and civic education does result, and further civic innovation like that described by Sirianni and Friedland has occurred. The City of Madison is now in the midst of developing a system of "Planning Councils." Planning Councils (PCs) are independent non-profit coalitions of neighborhood associations that receive city and private funds for a small staff and operations, with the goal of supporting neighborhood associations and increasing citizen participation in local decision-making. They will likely help formulate and implement the NSC plans. The first PC in Madison was initiated in 1993, with some of the members having recently served together on an NSC. In 1996 and 2000 the second and third PCs were formed, and many hope that the city will eventually be "covered" by five to ten contiguous PCs.

Planning councils and similar organizations exist or have been tried in a small number of other cities around the U.S.[14] In some cities, they have more power than in Madison, having for example "jurisdiction over zoning, authority over the distribution of various goods and services, and substantial influence over capital expenditures."[15] While Empowered Participatory Governance as Fung and Wright define it is certainly not everyone's goal for the PCs in Madison, the knowledge of cities where such groups are city-wide and have actual allocation power over the city budget influences the hopes and goals of some leaders.[16]

It appears, then, that the Madison case is characterized by gradual civic innovation toward increasingly empowered participatory deliberation, with deliberative bodies currently receiving moderate support from the state but not completely restructuring or "colonizing" state decision-making. While it is only one case, I suggest that exploring whether and how the Madison system could move further in the direction of empowered participatory governance and comparing it to the dynamics of reform in Porto Alegre can help assess the breadth of applicability of the EPG model. The key to this analysis is a shift in perspective: viewing EPG and related civic innovation as interventions into larger state–civil society systems and focussing on their relationships to the wider political context and the long-term effects on civil society.

III The System Dynamics of Participatory Reform

To understand this perspective, contrast planning in Madison with the Participatory Budget (PB) in Porto Alegre. Baoicchi's discussion of Porto Alegre emphasizes the importance of the relationship between the PB and the larger political regime and civil society. He describes a "virtuous cycle" that has led to the PB's increasing success over time. The cycle began when the lead party of a winning electoral alliance responded to deep popular grievances with a major institutional reform: the participatory budget. The resulting institutional structures were effective on a number of democratic fronts, including redressing grievances and strengthening civil society. These effects made the reforms even more thoroughgoing and legitimized the political regime.

Rather than viewing the EPG reform as a *fait accompli*, a one-time intervention in the institutional design, this perspective emphasizes the cycle of reinforcement and further reform that allows for the longevity of the system.[17] The more gradual participatory deliberation reforms like those in Madison can be viewed in a similar way. Instead of a dramatic win by a leftist coalition, the political context in Madison is mixed, with a history of progressivism, considerable cultural support for participatory democracy, and mild grievances, leading to a less unitary and less visionary reform agenda. The resulting innovation in governance involved both the NSC program and, somewhat later, experimentation with planning councils.

Both of these reforms have some positive long-term effects on civil society. For instance, participation in the NSC process increases participants' knowledge of city government and how to influence it. The process also creates new but often temporary relationships and networks among neighborhood leaders. In some cases, these connections have helped contribute to the creation and success of planning councils. PCs in turn create and strengthen longer-term relationships, networks, and organizations, and build the knowledge and capacity of citizens.

The effects on civil society appear to be more mixed, however, than in Porto Alegre. For instance, the NSC process can at least temporarily divert energy from neighborhood associations; it remains heavily "expert-driven" in some neighborhoods; and political interference with appointments to the committee, staff error, bureaucratic intransigence, and lack of implementation can contribute to cynicism rather than empowerment. The resulting legitimation and expansion of the participatory reform agenda in Madison is thus less strong than in Porto Alegre's virtuous cycle.

The creation of the planning councils and their slow spread suggests that it is possible, however, for gradualist participatory democratic reform and civic innovation to make headway. Our optimism ought to be cautious, for according to Berry *et al.* the exemplary planning-council-like systems in U.S. cities owe their success in part to the fact that they, like Porto Alegre, instituted city-wide systems at the outset and were able to reach strong levels of participation before confronting serious economic or political reversals.[18] Even with these factors, some of these successful systems have experienced setbacks due to funding cuts and conservative political swings. It remains to be seen whether the cycle of gradual reform in Madison is sufficiently "virtuous" to spread planning councils city-wide, much less lead to full-fledged empowered participatory governance of Fung and Wright's specification.

The future of Madison aside, this discussion points to a general model with which to understand the long-term and larger-system dynamics of EPG and related forms of civic innovation. In this general model, the political context influences the degree of institutional reform, which results in particular governance structures, which then have particular effects on civil society, which in turn act back upon the political context and the governance reform process. As with any model, of course, there are complexities this does not capture. In particular, there may be countervailing forces or cycles that influence its workings. There may also be thresholds of participation and legitimacy, a "critical mass" or "tipping point," in such systems that determine how far a reform can go and for how long. Although this analysis does not yet fully answer the question "how can it be done," it does give us some sense of the further questions we need to explore to do so.

IV Cautionary Tales from Madison

Additional empirical work must be done to assess the extent of similarity between the system dynamics of major reforms like the OP in Porto Alegre and more gradualist efforts like those in Madison. However, if I am right that many differences are a matter of degree rather than kind, then processes that I have observed in Madison may be relevant and important for the long-term prospects for EPG. In particular, I am concerned about the ways deliberation can be constrained when it is institutionally embedded in the state. I have observed several forms of such constraint, including scheduling and other bureaucratic exigencies and the logic of professional planning.

I will focus here on the problematic role of city staff as "experts." First, however, a few words about the positive side of embeddedness in state institutions. In addition to providing legitimacy and power, institutional embeddedness in the state can improve the deliberative process. For instance, anti-democratic factors such as status hierarchy and self-censorship often impair citizen deliberation. State regulation can help by imposing a more fair and open process.

The democratic effect of this *process* facilitation is impeded, however, when the same city staff also act as "experts" who "educate" citizens on matters of *content* under debate. In Madison, city staff members play such a dual role in the NSC program: in addition to forming the committee and facilitating the meetings, they are also sometimes the "experts" who teach citizens about the ins and outs of local government bureaucracy and urban planning methods, and make recommendations about specific land uses and other decisions.

Boaventura de Sousa Santos has discussed the role of expertise in the Porto Alegre case.[19] He claims that while technical expertise remains important there, the typical "technobureaucracy" has begun to be replaced by "technodemocracy," where citizens contest the dominance of the experts and technical staff members learn new ways of communicating with the public.

This effort is very much a contest, however, and its results are contingent, not given. Much of the interaction in the NSCs in Madison appears to stop short of Santos's hopes for technodemocracy. Many citizens treated "experts" who came to speak to their group as sources of information; only a few were able to critique the limitations of technocratic expertise, or see the solutions to neighborhood problems provided by experts as culturally or bureaucratically constrained. The antidemocratic nature of expertise in the NSC deliberations was particularly problematic, however, when the "expert" advice was being given by the staff member in charge of convening and facilitating the meetings.

An example of this occurred when members of one NSC were discussing the preservation of green space. Residents told Clyde, the city planner in charge of the committee, that they wanted the land to remain open, and ran up against his role as "expert" rather than process facilitator:

> **Katrina:** There's only one chance to preserve it, that's it, you can always develop it, can never reclaim it for green space once its developed.
>
> **Clyde:** If you did have development, how much of it would you keep for a park?
>
> **Janet:** Clyde, you're not hearing us, we're saying all green space, we're the committee, we're giving you our input.
>
> **Clyde:** (pausing) Yes, but I've got to balance your input with some professional expertise.
>
> **Alan:** (seconded by others) What's your professional expertise about it?
>
> **Clyde:** It's going to be developed, land is eventually developed, if you don't have a plan, you'll get something you don't want. I think you should think about trying to balance the real economic forces . . .

In the end, the neighborhood plan recommended preserving only a small fraction of the area as green space. Twenty-two months after this conversation, construction began on this site for a large development that would indeed leave a small corner green.[20]

In another neighborhood, a few NSC members were less willing to defer to the city planning staff facilitator as expert. For instance, while discussing recommendations regarding changes in zoning, the following exchange occurred between Ellen, the city planner and meeting facilitator, and committee members:

Ellen: My suggestion is to down-zone south of Page Street; this creates a buffer zone, single-family then mixed then commercial . . .

Pete: [points out that this would make owner-occupied 2-units illegal.]

Sandra: But we don't want 8-units.

Pete: Why don't we just say it [in the plan], no more than 3-units, we know the zoning code doesn't say it, but we want to preserve the character of the neighborhood.

Ellen: I want us to look at what kind of tools are available – the zoning code won't change soon [she reminds them this is accomplished through a larger political process, legislative changes].

Pete: I know that.

Ellen: You can say it verbally in your plan.

Frank: "Say it verbally" means it won't be in the plan, not a specific recommendation.

Ellen: It can be in the narrative.

Frank: You look more at –

Ellen: I look at what policy-makers are going to make of it.

Frank: (angrily) Don't policy-makers care what a neighborhood group meeting for fifteen months thinks?

Due to the persistent argumentation of Frank and Pete, occasionally supported by other committee members, a number of recommendations opposed by Ellen did remain in this neighborhood's plan.

Ellen was also responsible for facilitating the meeting and seeing to it that the process as a whole proceeded in a timely fashion, however.

This put her in a position of role-conflict, with potentially anti-democratic results. Frank and Pete frequently disagreed with the majority of the committee about recommendations in the plan. When disagreement among committee members occurred, it was Ellen's decision whether to allow discussion to continue in an effort to reach consensus, or to call for a vote. Since the majority of committee members were more swayed by "expert" opinion than were Frank and Pete, calling for a vote could have the effect, whether intentional or not, of influencing the outcome of the decision in the direction she preferred. It requires yet another level of empowerment on the part of citizens to take control of the meeting process itself. Attempts at such resistance did occur at times in the NSCs I observed, but the results were not always effective.

While the outcomes of these interactions between ordinary citizens and city staff "experts" have immediate consequences for how democratic the resulting neighborhood plans are, they may also have important implications for the long-term impact of the NSC program on civil society, and thus for the dynamic of further reform. Frank and Pete already had some of the knowledge, inclination, and cultural wherewithal necessary to resist the dominance of the "experts" they confronted. While other citizens on the NSC learned much from city staff about the workings of government, they did not necessarily learn that they could challenge the "experts," unless it was from the example of people like Frank and Pete.

If a participatory process educates people about decision-making without allowing them to question the process or the norms of bureaucratic and expert disciplines that constrain decisions, the process is less than fully deliberative, and the net effect on civil society could be one of co-optation rather than empowerment.[21] In Madison, improved institutional design could address some of these issues, for example by providing a facilitator who attends solely to group process, rather than combining facilitation with content expertise,[22] and by expanding the planning councils to increase citizen capacity to engage on a more equal footing with city staff and other experts.

In general, institutional design for participatory governance must not only create deliberative settings, it must do so in a manner that strengthens civil society; as my earlier analysis of the similarities between the system dynamics of reform in Porto Alegre and Madison suggests, such strengthening of civil society is necessary for the participatory reforms to be legitimated and furthered. If the more detailed evidence from Madison provided in this section is generalizable to EPG settings, the implications are that EPG designers ought to take care in the delineation of staff roles, and provide support for independent civil associations as well as for the more institutionally embedded EPG body itself.

If empowered participatory governance systems are to become more widespread, we must attend to the long-term dynamics of these and more gradual reforms, with special attention to their influence on civil society. Further exploration of the factors that contribute to or inhibit "virtuous cycles" of reform will be necessary, including detailed analyses of the deliberation process itself.

Notes

* Ph.D. Candidate in the Department of Sociology, University of Wisconsin, Madison.

1. In this context "generalizable" is used in a normative and practical sense, rather than a descriptive or explanatory one; Fung and Wright's question is how useful would the EPG institutional design be in a wider variety of settings, rather than how successfully the theoretical model describes or explains a wider variety of settings.

2. Chapter 2 in this volume, "Participation, Activism, and Politics: The Porto Alegre Experiment" by Gianpaolo Baiocchi.

3. They do not, of course, argue that the trend is universal or always unidirectional, and are agnostic as to whether it will eventually hold sway over countertrends.

4. See, for example, Doug McAdam and Dieter Rucht, "The Cross-National Diffusion of Movement Ideas," *Annals of the American Academy of Political and Social Science*, no. 528 (July 1993), pp. 56–74, and Margaret E. Keck and Kathryn Sikkink, *Activists Beyond Borders: Advocacy Networks in International Politics*, Ithaca, NY: Cornell University Press (1998).

5. Research is based on fieldwork including participant observation of over two hundred meetings and informal interactions from 1999 to 2001.

6. Thomas W. Still, "Madison Is the Ultimate in Citizen Involvement," *Wisconsin State Journal* (July 4, 1999), based on a study by Gregory Markus and Hanes Walton Jr., Michigan's ISR, Harwood Group.

7. All names are pseudonyms.

8. Source: personal interview, June 1, 2000.

9. The CDBG website describes the purpose of the program as follows: "Since 1974 CDBG has been the backbone of improvement efforts in many communities, providing a flexible source of annual grant funds for local governments nationwide – funds that they, *with the participation of local citizens*, can devote to the activities that best serve their own particular development priorities, provided that these projects either (1) benefit low- and moderate-income persons; (2) prevent or eliminate slums or blight; or (3) meet other urgent community development needs." http://www.hud.gov:80/progdesc/cdbgent.html, emphasis added.

10. Census tracts are small, relatively permanent statistical subdivisions of a county, defined by a committee of local data users for the U.S. government, for the purposes of enumerating the population and allocating services. Census tracts usually have between 2,500 and 8,000 persons, average about 4,000 people, and, when first delineated, are designed to be homogeneous with respect to population characteristics, economic status, and living conditions. The spatial size of census tracts varies widely depending on the density of settlement. Census tract boundaries are delineated with the intention of being

maintained over a long time so that statistical comparisons can be made from census to census (http://www.census.gov/td/stf3/append_a.html#CENSUSTRACT and http/ tier2.census.gov/ctsl/ctslinfo.htm#tract). Census tract boundaries can be very different from "neighborhood" boundaries as defined by the local culture, and can sometimes appear arbitrary to local residents. The NSCs I studied encompassed three or four "neighborhoods" as defined by local tradition and culture.

11. The city has particular difficulty getting racial diversity on the NSCs, and specific appointments are sometimes influenced by political factors. These and other questions as to how representative the NSCs really are inevitably arise, both for researchers and for participants. Any appointed group is potentially subject to the criticism that its members are not democratic representatives. However, given that voting and volunteerism both involve high degrees of self-selection and biases toward more empowered individuals, there is reason to believe that the NSC system, where this deliberate attempt at diversity of appointed representatives is made, is at least as representative as, and perhaps more representative than, many other deliberative bodies.

12. CDBG allocation amounts for Concentration Neighborhoods are 10 percent of the city's annual CDBG entitlement, allocated over a two-year period. During the period of this study the allocations were in the range given.

13. See the report of a study conducted by the Michelle Gregory, "Anatomy of a Neighborhood Plan: An Analysis of Current Practice," Chicago: American Planning Association Growing Smart Working Paper (1996), pp. 1–25, for a general assessment of the scarcity and difficulties of collaborative planning in the U.S.; Madison's uniqueness in this regard was first suggested to me in a personal communication with a Madison city planner.

14. See Jeffrey M. Berry, Kent E. Portney, and Ken Thomson, *The Rebirth of Urban Democracy*, Washington, DC: The Brookings Institution (1993) and Ira Katznelson, *City Trenches*, New York: Pantheon (1981). The planning bodies are variously named. In St. Paul, Minnesota they are "District Councils," in Dayton, Ohio "Priority Boards," in Birmingham, Alabama "Citizens Advisory Boards," and in Portland, Oregon "District Coalition Boards."

15. Berry *et al.*, *The Rebirth of Urban Democracy*, referring to St. Paul.

16. For instance, the recently hired head of the Department of Planning and Development in Madison worked for many years in Dayton, Ohio and frequently refers to the system there; a prominent aldermanic supporter of the planning councils has focussed on Portland, OR; and the former Mayor whose leadership helped get the PCs started took St. Paul as his model. The city is currently debating the proposed establishment of a city government "Office of Neighborhood Support," with a mission yet to be determined, creating fruitful ground for such hopes and goals to be discussed. City staff, elected officials, and citizens with experience in NSCs and PCs are using it as a forum to assess the strengths and weaknesses of these programs.

17. See the comment from Rebecca Abers, this volume. p. 200.

18. Berry *et al.*, *The Rebirth of Urban Democracy*, pp. 48–51.

19. Boaventura de Sousa Santos, "Participatory Budgeting in Porto Alegre: Toward a Redistributive Democracy," *Politics and Society*, vol. 26, no. 4 (December 1998).

20. At an elaborate groundbreaking ceremony the development was touted as a model of successful partnership and collaborative, neighborhood-friendly planning and development – despite the fact that no residents were in attendance.

21. A similar point was made years ago by Sherry R. Arnstein in "A Ladder of Citizen Participation," *Journal of the American Institute of Planners*, vol. 35, no. 4 (July 1969), pp. 216–24.

22. Strictly separating these roles, at least in time if not in different persons, is considered by many to be a basic tenet of good facilitation. See, for example, Roger M. Schwarz, *The Skilled Facilitator: Practical Wisdom for Developing Effective Groups*, San Francisco: Jossey-Bass (1994).

Power and Reason
*Joshua Cohen and Joel Rogers**

I Aims

For more than two decades the democratic Left has sought to clarify
the content of a "post-socialist" political project. The theory and case
studies gathered in this volume are part of that discussion, and their
contribution is best understood by reference to it.

The socialist project, including its more common social democratic
variant, was defined by a characteristic set of moral–political values
and an institutional and political strategy for advancing them. The values were egalitarian and participatory, with a strongly economic inflec-
tion. The institutional models included Keynesian macro-economic
steering, state regulation of market actors, workplace economic
democracy, and some measure of direct state ownership and planning.
The political strategy centered on the nation state, which was the chief
regulator, macro-economic manager, agent of income redistribution,
and sometime owner and planner.

Debate within the post-socialist Left begins from the conviction that
this statist and economistic approach to advancing egalitarian–democratic ideals is neither plausible nor adequate under contemporary
conditions. In part this conviction follows from greater appreciation of
the limits of the state, in part from a more expansive understanding of
those values themselves.

Appreciation of the limits of state competence and capacity flows
from at least two quarters. One, primarily concerning the economy,
draws negative lessons from the failures of much socialist planning, and
notes the fact that economic globalization – particularly given the
current distribution of political and military power – qualifies
the capacity of nation states, particularly small ones, to effectively
steer the economy within their borders. On the demand side of that
national economy, the Keynesian consensus at the foundation of social

democracy has substantially collapsed, leaving states much more cautious as economic actors promoting working-class well-being. On the supply side, central authorities typically lack the local knowledge needed to carry out potentially pro-worker policies in modernization, industrial adjustment, and training.

This last point generalizes beyond the economy to a second skepticism about the state, of great relevance to the work in this volume. These doubts follow from expansion in the scope and diversity of "local" problems that states are now routinely asked to remedy. Typically, though not always, such problems – in the environment, health, education, public safety, or countless other policy domains – present important inequalities in the power of affected actors. So leaving them to narrowly local solution is unacceptable; indeed, it commonly provides the first impetus to state involvement. But almost by definition, that involvement is immediately vexed. The most efficient solution to such problems requires knowledge of local circumstances and flexibility in adjusting general standards to them – something not easily achieved by central states. This problem only gets worse where, as is commonly the case, regulatory solutions in different policy domains or communities of interest are interdependent, and need to be reconciled. Such reconciliation requires a yet higher order of informed and flexible coordination by central authorities, a task that is typically beyond them.

Thus changes in the global economy undermine the state's capacity as economic manager. And what the state never claimed much capacity for – eliciting and acting on local knowledge, with nearly limitless monitoring and enforcement capacity for regulatory standards and solutions – it is increasingly asked to do. For both reasons, the nation state appears a less plausible agent of egalitarian–democratic advance.

On values, meanwhile, the gradual emergence of a more inclusive, tolerant, cosmopolitan understanding of the political public has undermined the appeal of a politics focussed on economic-class concerns, to the exclusion of interests in gender or racial justice, self-government by national groups, ethnic rights, the environment, and more. An egalitarian–democratic project must respect the heterogeneity of reasonable political demands. But this heterogeneity immediately creates a political problem – how to achieve collective focus, particularly among subordinate groups, on the achievement of any matter of shared concern.

Framed by these shifts in the world, debates in the post-socialist Left about models of a more just society have been dominated by two distinct, though compatible, lines of argument.

The first, growing out of appreciation of the state's limits as an economic manager, combines socialism's commitment to material equality with a renewed respect for markets as the preferred arena of economic coordination. Unlike social democracy, which left initial property positions largely intact, or state socialism, which abolished such positions entirely, it aims to promote greater equality through new forms and distributions of initial property assets,[1] which combine with markets to produce the desired result. In the Real Utopias series, John Roemer provides one example of such "asset egalitarianism." His "clamshell" socialism proceeds from an equalized *per capita* division of productive assets, and permits lifetime stock trades and consumption of dividends, if not principal.[2] Sam Bowles and Herb Gintis provide another example. Their work offers models that correct for inequalities in existing markets for essential goods not by direct regulation, but by endowing citizen consumers with new assets and special bargaining powers.[3]

The second line of argument grows out of an appreciation of the more general limits of the state's regulatory capacity. Building on the participatory, radical–democratic strand of traditional socialism, it seeks to construct models in which "local" players can be involved more directly in regulation and collective problem-solving, albeit with some form of center that coordinates local efforts. The idea is that empowering citizens, and then on more equal terms, is an intrinsic good, and a means of ensuring a fairer distribution of material resources. But it is also an important strategy for achieving more effective solutions to collective problems – informed by local knowledge, engaging local energies, and otherwise improving on the performance of a distant command-and-control central state.

Traditionally this radical democratic strand of the socialist project has been associated with ideas of economic democracy, including self-management and worker ownership, as well as more ambitious projects of democratic coordination above the level of the firm. But changes in firm and work organization and career patterns – more fluid firm boundaries, more discrete and shifting "communities of interest" within them, less sustained firm-specific employment, increased payoff to heterogeneous skills, greater integration of work and family life – suggest that the firm may not be the right locus of economic democracy. At the same time, the virtues of participatory, radical–democratic strategies are not confined to the economic arena. They seem to "travel" well to many areas of policy, including those areas of "local" coordination already noted. So the fact of political heterogeneity, while a challenge to socialism's traditionally privileged site for participatory democracy, here seems to invite its direct extension to a wider area of social life.

The work in this volume, and some of our own, exemplifies this participatory strand in post-socialist thought. Our work on associative democracy, which inaugurated the Real Utopias series with a volume on *Associations and Democracy*,[4] centered on the idea of improving democratic process and performance by a deliberate "politics of association." Instead of taking as fixed the strength and distribution of secondary organizations intermediate between state and market, liberal democratic governments would explicitly encourage an associational population better suited to representing underrepresented interests or adding to state capacities for regulation. In the concluding essay to that volume, we came around to the view that the point was not simply to foster associations of suitable kinds, but also to build new arenas for solving problems through citizen deliberation. Thus the idea was both to foster greater equality of power and to discipline the exercise of power directly through the common reason of citizens: to build a more democratic society, and a more deliberative democracy.

The present volume builds on this second strand of argument. Archon Fung and Erik Olin Wright offer a model of "Empowered Participatory Governance" (EPG), very much about the construction and use of citizen arenas for practically inclined democratic deliberation. The contributors then seek to assess the robustness and appeal of that model by considering some contemporary cases that arguably exemplify it. The cases vary widely: from Chicago schools and policing, to participatory budgeting in Porto Alegre, to the design of a range of public programs in West Bengal and Kerala, to the planning of complex regimes of habitat conservation in various parts of the United States. And at the very least, they present impressive evidence of social capacity for political invention. Across radically different circumstances, we see new forms of participation, all devised for attractively mundane purposes: making sure that schools work, that roads and water pipes get built where people need them, that jobs and endangered species both get protected, and that public safety improves in dangerous places.[5] These innovations are animated by and give evidence for the truth of the hopeful, radical–democratic assumption that explicitly animates this book – that ordinary people are capable of reducing the political role of untamed power and arbitrary preference and, through the exercise of their common reason, jointly solving important collective problems.

In our comments, we explore what more the book tells us about this hopeful assumption. In particular, we focus on the role in EPG of deliberation – the idea of subjecting collective decision to the rule of reason – and its relation to power. We find some important evidence here for the view that deliberative democracy is not, contrary to some of its critics, simply a way to empower the verbally agile and increase the returns to cultural capital, nor is its emphasis on reasons unduly respectful of the *status quo*. But we also criticize the presentation in the book for its inattention to conditions of background power. The cases discussed here differ sharply from one another in those background conditions, and on how they, or their remedy, figure in the activities under discussion here. By treating these cases as all instances of a common model, Fung and Wright may obscure the importance of this difference, and may exaggerate the capacity of deliberation itself to neutralize the effects of unequal power.

II The Empirics of Deliberation

The model of empowered participatory governance (EPG) comprises three conditions: focussed problem-solving, participation, and deliberation. We have EPG when parties who are affected by a certain area of policy come together to deliberate about which policies are most suitable to their case, and the results of their deliberation in fact determine the policies adopted. The ideas of focussed problem-solving and participation raise large questions.[6] But we put these issues aside here, and focus instead on what the cases tell us about the "deliberation" aspect of EPG.

Briefly, to deliberate means to debate alternatives on the basis of considerations that all take to be relevant; it is a matter of offering reasons for alternatives,[7] rather than merely stating a preference for one or another, with such preferences then subject to some rule of aggregation or submitted to bargaining. The exchange of reasons that a deliberative democracy puts at the center of collective decision-making is not to be confused with simple discussion, or the revelation and exchange of private information. Any view of intelligent political decision-making sees such discussion and exchange as important, if only because of initial asymmetries in the possession of relevant information. What is distinctive about a deliberative view is that the processing of this information is disciplined by the claims of reason – that arguments must be offered on behalf of proposals, and be supported by considerations that are acknowledged to provide relevant reasons, even though there may be disagreements about the weight and precise content of those considerations.

Consider, by way of illustration, the case of education. In deciding how to allocate resources, some relevant and potentially competing reasons might be: enabling each student to achieve his or her potential; promoting the performance of those who are performing least well; providing a common educational experience for students of diverse backgrounds. In the case of health care, they might be: benefiting those who are worst off; aiding those who would benefit most from medical resources; assisting the largest number of people; ensuring that all people have fair chances at receiving help, regardless of the urgency of their situation and of expected benefits from treatment.[8] As these examples suggest, the reasons relevant to particular domains can be complex, varied, and often competing, and there often will be no clear, principled basis for ranking them: reasonable people may reasonably disagree on how they should be weighted. And after the competing reasons are all aired, they may continue to disagree about the right result. Nevertheless, they accept the results of the deliberative process as legitimate in part in virtue of its having given due consideration to the relevant reasons.

The normative attraction of deliberation goes well beyond the prospect of public action based on the most complete relevant information, even the most complete information about possibly principled bases for action. In the ideal case, collective decision-making through deliberation also *neutralizes the political role of arbitrary preferences and power* by putting collective decisions on a footing of common reason. In ideal deliberation, the only power that prevails is, as Habermas puts it, the "force of the better argument"[9] – and that is a force equally available to all. If a commitment to deliberation in this way neutralizes power and equalizes chances to influence collective decision-making, moreover, it should also tend to produce more equitable outcomes than would otherwise result. The deliberative ideal of using common reason to discipline power and preference thus arguably connects to substantive norms of political equality (fairness of process) and distributive equity (fairness of result).[10]

Other effects and virtues are sometimes associated with deliberation: that it changes preferences in desirable, democracy-promoting, ways; that it encourages mutual respect among parties; that its connection to common reason fosters legitimacy in a way that bargaining, or majority rule with a simple counting of heads, do not; that it promotes more information revelation and, finally and simply, more intelligent decisions.[11] But the idea that deliberation helps to neutralize power is fundamental, and provides our focus here. What precisely is this claim, and what do the cases assembled here tell us about the possibilities of its achievement in the real world?

Two Prefatory Points

Before answering this question, however, we enter two prefatory points.

First, if the cases tell us anything hopeful at all, it will be largely news. Empirical literature on deliberation is thin, and not very promising in observed effects. As Rebecca Abers notes,[12] the "case study literature on experiments in direct citizen participation in governance is on the whole pessimistic," especially if measured against the standards of democratic deliberation proposed here. Either the full range of those affected by decisions – particularly the poor and less equipped with education and other "cultural capital" – did not actually participate in discussion. Or deliberative bodies were "talk shops," whose conclusions did not guide final policy decisions. More recent assessments also raise concerns about how deliberation may produce polarization, and about how reticence to express political judgements may lead to inequalities in deliberative participation.[13] But the concerns about polarization emerge most sharply in settings in which like-minded people deliberate, and the concerns about reticence have been studied in informal settings of discussion different from the problem-solving arenas that provide the focus for the case studies here.[14] One of the great strengths of this volume, indeed, is its wealth of examples from such arenas, presumably the most relevant to taking deliberative democracy seriously in actual public policy.

Second, however, a large caveat needs to be entered on the kinds of inference that can be supported by these cases. In selecting their cases, the editors sought to find illuminating illustrations of EPG, not to test a theory about it. In effect, they have sampled on a dependent variable. Given the immature state of theory and data in this area, this judgement made sense. Its downside, however, is that we lack the variation needed for testing hypotheses.

For example, in his treatment of participatory budgeting in Porto Alegre, Gianpaolo Baiocchi presents suggestive evidence in support of the claim that EPG has helped produce a fairer allocation of public-works spending in that city, one more attentive in particular to the needs of poorer neighborhoods. But the evidence presented, while consistent with this claim for EPG, is also consistent with the hypothesis that this fairer allocation results more directly from the Workers' Party

(PT) dominance of city government. Absent the pairing of cases with relevant variation – say, Porto Alegre with other cities run by the PT for comparable numbers of years, but without participatory budgeting; or different cities with participatory budgeting but with sustained differences in party control – we cannot decide this issue, or understand EPG's distinctive contribution. Similarly, the study of Kerala by T.M. Thomas Isaac and Patrick Heller finds increased popular participation as a result of institutionalization of the local grama sabhas, and fairer allocations of public resources following adoption of the Communist Party of India/Marxist's highly devolved program of economic development. Thomas Isaac and Heller do not find much deliberation in the grama sabhas, which meet infrequently, often at great distance from would-be participants, and are "too large and unwieldy for meaningful deliberation."[15] So we may simply have evidence for the idea that popular empowerment itself shifts the balance of political power to poorer citizens, and this – rather than reason-giving – generates shifts in public spending. In any case, the selection of cases counsels caution in drawing inferences.

This limitation acknowledged, the cases are instructive on the practical details of popular deliberation. In particular they suggest that at least some familiar objections to democratic deliberation are overstated, and at least some of its promised returns are in evidence – if overdetermined, or perhaps determined solely, by the supportive political organizations and movements that spurred the experiments in the first place.

III Two Common Objections to Deliberation's Promise

The cases presented here seem to offer good evidence against two common objections to deliberative democracy, or to power-neutralizing claims made on its behalf.[16]

The Power of the Word

The first objection – suggested by Pierre Bourdieu's skepticism about "linguistic communism" – departs from the observation that reasoning is an acquired capacity, not equally distributed among all. So collective decision-making through reason-giving may not *neutralize* power, but instead create new forms of unequally distributed power: a "logocracy," in which power goes to the rhetorically or laryngically gifted.

Moreover, this rule of the reasoners (not of reason) is likely to compound existing social inequalities. According to some critics, we can expect a preponderance of the economically advantaged, or men, or those otherwise possessed of cultural capital and argumentative confidence.

But from the evidence of the cases considered here – particularly those concerning the less educated and in the cases considered by Baiocchi (Porto Alegre participatory budgeting), Thomas Isaac and Heller (West Bengal and Kerala economic planning and budgeting), and Fung (Chicago policing and schools) – this objection is less than compelling. It overstates the weight of the feared effect, and underestimates the capacity of deliberative bodies and political officials to recognize and alleviate it, should it arise. Thus Fung finds that citizen participation in Chicago policing efforts is greater in poorer neighborhoods, and that the city, cognizant of concerns about cultural and class bias, invested resources in training participants in policing and schooling efforts. Baiocchi finds high rates of involvement by poorer, less-educated citizens, and a substantial role for women's participation in participatory budgeting bodies. And Thomas Isaac and Heller report high rates of participation by women, the poor, and less educated – indeed, if anything, an overrepresentation of the poor in the grama sabhas, owing to their higher stake in the decisions made there.

The case of Habitat Conservation Planning (HCP) is very different. Noting the great diversity in HCPs, and the difficulty of drawing any crisp lessons from the experience, Craig Thomas observes that many HCPs are "relatively small and elitist," and that internal deliberation is often dominated by experts, not ordinary citizens. What is not clear from his discussion, however, is whether the arenas are expert-dominated *because* they are deliberative, and thus unwelcoming to citizens who lack rhetorical confidence – or simply because the planning process has few democratic ambitions.[17]

Moreover, the cases suggest some support for the claim that decision-making through joint reasoning shifts *outcomes* and not only processes. In Porto Alegre and Kerala, there appear to be substantial shifts in the allocation of public resources to the poor, and in Chicago some redirection of police capacities to more pressing problems identified by citizens. It should be said, however, that Thomas Isaac and Heller do not find a great deal of deliberation in the Kerala case, so it may be that the results come from the dominance of the Left party, or from the sheer fact of broader participation. But deliberation may help in the other cases, and in any case does not seem to have the deficiencies identified by some critics.

Of particular interest are the arguments that deliberative bodies need not take rates and kinds of participation as given. When biases appear in citizens' capacity to participate, deliberative bodies can undertake affirmative measures to address those biases. In particular, they can help to train participants in the issues decided by the body and in how to frame arguments about the relevant policies. In Kerala, indeed, "a critical component of the Campaign has been an elaborate training program that has become one of the largest non-formal education programs ever undertaken in India,"[18] with several hundred thousand participants involved in multiple rounds of multi-day training focussed on one or another part of the planning process. On this, Jane Mansbridge is right that it would help to know more about the details of training offered to ensure deliberative equality.[19] Is the training really disinterested, and directed at increasing participant skills? Or is it abused for indoctrination or political control? This is a fair concern, perhaps especially when the deliberative body is sponsored by a political party. But then, some version of it might be applied to almost any program of civic education. Here, in any case, the straightforward capacity-building aims of training appear clearly dominant over any "political education."

A final observation on this first line of criticism: it needs to be acknowledged that the favorable findings presented here on the practice of deliberation may reflect something about the specific kinds of deliberative bodies under consideration. As Fung and Wright emphasize, the deliberative bodies studied in this volume aim to solve relatively concrete problems – to improve policy in relatively well defined areas – not to have open-ended public debate that sets political priorities, or to arrive at principles of political morality. So the cases do not show much about whether remedies for inequalities of deliberative capacity carry over to other cases, where (a critic might argue) inequalities of argumentative skills may be more recalcitrant to remedy. But it does seem that critics of deliberation were too quick to suppose that decision-making through joint reasoning would inevitably empower the verbally agile.

The Suppression of Self-Interest

A second objection to deliberation is that its conception of reason-giving as the favored form of political speech will work to the disadvantage of subordinate groups. Because those groups are subordinated, their particular interests may not be well understood or included within conventional understandings of the common good. To limit deliberation to arguments appealing somehow to that good, or to other considerations that are commonly cognized as reasons, boxes members of subordinate groups out of stating their interests at all; norms, according to the critic, reflect power, and are not an alternative basis of collective decision. Rather than playing this rigged game of deliberation, then, subordinate groups would do better to engage in straight-up bargaining. Thus Mansbridge observes that

> a single focus on the common good tends to make the assertion of self-interest illegitimate. Yet recognizing and asserting self-interest helps one figure out oneself what one wants. Recognizing and asserting self-interest helps in becoming understood (and respected) for what one wants and needs. Recognizing and asserting self-interest helps unveil hegemonic understandings of the common good when those understandings have evolved to mask subtle forms of oppression.[20]

But this objection rests on a conceptual confusion about deliberation, and has – at least from the cases considered here – almost no empirical basis.

Deliberation does not preclude statements of self-interest. The deliberative view holds that expressions of self-interest do not qualify as *justifications* for anything – as statements of reasons in the desired sense. But it admits them as ways to present *information*. For example, a relevant consideration in deliberation, and a possible justification or reason for a policy, is that it represents a fair accommodation of the interests of all, or advances the good of those who are in greatest need. But to know that it does either of these things, we need to know what those interests are, and expressions of self-interest by relevant persons are one way to find that out. Where the deliberative norm cuts is simply that saying "this policy is in my (my group's) interest(s)" is not itself a reason for adopting a policy, but again it may be very relevant information in choosing among different policies.

More immediately still, however, the objection lacks any empirical referent in the cases considered here. Even in those cases involving the most subordinate of groups, they suggest no evidence that members of those groups are reluctant to express their self-interests, or even to bring forth proposals specifically geared to meeting them. Nor is there any suggestion that statements are met with such criticism.

Why Reason Together?

But it is a third concern about deliberative democracy that needs more attention from proponents. The presentation in the book, however, is not very illuminating on this issue.

According to this objection, deliberation is a ruse unless substantial background equality of position is already assured. Or, conversely, under conditions of substantial inequality of power, a requirement of presenting reasons is unlikely to limit or neutralize power. Because constraints on what counts as a reason are not well defined, the advantaged will find some way to defend self-serving proposals with considerations that are arguably general. For example, they may make appeals to ideas of the common advantage, but press a conception of the common advantage that assigns great weight to the *status quo*. "Common advantage" will then consist in advantage relative to the existing framework of inequality, with that framework itself left off the deliberative table. Or if they fail in this, the advantaged will simply refuse to accept the discipline of deliberation. They will recognize, to paraphrase Hobbes, that reasons without the sword are but words with no force to tie anyone's hands. So actors with sufficient power to advance their aims without deliberating will not bother to deliberate. Or if for some reason they formally agree to deliberation, we can expect them only to offer "reasons" for action that in fact are purely self-serving proposals.

If this objection is right, then proposals for deliberative democracy that are inattentive to background relations of power will waste the time of those who can least afford its loss: those now subordinate in power. The time and energy they spend in argument, laboring under the illusion that sweet reason will constrain the power that suppresses them, is time and energy they could have spent in self-organization, instrumental efforts to increase their own power, or like efforts to impose costs on opponents.

What to make of this objection?

As a first response, let us be clear that observing the importance of background differences in power is not a criticism of the deliberative ideal *per se*, but a concern about its application. Deliberative democracy is a normative model of collective decision-making, not a universal political strategy. And commitment to the normative ideal does not require commitment to the belief that collective decision-making through mutual reason-giving – particularly reason-giving that expresses the democratic idea of members as equals – is always possible. So it may indeed be the case that some rough background balance of power is required before parties will listen to reason. But observing that does not importantly lessen the attraction of the deliberative ideal; it simply states a condition of its reasonable pursuit.

Thus, in Habermas's account of the ideal speech situation, or Cohen's account of an ideal deliberative procedure, inequalities in power are stipulated away for the sake of model construction.[21] These idealizations are intended to characterize the nature of reasoned collective decision-making and in turn to provide models for actual arrangements of collective decision-making. But actual arrangements must provide some basis for confidence that joint reasoning will actually prevail in shaping the exercise of collective power, and gross inequalities of power surely undermine any such confidence. In *Justice as Impartiality*, Brian Barry refers to the social and political conditions needed to actualize idealized deliberation as the "circumstances of impartiality."[22] In Barry's account, parties in the circumstances of impartiality need to be well informed, and prepared to listen to reasonable objections, regardless of the source of the objections. So discussion that expresses the deliberative ideal must operate with a background of free expression and association, thus providing minimal conditions for the availability of relevant information. Equally, if parties are not somehow constrained to accept the consequences of deliberation, if "exit options" are not foreclosed, it seems implausible that they will accept the discipline of joint reasoning, and in particular to reasoning informed by the democratic idea of persons as equals. Firms retaining a more or less costless ability to move investment elsewhere are not, for example, likely to accept the discipline of reasoned deliberation about labor standards, with workers as their deliberative equals.

Deliberation, then, is an ideal whose realization has preconditions. In the absence of those preconditions, we cannot expect the force of the better argument to prevail. And equally, when those preconditions are not met, we have a problem in the circumstances, not in the ideal that condemns them.

Specifying the conditions in which it can work is an empirical question, at the very heart of the concerns of this volume: What are the needed conditions? How widely can they be secured? Unfortunately, while the presentation of theory and cases in this book is consistent with acknowledging the importance of such questions – and of the underlying issue of differences in background power – the similar treatment of very diverse cases obscures the issue.

To be sure, Fung and Wright note important differences among the four cases.[23] But their principal emphasis is on *similarities*:

Though each of these cases differs from the others in its ambition, scope, and concrete aims, they all share surprising similarities in their motivating principles and institutional design features. They may have enough in common to describe them as instances of a novel, but broadly applicable, model of deliberative democratic practice that can be expanded horizontally . . . and vertically.[24]

And indeed, the cases do share some features. In each case, we have discussion aimed at problem-solving, rather than at the clarification of opinion. In each, the decisions more or less directly affect the allocation of public resources, rather than simply the decisions of non-public bodies. And in each, the participants in discussion are not territorial representatives with general responsibilities of representation, but ordinary citizens participating in person, or representatives with discrete responsibilities and policy bounds.

But on the issue that concerns us here, the relevance of background differences in power to deliberation, little is made of important differences among the cases. Those discussed by Fung (schools, policing) and Thomas (environmental regulation) are set against a background in which imbalances of power are not of obvious relevance to decision-making. Neither suggests that deliberation neutralizes power, but only because inequalities of power are not what stands in the way of achieving reasonable aims in these cases. Such inequalities of course exist in U.S. politics. But in both cases the issue is essentially one of achieving coordination for mutual benefit.

In the Chicago policing case, for example, the large problem is a lack of the information that is needed to target policing efforts. The role of the deliberative bodies is to provide that information, which citizens living in neighborhoods are assumed to have, and to provide it in the context of focussed, practical discussions aimed at addressing neighborhood security needs. But the deliberation does not address a fundamental conflict of interests. Instead it generates information and perhaps fosters greater trust between cops and citizens. And where there are conflicts of interest about neighborhood security – about how much to invest in police, and about the value of policing and other methods of improving community security (economic improvement, for example) – the community policing system described by Fung does not actually address those issues. In the case of HCPs, deliberation does not neutralize power but instead proceeds against the background of power-neutralizing threats of litigation or alternative EPA rule-making or decree available under the Endangered Species Act, a big stick that was "part of the background that brings actors to a common table,"[25] and that provided developers, in particular, an incentive to work with environmentalists.

In contrast, deliberative problem-solving arrangements in the non-U.S. cases do not result from such discrete innovations designed to address bounded policy problems – to be solved either through better information or through *de facto* "bargaining in the shadow of the law." They are instead part of much larger political projects, themselves aimed precisely at changing a more fundamental balance of power between large forces in society. In Porto Alegre and Kerala, the deliberative arenas and practices were established by leftist parties, with a broad social base and a program of mobilizing and activating the poor and dispossessed. The relevant participatory bodies are both effect and cause of a wider political mobilization that enabled groups to participate who had not participated before, and, importantly, those bodies have much wider powers than the more policy-specific bodies considered in the U.S. cases. Whereas the U.S. cases are arguably about achieving mutual gains through better coordination, and the point of the deliberation is to settle on a mutually beneficial plan, the non-U.S. cases are apparently about redistributing power and advantage. Indeed, they are as much about shifting the balance of power to create democratic conditions in the first place – including local democracy in traditionally centralized political systems – as they are about establishing specifically deliberative forms of democratic practice. Indeed, in the Kerala case, Thomas Isaac and Heller find only the empowerment, not the deliberation. In Porto Alegre, the shift in power achieved by the participatory budgeting arrangements appears to establish the social and political conditions that give a point to joint reasoning.

In emphasizing the common features of the different cases considered in this volume, Fung and Wright seem to overlook this difference, a difference that bears on the generalizability of deliberative problem-solving. Precisely because the U.S. cases are instances of deliberation aimed at improved coordination, we may – if we do not attend to the differences – lose the essential importance, in cases of distributive or redistributive politics, of shifting the relations of power as a precondition to enabling public deliberation to work its effects. The problem of generalizing deliberation is not that subordinate groups are unable to hold their own in deliberation, but that those with power advantages will not willingly submit themselves to the discipline of reason if that discipline presents large threats to their advantage.

Perhaps this relative inattention to the differences among the cases is simple oversight. But something more may be at work, and it is worth asking what that might be. That is, is there a more fundamental reason for thinking that deliberation *is* generalizable, making differences in background relations of power are less significant than we are supposing? Why might someone suppose that deliberation can work its power-neutralizing effects under a very broad range of political conditions, and not simply when there has been an explicit effort to redress profound background inequalities of power?

The most plausible rationale is an argument from uncertainty. Grant that actors will not hold their interests hostage to deliberative problem-solving if they have reasonable assurance of an ability to protect themselves and promote their interests without such submission. But what if they do not have that assurance? What if in fact they do not know yet what their interests are? The willingness to join in deliberation may derive precisely from uncertainty on these essentials.

Here is how this might go. First, even an agent who apparently has large resources and power will want to generate new information. Second, that agent will recognize that other agents have information relevant to his or her own protection and advantage. But then suppose, third, that the environment is not very stable and that information relevant to advancing interests changes rapidly. Then apparently more powerful agents will have strong incentives to elicit the willing cooperation of apparently less powerful agents so that the latter reveal the information they have that bears on the interests of the more powerful. And one strategy for eliciting that cooperation will be to offer reasons rather than force to the subordinate. Moreover, because the relevant information cannot be provided on a one-shot basis (this is the force of the assumption about the shifting environment), the incentive is actually to establish some form of ongoing discussion in which information will regularly be gathered and reported. So even the apparently powerful agents emerge from reflection on the circumstances of uncertainty with an interest in establishing ongoing arenas of deliberative discussion aimed at exploring solutions to practical problems.

Now this uncertainty-based argument may seem not to get us all the way to deliberation. If the aim is simply to elicit information, it may be possible simply to pay for it, that is, to ensure some form of mutual gains, in the way that bargaining does. But the acknowledgement of pervasive, persistent, and profound uncertainty, and the associated recognition of mutual dependence, may throw into question our sense of our own interests. After all, even the powerful come to see their own fate as dependent on securing the willing cooperation of others, as the fate of the weak depends on the willing cooperation of the strong. And this recognition of commonality of circumstance and mutual dependence – of a sense of being "in it together" – may produce a sense of shared identity and shared fate, which in turn changes the understanding of interests. How I think about my good, after all, plausibly depends on how I understand myself; and the facts of pervasive inter-dependence, constantly reinforced in arenas of discussion with diverse others, is bound to change that self-understanding.

Or so the uncertainty argument might go.

But note two things about this argument, as it bears our focus on the neutralizing effects of deliberation on power. First, uncertainty's effects here are felt directly, not *via* deliberation. The argument is not about the power-neutralizing effects of deliberation itself, under background conditions of uncertainty, but about how pervasive uncertainty itself undermines differences of power, leading to acceptance of delibera-tion. Deliberation emerges as a way to pool information and explore strategies of coordination given the power-neutralizing effects of uncertainty. Second, and more to the point, it seems clear that the pro-found, pervasive, and sustained uncertainty required to achieve this direct effect – that is, to make substantial differences of power only apparent, and of no real effect in protecting and advancing interests – is a very special case. We cannot assume that, as a general matter, uncertainty takes that distinctive form. And if it does not, then gaining the benefits of deliberation may well require direct efforts to address inequalities of power.

Moving Forward

Creating a deliberative democracy is an important part of the post-socialist, egalitarian–democratic project. And much of the evidence presented in this book indicates that efforts to make democracy more deliberative have considerable promise: they appear not to be vexed by inequalities in deliberative capacities, or to silence historically excluded groups; moreover, the promise of deliberative democracy appears to resonate, under a broad range of circumstances.

But the project of constructing a more deliberative democracy should not be based on naive expectations about the autonomy of reason from political reality or the capacity of reason to defeat naked power. A central aim of the democratic project, indeed one way of expressing the democratic ambition itself, is to ensure a place for the shared reason of equals in practical politics. This place cannot be claimed at all, however, unless the inequalities of power that would thwart an expansive role for such reason are defeated, or at least momentarily kept at bay. The Fung–Wright model of EPG is consistent with this observation, but its application – its like treatment of the very different cases, involving different roles for background differences in power – is insufficiently disciplined by attention to these inequalities.

Cases in which deliberation emerges as a way to exploit possibilities of mutually beneficial coordination differ substantially from cases in which deliberative problem-solving depends on and follows from a broader democratization of social power. The project of deliberative democracy must respect that difference. Neglecting it invites illusions about the present place of reason in our politics, and about what would be required to increase its prominence.

Notes

* Respectively, Goldberg Professor of the Humanities, Professor of Philosophy and Political Science at Massachusetts Institute of Technology; Macarthur Professor of Law, Political Science, and Sociology at University of Wisconsin-Madison.

1. The social democratic project left the inequality of property holdings largely intact, and thereby guaranteed eternal contest over achievement of a passably equal income distribution, which required a "taking" from those who had benefited from initial property inequalities.

2. John Roemer, *Equal Shares: Making Market Socialism Work*, New York and London: Verso (1996).

3. Samuel Bowles and Herbert Gintis, *Recasting Egalitarianism: New Rules for Communities, States and Markets*, New York and London: Verso (1999).

4. Joshua Cohen and Joel Rogers, *Associations and Democracy*, New York and London: Verso (1995).

5. Hannah Arendt might have shuddered to think that the noble activity of political innovation could be brought so low, but so much the worse for Arendt.

6. In his discussion of Chicago policing, Fung says that "17–21 residents generally attend each meeting in addition to five or six beat officers." With four to six thousand adults living in each beat, these numbers may seem very small, but they are, he says, "more than enough for problem-solving planning and implementation" (p. 128). Without disputing this assertion about sufficiency for solving problems, we might naturally wonder what such low participation rates indicate about democratic promise, and what would be required to show that participants are sufficiently representative or accountable to answer those concerns.

7. Of course, the availability of such shared reason may itself be in doubt. Much of the recent literature on deliberative democracy aims to clarify just what the relevant idea of a reason is, particularly when participants in deliberation are assumed to have basic disagreements in their respective philosophies of life. We will not pursue this issue here, but recommend the wide-ranging and illuminating discussion in Samuel Freeman, "Deliberative Democracy: A Sympathetic Comment," *Philosophy and Public Affairs*, vol. 29, no. 4 (Fall 2000), pp. 371–418.

8. See Norman Daniels, "Limits to Health Care: Fair Procedures, Democratic Deliberation, and the Legitimacy Problem for Insurers," *Philosophy and Public Affairs*, vol. 26, no. 4, pp. 303–51.

9. Jürgen Habermas, *Theory of Communicative Action*, trans. Thomas McCarthy, Boston: Beacon Press (1984), p. 25.

10. Joshua Cohen, "Procedure and Substance in Deliberative Democracy," in Seyla Benhabib, ed., *Democracy and Difference: Changing Boundaries of the Political*, Princeton: Princeton University Press (1996).

11. Freeman, "Deliberative Democracy."

12. This volume, p. 200.

13. See Cass Sunstein, *Designing Democracy: What Constitutions Do*, Oxford:

Oxford University Press (2001), chapter 1; Pamela Johnston Conover *et al.*, "The Deliberative Potential of Political Discussion," *British Journal of Political Science*, vol. 32 (2002), pp. 21–62.

14. Conover *et al.* suggest that some familiar barriers to deliberative discussion – inexperience in argument, failures of education, a general lack of social confidence, and so on – may be remediable through education (ibid., pp. 59–60) and, as we indicate below, the case studies reported in this volume provide some suggestive support for this claim. They also find a large source of reticence in the unwillingness of individuals to state their political views, and expose them to criticism. In the problem-solving settings studied here, that reticence seems not to be in evidence, though it is not easy to tell whether the reduced reticence reflects self-selection or a sense that in these settings reticence is not appropriate and political views are not properly construed as private matters.

15. Thomas Isaac and Heller, this volume, p. 103.

16. For critical discussion of deliberative democracy, see Lynn Sanders, "Against Deliberation," *Political Theory*, vol. 25 (1997), pp. 347–76; Iris Young, "Communication and the Other: Beyond Deliberative Democracy," in Seyla Benhabib, ed., *Democracy and Difference: Contesting the Boundaries of the Political*, Princeton: Princeton University Press (1994); and the essays by Susan Stokes, James Johnson, and James Fearon in Jon Elster, ed., *Deliberative Democracy*, Cambridge: Cambridge University Press (1998).

17. On this point, see Thomas's footnote 22, p. 170 on the guidelines for public participation.

18. Thomas Isaac and Heller, this volume, p. 83.

19. Mansbridge, this volume, p. 185.

20. Mansbridge, this volume, p. 179.

21. See the essays by Cohen and Habermas in James Bohman and William Rehg, ed., *Deliberative Democracy*, Cambridge, MA: MIT Press (1997).

22. Brian Barry, *Justice as Impartiality*, Oxford: Oxford University Press (1995), pp. 99–111.

23. Fung and Wright, Introduction to this volume, p. 5.

24. Fung and Wright, Introduction to this volume, p. 15.

25. Thomas, this volume, p. 161.

PART IV
Epilogue

Countervailing Power in Empowered Participatory Governance
Archon Fung and Erik Olin Wright*

The chapters of this volume focus upon the institutional designs of Empowered Participatory Governance. Fair, effective, and sustainable deliberation and participation in institutions depend, however, not just on the details of their design but also upon background contexts, and in particular upon the constellation of social forces that maneuver in and around EPG institutions. In particular, as Cohen and Rogers write,

> Deliberation . . . is an ideal whose realization has preconditions. In the absence of those preconditions, we cannot expect the force of the better argument to prevail . . . What are those needed conditions? Unfortunately, while the presentation of the theory and cases in this book are consistent with acknowledging the importance of such questions – and of the underlying issue of differences in background power – the similar treatment of very diverse cases obscures the issue.[1]

By focussing upon similarities across institutional designs, our presentation of EPG may share a fault with other proposals for collaborative and participatory governance. Such schemes are often inattentive to problems of powerlessness and domination, thus seeming to suggest that if only the institutional designs can be constructed just right, then gross imbalances of power in the contexts of these institutions will be neutralized.

That is certainly not our considered view. In this epilogue, we begin to address this crucial question regarding the social circumstances necessary for EPG to contribute to just governance by engaging the central problem raised by Cohen and Rogers in their comment – the ways in which inequalities of background power can subvert the democracy-enhancing potential of institutional designs such as EPG. Our discussion will revolve around the concept and role of what we term *countervailing power* – a variety of mechanisms that reduce, and perhaps even neutralize, the power-advantages of ordinarily powerful actors.[2] We contend that in nearly all contexts significant countervailing power is necessary for EPG to yield the benefits for democratic governance that we have claimed for it. The absence of mobilized countervailing power jeopardizes both EPG institutions that aim to solve bounded policy challenges – as in the Chicago schools and policing – as well as those that aim to transform fundamental balances of social power – such as the Porto Alegre and Kerala cases.[3] The key question, then, is whether or not it is plausible that the required kind of countervailing power can emerge in the contexts of EPG institutions to enable them to function in a robust, sustainable manner.

Countervailing power is the too-simple concept that describes how powerful actors with privileged access to decision-making venues may be challenged and even defeated from time to time by the weak and less organized. Countervailing power conjures images of organizations of patients facing down health maintenance organizations, "citizens [circling] their wagons against the onslaught of some power elite" or "the activities of blacks, women, and environmentalists . . . against the Reagan administration."[4] In such conventional, adversarial, arenas, the forms of countervailing power (which we will term "*adversarial countervailing power*") are quite familiar. They appear as interest groups, public interest litigators, social movements, or perhaps cross-cutting networks of professionals and officials.[5]

The forms and functions of countervailing power relevant to empowered participatory governance are, however, much less clear. Indeed, it might seem at first glance that the deliberative ideals of empowered participatory governance are deeply at odds with the very idea of countervailing power, since countervailing power suggests the use of threats and mobilization, rather than reason, to settle issues in dispute. It is for this reason that defenders of the ideals of popular empowerment are generally skeptical about the prospects of somehow combining effective countervailing power with meaningful forms of collaboration. These concerns raise a number of important questions. What, precisely, does it mean to talk about mobilized forms of power of disadvantaged groups in a decision-making setting that is meant to engender collaborative, deliberative problem-solving? What are the obstacles to creating such forms of countervailing power? And how can those obstacles be overcome? How might such countervailing power be cultivated, and what would prevent it from fostering adversarial confrontations that undermine the deliberations of EPG? These are the issues we will address in this epilogue.

We will begin, in section I, by clarifying the concept of countervailing power, especially as it relates to collaborative settings of decision-making. Section II explores four general propositions about the relationship between collaborative governance and countervailing power. Section III examines a number of empirical examples in light of these propositions. Section IV examines the difficulty of using adversarial countervailing power for collaborative purposes, and section V more speculatively discusses ways in which collaborative countervailing power might be constructed.

I Governance and Countervailing Power

Two Governance Modes: Top-Down Adversarial and Participatory-Collaborative

The forms and consequences of countervailing power, and social power generally, depend upon the shape of political institutions in which that power operates. Two dimensions on which these institutions vary are especially salient: first, the extent to which they are organized primarily as *adversarial* or *collaborative* forms of decision-making, and second, whether the governance process is primarily *top-down* or *participatory*. In adversarial decision-making, interest groups seek to maximize their interests by winning important government decisions over administrative and legal programs and rules, typically through some kind of bargaining process. In collaborative decision-making, by contrast, the central effort is to solve problems rather than to win victories, to discover the broadest commonality of interests rather than to mobilize maximum support for given interests. In top-down governance structures decisions are made by actors at the peak of an organizational structure and then imposed on lower levels; in participatory governance, decisions involve substantial direct involvement of actors from the bottom tiers.

Taking these two dimensions together generates the four types of governance in figure 11.1 (page 262).

For our purposes, the two most important cells in this typology are top-down adversarial governance and participatory collaborative governance. Many scholars have developed criticisms of top-down

Character of decision-making process

		Adversarial	Collaborative
	Top down	Conventional interest group politics	Expert/elite problem-solving (e.g. negotiated rulemaking)
	Participatory	Some town meetings	Empowered participatory governance

Governance structure (vertical label, left side)

Figure 11.1 Varieties of Governance Structures and Processes

adversarial governance.[6] Adversarialism emphasizes the differences between groups rather than their commonalities, and so potentially generates excess conflict. This conflict reduces the *legitimacy* of the rule-making process on one hand, and the *creativity* of governance on the other.[7] Because interests face different barriers to collective action, some interests dominate others and can capture the "subgovernments" or "policy subsystems" that are most vital to them.[8] Because those who formulate the rules and programs are often far from those who must live under them, top-down governance solutions often suffer from lack of relevant information and local knowledge, and long feedback loops. Similarly, the long chain of command connecting decision to implementation exacerbates the familiar principal-agent problems that plague the public sector. Finally, top-down governance methods have been thought to generate fixed rules that are inappropriate for governance contexts of high local diversity, volatility, and scientific uncertainty.[9]

Partially in response to these failures, practitioners and scholars have offered forms of collaborative governance, of which our proposal for empowered participatory governance is one kind, as alternatives to adversarial interest-group politics. The "field" of collaboration contains many flavors of non-adversarial governance, including regulatory negotiation, alternative dispute resolution, stakeholder negotiation, and grass-roots community problem-solving.[10] Many of these forms of collaborative governance, however, primarily involve elites and experts, thus retaining the top-down quality typical of much adversarial governance. The introduction to this volume explains how empowered participatory governance is a form of collaborative governance that distinctively combines popular participation, decentralized decision-making, practical focus, continuous deliberation and engagement, and cooperation between parties and interests that frequently find themselves on opposite sides of political and social questions.

The Problem of Countervailing Power in Collaborative Decision-Making

Both collaborative and adversarial modes of governance suffer from the characteristic danger that some interests and parties may be improperly subordinated for the sake of more powerful interests and groups. In adversarial arenas, this problem has been well explored theoretically and empirically by students of collective action, interest-group politics,[11] and social movements. The relevance, shape, functions, and effects of countervailing power in collaborative arenas are much less well understood. Perhaps because the topic of collaborative governance is relatively new and because those who study collaboration may be less disposed to ponder the difficulties of conflict, there has been very little empirical investigation of these questions. Another difficulty may be that there are not many forms of collaborative countervailing power to study yet. In areas where collaborative governance is novel, organizations, interest groups, and individuals may have not yet recognized the importance of countervailing power or enjoyed opportunities to develop appropriate organizations and strategies. Indeed, for many people the expression "collaborative countervailing power" may seem a bit of an oxymoron: if a governance process is truly collaborative, then how can it involve *counter*vailing power of one group against another? Does this not somehow contradict the very spirit of collaboration?

We believe that, in general, collaborative governance without an appropriate form of countervailing power is likely to fail for at least three overlapping reasons. First, in areas where countervailing power is already well organized in adversarial forms – for example the environmental and labor movements – these organizations are likely to oppose institutional movements from adversarial to collaborative forms of governance. Their capacities and approaches are well adapted to adversarialism, and the shift to collaboration may be seen as risky, costly, and demobilizing. Second, the specific designs of institutions of collaboration are themselves generally the result of endogenous political processes. Where countervailing power is weak or nonexistent, the rules of collaboration are likely to favor entrenched, previously organized, or concentrated interests. They may do so by limiting the agenda of issues that is open to collaboration, restricting the range of participants to a select few, and reducing the influence of collaboration to mere advice that can be heeded or ignored. Collaboration, under these conditions, is much more likely to become top-down collaborative governance involving experts and powerful interests even if its impulse originated from bottom-up initiatives. Third, even with fair institutional rules for collaboration, concentrated or entrenched interests will more ably advance their interests over those of others unless countervailing forms of power mitigate these general advantages. With collaborative forms of regulation, for example, firms and industry groups usually enjoy advantages over workers and consumers. When collaborative reforms aim to open service agencies – schools or police departments – to broader participation, street-level bureaucrats who are trained, full-time professionals can protect their prerogatives even as they ostensibly collaborate with parents, residents, and other lay participants. For these reasons, therefore, we feel that robust, democracy-enhancing col-laboration is unlikely to emerge and be sustained in the absence of effective countervailing power.

Four Governance Regimes

Dichotomizing these two concepts – top-down administrative versus participatory-collaborative governance institutions and high versus low countervailing power – yields a simple four-fold schema that maps both concrete public policy reforms and the debate between propo-nents and critics of collaboration. Consider that space in figure 11.2.

The upper right-hand corner characterizes the familiar contested areas of public policy in which diffused, general interests are mobilized as countervailing power in order to defend their interests within adver-sarial political arenas. Environmental politics of the 1970s and 1980s exemplifies such adversarial pluralism, as does racial politics since the civil rights movement, and labor politics for most of the twentieth century.

The upper left-hand corner describes top-down governance arrange-ments in which broadly held or subordinated interests are not mobi-lized. If, as most of the group literature argues, concentrated, powerful interests will be able to advance their interests in government, the result will be that those powerful groups with the deepest interests in particu-lar parts of policy will capture the relevant agencies, or form mutually beneficial alliances with relevant administrators and lawmakers. This situation is sometimes described as "captured subgovernment."[12]

Frustration with governance under these top-down institutions has

Degree of countervailing power

		Low	*High*
Top-down administration		I Captured sub-government	II Adversarial pluralism
Participatory collaboration		III Co-optation, participatory window dressing	IV Empowered participatory governance

Governance institutions

Figure 11.2 Four Governance Regimes

led some policy-makers, practitioners, and academics to reject top-down and adversarial governance methods in favor of participatory collaboration. But critics of collaboration have highlighted the possibilities depicted in the lower left hand region of figure 11.2. A shift of governance from the top-down adversarial to the participatory collaborative form involves the delegation of power from higher to lower levels of governance and to a broader array of participants. When countervailing power is well organized for adversarial contests but not well organized to collaborate (a shift from cell II to III in figure 11.2), the outcomes for the interests they defend can suffer as a result. When there are no local environmentalists, a federal program to reduce pollution through local negotiation between firms and community residents may amount to abdication of federal oversight over that program. Writ large, the shift from top-down adversarial governance to collaborative governance, when there is no countervailing power or capacity, can amount in practice to a state-shrinking, deregulatory maneuver in which oppositional forces are co-opted and neutralized and the collaborative participation becomes mere window dressing.[13]

Finally, consider governance and politics in the lower right-hand region of figure 11.2. Like region III, the institutions here confer power to decentralized units of government, open decision-making to a broad array of interests that includes ordinary citizens, and aim at solving concrete public problems rather than imposing external rules or issuing commands. Unlike III, however, otherwise subordinated or diffuse interests are well organized and backed by countervailing forms of power that enable them to engage in collaboration on more equal terms. In the ideal, empowered participatory governance occupies this region.

II Four Claims

The rest of this chapter will provide evidence in support of four claims regarding collaborative governance and countervailing power.

Proposition 1. Forms of participatory collaboration, including EPG institutions, will in general fail to yield the benefits that their proponents desire without the substantial presence of countervailing power. The benefits of deliberation, participation, and collaboration are likely to result only from genuinely collaborative processes that are inclusive, fair, and free from domination. Formal institutions of participatory collaboration are usually characterized by large asymmetries in prior organization, knowledge, intensity of interest, and capabilities. These asymmetries create temptations for advantaged parties to exclude and subject others, and so fair collaboration is frequently difficult to achieve. The presence of countervailing power – for example parent organizations to check school administrators or environmental groups to balance industrial or development interests – can level some of these differences and so create conditions for fair collaboration.

Proposition 2. The sources and forms of countervailing power that are appropriate in collaborative contexts are in general quite different from those found in adversarial ones. The assertion that countervailing power is necessary to reap the benefits of collaboration might suggest that the most promising policy areas for the development of participatory-collaborative institutions would be those adversarial areas in which substantial countervailing power already exists. This suggestion may indeed sometimes be correct, but the inference is too quick. Adversarial interest organizations have developed competencies, methods of organizational maintenance, and mobilization strategies that depend upon victory in conflict. Participatory collaboration requires organizations with very different skills, sources of support, and bases of solidarity.

Proposition 3. These two broad varieties of countervailing power – adversarial and collaborative – are not easily converted from one to the other. In particular, countervailing power that has been effectively organized for adversarial contests cannot easily be redeployed for collaborative purposes. As we shall see below, powerful organizations that supply crucial countervailing power in adversarial arenas are frequently ineffective in collaborative ones. In part due to their comparative advantages, those organizations thus often oppose reform programs to move governance from top-down adversarial to participatory-collaborative modes. Mark Sagoff observes, for example, that the

> single issue strategies of many lobbying groups routinely "gridlock" policy in the Iron Triangle. For these groups, conflict provides the principal method to deal with issues and mobilize support. Deliberating with others undermines the group's mission, which is to press its purpose or concerns as far as it can in a zero-sum game with its political adversaries . . . When an interest group joins with its enemies to solve a problem, it loses the purity of its position; it ceases to be a cause and becomes a committee.[14]

Proposition 4. The problem of generating countervailing power suitable for collaborative governance is not easily solved through clever public policies and institutional designs. Typically, even well-designed collaborative procedures, rules, and regulations will not in and of themselves yield substantial collaborative countervailing power. Countervailing sources of power usually arise from the polity, outside the boundaries of the institutions themselves, and their presence is contingent upon capricious factors such as those that give rise to interest groups, social movements, and lower barriers to collective action generally. Appropriate institutional designs can facilitate the rise and entry of countervailing voices. However, explanations of their presence and strength are separate from, though linked to, questions about the shape of collaborative institutions themselves.

III Applications

To support these propositions we will briefly explore attempts to generate collaborative, participatory forms of governance in four arenas: civic environmentalism, workplace anti-discrimination strategies, parental and community engagement in public education, and new forms of policing. Some of these intersect the case studies in this book and others are somewhat different. In each case our concern here will be the interaction between the actual practices in these efforts and the character of countervailing power in these new governance institutions.

Civic Environmentalism

Critics of current practices of environmental regulation contend that top-down, adversarial environmental governance has been dominated by industrial and environmental special interests. As a result it is excessively conflictual, unresponsive to local needs and priorities, insensitive to emergent concerns such as those of racial minorities, and incapable of dealing with the "unfinished business" of non-point source pollution, pollution prevention, and ecosystem integrity.[15] Some of these critics believe that a style of environmentalism that is at once more local, participatory, focussed on problem-solving, and collaborative – what they call *civic environmentalism* – can address many of these difficulties.[16] Civic environmentalism covers a wide range of activities including watershed management and restoration, forest management, urban planning and redevelopment, agricultural pollution, and community-driven industrial regulation.[17] Two prominent experiences highlight the disputes between civic environmentalists and skeptics of this novel approach.[18]

The first comes from the forests in the Sierra Nevada country of California.[19] After decades, a familiar struggle between environmentalists and timber harvesting interests had played itself out to bitter, sometimes violent, conflict in the logging town of Quincy. These conflicts were compounded by resource management policies of fire suppression that actually exacerbated the possibilities of devastating conflagration. After a large fire destroyed a nearby spotted-owl habitat, one resident environmental activist commented that it "wasn't loggers versus owls that was the unresolved issue . . . it was the owls versus fire."[20]

A small but diverse group of about twenty individuals – environmentalists, timber businessmen, and local officials – began to meet at a local library to explore solutions to this triple dilemma of environmental protection, economic development, and forest fires. An expanded version of this group became known as the Quincy Library Group. Over several months, the group developed a forest management plan for some 2.5 million acres around the town that attempted to satisfy all of the involved interests. For the environmentalists, the plan put one million roadless acres of forest, much of that old-growth, into a protected status. But the plan would also allow loggers to harvest forty to sixty thousand acres of dead leaning trees, young ones, and deadwood on the ground, while protecting larger trees. To control the threat of fires, the plan provided for loggers to harvest in targeted areas to create fuel breaks, now called "Defensible Fuel Profile Zones," that would use logging to simulate non-human processes of forest thinning.[21]

National environmental organizations coalesced to oppose the

Quincy Library Group. This formidable coalition eventually included the Sierra Club, the Wilderness Society, the Natural Resources Defense Council, and the Audubon Society. The Quincy Library Group proposal thus created a set battle between the proponents of local, participatory collaborative problem-solving and the nationally organized adversarial countervailing power of the large environmental interest groups. Indeed, a local chapter of the Audubon Society actually supported the Quincy Library Group proposal. Its members saw the actions of the national organization as patronizing, ignorant of local conditions, and insensitive to place-based attachments.[22]

Why did national environmental groups reject the possibility that local environmental collaborative problem-solving groups might contribute to the national interest in environmental protection in this way? The problem was principally one of power and precedent. Rightly or not, national organizations felt that environmental interests were more likely to prevail at the national level rather than in thousands of local arenas. Sierra Club President McCloskey wrote,

> Industry thinks its odds are better in these [participatory collaborative] forums. It is ready to train its experts in mastering this process. It believes it can dominate them over time and relieve itself of the burden of tough national rules. It has ways to generate pressures in communities where it is strong, which it doesn't have at the national level.[23]

From this perspective, Congressional adoption of the Quincy Library Group plan would set a dangerous precedent for participatory collaboration for the management of national forests. While this particular plan might work well in the case of Quincy and the surrounding Plumas, Lassen, and Tahoe National Forests, environmental interests are less organized or entirely absent in countless other locales. As precedent, the Quincy plan would be dangerous precisely because of the absence of countervailing power in other sites where collaboration might be proposed.

Despite substantial mobilization and objection, the national environmental groups lost in Congress. They were, however, not without force. Senator Barbara Boxer originally supported the bill, but withdrew due to pressure. In 1998, however, the "Quincy Library Group Forest Recovery and Economic Stability Act" was incorporated into the omnibus appropriations for fiscal year 1999.

Figure 11.3 below maps these changes and debates in terms of the distinctions depicted in figure 11.2. The regime of forest policy determined through centralized interest-group contests and then enforced by the U.S. Forest Service is squarely in the upper right-hand quadrant of adversarial governance backed by the mobilized countervailing power of the large environmental organizations. The large environmental organizations viewed the Quincy plan as precedent for a broader shift from quadrant II to quadrant III governance: a regime of largely empty participatory collaboration in thousands of locales without substantial countervailing collaborative power in most of them. The Quincy Library Group, by contrast, viewed the change as moving from region II to region IV. The Quincy environmentalists saw themselves as well organized and quite capable of collaborating on fair terms with other local interests. Enthusiastic observers of the Quincy process saw it as a harbinger of a larger shift to civic environmental modes of governance more broadly.[24] From this perspective, local environmentalists would rise up to participate in decentralized environmental problem-solving bodies around forests, watersheds, and industrial facilities if such opportunities existed (a shift from quadrant II to IV in figure 11.3).

Critics disagree about whether or not the national environmental

Presence of countervailing power

		Low	*High*
Top-down administration		I The Forest Service before the environmental movement: professional ecosystem management insulated from environmentalist pressures	II Pre-QLG plan: industry and environmental interests bargain for policy position
Participatory collaboration		III Devolution of environmental policy to stakeholder processes dominated by industry	IV Diffusion of robust civic environmental problem-solving, exemplified by Quincy process

Governance institutions

Figure 11.3 Forest Management and The Quincy Library Group Plan

groups were themselves parochial in failing to recognize the substantial power and potential of local environmental organizations[25] or whether they were indeed generally correct and that groups like the one in Quincy were exceptional in their capability and organization.[26] Single local initiatives like the Quincy Library Group plan are likely to arise where there is already substantial local countervailing power in place. As such, these initiatives do not test the question posed by McCloskey and other environmental skeptics of participatory collaboration: if collaboration were to become a more widespread mode of governance, would industry's odds improve? Would it dominate over time? To gain some purchase on this larger question, consider the policy described by Craig Thomas and Bradley Karkkainen in this volume: habitat conservation planning in the Endangered Species Act.

As Thomas and Karkkainen discuss in their chapters, Habitat Conservation Plans are very promising from the point of view of proponents of participatory collaboration. However, the quality of participation in plan formulation, the plans themselves, and very likely their implementation, has been quite uneven.[27] Very little is known about the factors that make some HCPs more democratically inclusive and scientifically rigorous, while others fail. At the local level, a working hypothesis in line with the argument offered above is that areas with mobilized environmental interests will have more inclusive and comprehensive habitat conservation plans. Nationally, environmental organizations have not for the most part mobilized to support habitat conservation planning or effectively lobbied for a vision of habitat conservation planning that prioritizes environmental interests. Perhaps as a consequence of this political weakness or inattention, the Department of the Interior has been quite lackadaisical in its efforts to make the process of habitat conservation planning more participatory and to monitor plan implementation to assure that they protect endangered species.

The move from strict ESA enforcement to habitat conservation planning, then, illustrates a shift from a regulatory regime with environmentally mobilized countervailing power and adversarial governance rules to one with collaboration but little supporting countervailing power. The price of collaboration without power is evident at both the national and local levels: weak oversight and procedural structure at the national center of regulation and lack of environmentalist capacity to utilize plasticity at the local level. The actual outcomes – for species protection, accountability, and democratic participation – will continue to fall short of the expectations of its supporters unless environmental interests mobilize at both the national and local levels.

Nationally, the regulatory regime will remain ineffective unless it includes substantial monitoring, information-sharing, and enforcement mechanisms. The plans for particular ecosystems are unlikely to protect species well or be monitored and enforced unless local environmental constituencies mobilize and gain the capacities necessary to participate in sophisticated habitat conservation planning processes.

Second-Generation Workplace Discrimination

Though the problems and policies are a world away, similar governance shifts and disputes have characterized the field of workplace anti-discrimination. The familiar public strategies for ending employer racial and gender-based discrimination grew out of the hot social movements of the 1950s and 1960s. This "first generation" of anti-discrimination law resulted from adversarial struggles that pressed the state to deploy its resources against employers who egregiously violated norms of fairness and equity. The discrimination that these laws sought to stop was clear, intentional, and well established. The laws themselves were forceful, simple, and top-down in formulation and implementation. Some of these laws prohibited employers from engaging in forms of intentional discrimination such as exclusionary testing and using irrelevant characteristics such as race and gender in hiring and promotion decisions. Others required employers to adopt affirmative measures to desegregate workplaces, provide back pay to those who have been discriminated against, and seek employees from excluded communities.

These measures have been effective in stemming the most blatant kinds of racial and gender discrimination. However, this strategy has its limitations. In particular, many contemporary forms of discrimination and harassment are subtler than those of the first generation. They stem from complex patterns of individual interaction and organizational culture rather than explicit and deliberate bias. Susan Sturm, one of the closest analysts of this "second-generation discrimination," puts it this way:

> Exclusion increasingly results not from an intentional effort to formally exclude, but rather as a byproduct of ongoing interactions shaped by the structures of day-to-day decisionmaking and workplace relationships. The glass ceiling remains a barrier for women and people of color largely because of patterns of interaction, informal norms, networking, training, mentoring, and evaluation . . .

> Claims of hostile workplace environment, exclusionary subjective employment practices, and glass ceilings are, by their nature, complex. Their complexity lies in multiple conceptions and causes of harm, the interactive and contextual character of the injury, the blurriness of the boundaries between legitimate and wrongful conduct . . . This complexity resists definition and resolution through across-the-board, relatively specific commands and an after-the-fact enforcement mechanism.[28]

The inability of traditional top-down measures to meet these challenges has led to the proliferation of participatory-collaborative anti-discrimination measures. Rather than follow rigid legal prescriptions or prohibitions against clear discriminatory action, many employers have embarked on intensive problem-solving efforts to identify and root out subtle causes of discrimination and hostility in workplaces and to increase the diversity of workforces. These programs often involve not only human resource professionals, outside diversity consultants, and training providers, but also directly engage employees of all kinds. Those workers, after all, know best the subtle patterns of human interaction, corporate culture, and workplace practice that generate hostile environments and discriminatory outcomes in their workplaces. For example, Sturm describes how Deloitte and Touche created ongoing participatory task forces to investigate the gender gap in hiring and promotion. After many of the recommendations of these committees were incorporated into management practice throughout the company, the percentage of female senior managers and partners increased dramatically, and the company-wide turnover rate dropped for both men and women.[29]

These participatory-collaborative strategies to solve workplace problems of diversity and discrimination have many advantages over conventional top-down, adversarial approaches. They utilize the highly contextual knowledge of workers in particular employment settings. They harness the affirmative energies of management and workforce in ways that commanding legislation could never do. They reach deeply into realms that are impenetrable for conventional regulation, yet central to second-generation discrimination: seemingly innocuous details of management policies and practices, corporate cultures, and the minutiae of human interaction at work.

Despite these advantages, critics who are at home with the adversarial approach have been less enthusiastic about shifting to a regime that encourages participatory-collaborative solutions to harassment and discrimination. For every Deloitte and Touche, there may be many more employers whose primary motivation is to avoid legal liability rather than seriously address second-generation discrimination. As an alternative to more adversarial and commanding legal forms, a regulatory and governance regime that emphasizes management-centered collaborative problem-solving may create the space for such employers to avoid responsibility for harassing behavior. Susan Bisom-Rapp, for example, argues that the contemporary jurisprudence around sexual harassment and racial discrimination creates a liability shield for employers who take two affirmative steps: creating a grievance procedure and offering diversity training programs.[30] These two measures, by themselves, do little to address second-generation discrimination and pale in comparison to robust participatory collaboration.

The structure of concrete alternative approaches to discrimination and the debates surrounding the wisdom of those alternatives closely resemble developments in environmental regulation discussed above. First-generation, top-down regulatory strategies motivated by adversarial social movements made enormous progress against the problems they sought to address: explicit and egregious forms of racial and sexual discrimination (a shift from quadrant I to II in figure 11.4). They have been, however, much less effective against the more subtle forms of second-generation discrimination. The emerging alternative of participatory collaboration between managers and employees offers an attractive solution. As with the Quincy Library Group, the benefits of this strategy are manifest where conditions are favorable, as they were with the supportive management at Deloitte and Touche. The current governance regime is highly permissive, and so includes both those firms who develop impressive programs to address second-generation discrimination and those who enact the bare minimum necessary to construct legal shields (a shift from quadrant II to III in figure 11.4).

As a general strategy of regulation that governs not only enthusiastic firms but also recalcitrant ones, then, the wisdom of participatory collaboration is uncertain. Increased countervailing power to confront the reluctant employers would certainly be necessary to press them to move from minimal grievance and education procedures to innovative participatory collaboration around diversity and discrimination issues. Countervailing power might come in the form of judicial standards that require employers to adopt more pro-active, less minimal, antidiscrimination programs in order to reduce their liability or laws that press judges to enact such standards. They might also come in the form of social movement organizations, professional groups, and other intermediary associations that press employers to explore these novel approaches and help to implement them.[31] This unrealized possibility is depicted as region IV of figure 11.4.

Presence of countervailing power

Governance institutions

	Low	*High*
Top-down adversarialism	I Pre civil-rights private ordering: deliberate practices of racial and gender discrimination	II Long civil rights era, first generation anti-discrimination: clear goals, standards, and enforcement methods
Participatory collaboration	III Employer-driven diversity initiatives	IV Legally required employer diversity initiatives + local diversity partnerships

Figure 11.4 Racial and Gendered Employment Discrimination

Parental and Community Engagement in Public Education

Contending reforms in public education can also be fruitfully mapped along these dimensions of participatory collaboration and countervailing power. The long development of public education systems lies squarely in the bureaucratic ideal type of organizations that are managed in top-down fashion and insulated from countervailing power and public influence generally: the upper left-hand region of figure 11.5.[32] In many school systems, interest groups such as teachers' unions join professional educators and school boards in governing the schools system. These arrangements generate captured policy subsystems depicted as (ii) in region I of figure 11.5. Criticisms of these policy subsystems abound, as do suggestions for how public education might be made more effective, fair, and accountable. Reform proposals occupy all four quadrants of the policy matrix in figure 11.5.

As with anti-discrimination in employment contexts, the most familiar strategies to address racial and economic disparities in public education follow the classic civil rights strategy of mobilizing adversarial countervailing power – either through grass-roots support or litigious

Presence of countervailing power

	Low	High
Top-down administration	I (i) Classic education bureaucracy (ii) Subgovernment captured by narrow interests (unions, educators) (iii) Some high stakes testing and accountability reforms	II (i) Court ordered desegregation (ii) State school finance cases
Participatory collaboration	III Professional site-based school reform efforts	IV (i) Chicago Local School Councils (ii) Texas Interfaith Alliance (iii) Oakland small schools

Governance institutions

Figure 11.5 Governance in Public Education

strategies – followed by top-down legal or policy mandates to establish fairness. These strategies are depicted in the upper right-hand corner of figure 11.5. Such strategies include court-ordered desegregation decisions, federal education equity cases, and then a host of court decisions rooted in the constitutions of individual states that attempt to level public education spending across rich and poor districts. Though legal decisions receive the bulk of media and scholarly attention, grass-roots advocacy campaigns for school equity and access comprise another important set of adversarial, top-down, strategies. Community organizations such as the Texas IAF and Oakland Community Organizations, for example, frequently mobilize to support increasing public education investment in poor areas.[33]

Though these active adversarial strategies have importantly increased educational opportunities of minority and poor children, they cannot reach into the organization and practices of schools themselves. Problems of education are not limited to resource deficiencies and invidious exclusions, but also include defects in school management, instruction, curriculum, governance, and community integration. As an alternative to top-down reform strategies, some reformers have urged varieties of participatory collaboration that aim to improve school performance by involving those most closely associated with students: their teachers and parents.

The best of these efforts combine participatory collaboration with countervailing parental and community power (depicted in the lower right-hand quadrant of figure 11.5). Sometimes, as with the Chicago School reforms described in chapter 4, these reforms are institutionalized into formal governance procedures. Though these reforms were intended to create robust collaboration between parents and professional educators, the Chicago experience illustrates many of the difficulties of participatory collaboration. Principals and school administrators sought to protect their professional prerogatives and spheres of insular control. Furthermore, leaders of the school system and City Hall were ambivalent regarding participatory collaboration. As a result, Local School Councils and their community-based supporters struggled with hostile central school administrators in a series of administrative street-fights over formal authority and informal control between 1995 and 2000. Though particular leaders at the top of the Chicago Public Schools rejected collaboration between 1995 and 2000, not all administrators share this disposition. By mid 2002, the CPS leadership indicated a desire for more cooperative arrangements, and these attitudes may yet be translated into action.

The faith that drove the Chicago school reform movement was that residents would be willing and able to participate in the complicated business of educational governance if only the opportunities were available to them. Community organizing projects in education reform frequently aim toward the same end of participatory collaboration, but begin from the opposite premise. For them, large institutional reforms like the Chicago local school councils cannot succeed without first developing the interests and abilities of individual parents, teachers, and principals.

The Texas Interfaith Alliance Schools project offers one of the most successful examples of this type of collaborative school organizing.[34] Closely associated with Ernesto Cortes and the Texas Industrial Areas Foundation, the Alliance Schools Project consists of some ninety schools across Texas. In those schools, organizers have developed finely tuned strategies that link parents to teachers in resource-intensive efforts to improve schools in widely ranging dimensions that include instruction, school safety, physical plant, educational mission, equity, and access to further educational opportunities. By most accounts from close observers, the Alliance Schools project is highly effective in fostering collaboration between parents and educators at individual schools in ways that fundamentally transform the organizational cultures in these schools and make possible deep and innovative reforms.

Another example comes from Oakland, California, where an educational reform initiative combines the bottom-up school organizing of the Alliance Schools with Chicago-style institutional reforms. In 1999, the Oakland Unified School District joined with the Oakland Community Organization (OCO) – a grass-roots organizing entity affiliated with the Pacific Institute for Community Organizing – and the Bay Area Coalition for Equitable Schools (BayCES) – a non-governmental group with substantial education reform expertise. This tripartite partnership launched an initiative that will create ten small schools in low-income Latino, Asian-American, and African-American neighborhoods. In each of these schools, BayCES will bring crucial expertise regarding instruction and curriculum while OCO will help develop community and parental engagement and support. For its part, the district hopes to improve the system both by beginning with these ten schools and by learning lessons from their experience. This partnership is a city-wide collaborative governance effort that attempts to create high-performing small schools in which organized parents – school-level countervailing power – collaborate with self-selected public school teachers and principals.

These three cases – the Chicago school reform, the Texas Interfaith Schools Project, and the Oakland school innovations – show how well-organized parent and community-based countervailing power can operate through different paths and grow from different origins to sustain participatory collaboration in educational governance.

The New Policing

In a path of development that follows public school systems, big city police organizations converged on the corporate model of hierarchical, professional, and politically insulated bureaucracy in the first part of the twentieth century. These methods, combined with other criminal justice policies such as stricter sentencing and anti-drug offensives, have generated a wave of criticisms from within policing and outside of it. Skeptics charge that policing, sentencing, and incarceration practices fail dismally on two of their central objectives: keeping neighborhoods safe and treating individuals with respect and dignity. With some veracity, Roberto Unger once described the American criminal justice system as a mechanism for deciding which members of the underclass to incarcerate. One might think this repression, as horrible as it is for particular individuals and society as whole, would at least yield the benefit of making neighborhoods, especially "underclass" neighborhoods, safer. But, for a variety of well-known reasons, modern policing has failed in this regard as well.[35]

These two branches of the problem have spurred separate reform movements. Traditional progressive movements have focussed on large and small structural inequities in criminal justice policy and organization and used traditional methods of adversarial social mobilization to reform those institutions. Prisoners' rights movements belong in this broad category, as do those who advocate less investment in prison construction and more in education, and those who press for centralized community review boards to check abuses of police power. These adversarial movements tend to be rigid in how they frame political issues and mobilize political support, and in their policy demands. Techniques for this mobilization often involve constructing an image of the state, or that part of it involved in criminal justice, as incorrigible and inherently repressive or racist.

A second response has been to introduce the mechanisms of participatory collaboration into policing. Chapter 4 of this volume describes the participatory variant of community policing in Chicago, where residents regularly join with police in deliberating public safety problems and solving them together.[36] Despite its attractive features and successes, the experience of community policing in Chicago illustrates the problem of countervailing power in collaborative governance. Though strong community organizations moved the original institutional design of Chicago community policing in a participatory direction, the Mayor and police department eventually moved to exclude those organizations. Like the Chicago school reform experience, police and politicians were uncomfortable with a mode of collaboration in which community organizations possessed substantial countervailing power and used it to challenge their institutional and professional prerogatives. The quality of deliberation and problem-solving in neighborhood community beat meetings has likely suffered from this exclusion in two respects. Community organizations had provided substantial facilitation and training to residents, and so those capacities are in shorter supply. Furthermore, community organizers are less easily intimidated by police officers than many community residents. They thus checked police authority and domination in neighborhood discussions and helped to build the self-confidence of residents so that they themselves could provide this source of countervailing power. Absent the contribution of community-based organizations, many residents are less likely to press their distinctive priorities or offer their own solutions to local problems. More generally, weak social movement involvement in city-level reforms to policing means that police professionals determine the substantive focus of community policing. Consequently, community policing is usually about public safety understood in fairly narrow terms, and the solutions to public safety generally employ relatively conventional police methods.

IV Redeploying Adversarial Countervailing Power in Collaborative Contexts

If what we have said so far is correct, the prospects for sustainable, meaningful empowered participatory governance and other forms of participatory collaboration are fairly dismal in the absence of robust countervailing power. Where is this countervailing power going to come from? One possibility is that it may be generated by a simple redeployment of adversarial countervailing power. Substantial organizations representing disadvantaged interests contest policy in environment, civil rights, labor, and many other areas. Though most of these organizations have developed in sharply adversarial governance contexts, they would seem to be the most promising source of collaborative countervailing power. Might their resources be redeployed to support disadvantaged interests in participatory-collaborative forms of governance? Unfortunately, three general barriers prevent the smooth conversion of adversarial countervailing power to collaborative forms. Compared to adversarial organizations, collaborative groups typically operate at incompatible scales, require distinctive competencies, and build upon very different cognitive frames and sources of solidarity.

The first mismatch concerns political scale. In top-down, adversarial governance systems, groups are organized to engage at centralized points of decision-making. By contrast, collaborative countervailing organizations must operate at very local levels *and* at larger scales of political decision. This difference of operational scale grows naturally from the distinctive logics of top-down and participatory governance. In the former, groups primarily aim to influence high-level policy and legislation and consider the challenges of administration to be secondary. The contemporary environmental movement perhaps best illustrates this pattern. Those groups are well organized – through

Washington offices, lobbying capabilities, networks of allies and contacts, and campaign strategies – to influence national regulations around air and water quality, land management, endangered species protection, and the like. When civic environmentalists argue that local participation, information, and engagement will make environmental policy more just and effective, national organizations are simply not organized to support, much less lead, these local efforts.

A second mismatch concerns organizational competencies. Adversarial countervailing organizations aim to influence peak policy and legislative decisions, and their competencies flow from this aim. Some pursue narrow strategies of communication, information provision, and persuasion. Others, such as social movement organizations, attempt to mobilize broad popular support and pressure. Whereas these strategies require a variety of capacities that sway policy-makers, participatory collaboration requires competencies of problem-solving and implementation. Habitat conservation planning and the Quincy Library Group plan for forest management raised thorny political challenges, but these collaborative governance experiences also required participants to have deep local knowledge, ecological expertise, and analytic capacities. Similarly, adversarial education and police reform organizations are skilled at pressuring or persuading top administrators, municipal legislators, and city halls. Participatory collaboration, however, requires organizations that can facilitate close problem-solving with individual principals, teachers, and police officers on the beat. As with the problem of scale mismatch, adversarial countervailing organizations would have to acquire entirely new kinds of organizational competencies in order to function effectively in collaborative governance arrangements.

Third, differences in constructions of political meaning and psychological sources of solidarity also prevent adversarial countervailing organizations from redeploying their powers to support collaboration. Recent work in the sociology of social movements has stressed the importance of cognitive factors such as the construction of meaning and issue framing in processes of political mobilization.[37] Social movements overcome apathy and barriers to collective action in part by constructing "shared understandings of some condition or situation they define as in need of change."[38] In the case of adversarial countermovements and organizations, these understandings involve narratives of inequity and disrespect – "injustice frames" – that generate common diagnoses (diagnostic framing), approaches to solutions (prognostic framing), and reasons for action (motivational framing).[39] Many adversarial groups and their constituencies embrace cognitive frames that do not lend themselves to collaborative problem-solving approaches. These frames can unambiguously assign culpability (e.g. an authoritarian city government and police department), depict Manichean protagonists and antagonists (e.g. brutal police officers and defenseless youth), and prescribe simple and direct policy solutions.

Participatory collaboration, by contrast, requires much less rigid diagnostic, prognostic, and therefore motivational cognitive frames. Decentralized governance activities around public safety, education, ecosystem management, and second-generation discrimination aim in large measure to discover and test hypotheses about the complex causes of public problems and create, on the fly, locally tailored solutions to those problems. Rigid diagnoses and prognostications inhibit this flexible problem-solving. Furthermore, participatory collaboration frequently depends upon sustained and deep cooperation between diverse parties such as police officers and minority residents, parents and educators, workers and managers, and environmentalists and developers. "Injustice frames" that demonize or recriminate adversaries again obstruct such joint action. In order to provide countervailing power for collaborative governance, many adversarial organizations would be required to dramatically transform the cognitive frames through which they understand the political world, articulate solutions to the urgent problems in it, and mobilize support for themselves and for social change more broadly. Unsurprisingly, many adversarial organizations resist such revolutionary transformations. They not only erode bases of solidarity and support, but also call into question the deep purposes of leaders and the very reasons that those organizations exist.

V Sources of Collaborative Countervailing Power

In most participatory-collaborative governance arrangements, then, countervailing power will not grow easily from either supportive public policies or existing adversarial organizations. Are there more likely sources of collaborative countervailing power? Here we must be more speculative. Contemporary forms of participatory collaboration are fairly young, and so most practitioners and scholars in this area have focussed on institutional analysis rather than upon the political and social conditions that are necessary for these institutions to operate fairly and effectively. Tentatively, then, consider three potential paths to the generation of collaborative countervailing power: local adversarial organizations, political parties, and larger social movement organizations.

Though neither ubiquitous nor dominant, the strongest forms of collaborative countervailing power in the experiences described in section III above came from locally organized adversarial entities. For example, indigenously local rather than nationally affiliated environmental groups engaged developers and industrial interests in the forest management and habitat conservation programs. In cases of participatory collaboration in public services – education and policing – coalitions of neighborhood groups and their city-level umbrella organizations provided some countervailing force against city government. Generally, locally organized entities can shift more easily from adversarial to collaborative modes of participation. Unlike their national counterparts, they do not suffer from scale-mismatch; most are already organized for action at the levels of government and society most appropriate for decentralized problem-solving. In part because they act at this scale, adversarial groups frequently also possess some of the organizational competencies necessary to participate in collaborative governance. For example, they have deep local knowledge of the particular environmental, educational, and economic challenges in their communities. Many already engage in direct service provision, and so are familiar with the details and difficulties of implementing programs. When local groups make demands upon public or private entities, these demands often concern inclusion and representation in governance and problem-solving. They frequently demand to be allowed to collaborate rather than pressing for specific policy solutions. Cress and Snow report, for example, that one of the major demands of homelessness prevention social movement organizations is to be represented on the boards and bodies that make and implement local policies in this area.[40]

Perhaps the cognitive issues of framing and psychological sources of solidarity and motivation present the greatest obstacle to participating in collaborative governance for local adversarial organizations. Like their national counterparts, local frames of political understanding frequently rely upon unambiguous narratives of injustice and culpability. Such frames lead participants to be suspicious – often for good reasons – of proposals for collaboration. Nevertheless, some of the most innovative and successful local organizing entities have developed alternative frames that capaciously include both adversarial and collaborative strategies. For example, Mark Warren describes how the Texas Industrial Areas Foundation moved beyond Alinskyite understandings and strategies to develop a less myopic organizing approach that stressed common values and allowed for constructive engagement.[41] This approach grounded the participatory-collaborative school organizing strategy of the Interfaith Alliance described above. Similarly, the Oakland Community Organization has used tactics of disruption and protest to secure increased funding for schools in poor neighborhoods while simultaneously engaging in partnership with the educational administration to participate in the governance of some of those schools. Though not without difficulty, they have developed political frames and narratives that understand both kinds of tactics as stemming from a common approach to building constructive power and organizing defective social institutions.

As a general matter, however, local adversarial organizations are strong in some areas and weak in others. Broadly imposing structures of collaborative governance will, as we have seen in the case of habitat conservation planning, create opportunities for some of these groups, but may also produce many other venues in which, in the assessment of environmental leader Michael McCloskey, industry has better odds.

A second source of more reaching countervailing power may come from political leaders who view participatory collaboration as good politics as well as good policy. A politician or party might champion policies that open top-down agencies, create venues for popular voice and problem-solving, and so attempt to reap the democratic and technical benefits commonly attributed to participatory collaboration. In doing so, he or she may construct constituencies of beneficiaries from the policies, who in turn support the officials who championed them. Such a politician or party would irritate administrators and entrenched interests, but that would be the price of generating participatory-populist support. In a tepid version of this strategy, Chicago Mayor Richard M. Daley strongly supported the city's community policing program. A fully blown example of this path to countervailing power comes from outside the borders of the United States. Chapters 2 and 3 above illustrate how left political parties in Porto Alegre, Brazil, and Kerela, India campaigned to implement participatory governance and provided effective countervailing power for activists involved in the process.

Perhaps more squarely within the boundaries of the American political imagination, a third path to collaborative countervailing power lies in the slow transformation of traditional adversarial organizations. The barriers outlined above are formidable, but perhaps not insuperable, for some large interest groups and social movement organizations. The large labor unions, the NAACP, some women's organizations, and some environmental organizations have both national offices and local affiliates. The barriers of scale and competence will be lower for organizations with local affiliates that exercise the autonomy and possess the kinds of capability that are common in local adversarial organizations. The perennial conflicts over local autonomy versus national mission that occur in labor, environmental, and other movements has taken on a new dimension with the emergence of participatory collaboration as a mode of governance.

The chorus of support in favor of participatory collaboration is growing. Its natural constituents are local organizations, such as the civic environmentalists in Quincy, California and the environmental justice movement, the more energetic locals and County Labor Councils in organized labor, and local civil rights and racial justice organizations. Pressed from below by these sources and perhaps also by the disappointments of their own approaches, leaders of national adversarial organizations may eventually accept the limitations of top-down governance strategies. When they do so, they may begin to make the difficult transformations of scale, competence, and political framing necessary for them to become effective actors in participatory collaborative governance schemes.

VII Conclusion

Across a vast range of policy questions, both proponents of participatory collaboration and its critics are united by a set of deep commitments to democratic government and social justice. They are divided principally regarding the means with which these general goals are best realized. The gulf between them, however, is deeper than most strategic disagreements, for it concerns the very structure and institutions of governance and politics. Most of the work in political science and sociology is not terribly helpful in bridging that gulf. As has been oft noted but seldom addressed, the former focusses on formal avenues of participation and influence – voting and interest groups – usually in centralized venues while social movements scholars in the latter discipline focus squarely on informal methods such as protest and disruption.[42] Participatory collaboration lies between these two domains, and so has largely escaped the analytic gaze of social scientists. As a consequence, there are few conclusive findings regarding the operations, outcomes, or even prevalence of this emergent governance mode.

Proponents and critics have thus relied upon their intuitions to guide them regarding crucial points of disagreement such as the role and potential for collaborative countervailing power. Many proponents of participatory collaboration have ignored asymmetric power and so implicitly supposed that power can be bracketed away and is therefore unimportant in these venues. Others embrace a naive pluralism that supposes that interests are all sufficiently well resourced and organized to participate and that none will be systematically excluded. Critics, many of whom have studied or worked in contexts of top-down adversarial governance, frequently make the opposite but equally naive supposition. They recognize that collective action problems are extremely difficult to overcome and robust organizations hard to build. They see the impossibility of constructing countervailing power in locales where it is weak or absent. They consequently reject participatory collaborative governance from the fear that it will bring local domination and co-optation.

The best prospects for participatory collaboration lie between these extremes. Critics should recognize first that, whatever their other failings, the emergent governance structures offer possibilities of solving complex problems that are unavailable to top-down methods. Conversely, proponents should acknowledge that many of these benefits fail to accrue in the absence of sufficient countervailing collaborative power. With these common understandings, both can begin the hard work of understanding the roles, forms, and sources of political power in the distinctive structure and politics of empowered participatory governance.

Notes

* A longer version of this epilogue was originally written as a stand-alone paper by Archon Fung about six months after the completion of the rest of the chapters in this book. It was only after rereading the book in page-proofs that we realized that the ideas in that paper would constitute a useful epilogue to the book itself, following up on some of the central issues raised by the commentators, especially by Cohen and Rogers in chapter 10. We therefore decided to revise and shorten it for that purpose. We wish to thank David Barron, Gene Corbin, Michael Dorf, Bradley Karkkainaen, James Liebman, Dara O'Rourke, and Charles Sabel for comments on previous versions of this chapter.

1. Chapter 10 of this volume, p. 249.

2. There is no standard term in the literature for the potential power of normally weak and disadvantaged groups as they confront the powerful. The term "countervailing power" is also used in quite different contexts – as in the countervailing power of different institutions in a system of governmental checks and balances. We are adopting it here because it suggests a form of power that develops to counter some well-established form of power advantage.

3. Cohen and Rogers (chapter 10 of this volume, pp. 250–3) argue that the problem of power imbalance may not be as relevant for policy-directed versions of EPG as for the more ambitious cases drawn from developing countries in this volume. Though the balancing of social forces occurs at very different scales in these two kinds of cases, we

contend that the balance of power, and the presence of countervailing power, are important in both kinds of cases, and for EPG generally.

4. Andrew McFarland, "Interest Groups and the Policymaking Process: Sources of Countervailing Power in America," in Mark P. Petracca, ed., *The Politics of Interests: Interest Groups Transformed*, Boulder, CO: Westview Press, 1992, p. 58.

5. Hugo Helco, "Issue Networks and the Executive Establishment," in Anthony King, ed., *The New American Political System*, Washington, DC: American Enterprise Institute, 1978.

6. See Theodore Lowi, *The End of Liberalism: The Second Republic of the United States*, New York: Norton, 1979; Richard B. Stewart, "The Reform of American Administrative Law," *Harvard Law Review*, vol. 88, no. 8 (June 1975); Jody Freeman, "Collaborative Governance in the Administrative State," *University of California, Los Angeles Law Review*, vol. 45 (October 1997); Mark Petracca, ed., *The Politics of Interests: Interest Groups Transformed*, Boulder, CO: Westview Press, 1992; Frank Baumgartner and Beth L. Leech, *Basic Interests: The Importance of Groups in Politics and Political Science*, Princeton: Princeton University Press, 1998.

7. Freeman "Collaborative Governance in the Administrative State," p. 18.

8. Mancur Olson, *The Logic of Collective Action: Public Goods and the Theory of Groups*, Cambridge, MA: Harvard University Press, 1965; Claus Offe and Helmut Wiesenthal, "Two Logics of Collective Action," in John Keane, ed., *Disorganized Capitalism: Contemporary Transformations of Work and Politics*, Cambridge, MA: MIT Press, 1985; James Q. Wilson, "The Politics of Regulation," in James Q. Wilson, ed., *The Politics of Regulation*, New York: Basic Books, 1985; Lowi, *The End of Liberalism*.

9. Joshua Cohen and Charles Sabel, "Directly-Deliberative Polyarchy," *European Law Journal*, vol. 3, no. 4 (December 1997).

10. Xavier de Souza Briggs, *Community Building: The New (and Old) Politics of Urban Problem-Solving*, Working Paper RWP02-003, Cambridge, MA: John F. Kennedy School of Government, 2002, p. 3.

11. Olson, *The Logic of Collective Action*; E.E. Schattschneider, *The Semisovereign People: A Realist's View of Democracy in America*, New York: Holt, Rinehart, and Winston, 1960; Kay Lehmann Schlozman, "What Accent the Heavenly Chorus: Political Equality and the American Pressure System," *Journal of Politics*, vol. 46, no. 4 (November 1984); Lowi, *The End of Liberalism*; Wilson, "The Politics of Regulation."

12. See Richard B. Stewart, "Madison's Nightmare," *University of Chicago Law Review*, vol. 57 (Spring 1990).

13. Under special circumstances – where there are no deep conflicts of interest among actors engaged in the problem-solving process, or where, for some contingent reason, powerful groups adopt an altruistic moral stance toward collaboration and voluntarily refrain from using their power – it may happen that even in the absence of countervailing power, genuine participatory collaboration can take place. But the usual political context of decision-making is not so benign, and thus, as with the more familiar forms of top-down governance, power matters and the presence or absence of countervailing power will produce very different outcomes given the very same collaborative governance institutions.

14. Mark Sagoff, "The View from Quincy Library: Civic Engagement and Environmental Problem Solving," in Robert K. Fullinwider, ed., *Civil Society, Democracy, and Civic Renewal*, New York: Rowman Littlefield, 1999, p. 161.

15. Daniel Kemmis, *Community and The Politics of Place*, Norman: University of Oklahoma Press, 1990; DeWitt John, *Civic Environmentalism: Alternatives to Regulation in States and Communities*, Washington, DC: Congressional Quarterly Press, 1994; William Shutkin, *The Land That Could Be: Environmentalism and Democracy in the Twenty-First Century*, Cambridge, MA: MIT Press, 2000; Bradley C. Karkkainen, Charles Sabel, and Archon Fung, *Beyond Backyard Environmentalism*, foreword by Amory and Hunter Lovins, Boston: Beacon Press, 2000.

16. John, *Civic Environmentalism*; Shutkin, *The Land That Could Be*; Marc Landy, *Civic Environmentalism in Action: A Field Guide to Regional and Local Initiatives*,

Washington, DC: Progressive Policy Institute, 1999; Carmen Sirianni, and Lewis Friedland, *Civic Innovation in America: Community Empowerment, Public Policy, and the Movement for Civic Renewal*, Berkeley: University of California Press, 2001.

17. Edward Weber, "The Question of Accountability in Historical Perspective: From Jacksonian to Contemporary Grassroots Ecosystem Management," *Administration and Society*, vol. 41, no. 4 (1999).

18. Rena Steinzor, "The Corruption of Civic Environmentalism," *Environmental Law Reporter*, vol. 30. (October 2000).

19. This account is drawn from Sagoff, "The View from Quincy Library"; Timothy P. Duane, "The Ecosystem Approach: New Departures for Land and Water: Practical Legal Issues in Community Initiated Ecosystem Management of Public Land: Community Participation in Ecosystem Management," *Ecology Law Quarterly*, vol. 24 (1997).

20. Sagoff, "The View from Quincy Library," p. 167.

21. Sagoff, "The View from Quincy Library," pp. 167–8; Duane, "The Ecosystem Approach."

22. Sagoff, "The View from Quincy Library."

23. Michael McCloskey, "The Skeptic: Collaboration Has Its Limits," *High Country News*, vol. 28, no. 9 (May 13, 1996); see also Michael McCloskey, "Problems With Using Collaboration to Shape Environmental Public Policy," *Valparaiso University Law Review*, vol. 34 (Spring 2000).

24. Sagoff, "The View from Quincy Library."

25. Sagoff, "The View from Quincy Library."

26. Steinzor, "The Corruption of Civic Environmentalism"; William Ratliff, "The Devolution of Environmental Organization," *Journal of Land Resources and Environmental Law*, vol. 17 (1997).

27. See Thomas, chapter 5 of this volume; Peter Kareiva, *Using Science in Habitat Conservation Planning*, Washington, DC: American Institute of Biological Sciences, 1999; Stephen Yaffee *et al.*, *Balancing Public Trust and Private Interest: Public Participation in Habitat Conservation Planning*, Ann Arbor: University of Michigan, School of Natural Resources and Environment, 1998; see Karkkainen, chapter 8 of this volume, for response.

28. Susan Sturm, "Second Generation Employment Discrimination: A Structural Approach," *Columbia Law Review*, vol. 101 (April 2001): p. 469.

29. Sturm, "Second Generation Employment Discrimination."

30. Susan Bisom-Rapp, "An Ounce of Prevention is a Poor Substitute for a Pound of Cure: Confronting the Developing Jurisprudence of Education and Prevention in Employment Discrimination Law," *Berkeley Journal of Employment and Labor Law*, vol. 22 (2001).

31. Sturm, "Second Generation Employment Discrimination"; Michael Dorf and Charles Sabel, "A Constitution of Democratic Experimentalism," *Columbia Law Review*, vol. 98 (March 1998).

32. See, for example, David Tyack, *The One Best System: A History of American Urban Education*, Cambridge, MA: Harvard University Press, 1974.

33. Research for Action and Cross Cities Campaign for Urban School Reform, *Strong Neighborhoods, Strong Schools: The Indicators Project on Education Organizing*, Chicago: Cross Cities Campaign for Urban School Reform, March 2002.

34. Frank Levy and Richard Murnane, *Teaching the New Basic Skills: Principles for Educating Children to Thrive in a Changing Economy*, New York: Free Press, 1996; Dennis Shirley, *Community Organizing for Urban School Reform*, Austin: University of Texas Press, 1997 and Dennis Shirley, *Valley Interfaith and School Reform: Organizing for Power in South Texas*, Austin: University of Texas Press, 2002; Mark Warren, *Dry Bones Rattling: Community Building to Revitalize American Democracy*, Princeton: Princeton University Press, 2001.

35. Malcolm Sparrow *et al.*, *Beyond 911: A New Era for Policing*, New York: Basic Books, 1990.

36. Wesley G. Skogan and Susan M. Hartnett, *Community Policing: Chicago Style*, New York: Oxford University Press, 1997.

37. David Snow and Robert Benford, "Frame Alignment Processes, Mobilization, and Movement Participation," *American Sociological Review*, vol. 51, no. 4 (August 1986).

38. Robert Benford and David Snow, "Framing Processes and Social Movements: An Overview and Assessment," *Annual Review of Sociology*, vol. 26 (2000).

39. Snow and Benford, "Frame Alignment Processes."

40. Daniel Cress and David Snow, "The Outcomes of Homeless Mobilization: The Influence of Organization, Disruption, Political Mediation, and Framing," *American Journal of Sociology*, vol. 105, no. 4 (January 2000).

41. Warren, *Dry Bones Rattling*.

42. Cathy Cohen and Fred Harris, "Social Capital and Political Activism Among Marginal Groups," prepared for Conference on Social Capital and Political Activism, Harvard University (May 23–24, 2002); Douglas McAdam, Sidney Tarrow, and Charles Tilly, *Dynamics of Contention*, New York: Cambridge University Press, 2001.

References

Abers, Rebecca N., "From Ideas to Practice: The Partido dos Trabalhadores and Participatory Governance in Brazil," *Latin American Perspectives*, vol. 91, no. 23 (1996), pp. 35–53.

Abers, Rebecca N., "From Clientelism to Cooperation: Participatory Policy and Civic Organizing in Porto Alegre, Brazil," *Politics and Society*, vol. 26, no. 4 (December 1998), pp. 511–37.

Abers, Rebecca N., *Inventing Local Democracy: Grassroots Politics in Brazil*, Boulder, CO: Lynne Rienner (2000).

Alvarez, Sonia, "Deepening Democracy: Popular Movement Networks, Constitutional Reform, and Radical Urban Regimes in Contemporary Brazil," in Robert Fisher and Joseph Kling, eds., *Mobilizing the Community*, Newbury Park: Sage Publications (1993).

Arnstein, Sherry R., "A Ladder of Citizen Participation," *Journal of the American Institute of Planners*, vol. 35, no. 4 (July 1969), pp. 216–24.

Austen-Smith, David, "Strategic Models of Talk in Political Decision Making," *International Political Science Review*, vol. 13, no. 1 (1992), pp. 45–58.

Avritzer, Leonardo, "Public Deliberation at the Local Level: Participatory Budgeting in Brazil," paper presented at *Experiments in Deliberative Democracy* Conference, Madison, WI, January 2000.

Babbitt v. Sweet Home Chapter of Communities for a Greater Oregon, U.S. (Scalia, J., dissenting), 515 U.S. 687 (1995).

Bachrach, Peter, "Interest, Participation and Democratic Theory," in J. Roland Pennock and John W. Chapman, eds., *Participation in Politics: NOMOS XVI*, New York: Lieber-Atherton (1974).

Bachrach, Peter and Baratz, Morton, "Two Faces of Power," *American Political Science Review*, vol. 56, no. 4 (December 1962), pp. 947–52.

Bachrach, Peter and Baratz, Morton, "Decisions and Non-Decisions: An Analytical Framework," *American Political Science Review*, 57 (1963), pp. 632–42.

Baierle, Sergio, *A explosao da experiencia; a emergencia de um novo principio etico-politico em Porto Alegre*, UNICAMP, unpublished manuscript (1991).

Baiocchi, Gianpaolo, "Militance and Citizenship: The Workers' Party, Civil Society, and Participatory Governance in Porto Alegre, Brazil," Ph.D. dissertation, University of Wisconsin, Dept. of Sociology (2001).

Baiocchi, Gianpaolo, ed., *Radicals in Power: Experiments in Urban Democracy in Brazil*, London: Zed Press, forthcoming.

Barber, Benjamin, *Strong Democracy*, Berkeley: University of California Press (1984).

Barber, Benjamin, "Three Challenges to Reinventing Democracy," in Paul Hirst and Sunil Khilnani, eds., *Reinventing Democracy*. Cambridge, MA: Blackwell (1998).

Barcellos, Tanya, *Segregaçao urbana e mortalidade infantil em Porto Alegre*, Porto Alegre: FEE (1986).

Bardhan, Pranab, "Sharing the Spoils: Group Equity, Development, and Democracy," unpublished paper, University of California, Berkeley (1997).

Bardhan, Pranab, "The State against Society: The Great Divide in Indian Social Science Discourse," in Sugata Bose and Ayesha Jalal, eds., *Nationalism, Democracy and Development*, New York: Oxford University Press (1999), pp. 184–95.

Barrows, Cameron, "An Ecological Model for the Protection of a Dune System," *Conservation Biology*, no. 10 (1996), pp. 888–91.

Barry, Brian, *Political Argument*, London: Routledge & Kegan Paul (1965).

Barry, Brian, *Justice as Impartiality*, Oxford: Oxford University Press (1995).

Baumgartner, Frank and Leech, Beth L, *Basic Interests: The Importance of Groups in Politics and Political Science*, Princeton: Princeton University Press (1998).

Bean, Michael J., Fitzgerald, Sarah G., and O'Connell, Michael A., *Reconciling Conflicts under the Endangered Species Act: The Habitat Conservation Planning Experience*, Washington, DC: World Wildlife Fund (1991).

Beatley, Timothy, "Balancing Urban Development and Endangered Species: The Coachella Valley Habitat Conservation Plan," *Environmental Management*, no. 16 (1992), pp. 7–19.

Beatley, Timothy, *Habitat Conservation Planning: Endangered Species and Urban Growth*, Austin, TX: University of Texas Press (1994).

Beitz, Charles, *Political Equality: An Essay in Democratic Theory*, Princeton: Princeton University Press (1989).

Benford, Robert and Snow, David, "Framing Processes and Social Movements: An Overview and Assessment," *Annual Review of Sociology*, vol. 26 (2000), pp. 611–39.

Benhabib, Selya, ed., *Democracy and Difference: Contesting the Boundaries of the Political*, Princeton: Princeton University Press (1996).

Berry, Jeffrey M., Portney, Kent E., and Thomson, Ken, *The Rebirth of Urban Democracy*, Washington, DC:, Brookings Institution (1993).

Bisom-Rapp, Susan, "An Ounce of Prevention is a Poor Substitute for a Pound of Cure: Confronting the Developing Jurisprudence of Education and Prevention in Employment Discrimination Law," *Berkeley Journal of Employment and Labor Law*, vol. 22 (2001), pp. 1–47.

Bittar, Jorge, *O modo petista de governar*, São Paulo, Brazil (1992).

Boaventura Leite, Ilka, *Negros no Sul do Brasil*, Ilha de Santa Catarina, SC: Letras Contemporaneas (1996).

Boggs, Carl, *Social Movements and Political Power*, Philadelphia: Temple University Press (1986).

Bohman, James and Rehg, William, ed., *Deliberative Democracy*, Cambridge, MA: MIT Press (1997).

Bourdieu, Pierre, *Language and Symbolic Power*, Cambridge: Polity (1991).

Bowles, Samuel and Gintis, Herbert, *Recasting Egalitarianism: New Rules for Communities, States and Markets*, New York and London: Verso (1999).

Boyte, Harry, *Backyard Revolution: Understanding the New Citizen's Movement*, Philadelphia: Temple University Press (1980).

Brewer, Marilynn B. and Brown, Rupert J., "Intergroup Relations," in D. Gilbert, S. Fiske, and G. Lindzey, eds., *Handbook of Social Psychology* (1998).

Briggs, Xavier de Souza, *Community Building: The New (and Old) Politics of Urban Problem-Solving*. Cambridge, MA: Kennedy School (2002) (RWP02-003).

Bryk, Anthony S., Thum, Yeow Meng, Easton, John Q., and Luppescu, Stuart, *Academic Productivity of Chicago Public Elementary Schools: A Technical Report Sponsored by the Consortium on Chicago School Research*, Chicago: Consortium on Chicago School Research (March 1998).

Buchanan, James and Tullock, Gordon, *The Calculus of Consent: Logical Foundations of Constitutional Democracy*, Ann Arbor, Michigan: University of Michigan Press (1965).

Cabral, John T. and Sobreira de Moura, Alexandrina, "City Management, Local Power and Social Practice: An Analysis of the 1991 Master Plan Process in Recife," *Latin American Perspectives*, vol. 23, no. 4 (1996), pp. 54–70.

Cassel, Guilherme and Verle, João, "A politica tributaria e de saneamento financeiro da administração popular," in Carlos Henrique Horn, ed., *Porto Alegre: o desafio da mudança*, Porto Alegre: Ortiz (1994).

Catalyst Staff, "Local School Council Elections," *Catalyst: Voices of Chicago School Reform*, vol. 7, no. 8 (May 1996), p. 26.

Chalmers, Doug, Martin, Scott, and Piester, Kerianne, "The Associative Network: Emerging Patterns of Popular Representation," in Douglas Chalmers, Carlos M. Vilas, and Katherine Roberts Hite, eds., *The New Politics of Inequality in Latin America*, New York: Oxford University Press (1997).

Chicago Community Policing Evaluation Consortium, *Community Policing in Chicago, Years Five–Six: An Interim Report*, Evanston, IL: Institute for Policy Research (1999).

Chicago Community Policing Evaluation Consortium, *Community Policing in Chicago, Year Seven: An Interim Report*, Springfield: Illinois Criminal Justice Authority (2000).

Chicago Public Schools, Office of Accountability, *The Illinois State School Report Card Data Book for 1995–96: An Analysis of Student, School, District, and State Characteristics*, Chicago: Chicago Public Schools (1996).

Chicago Tribune Staff, *Chicago Schools: "Worst in America": An Examination of the Public Schools that Failed Chicago*, Chicago, IL: Chicago Tribune (1988).

CIDADE, "Ciclo do orçamento participativo," in *De Olho no orçamento*, Porto Alegre: CIDADE (1995).

CIDADE, "Orçamento participativo – quem e a populacao que participa e que pensa do processo," Porto Alegre: Centro de Assessoria e Estudos Urbanos (unpublished report, 1999).

City Council of Chicago, "Amendments of Titles 8 and 13 of Municipal Code of Chicago Concerning Liability of Property Owners and Management for Unlawful Activities on Property," *Chicago City Council Journal* (July 31, 1996), pp. 27, 730–35.

Cohen, Cathy and Harris, Fred, "Social Capital and Political Activism Among Marginal Groups," prepared for Conference on Social Capital and Political Activism, Harvard University (May 23–24, 2002). Manuscript on file with author.

Cohen, Joshua, "Deliberation and Democratic Legitimacy," in A. Hamlin and Phillip Petit, eds., *The Good Polity: Normative Analysis of the State*, Cambridge: Basil Blackwell (1989).

Cohen, Joshua, "Procedure and Substance in Deliberative Democracy," in Selya Benhabib, ed., *Democracy and Difference: Contesting the Boundaries of the Political*, Princeton: Princeton University Press (1996), pp. 95–109.

Cohen, Joshua and Rogers, Joel, "Secondary Associations and Democratic Governance," *Politics and Society*, vol. 20, no. 4 (1992), pp. 393–472.

Cohen, Joshua, and Rogers, Joel, *Associations and Democracy*, New York and London: Verso (1995).

Cohen, Joshua and Sabel, Charles, "Directly-Deliberative Polyarchy," *European Law Journal*, vol. 3, no. 4 (December 1997), pp. 313–42.

Coit, Katharine, "Local Action, Not Citizen Participation." in William K. Tabb and Larry Sawyers, eds., *Marxism and the Metropolis: New Perspectives in Urban Political Economy*, New York: Oxford University Press (1978).

Conover, Pamela Johnston, Searing, Donald D., and Crewe, Ivor M., "The Deliberative Potential of Political Discussion," *British Journal of Political Science*, vol. 32 (2002), pp. 21–62.

Conselho Popular do Partenon, *Regimento interno*, Porto Alegre (1992).

Cortes, Ernesto, Jr., "Reweaving the Social Fabric," *The Boston Review*, vol. 19, no. 3&4 (June–September 1994), pp. 12–14.

County of San Diego, Multiple Species Conservation Program, *Plan Summary* (1998). Available at htp//www.co.sandiego.ca.us/cnty/cntydepts/landuse/-planning/mscp/1_plansum/1_plsum.html (accessed on July 25, 2002).

Couto, Cláudio Gonçalves, *O desafio de ser governo: O PT na Prefeitura de São Paulo*, São Paulo: Paz e Terra, 1995.

Coy, Patrick, ed., *Conflicts and Consensus Decision-Making in Social Movements*, Volume 24/5 of *Research in Social Movements, Conflicts and Change*, Elsevier Science/ JAI Press (forthcoming).

Cress, Daniel and Snow, David, "The Outcomes of Homeless Mobilization: The Influence of Organization, Disruption, Political Mediation, and Framing," *American Journal of Sociology*, vol. 105, no. 4 (January, 2000), pp. 1063–1104.

Dahl, Robert, *Democracy and its Critics*, New Haven: Yale University Press (1989).

Daniels, Norman, "Limits to Health Care: Fair Procedures, Democratic Deliberation, and the Legitimacy Problem for Insurers," *Philosophy and Public Affairs*, vol. 26, no. 4, pp. 303–51.

Darin, Thomas F., "Designating Critical Habitat under the Endangered Species Act: Habitat Protection Versus Agency Discretion," *Harvard Environmental Law Review*, vol. 24, no. 1 (2000), pp. 209–35.

Dawson, Michael C., *Behind the Mule: Race and Class in American Politics*, Princeton: Princeton University Press (1994).

De Sousa Santos, Boaventura, "Participatory Budgeting in Porto Allegre: Toward a Redistributive Democracy," *Politics and Society*, vol. 26, no. 4 (December 1998), pp. 461–510.

Designs for Change, *The Untold Story: Candidate Participation in the 1991 Chicago Local School Council Elections*, Chicago: Designs for Change (1991), p. 7.

Dietz, Henry, *Urban Poverty, Political Participation and the State*, Pittsburgh, PA: University of Pittsburgh Press (1998).

Dorf, Michael and Sabel, Charles, "A Constitution of Democratic Experimentalism," *Columbia Law Review*, vol. 98 (March, 1998), pp. 267–473.

Dorf, Michael C. and Sabel, Charles, "Drug Treatment Courts and Emergent Experimentalist Government," *Vanderbilt Law Review*, vol. 53, no. 3 (2000).

Drèze, Jean and Sen, Amartya, *India: Economic Development and Social Opportunity*, Delhi: Oxford University Press (1995).

Druffin, Elizabeth, "Spotlight Brings Focus: One School's Probation Story," in *Catalyst: Voices of Chicago School Reform*, vol. 9, no. 9 (June 1998), pp. 12–15.

Duane, Timothy P, "The Ecosystem Approach: New Departures for Land and Water: Practical Legal Issues in Community Initiated Ecosystem Management of Public Land: Community Participation in Ecosystem Management," *Ecology Law Quarterly*, vol. 24 (1997), pp. 771–97.

Ebbin, Marc J., "Is the Southern California Approach to Conservation Succeeding?" in *Ecology Law Quarterly*, vol. 24, no 4 (1997), pp. 695–706.

Elster, Jon, *Sour Grapes: Studies in the Subversion of Rationality*, Cambridge: Cambridge University Press (1983).

Elster, Jon, "Selfishness and Altruism," in Jane Mansbridge, ed., *Beyond Self-Interest*, Chicago: University of Chicago Press (1990).

Elster, Jon, ed., *Deliberative Democracy*, Cambridge: Cambridge University Press (1998).

Elster, Jon, *Alchemies of the Mind: Rationality and the Emotions*, Cambridge: Cambridge University Press (1999a).

Elster, Jon, *Strong Feelings: Emotion, Addiction, and Human Behaviour*, Cambridge, MA: MIT Press (1999b).

Endangered Species Act 16 U.S. Code, Chap. 35, Sec. 1531 et seq.

Endangered Species Recovery Act of 1999, H.R. 960, 106th Congress.

Evans, Peter, "Government Action, Social Capital and Development: Reviewing the Evidence on Synergy," *World Development*, vol. 24, no. 6 (1996), pp. 1119–32.

Fedozzi, Luciano, *Orçamento participativo: reflexoes sobre a experiencia de Porto Alegre*, Porto Alegre: Tomo Editorial (1997).

Ferguson, James, *The Anti-Politics Machine: "Development," Depoliticization and Bureaucratic Power in Lesotho*, New York: Cambridge University Press (1994).

Ferree, Myra Marx and Martin, Patricia Yancey, eds, *Feminist Organizations:*

Harvest of the New Political Women's Movement, Philadelphia, PA: Temple University Press (1995).

Filho, Arno Agostin, "A Experiencia do orçamento participativo na administracao popular da prefeitura municipal de Porto Alegre," in Carlos Henrique Horn, ed., *Porto Alegre: o desafio da mudanca*, Porto Alegre: Editora Ortiz (1994).

Frampton, George, "Environmental Law Faces the New Ecology: Ecosystem Management in the Clinton Administration," *Duke Environmental Law and Policy Journal*, vol. 7 (Fall 1996), pp. 39–48.

Franke, Richard and Chasin, Barbara, "Power to the Malayalee People," *Economic and Political Weekly*, vol. 31, no. 10 (1997), pp. 625–30.

Freeman, Jo, "The Origins of the Women's Liberation Movement," *American Journal of Sociology*, vol. 78 (1973), pp. 792–811.

Freeman, Jody, "Collaborative Governance in the Administrative State," *University of California, Los Angeles Law Review*, vol. 45 (October, 1997), pp. 1–98.

Freeman, Samuel, "Deliberative Democracy: A Sympathetic Comment," *Philosophy and Public Affairs*, vol. 29, no. 4 (Fall 2000), pp. 371–418.

Friere, Paolo, *Pedagogy of the Oppressed*, trans. Myra Bergman Ramos, New York: Herder and Herder (1970).

Fung, Archon, "Contract Expired: Is Chicago Poised to Take the Community out of Community Policing?" *Neighborhood Works* (March/April 1997), pp. 8–9.

Fung, Archon, "Street Level Democracy: A Theory of Popular Pragmatic Deliberation and Its Practice in Chicago School Reform and Community Policing, 1988–1997," Ph.D. dissertation, Massachusetts Institute of Technology, Department of Political Science (1999).

Gadgil, Madhav and Guha, Ramachandra, *This Fissured Land: An Ecological History of India*, Delhi: Oxford University Press (1992).

Gastil, John, *Democracy in Small Groups: Participation, Decision Making, and Communication*, Philadelphia: New Society Publishers (1993).

Gastil, John and Dillard, J.P., "Increasing Political Sophistication through Public Deliberation," *Political Communication*, vol. 16 (1999), pp. 3–23.

Genro, Tarso and de Souza, Ubiratan, *Orçamento participativo: a experiencia de Porto Alegre*, Porto Alegre: Fundação Perseu Abramo (1997).

Ghatak, Maitreesh and Ghatak, Maitreya, "Grassroots Democracy: A Case Study of the Operation of the Panchayat System in West Bengal, India," Manuscript (2000).

Gilbert, Alan and Ward, Peter, "Community Action by the Urban Poor: Democratic Involvement, Community Self-help or a Means of Social Control?" *World Development*, vol. 12, no. 8 (1984), pp. 769–82.

Gittell, Marilyn, *Participants and Participation: A Study of School Policy in New York City*, New York: F.A. Praeger (1967).

Goldstein, Herman, *Problem Oriented Policing*, Philadelphia: Temple University Press (1992).

Government of India, *Guidelines for the Formulation of District Plans*, New Delhi: Planning Commission (1969).

Government of India, *Report of the Working Group on Block Level Planning*, New Delhi: Planning Commission (1978).

Government of India, *Report of the Working Group on District Planning*, New Delhi: Planning Commission (1984).

Government of Kerala, *Budget 1997–98*, Thiruvananthapuram: Ministry of Finance (1997).

Gregory, Michelle, "Anatomy of a Neighborhood Plan: An Analysis of Current Practice," Chicago: American Planning Association Growing Smart Working Paper (1996).

Grimshaw, William J., *Bitter Fruit: Black Politics and the Chicago Machine, 1931–1991*, Chicago: University of Chicago Press (1992).

Guinier, Lani, *The Tyranny of the Majority: Fundamental Fairness in Representative Democracy*, New York: Free Press (1995).

Gutmann, Amy, *Liberal Equality*, Cambridge: Cambridge University Press (1980).

Gutmann, Amy and Thompson, Dennis, *Democracy and Disagreement*, Cambridge, MA: Harvard University Press (1996).

Habermas, Jürgen, *Theory of Communicative Action*, trans. Thomas McCarthy, Boston: Beacon Press (1984).

Hall, Anthony, "Community Participation and Development Policy: A Sociological Perspective," in A. Hall and J. Midgley, eds., *Development Policies: Sociological Perspectives*, New York: Manchester University (1988), pp. 91–107.

Harnecker, Marta, *Frente amplio: los desafíos de un izquierda legal. Segunda parte: los hitos mas importantes de su historia*, Montevideo: Ediciones La Republica (1991).

Harvey, Jerry, *The Abilene Paradox*, Lexington, MA: Lexington Books (1988).

Helco, Hugo, "Issue Networks and the Executive Establishment," in Anthony King, ed., *The New American Political System*, Washington, DC: American Enterprise Institute (1978).

Heller, Patrick, *The Labor of Development: Workers in the Transformation of Capitalism in Kerala, India*, Ithaca: Cornell University Press (1999).

Heller, Patrick, "Degrees of Democracy: Some Comparative Lessons from India," *World Politics*, vol. 52 (July 2000), pp. 484–519.

Heller, Patrick, "Moving the State: The Politics of Decentralization in Kerala, South Africa and Porto Alegre," *Politics and Society*, vol. 29, no. 1 (2001), pp. 131–63.

Hibbing, John R. and Theiss-Morse, Elizabeth, *Stealth Democracy: Americans' Beliefs about How Government Should Work*, Cambridge: Cambridge University Press (2002).

Hirst, Paul, *Associative Democracy: New Forms of Economic and Social Governance*, Cambridge: Polity Press (1994).

Holing, Dwight, "Lizard and the Links," *Audubon*, no. 89 (1987), pp. 39–49.

Holling, C.S., *Adaptive Environmental Management and Assessment*, Chichester, NY: Wiley (1978).

Honig, Bonnie, *Political Theory and the Displacement of Politics*, Ithaca: Cornell University Press (1993).

Hood, Laura C., *Frayed Safety Nets: Conservation Planning under the Endangered Species Act*, Washington, DC: Defenders of Wildlife (1998).

Hutcheson, J.D., "Citizen Representation in Neighborhood Planning," *Journal of the American Planning Association*, no. 50 (1984), pp. 175–82.

Illinois Compiled Statutes, Ch. 720, Sec. 37–4 (1996).

Illinois State Police, Division of Administration, Crime Studies Section, *Crime in Illinois – 1998*, Springfield, IL: State of Illinois (April 1999).

Jackman, Robert and Miller, Ross, "Voter Turnout in the Industrial Democracies during the 1980s," *Comparative Political Studies*, vol. 27, no. 4 (1995), pp. 467–92.

Jackson, J.S. and Shade, W.L., "Citizen Participation, Democratic Representation, and Survey Research," *Urban Affairs Quarterly*, vol. 9 (1973), pp. 57–89.

Jacobson, Louis, "Local Timber Collaboration Stalls in National Arena," *Planning*, vol. 61, no. 11, (November 1998), pp. 22–23.

Janis, Irving L., *Groupthink: Psychological Studies of Policy Decisions and Fiascos*, Boston: Houghton Mifflin (1982).

John, DeWitt, *Civic Environmentalism: Alternatives to Regulation in States and Communities*, Washington, DC: Congressional Quarterly Press (1994).

Kahn, Mark E., *Middle Class Radicalism in Santa Monica*, Philadelphia, PA: Temple University Press (1986).

Kareiva, Peter, Andelman, Sandy, Doak, Daniel, Elderd, Bret, Groom, Martha, Hoekstra, Jonathan, Hood, Laura, James, Frances, Lamoreux, John, LeBuhn, Gretchen, McCulloch, Charles, Regetz, James, Savage, Lisa, Ruckelshaus, Mary, Skelly, David, Wilbur, Henry, and Zamudio, Kelly, *Using Science in Habitat Conservation Plans*, Washington, DC: American Institute of Biological Sciences (1999).

Karkkainen, Bradley C., Sabel, Charles, and Fung, Archon, *Beyond Backyard Environmentalism*, ed. Joshua Cohen and Joel Rogers, foreword by Hunter Lovins and Amory Lovins, Boston: Beacon Press (2000).

Karkkainen, Bradley C., Fung, Archon, and Sabel, Charles F., "After Backyard Environmentalism: Toward a Performance-Based Regime of Environmental Protection," *American Behavioral Scientist*, vol. 44 (2000), pp. 692–711.

Katznelson, Ira, *City Trenches*, New York: Pantheon Press (1981).

Kaufman, Arnold, "Human Nature and Participatory Democracy," in Carl J. Fridrich, ed., *Responsibility: NOMOS III*, New York: Lieber-Atherton (1960).

Kaufman, Arnold, "Participatory Democracy: Ten Years Later," *La Table Ronde*, no. 251–252 (1968), pp. 216–28, reprinted in William E. Connolly, ed., *The Bias of Pluralism*, New York: Atherton Press (1971).

Keane, John, "The Philadelphia Model," in Takasi Inoguchi, Edward Newman, and John Keane, eds., *The Changing Nature of Democracy*, Tokyo: United Nations University Press (1998).

Keck, Margaret E., *The Worker's Party and Democratization in Brazil*, New Haven: Yale University Press (1992).

Keck, Margaret E. and Sikkink, Kathryn, *Activists Beyond Borders: Advocacy Networks in International Politics*, Ithaca, NY: Cornell University Press (1998).

Kemmis, Daniel, *Community and The Politics of Place*, Norman: University of Oklahoma Press (1990).

Knight, Jack and Johnson, James, "Aggregation and Deliberation: On the Possibility of Democratic Legitimacy," *Political Theory*, vol. 22 (1994), pp. 277–98.

Kowarick, Lucio and Singer, Andre, "The Workers' Party in Sao Paulo," in Lucio Kowarick, ed., *Social Struggles and the City*, New York: Monthly Review Press (1994).

Landy, Marc, *Civic Environmentalism in Action: A Field Guide to Regional and Local Initiatives*, Washington, DC: Progressive Policy Institute (1999).

Lee, Kai N., *Compass and Gyroscope: Integrating Science and Politics for the Environment*, Washington, DC: Island Press (1993).

Leidner, Robin, "Stretching the Boundaries of Liberalism: Democratic Innovation in a Feminist Organization," *Signs*, vol. 16 (1991), pp. 263–89.

Leidner, Robin, "Constituency, Accountability, and Deliberation: Reshaping Democracy in the National Women's Studies Association," *National Women's Studies Association Journal*, vol. 5 (1993), pp. 4–27.

Leite, Ilka Boaventura, *Negros no sul do Brasil*, Ilha de Santa Catarina, SC: Letras Contemporaneas (1996).

Lesbaupin, Ivo, *Prefeituras do povo e para o povo*, São Paulo, Brazil: Edições Loyola (1996).

Levy, Frank and Murnane, Richard, *Teaching the New Basic Skills: Principles for Educating Children to Thrive in a Changing Economy*, New York: Free Press (1996).

Lewis, Michael and Haviland-Jones, Jeanette, eds., *Handbook of Emotions*, New York: Guilford (2000).

Lieten, G.K., *Development, Devolution, and Democracy: Village Discourse in West Bengal*, New Dehli: Sage Publications (1996).

Lijphart, Arend, *Patterns of Democracy*, New Haven: Yale University Press (1999).

Lindblom, Charles E., "The Science of Muddling Through," *Public Administration Review*, vol. 19 (1959), pp. 79–88.

Lipsky, Michael, *Street-Level Bureaucracy: Dilemma of the Individual in the Public Services*, New York: Russell Sage Foundation (1980).

Lovell, Peggy, "Race, Gender, and Development in Brazil," *Latin American Research Review*, vol. 29, no. 3 (1994), pp. 7–35.

Lowi, Theodore, *The End of Liberalism: The Second Republic of the United States*, New York: Norton (1979).

Lukes, Stephen, *Power: A Radical View*, London: Macmillan (1974).

Luskin, Robert C. and Fishkin, James, "Does Deliberation Make Better Citizens?," paper presented at the meeting of the European Consortium for Political Research, Turin, Italy (March 22–27, 2002).

McAdam, Doug and Rucht, Dieter, "The Cross-National Diffusion of Movement

Ideas," *Annals of the American Academy of Political and Social Science*, no. 528 (July 1993), pp. 56–74.

McAdam, Douglas, Tarrow, Sidney, and Tilly, Charles, *Dynamics of Contention*, New York: Cambridge University Press (2001).

McCloskey, Michael, "The Skeptic: Collaboration Has Its Limits," *High Country News*, vol. 28. no. 9 (May 13, 1996), p. 7.

McCloskey, Michael, "Problems With Using Collaboration to Shape Environmental Public Policy," *Valparaiso University Law Review*, vol. 34 (Spring 2000), pp. 423–34.

McFarland, Andrew, "Interest Groups and the Policymaking Process: Sources of Countervailing Power in America," in Mark P. Petracca, ed., *The Politics of Interests: Interest Groups Transformed*, Boulder, CO: Westview Press (1992).

McKersie, William S., "Private Funding Down for LSC Elections," *Catalyst: Voices of Chicago School Reform*. vol. 7, no. 6 (March 1996), p. 15.

Manjula, B., "Voices from the Spiral of Silence: A Case Study of Samatha Self-Help Groups of Ulloor," paper presented at the International Conference on Democratic Decentralization, Thiruvananthapuram, May 23–27, 2000.

Manor, James, *The Political Economy of Decentralization*, Washington, DC: The World Bank (1999).

Mansbridge, Jane, *Beyond Adversary Democracy*, Chicago: University of Chicago Press (1980).

Mansbridge, Jane, "A Deliberative Theory of Interest Representation," in Mark Petracca, ed., *The Politics of Interests: Interest Groups Transformed*, Boulder, CO: Westview Press (1992).

Mansbridge, Jane, "Feminism and Democratic Community," in John W. Chapman and Ian Shapiro, eds., *Democratic Community: NOMOS XXXV*, New York: New York University Press (1993).

Mansbridge, Jane, "Using Power/Fighting Power: The Polity," in Seyla Benhabib, ed., *Democracy and Difference*, Princeton: Princeton University Press (1995).

Mansbridge, Jane, "Reconstructing Democracy," in Nancy J. Hirschmann and Christine Di Stefano, eds., *Revisioning the Political: Feminist Reconstructions of Traditional Concepts in Western Political Theory*, New York: Westview Press (1996).

Mansbridge, Jane, "On the Contested Nature of the Public Good," in Walter W. Powell and Elisabeth S. Clemens, eds., *Private Action and the Public Good*, New Haven: Yale University Press (1998).

Mansbridge, Jane, "On the Idea that Participation Makes Better Citizens," in Stephen L. Elkin and Karol E. Soltan, eds., *Citizen Competence and Democratic Institutions*, University Park: Pennsylvania State University Press (1999).

Marcus, George E., *The Sentimental Citizen: Emotion in Democratic Politics*, University Park: Pennsylvania State University Press (2002).

Marquetti, Adalmir, *Orçamento participativo de Porto Alegre*, unpublished manuscript (2001).

Marris, Peter and Rein, Martin, *Dilemmas of Social Reform*, Chicago: University of Chicago Press (1982, originally published 1967).

Marsh, Lindell L. and Thornton, Robert D., "San Bruno Mountain Habitat Conservation Plan," in David J. Brower and Daniel S. Carol, eds., *Managing Land-Use Conflicts: Case Studies in Special Area Management*, Durham, NC: Duke University Press (1987).

Martinez, Michael, "Clement's Council Renews Principal War," *Chicago Tribune* (November 18, 1997).

Medoff, Peter and Sklar, Holly, *Streets of Hope: The Fall and Rise of an Urban Neighborhood*, Boston, MA: South End Press (1994).

Mendelberg, Tali and Oleske, John, "Race and Public Deliberation," *Political Communication*, vol. 17 (2000), pp. 169–91.

Mendelberg, Tali, "The Deliberative Citizen: Theory and Evidence," in Michael Delli Carpini, Leonie Huddy, and Robert Y. Shapiro, eds., *Research in Micropolitics, Volume 6*, New York, Elsevier Press (forthcoming).

Mill, John Stuart, *Considerations on Representative Government*, ed. with an Introduction by Currin V. Shields, Indianapolis: Bobbs-Merrill (1958, originally published 1861).

Mills, C. Wright, *The Power Elite*, New York: Oxford University Press (1959, originally 1956).

Nagel, Jack, *Participation*, New York: Prentice Hall (1987).

National Research Council, *High Stakes: Testing for Tracking, Promotion, and Graduation*, Washington, DC: National Academy Press (1999).

Noss, Reed F. and Cooperrider, Allen Y., *Saving Nature's Legacy: Protecting and Restoring Biodiversity*, Washington, DC: Island Press (1994).

Noss, Reed F., O'Connell, Michael A., and Murphy, Dennis D., *The Science of Conservation Planning: Habitat Conservation under the Endangered Species Act*, Washington, DC: Island Press (1997).

Nussbaum, Martha Craven, "Emotions and Women's Capabilities," in Martha Craven Nussbaum and Jonathan Glover, eds., *Women, Culture, and Development*, Oxford: Oxford University Press (1995).

Nylen, William, "Popular Participation in Brazil's Workers' Party: Democratizing Democracy in Municipal Politics," *The Political Chronicle*, vol. 8, no. 2 (1998), pp. 1–9.

Offe, Claus and Wiesenthal, Helmut, "Two Logics of Collective Action," in John Keane, ed., *Disorganized Capitalism: Contemporary Transformations of Work and Politics*, Cambridge, MA: MIT Press (1985).

Oliveira, Ney dos Santos, "Favelas and Ghettos: Race and Class in Rio de Janeiro and New York City," *Latin American Perspectives*, vol. 23, no. 4 (1996), pp. 71–89.

Oliver, Pamela, "'If You Don't Do It, Nobody Else Will': Active and Token Contributors to Local Collective Action," *American Sociological Review*, vol. 49 (1984), pp. 601–10.

Olson, Mancur, *The Logic of Collective Action: Public Goods and the Theory of Groups*, Cambridge, MA: Harvard University Press (1965).

Petracca, Mark, ed., *The Politics of Interests: Interest Groups Transformed*, Boulder, CO: Westview Press (1992).

Pflepsen, Alison, "LSCs Lose 182 Members Who Didn't Complete Training," *Catalyst: Voices of Chicago School Reform*, vol. 10, no. 8 (May 1999), pp. 24–25.

Phillips, Anne, *Engendering Democracy*, Cambridge: Polity Press (1991).

Polanyi, Karl, *The Great Transformation*, New York: Rinehart & Co. (1944).

"The Port Huron Statement," in Paul Jacobs and Saul Landau, eds., *The New Radicals*, New York: Random House (1966, originally published 1962).

Pozzobon, Regina, *Porto Alegre: os desafios da gestao democratica*, São Paulo: Instituto Polis (1998).

Prefeitura Municipal de Porto Alegre, *Anuario estatistico*, Porto Alegre: GAPLAN (1997).

Prefeitura Municipal de Porto Alegre, *Regioes do orçamento participativo de Porto Alegre – Alguns Indicadores Sociais*, Porto Alegre: Fundacao de Educacao Social e Comunitaria (1999).

Putnam, Robert. D., *Making Democracy Work, Civic Traditions in Modern Italy*, Princeton: Princeton University Press (1993).

Putnam, Robert, *Bowling Alone: The Collapse and Revival of American Community*, New York: Simon and Schuster (2000).

Rakove, Milton L., *Don't Make No Waves, Don't Back No Losers*, Bloomington: Indiana University Press (1975).

Ratliff, William, "The Devolution of Environmental Organization," *Journal of Land Resources and Environmental Law*, vol. 17 (1997), pp. 45–91.

Rawls, John, *A Theory of Justice*, Cambridge, MA: Harvard University Press (1971).

Research for Action and Cross Cities Campaign for Urban School Reform, *Strong Neighborhoods, Strong Schools: The Indicators Project on Education Organizing* (March, 2002) Chicago: Cross Cities Campaign for Urban School Reform.

Riker, William, *Liberalism against Populism: A Confrontation between the Theory of Democracy and the Theory of Social Choice*, Prospect, IL: Waveland Press (1982).

Riker, William and Ordeshook, Peter, "A Theory of the Calculus of Voting," *American Political Science Review*, vol. 62, no. 1 (March 1968), pp. 25–42.

Riger, Stephanie, "Challenges of Success: Stages of Growth in Feminist Organizations," *Feminist Studies*, vol. 20 (1994), pp. 275–301.

Roemer, John, *Equal Shares: Making Market Socialism Work*, New York and London: Verso (1996).

Rorty, Amélie Oksenberg. "Varieties of Rationality, Varieties of Emotion," *Social Science Information*, vol. 24 (l985), pp. 343–53.

Rosenstone, Steven J. and Hansen, John Mark, *Mobilization, Participation, and Democracy*, New York: Macmillan (1993).

Rossi, Rosalind, "School Races Attract Few Candidates," *Chicago Sun Times* (April 6, 1998), p. 8.

Rousseau, J.-J., *Social Contract*, trans. Donald A. Cress, Cambridge: Hackett Publishing (1987).

Ryan, Susan P., Bryk, Anthony S., Lopez, Gudelia, Williams, Kimberley P., Hall, Kathleen, and Luppescu, Stuart, *Charting Reform: LSCs – Local Leadership at Work*, Chicago: Consortium on Chicago School Research (1999).

Sabel, Charles, Karkkainen, Bradley, and Fung, Archon, *Beyond Backyard Environmentalism*, foreword by Amory and Hunter Lovins, Boston: Beacon Press (2000).

Sagoff, Mark, "The View from Quincy Library: Civic Engagement in Environmental Problem Solving," in Robert K. Fullinwider, ed., *Civil Society, Democracy, and Civic Renewal*, New York: Rowman Littlefield (1999).

Sanders, Lynn M., "Against Deliberation," *Political Theory*, vol. 25 (1997), pp. 347–76.

Sartori, Giovanni, *The Theory of Democracy Revisited*, Chatham: Chatham House (1987).

Schattschneider, E.E., *The Semisovereign People: A Realist's View of Democracy in America*, New York: Holt, Rinehart, and Winston (1960).

Scheid, Dan, "Board Bumps Reform Groups from LSC Training," *Catalyst: Voices of Chicago School Reform*, vol. 10, no. 1 (September 1998), pp. 1, 20–21.

Schlozman, Kay Lehmann, "What Accent the Heavenly Chorus: Political Equality and the American Pressure System," *Journal of Politics*, vol. 46, no. 4 (November, 1984), pp. 1007–32.

Schonwalder, Gerd, "Local Politics and the Peruvian Left," *Latin American Perspectives*, vol. 33, no. 2 (1998).

Schwarz, Roger M., *The Skilled Facilitator: Practical Wisdom for Developing Effective Groups*, San Francisco: Jossey-Bass (1994).

Schweik, Charles and Thomas, Craig W., "Using Remote Sensing to Evaluate Environmental Institutional Designs: A Habitat Conservation Planning Example," *Social Science Quarterly* (forthcoming).

Scott, James, *Seeing Like a State: How Certain Schemes to Improve the Human Condition Have Failed*, New Haven: Yale University Press (1998).

Seema, T.N. and Mukherjee, Vanitha, "Gender Governance and Citizenship in Decentralized Planning," paper presented at the International Conference on Democratic Decentralization, Thiruvananthapuram, May 23–27, 2000.

Selznick, Phillip, *T.V.A. and the Grassroots*, Berkeley: University of California Press (1949).

Shirley, Dennis, *Community Organizing for Urban School Reform*, Austin: University of Texas Press (1997).

Shirley, Dennis, *Valley Interfaith and School Reform: Organizing for Power in South Texas*, Austin: University of Texas Press (2002).

Shutkin, William, *The Land That Could Be: Environmentalism and Democracy in the Twenty-First Century*, Cambridge, MA: MIT Press (2000).

Sirianni, Carmen, "Learning Pluralism: Democracy and Diversity in Feminist

Organizations," in Ian Shapiro and John Chapman, eds., *Democratic Community: NOMOS XXXV*, New York: New York University Press (1993a).

Sirianni, Carmen, "Feminist Pluralism and Democratic Learning: the Politics of Citizenship in the National Women's Studies Association," *National Women's Studies Associatio Journal*, vol. 5 (1993b), pp. 367–84.

Sirianni, Carmen and Friedland, Lewis, *Civic Innovation in America: Community Empowerment, Public Policy, and the Movement for Civic Renewal*, Berkeley: University of California Press (2001).

Skocpol, Theda, "Feminist Pluralism and Democratic Learning: The Politics of Citizenship in the National Women's Studies Association," *National Women's Studies Association Journal*, vol. 5 (1993), pp. 367–84.

Skocpol, Theda and Fiorina, Morris P., eds., *Civic Engagement in American Democracy*, Washington, DC: Brookings Institution Press (1999).

Skogan, Wesley G. and Hartnett, Susan M., *Community Policing: Chicago Style*, New York: Oxford University Press (1997).

Smith, Andrew A., Moote, Margaret A., and Schwalbe, Cecil R., "The Endangered Species Act at Twenty: An Analytical Survey of Federal Endangered Species Protection," *Natural Resources Journal*, vol. 33 (1993), pp. 1,027–75.

Snow, David and Benford, Robert, "Frame Alignment Processes, Mobilization, and Movement Participation," *American Sociological Review*, vol. 51, no. 4 (August, 1986) pp. 464–81.

Sparrow, Malcolm K., Moore, Mark H., and Kennedy, David M., *Beyond 911: A New Era for Policing*, New York: Basic Books (1990).

Steinzor, Rena, "The Corruption of Civic Environmentalism," *Environmental Law Reporter*, vol. 30 (October, 2000), pp. 10,909–21.

Stewart, Richard B., "The Reform of American Administrative Law," *Harvard Law Review*, vol. 88, no. 8 (June, 1975), pp. 1667–1813.

Stewart, Richard B., "Madison's Nightmare," *University of Chicago Law Review*, vol. 57 (spring, 1990), pp. 335–56.

Stiefel, Matthias and Wolfe, Marshall, *A Voice for the Excluded. Popular Participation in Development: Utopia or Necessity?* London: Zed Books (1994).

Still, Thomas W., "Madison Is the Ultimate in Citizen Involvement," *Wisconsin State Journal* (July 4, 1999).

Strahler, Steven R., "It's Back-To-School Time: Daley's Crisis Plan Begins to Take Shape," *Craine's Chicago Business* (April 10, 1995) p. 3.

Sturm, Susan, "Second Generation Employment Discrimination: A Structural Approach," *Columbia Law Review*, vol. 101 (April, 2001), pp. 458–568.

Sunstein, Cass, *Designing Democracy: What Constitutions Do*, Oxford: Oxford University Press (2001).

Szasz, Andrew, *Ecopopulism: Toxic Waste and the Movement for Environmental Justice*, Minneapolis: University of Minnesota Press (1994).

Szasz, Andrew, "Progress through Mischief: The Social Movement Alternative to Secondary Associations," in Erik O. Wright, ed., *Associations and Democracy*, London: Verso (1995).

Telles, Edward, "Residential Segregation and Skin Color in Brazil," *American Sociological Review*, vol. 57, no. 2 (1992), pp. 186–97.

Thomas, Craig W., *Bureaucratic Landscapes: Interagency Cooperation and the Preservation of Biodiversity*, Cambridge, MA: MIT Press (2003).

Thomas, Craig W., "Public Management as Interagency Cooperation: Testing Epistemic Community Theory at the Domestic Level," *Journal of Public Administration Research and Theory*, vol. 7 (1997), pp. 221–46.

Thomas, Craig W. and Schweik, Charles, "Regulatory Compliance under the Endangered Species Act: a Time-Series Analysis of Habitat Conservation Planning Using Remote-Sensing Data," paper presented at the *Association for Public Policy Analysis and Management (APPAM) Annual Research Conference*, Washington, DC (1999).

Thomas Isaac, T.M., with Richard Franke, *Local Democracy and Development: People's Campaign for Decentralised Planning in Kerala*, New Delhi: Leftword (2000).

Thomas Isaac, T.M., The Socio-Economic and Political Context of People's Planning Campaign, National Workshop on Decentralised Governance, Organised by Kerala Institute of Local Administration and Swiss Agency for Development and Co-operation, Thrissur (1999a).

Thomas Isaac, T.M., "People's Planning – Towards a Handbook," presented at the Workshop organised by State Planning Board, Tripura, Agarthala on May 3 and 4, 1999 (1999b).

Thomas Isaac, T.M., "Janakeeyasoothranavum Ayalkoottangalum – Anubhavangalum Padangalum" [People's Planning and Neighbourhood groups – Lessons from Experience], in *Ayalkootta Sangamam* [Neighborhood Groups] vol. I, Kerala State Planning Board, Thiruvananthapuram (1999c).

Thomas Isaac, T.M., "Gunabhokthra Samithikalude Anubhava Padangal" [People's Planning and Beneficiary Committees – Lessons from Experience], in *Gunabhokthra Samithikalum Janakeeyasoothranavum* [People's Planning and Beneficiary Committees] Kerala State Planning Board, Thiruvananthapuram (1999d).

Thomas Isaac, T.M., Seema, T.N, Thampy, Binitha, and Antony, Margaret, "Gender and Decentralised Planning – The Experience of People's Campaign" (unpublished working paper), Center for Development Studies, Thiruvananthapuram (1999).

Thompson, Robert, "Coachella Valley Habitat Conservation Plan," in Judith Innes, Judith Gruber, Michael Neuman, and Robert Thompson, eds., *Coordinating Growth and Environmental Management through Consensus Building*, Berkeley: California Policy Seminar, University of California (1994).

Turner, John C., *Rediscovering the Social Group: A Self-Categorization Theory*, Oxford: Basil Blackwell (1987).

Tyack, David, *The One Best System: A History of American Urban Education*, Cambridge, MA: Harvard University Press (1974).

U.S. Fish and Wildlife Service and National Marine Fisheries Service, "Habitat Conservation Plan Assurances ('No Surprises') Rule," *Federal Register*, vol. 63, no. 35 (1998), pp. 8, 859–73.

U.S. Fish and Wildlife Service and National Marine Fisheries Service, *Habitat Conservation Planning Handbook*, Washington, DC: U.S. Fish and Wildlife Service and National Marine Fisheries Service (1996).

U.S. Fish and Wildlife Service and National Marine Fisheries Service, "Notice of Availability of a Final Addendum to the Handbook for Habitat Conservation Planning and Incidental Take Permitting Process," *Federal Register*, vol. 65, no. 106 (2000), pp. 35, 241–57.

U.S. Fish and Wildlife Service and National Marine Fisheries Service, "Safe Harbor Agreements and Candidate Conservation Agreements with Assurances," *Federal Register*, vol. 64, no. 116 (1999), pp. 32, 705–16.

Utzig, Jose, "Notas sobre of governo do PT em Porto Alegre," *Novos Estudos Cebrap*, vol. 45, pp. 209–22 (1996).

Verba, Sidney and Nie, Norman H., *Participation in America: Political Democracy and Social Equality*, New York: Harper and Row (1972).

Verba, Sidney, Schlozman, Kay Lehman, and Brady, Henry E., *Voice and Equality: Civic Voluntarism in American Politics*, Cambridge, MA: Harvard University Press (1995).

Walton, Douglas, *The Place of Emotion in Argument*, University Park: Pennsylvania State University Press (1992).

Warren, Mark E., "Democratic Theory and Self-Transformation," *American Political Science Review*, vol. 86 (1992), pp. 8–23.

Warren, Mark E., "Psychological Dimensions of Habermas's Discursive Model of Democracy," *Political Psychology*, vol. 14 (1993), pp. 209–34.

Warren, Mark E., "Deliberative Democracy and Authority," *American Political Science Review*, vol. 90 (1996), pp. 46–60.

Warren, Mark E., "What Should We Expect from More Democracy? Radically Democratic Responses to Politics," *Political Theory*, vol. 24 (1996), pp. 241–70.

Warren, Mark R., *Dry Bones Rattling: Community Building to Revitalize American Democracy*, Princeton: Princeton University Press (2001).

Watchman, Laura H., Groom, Martha, and Perrine, John D., "Science and Uncertainty in Habitat Conservation Planning," *American Scientist*, vol. 89, no. 4 (2001), p. 351–9.

Weber, Edward, "The Question of Accountability in Historical Perspective: From Jacksonian to Contemporary Grassroots Ecosystem Management," *Administration and Society*, vol. 41, no. 4 (1999), pp. 451–94.

Weissmann, Dan, Randall, Jennifer, Lewis, Lisa, and Grotto, Jason, "Did Community Groups Have an Impact," in *Catalyst: Voices of Chicago School Reform*, vol. 7, no. 8 (May 1996), pp. 1, 25–26.

Williams, John E. and Best, Deborah L., *Measuring Sex Stereotypes*, Beverly Hills, CA: Sage (1982).

Wilson, James Q., "The Politics of Regulation," in James Q. Wilson, ed., *The Politics of Regulation*, New York: Basic Books (1980).

Yaffee, Steven L., *Prohibitive Policy: Implementing the Federal Endangered Species Act*, Cambridge, MA: Massachusetts Institute of Technology Press (1982).

Yaffee, Steven L., *The Wisdom of the Spotted Owl: Policy Lessons for a New Century*, Washington, DC: Island Press (1994).

Yaffee, Steven L., Aengst, Peter, Anderson, Jeremy, Chamberlin, Jay, Grunewald, Christopher, Loucks, Susan, and Wheatley, Elizabeth, *Balancing Public Trust and Private Interest: Public Participation in Habitat Conservation Planning*, Ann Arbor: School of Natural Resources and Environment, University of Michigan (1998).

Young, Iris Marion, *Justice and the Politics of Difference*, Princeton: Princeton University Press (1990).

Young, Iris Marion, "Communication and the Other: Beyond Deliberative Democracy," in Seyla Benhabib, ed., *Democracy and Difference: Contesting the Boundaries of the Political*, Princeton: Princeton University Press (1996).

Young, Iris Marion, *Inclusion and Democracy*, Oxford: Oxford University Press (2000).

Index